CULTURAL HERITAGE AND CONTEMPORARY CHANGE
SERIES VI. FOUNDATIONS OF MORAL EDUCATION, VOL. 1

General Editor
George F. McLean

PHILOSOPHICAL FOUNDATIONS FOR MORAL EDUCATION AND CHARACTER DEVELOPMENT:

Act and Agent

Edited by

George F. McLean

Frederick E. Ellrod

Second edition expanded

THE COUNCIL FOR RESEARCH IN VALUES AND PHILOSOPHY

Copyright © 1992 by
The Council for Research in Values and Philosophy

Box 261
Cardinal Station
Washington, D.C. 20064

All rights reserved

Printed in the United States of America

Library of Congress Cataloging-in-Publication

Philosophical Foundations for Moral Education and Character Development-- 2nd ed., rev. and expanded
p. cm. -- (Cultural heritage and contemporary change, George F. McLean, Gen. ed.; Series VI, Foundations of Moral Education; vol. 1)
Includes bibliographical references and index.
1. Ehics. 2. Moral education. 3. Moral development. 4. Act (Philosophy 5. Agent (Philosophy)
I. Ryan, Kevin; II. Lickona, Thomas; III. Series.
BJ1012.A26 1992
170--dc20　　　　　　　　　　　　　　　　　　　　　　　　　91-30829
　　　　　　　　　　　　　　　　　　　　　　　　　　　　　　CIP

ISBN 1-56518-001-1
ISBN 1-56518-000-3(pbk.)

THE COUNCIL FOR RESEARCH IN VALUES AND PHILOSOPHY

S. Avineri, Israel	H.D. Lewis, UK
P. Balasubramaniam, India	S. Lokuang, Taipei
P. Bodunrin, Nigeria	A. Lopez Quintas, Spain
V. Cauchy, Canada	M. Markovic, Yugoslavia
M. Chatterjee, India	H. Nasr, USA/Iran
R. De George, USA	Ngwey Ngond'a Ndenge, Zaire
M. Dy, Philippines	J. Nyasani, Kenya
I.T. Frolov, USSR	C. Pan, Singapore
H.G. Gadamer, BDR	Paulus Gregorios, India
A. Gallo, Guatemala	O. Pegoraro, Brazil
K. Gyekye, Ghana	C. Ramirez, Costa Rica
P. Henrici, Italy	P. Ricoeur, France
J. Hoyos Vellez, Colombia	M. Sastrapatedja, Indonesia
T. Imamichi, Japan	J. Scannone, Argentina
A. Irala Burgos, Paraguay	K. Schmitz, Canada
J. Kellerman, Hungary	V. Shen, Taipei
M. Kente, Tanzania	W. Strozewski, Poland
R. Knowles, USA	Tang Yi-jie, Peking
J. Kromkowski, USA	J. Teran-Dutari, Ecuador
J. Ladrière, Belgium	G. Tlaba, Lesotho
P. Laleye, Senegal	Wang Miao-yang, Shanghai

George F. McLean, Secretary

Cardinal Station, P. O. Box 261
Washington, D.C. 20064
Tel. 202/319-5636; Fax. 202/319-6089

ACKNOWLEDGEMENTS

Grateful acknowledgement is made to Silver Burdett Co., Morristown, N.J., for permission to quote from F. Clark Power and Lawrence Kohlberg, "Religion and Religious Maturity" in J. Fowler and A. Vergote, eds., *Toward Moral and Religious Maturity*; to Houghton Mifflin Co., Boston, Mass., for permission to quote from Lawrence Kohlberg, "State and Sequence" in D. Goslin, ed., *Handbook of Socialization Theory and Research*; to Macmillan Publishing Co., New York and Routledge & Keegan Paul, Ltd., London, for permission to quote from Martin Buber, *Between Man and Man*; to Plenum Press, New York, for permission to quote from D. Callahan and S. Bok, eds., *Ethics Teaching in Higher Education*; to *The International Philosophical Quarterly* for permission to quote from R. Peters, "Moral Development: A Plea for Pluralism"; and to John Wilson for permission from his *Practical Methods of Moral Education*.

TABLE OF CONTENTS

CONTENTS	v
PREFACE	vii
INTRODUCTION	

PART I. PHILOSOPHICAL RESOURCES

1. Contemporary Philosophies of Moral Education by *Frederick E. Ellrod*	9
2. Backgrounds in American Philosophers for a Theory of Moral Development by *Jesse A. Mann*	43
3. Affectivity: The Power Base of Moral Behavior by *Sebastian A. Samay*	61
4. Traditions, Cultures and Values by *George F. McLean*	99

PART II. ASPECTS OF AN INTEGRATED THEORY OF THE MORAL AGENT

5. Freedom and Moral Choice by *Frederick E. Ellrod*	123
6. Moral Character by *Walter Nicgorski* and *Frederick E. Ellrod*	143
7. Moral Reasoning by *Joseph M. Boyle, Jr.*	163
8. A Phenomenology of Moral Sensibility: Moral Emotion by *John D. Caputo*	191
9. The Human Good and Moral Choice by *John Farrelly*	211
10. On the Foundations of Moral Judgment by *David Schindler*	251
11. The Moral Environment by *Walter Nicgorski*	281
12. On the Integrity of Morality in Relation to Religion by *David Schindler*	303

PART III. THE UNITY OF THE MORAL AGENT

13. The Person, Moral Growth and Character Development by *George F. McLean*	327
CONCLUSION	357
INDEX	361

PREFACE TO THE SECOND EDITION

This series of studies on The Foundations of Moral Education, having met full success, is now in the process of being reprinted. The occasion makes possible an important addition to the present volume.

The project was undertaken in response to an emerging awareness of the importance of value horizons for education and personal development. Values Clarification was the first of the recent efforts to fill this need. It attempted merely to make evident and effective the guiding choices latent in one's life. This was succeeded by the more technical efforts of J. Piaget and L. Kohlberg to chart the dynamics of the development of moral reasoning toward more abstract and principled levels.

However, the issue was broader and deeper than one of techniques. Persons are complex physical realities with sensation and perceptions, feelings and emotions, intellect and insight, will and love--and, of course, their contraries. Over time and interacting with family and community they shape their raw capabilities into a character which gives shape and consistency to their personal and social life. To better understand this and to help in its development requires not only ancient wisdom, but really new understanding. This challenged teams of specialists in philosophy, psychology and education to work together over a two year period to carry out the creative work required to generate the needed new insight.

The work was begun by a team of nine philosophers who, after surveying the state of the question and the resources available in North American and European philosophy, proceeded to develop an integrated understanding of the person with special attention to one's capacity for moral action. They looked into the classical patterns of ethical reasoning in relation to moral principles, the more recent phenomenological understandings of the development of purpose and commitment in the process of one's complex and multileveled interrelations with family and community, and the relation of both to one's overall religious and philosophical horizons. This made possible a better understanding of moral growth as a process of developing personal character, consisting of values and virtues, which enables and orients responsible and creative moral action. The work of this team of philosophers constitutes the present volume.

In the few intervening years since its publication there has been increased understanding of how these values and virtues are not only individual, but over time are shaped by the experience, modes of understanding and creative life of a people. Just as in the individual this forms character, in a people it forms culture, within which individuals grow and shape themselves and their life. From generation to generation this sense of what promotes a good life and hence of what is decent *(decet)* in human interaction is continually reevaluated, selectively passed on *(tradita)*, and hence comes to constitute a cultural tradition. This constitutes the humanizing patrimony with which each one sets out on his or her life pilgrimage. The studies of hermeneutics by such figures as H.G. Gadamer and J. Habermas, which followed upon the extended basic studies of the person by M. Heidegger and others, have made possible new understanding. This promises to be most fruitful for understanding ways in which education broadly understood can and should be also a process of value and character development. Chapter four has been added to this second edition of *Act and Agent: Philosophical Foundations of Moral Education and Character Development* to present these crucial recent developments.

The second volume in the project is the work of a team of psychologists who began work one year after the philosophers and carried out a similar investigation in their own field. In the process they developed new dimensions of psychology relating especially to the way personal responsibility extends beyond conditioning by the environment, to the properly moral aspect of emotions, and to the significance for character development of interpersonal example and its imaginative mode as story telling. The resulting volume, edited by R. Knowles, is entitled *Psychological Foundations for Moral Education and Character Development: An Integrated Theory of Moral Development*. Two major accomplishments complete the volume: an integrated psychological theory of moral development and the sketch of life-long moral development from infancy to old age, identifying at each stage what one can hope to accomplish and how others can help. This serves as a bridge from the more theoretical work of the philosophers and psychologists to that of the team in education begun one year later.

With the resources of the two studies described above this team from schools and research institutes of education in the United States and Canada undertook to survey the history and concrete challenge of moral education to the process of education itself (T. Lickona). The school was studied not only as an institution of learning, but also as an ordered community central to the formation of the moral outlook and capacitation of students during their most formative years. The study focused on the challenges and on approaches which could best serve at the elementary, junior high, high school and college levels. It reached further to study the role of parents, religion and the media in this work. This volume, edited by Kevin Ryan, is entitled *Character Development in Schools and Beyond*. The Association for Supervision and Curriculum Development booklet, *Moral Education in the Life of the School*, is shorter but very similar to this work.

Other related studies have been and are being carried out. A volume entitled *The Social Context of Values, Perspectives of the Americas*, largely by Latin America authors, looks into the psycho-social and socio-cultural bases of value formation, whose liberative effect it then studies in relation to history, technology, aesthetics and religion. Other volumes such as *Chinese Foundations for Moral Education and Character Development* mine related resources in other cultural traditions.

On a continuing basis Duquesne University has instituted the Center for Character Education, Civic Responsibility and Teaching. Its work has been especially concerned with the way moral and character education draws on the resources of a culture and creatively bears that forward for a new generation. The Center has been holding workshops with teachers to develop teaching materials which will enable the content in the volumes of this series to contribute concretely to work in the classroom at the different levels.

Each generation must struggle to understand its own life and to prepare its offspring to shape their own. This is the central and on-going human challenge envisaged by The Foundations of Moral Education project of which the present volume is the first step.

G. McLean

INTRODUCTION

FREDERICK E. ELLROD III

In recent years rapid cultural change and intense social pressures have created a number of urgent and deeply felt concerns in the area of moral education. Parents have found particularly difficult the question of transmission of values to their children; young people have found themselves in a quandary when it comes to determining the importance of a moral outlook and shaping one that will handle the new problems they face. At the same time heated debates over social issues have brought into sharp relief the need for good moral qualities, along with questions about exactly what those qualities are, so that the public is now broadly concerned about the moral fabric of American life. Hence, a major request of parents to school boards in recent years has been for the development of the overall educational program in a way that will contribute to good character formation for their children.

This has moved many school systems to introduce significant programs of moral education, even in the early grades, generally either on the model of Lawrence Kohlberg's "cognitive-developmental" approach or on that of the "values clarification" methods devised by Sidney B. Simon, Howard Kirschenbaum, and others. These programs have been beneficial in assisting students in some cases to become more conscious of the values they actually hold and to grow in moral sensitivity and maturity. Experience with these programs, however, has indicated that there are dimensions of moral education to which they do not attend and that, among other problems, this has encouraged a tendency toward moral relativism in society. Hence teacher formation leaders have noted as the most urgent needs: the laying of a firm and universal foundation for morality, the elaboration of a broader understanding of the moral person which integrates both cognitive and affective dimensions of character development, the determination of the related psychological dynamics of personal growth, and the development of related educational policies and teacher training programs.

This calls for coordinated contributions from ethics, developmental psychology, and education, designed to complement, enrich and promote existing moral education approaches. Accordingly, a research project was initiated to outline a new and more comprehensive account of what is involved in moral knowledge and action, how the person develops to attain maturity in these respects, and how an educational system may assist that development in practice.

The work of the four-year project, "Foundations of Moral Education," has involved three ten-person teams of philosophers, psychologists, and specialists in education, most working for two years. Each group has combined periods of personal research on component issues with seminar-type meetings to plan, discuss and advance that research, ensuring that the result is not simply a collection of essays, but a systematic, well researched, critically examined approach to moral education. Each team has produced a volume with its separate integrity, developed in view of the others. The three volumes, of which this is the first, are entitled:

1. *Act and Agent: Philosophical Foundations of Moral Education and Character Development*
2. *Psychological Foundations of Moral Education and Character Development* (Washington: University Press of America, 1986)
3. *Character Development in Schools and Beyond* (New York: Praeger, 1986)

Volumes now in preparation on the social context and values and on related issues in the Latin American, Chinese and other cultural contexts will carry forward this work.

II

The current volume concentrates upon questions which precede precise definition of psychological stages and educational techniques: What is it that constitutes a morally mature person? What is the nature and what are the conditions of the "moral action" which such a person must be able to carry out? With this clearly in view the subsequent volumes will proceed to examine the actual development of the person through the stages revealed by psychological study, and design educational methods for promoting such developments.

The project, then, is an attempt to propose a distinctive paradigm or general approach to moral education. It is, of course, not entirely new; it stands close to what might be called common sense in moral training, and is indebted both to contemporary theories of moral education and to the tradition of Western thought on which it draws. For this reason each section involves criticism and discussion of earlier work as well as a constructive account of its proper contribution. This account is not, of course, presented as final and conclusive, for discussion and application of the approach here described will no doubt lead to further progress. Nonetheless, it does hope to make a significant contribution to the elaboration of a more adequate view of moral development.

The approach presented here is unified in its basic claims. The authors have not come to agreement on every issue raised, nor need they have done so; but together and over the period of their collaboration they have worked out a framework sufficiently unitary to make of their contributions not merely a collection of essays, but a cohesive step ahead.

This framework may be called an *integrative* one, for it combines what is valid in several approaches to the moral person, all of which elements are necessary to make possible our public and private human lives. It makes the claim that there is an objective foundation for ethics in the human good; but the person grows slowly in his *ideas* concerning that good, and must thus be approached differently at different stages. It holds that cognitive elements are extremely important in moral action, but not the *only* factors at work; the emotional life and the relatively fixed character traits of the agent have parts to play as well in moral decision and in the execution of moral action.

The integrative approach includes the assertion that the human person is fundamentally free in those deeds which can be evaluated according to moral criteria, along with the understanding that the social environment in which moral development takes place is extremely important, but not all-determining, for that development. In addition, it asserts, in line with recent writings in cognitive-developmental psychology, that the individual's religious life plays a foundational role of a certain sort in his attention to moral concerns, although it is not identical with morality. Finally, the general approach of the investigations which follow may be described as *person-centered*: the notion of the human person is taken as a central idea around which the various facets of moral action described above may fruitfully be organized. These points are argued in detail in the articles that follow.

All of the current approaches to moral education are in possession of valuable insights and crucial data. Their main defect lies in a tendency to oversimplify, to avoid or ignore certain aspects of the moral life and to overemphasize others. The task we have set ourselves is, first, that of the appreciation of work done; second, that of adding the elements needed for a comprehensive vision; and third, that of integrating all these elements in a more adequate understanding of the moral agent.

The organization of our approach may be clarified by considering an example of moral action. For this purpose we may employ a simple case, so that the main lines of the theory may be displayed in a situation where most would agree on the appropriate resolution. It should be taken not as a paradigm for all such action, but only as a case in which the various elements discussed may be seen at work. Here the approach is merely described; the details of our analysis are worked out in the articles that follow. The case is developed explicitly in a particular context in Chapter VIII below.

Let us suppose that an employer is faced with a decision: whether to use racial factors to discriminate among job applicants. We may then distinguish a number of factors in the situation to which attention must be drawn in understanding how the employer acts as a moral agent. The individual is faced with a *choice* among possible actions; but this choice is not made in a vacuum, for both his own prior inclinations or *character*, and the *social context*, will encourage certain actions over others. His *reasoning* about the problem is essential to solving it as a moral agent; but that reasoning cannot be complete without reference to judgments about objective *good*, to the goals or ends of action. His *emotional* response may play several sorts of roles in shaping the act; and the *religious* convictions of the agent about the rights and wrongs of discriminating among persons on such grounds will also play a major role.

III

The plan of this volume is built upon the need to attend to the above considerations.

The first section examines the current state of moral education, with emphasis upon its theoretical resources rather than upon actual research and techniques, which will be treated more fully in the corresponding parts of the later volumes. Chapter II, "Backgrounds in American Philosophy for the Theory of Moral Development," sets this in historical context by discussing certain major North American philosophical influences operative on these modern theories, such as Dewey and Royce. Chapter III on affectivity develops insights suggested by Continental philosophy which challenge the theories based upon the development of knowledge and judgment that have been influential in contemporary moral education. Together these papers invite the reader to rethink the whole basis for the development of responsible students and citizens in our times (see Ch. III, Epilogue).

The next section engages this rethinking by taking up one by one the various aspects of an integrated account of the moral agent. Each starts from current debates on one aspect of the issue and attempts to show how they should be resolved to provide an adequate picture of the acting person: freedom of choice, training of character, correctness of reasoning, rightness of emotion, affectivity and value-judgment, and proper relations to the social, cultural and religious environment. The various papers attempt to draw upon the resources of many philosophical traditions to elaborate a more adequate understanding of the essential aspects of the person. From their diverse philosophical positions, through alternating periods of intensive seminar discussion and research, the authors were able to elaborate chapters which are mutually complementary, though not without creative mutual tensions. The resulting work integrates these multiple philosophical resources and brings them to bear in a coordinated manner to identify, understand and interrelate the various dimensions of the person who would act morally and responsibly as citizen in our world.

The final section draws all of this together by elaborating the multiple dimensions of the concept of the person, often used as a standard or even as basis for a moral theory without sufficient analysis. In this way the various strands or facets of the second part are shown to be aspects of a single acting being, the subject of moral action. Subsequent volumes in this series from the Latin American (*The Social Context and Values: Perspectives of the Americas*), Chinese (*Chinese Foundations of Moral Education and Character Development*) and other cultures add substantively to this Western focus upon the person by elaborating the implications for moral education of the insights of their rich heritages into the importance of the social and communitary dimensions of human life.

IV

The intense discussion of the papers that make up this volume has added immeasurably to their individual quality and collective integrity. Each of the members of the group, therefore, along with those of the psychological and educational committees, has made important contributions to all of the papers. The series of meetings was made possible by grants from the Dyson Corporation and from the Council for Research in Values and Philosophy. Indispensable secretarial work in managing this enterprise was accomplished by Bonnie Kennedy.

Finally, acknowledgement must be made to all those who have worked, often brilliantly, on the topics of moral education, including those with whom we have found reason to disagree. Such people as Lawrence Kohlberg, Jean Piaget, Howard Kirschenbaum, Paul J. Philibert, and others have made important contributions to the integrated view represented by this volume and those to follow.

PART I

PHILOSOPHICAL RESOURCES

CHAPTER I

CONTEMPORARY PHILOSOPHIES

OF

MORAL EDUCATION

FREDERICK E. ELLROD III

INTRODUCTION

Moral education is an activity which must draw upon two theoretical studies and apply their results to action. On the one hand, the notion of morality, traditionally the province of philosophy, gives moral education its goal; a theory of moral education will obviously depend heavily on the understanding of the person and of ethics or morality it takes to be correct. On the other, the makeup and dynamics of the human person as stated in psychology determine how this person can become a moral agent, able to think and act according to philosophically determined standards of morality. Finally, education is the act which puts this theoretical background to work and determines programs, procedures, methods, and tests relating to the development of good moral agents.

In considering the present state of moral education, we shall examine four currently influential views with regard to their background and assumptions. Our approach in this volume will focus on the underlying philosophies of these movements; they will be reviewed more closely from psychological and educational standpoints in succeeding volumes of this work. In the treatment here, each one will be considered in five steps. First of all, we will ask (1) what sorts of human activity, according to this particular view, fall within the range of moral evaluation and thus of moral education. When combined with (2) the practical methods it recommends, this may allow us to see the underlying (3) philosophical and (4) psychological background of each view, even if this is not stated explicitly by proponents of that view. We shall then (5) evaluate the overall adequacy of each approach as an account of the development of the moral agent. From this will become apparent the strengths and weaknesses of the various movements, and the problems which must be resolved in delineating a comprehensive and adequate view.

But to judge the adequacy of an approach we need a standard of adequacy; even to pick out "moral education theories" to discuss we must employ some tacit understanding of the kind of thing we are talking about. This general background, rooted in the commonplace moral experience which every person shares, will be assumed in all that follows. We find ourselves making moral judgments and acting on them: these are the data from which we begin. We want to know how to become better at doing these things, and to help others, especially young people, to do so. It is appropriate, then, to consider briefly and at the beginning what we mean by "morality."

Morality has to do with human action, and with evaluating action: how to act or to live *well* in some respect. On some accounts all kinds of actions are included in the scope of morality, from eating a sandwich to dying for a cause; on others only certain actions are "moral actions," others being nonmoral or unmoral (not *im*moral). Though moralists disagree on what it is about actions that makes them moral or immoral, it seems clear that action is fundamental. "Moral judgment," "moral theory," "moral development," and certainly "moral education" are all defined by reference to the idea of better or worse action.

Equally elementary is the fact that human action, though it is the action of a single unified person and not a committee, is not simple. It depends on a complex web of processes and abilities, from neural firing to formal-operational judgment. "Moral education," then, may be used to refer to the ways in which people acquire whatever abilities are necessary to act well in these respects, to become good moral agents. Many necessary abilities are studied in other connections by, for example, the neurobiologist and the efficiency expert, but the study of moral psychology and moral education is usually confined to those aspects of the person which are peculiar to moral functioning or play a central role there. Moral psychology asks the question: What is it in the person that makes one a moral agent?--assuming from philosophical ethics a conception of morality on which this question is based. Moral education then builds upon this to ask: How, in practice, can we develop these abilities in people?

Our purpose here is not to examine every such theory that has ever been proposed, but rather to focus on those with considerable influence here and now: the values clarification, cognitive-developmental, cognitive-analytic, and traditional theories. On the basis of this survey we may be able to reach conclusions with more far-reaching application.

THE VALUES CLARIFICATION THEORY OF MORAL EDUCATION

The movement known as "values clarification" had its start in the work of Louis Raths and others during the 1950s and 1960s, first set forth in book-length form by Raths with Merrill Harmin and Sidney B. Simon in *Values and Teaching* (1966).[1] Its theoretical structure remained relatively unchanged in succeeding years, as remarked by Howard Kirschenbaum in a later collection of essays, *Readings in Values Clarification* (1973).[2] Some suggestions toward revising the approach were made by Kirschenbaum at that time, and in his more recent work *Advanced Values Clarification* (1977).[3] In general, though the movement's founders have occasionally drawn attention to its theoretical and research base,[4] the values clarification school of thought has been relatively loose and pluriform; it has tended more to practical technique than to theory[5]. The following is a brief summary, noting its implications and presuppositions.

(1) The range of application for values clarification methods extends beyond "moral issues" narrowly conceived into various sorts of life decisions. The proponents of values clarification point to the presence of values in every choice and selection; thus while attention is restricted to the "values aspects" of things, practically everything has such aspects.[6] The focus of the movement, however, is not on the specific valuations made, and in fact its techniques tend to lead away from any judgment about individuals' evaluations. Instead, values education in this form attempts to teach strategies for straightening out or making consistent one's personal system or hierarchy of values.

It is assumed that a person already holds certain things to be important or valuable, but that one's understanding of this set of values and how they are related is often confused, so that a person's values may contain incompatible elements without a clear order of priority. Similarly, action in accordance with these values may be inhibited by reluctance to acknowledge publicly what one values, or to accept it where it conflicts with those value-judgments which are emphasized by authority or by a peer group. Thus values clarification is a way of removing inconsistencies, making clear to oneself one's deep preferences, and developing pride and confidence in whatever values one espouses. The emphasis is on the special expertise of *valuing,* but how one performs this valuing will make a difference in all areas of life. In this commitment first of all to a general principle of self-examination, rather than to any particular conclusions or value-judgments, the values clarification approach reflects one aspect of the Socratic tradition of the "examined life."

(2) The sort of moral instruction offered under values clarification, then, is not the statement of rules or principles of a substantive sort. Instead, good valuing *methods* are emphasized, including a seven-step procedure for bringing to light the coherence and sincerity of one's value-commitments.

> The valuing process as defined here is a process by which we increase the likelihood that our living in general or a decision in particular will first, have positive value for us, and, second, be constructive in the social context.

> The most important and inclusive objective, stated in strict behavioral terms, might be: When confronted by an important decision, the student will select and skillfully utilize the appropriate valuing processes. The processes chosen will meet the criteria of 'appropriate selection' and 'skillful integration' if the actual consequences of these processes are both personally satisfying and socially constructive.[7]

12 Contemporary Philosophies of Moral Education

These valuing processes include the following:

A. Choosing:

1. Choosing from Alternatives. One considers a number of possible alternatives in deciding what one values, rather than fixing on something without considering possible competing values.
2. Choosing after considering consequences. One adopts a value after taking note of its long range results as well as its immediate appeal, along with the consequences of other alternatives.
3. Choosing Freely. The choice of what is valued is made according to one's own lights, not under pressure from peers or figures of authority.

B. Prizing:

4. Prizing and Cherishing. One prizes or holds important that which one values, and is concerned to seek and protect it.
5. Publicly Affirming. One acknowledges one's values in the presence of others rather than concealing or denying them.

C. Acting:

6. Acting. One does not merely passively "cherish" what is valued, but rather puts it into practice, acting in accord with one's valuational priorities.
7. Acting with a Pattern, Repetition, and Consistency. If something is truly valued, it will not merely stimulate a single impulsive effort on its behalf, but will continue to inform one's action over a period of time, consistent in its importance and in its relation to other values.[8]

The techniques to be used, then, involve more than simply free-flowing discussions where values are exhibited: imaginative and personally involving ways of getting people to order and schematize their value-beliefs are emphasized.[9]

This procedure allows a person to carry out a certain sort of criticism of value-commitments, but any such criticism must be internal to the person's system of values. Two of my values may conflict with each other, as revealed by the above methods, and thus force me to choose or somehow arbitrate between them. My consistency, sincerity, or autonomy in value-selection may be examined; but the method does not necessarily lead me to compare my values directly to any standard outside my existing system of values (though it does refer to the consequences my choices have for others).[10] The many techniques for values clarification are means of making clear one's actual current values; only secondarily are they means for criticizing or altering them. Even my public affirmation and communication of values, which might normally arouse challenge or disagreement and thus stimulate change, is deflected to some extent from encouraging any change in my value-commitments by the admonition to choose autonomously and to be wary of others' pressure.

There is no suggestion here that any values might be incorrect or wrong in themselves, aside from their conflict with other values.[11] In fact, the early forms at least of values clarification made it explicit that they were *not* based on any assumption that there were real objective goods against which personal commitments could be measured. While they did not actually deny the possibility of such goods, the operating assumption seemed to be one of value-relativism, insofar as any criticism of a person's valuing was sharply discouraged.[12] This tendency has been mitigated somewhat in more recent formulations of the approach, in acknowledging that the approach itself assumes certain values to be correct, as will be discussed below.[13]

(3) These methods of moral education are designed around certain basic assumptions. The teacher seeks to lead students to think about their own values, to look for them in ways likely to reveal them; it is assumed that everyone *has* such values and that the business of moral education is more to unearth and clarify them than to change them. In this way values clarification attempts to respect the autonomy and freedom of students by refusing to tamper with their values; it merely helps them to elucidate these values and leaves any possible reevaluation entirely to the individual.[14]

There is a close kinship here with contemporary analytic philosophy, which often claims not to discover new truths or to solve substantive problems, but only to clarify and untangle the confusions of ordinary language. But there is also a similarity to modern phenomenological philosophy where the pure description of the given, without judgment as to its reality, becomes paramount in some cases. Yet again, existentialistic ethical notions can easily be fitted into the values clarification framework, since on this account there is no absolute standard for value but, in at least some formulations, only a radical decision by the individual whether to accept a value or not.[15]

In values clarification methods, no judgment is generally passed on a proclaimed value, and no standard mentioned by which a confused individual may choose even among his own confused valuations; the notion of a pure and arbitrary decision could readily find a home here. The approach attempts to avoid what its supporters consider to be the provincialism and dogmatism of claiming universal validity for a single set of values, an attitude which they found highly objectionable in traditional moral education. For those influenced by these philosophical lines of thought, values clarification may appear as a useful and "neutral," nonindoctrinative method.

The techniques of values clarification are thus "formal" in this sense: they describe a format or procedure for arriving at answers about what is valued, rather than giving a set of specific answers directly.[16]

Such a distinction between the "form" of moral thought and its "matter" or "content" (the particular judgments of value or disvalue) is prominent in modern moral thought. It functions often as a way of respecting the autonomy of the individual, since one teaches merely *how* to think, not *what* to think: the same form can apply to many sorts of content, as the seven-phase clarification procedure can be used no matter what the specific values of the individual. The outcome of the clarification procedure would normally be a set of "material" moral principles, specific values, endorsing particular goods, for it is assumed that the one who values will in the end find himself committed to some values or other.[17] But insofar as no conditions beyond these formal ones are imposed, it is evident that different individuals could choose varied and conflicting hierarchies of value, each meeting the requirements of the seven-step method and each "clarifiable."

One might argue that certain values are implicit in the method itself, and in the positive decision that it ought to be adopted. The refusal to impose one person's value-choices on another, and the positive injunction to "choose freely," evince a respect for democratic tolerance-- a fairly unsurprising value in a pluralistic society which must nonetheless continue to function harmoniously. As Kirschenbaum observes:

> there are certain value judgments implicit in each process. If we urge critical thinking, then we value rationality. If we support moral reasoning, then we value justice. If we advocate divergent thinking, then we value creativity. If we uphold free choice, then we value autonomy or freedom. If we encourage "no-lose" conflict resolution, then we value equality.[18]

The method reflects, in addition, a demand for personal authenticity and sincerity, both in freely choosing one's commitments and in publicly affirming them;[19] the judgment that authenticity is a vital value is a major existentialist theme.

There is also a different sort of "value" that might be claimed for the clarification process itself, the value of clear valuing: the clarification helps one achieve one's values, whatever they may be, more *effectively*. Thus writers in the movement will occasionally speak vaguely of its assistance in finding values that "best suit" one's environment, in "adjusting" them or making "intelligent" choices--values that "work" or are "effective."[20] Values clarification is claimed to be a means to certain ends: "we experience a stronger self-esteem; we experience greater meaning in our lives; we are less apathetic and flighty, more purposeful and committed."[21] The processes themselves are means to these ends, which are themselves primarily qualities that help toward further ends which can be better accomplished through purposefulness and commitment.

This sort of recommendation depends on a different philosophical strain: the pragmatist emphasis on the value of means toward an end.[22]

On occasion a further link is made with humanistic psychology in the reference to "fulfilled, self-actualizing" values.[23] Each of these ways of providing rational grounds for entering upon the examination of values assumes some other particular value which is to be served by the resulting clarification: democracy, authenticity, efficiency, self-fulfillment. But these assumed values are not always made explicit, although more attention has been paid to this point in recent discussion.

(4) If it is possible to extract an underlying moral psychology as well from the values clarification view, it, too, would seem to be that of humanistic psychology (as represented, for example, by Carl Rogers).[24] Attention seems to be focused entirely on the achievement of value-*knowledge* of a sort, on discovering that something "is a value for" (is valued by) me, and on making sure that such acceptance is sincere, that is, that I put it into action as well as hold it in theory.

But, while it is claimed that one must *act* on a true value, this action itself is seen as relatively unproblematic. Active pursuit of values is taken more as a measure of true commitment than as something with its own difficulties and complications. While rank-ordering of values is a common strategy, for instance, the more complex procedures for choice involved in principles such as that of marginal utility, or the traditional principle of double effect, are neglected.[25] Much less are "weakness of will" or excessive stubbornness addressed as problems toward which moral education might be directed. Thus, except for the warnings against adverse peer pressure in public affirmation, little attention is given to internal difficulties in actualizing one's values. The injunction seems more to warn against possible failure to make a real, active commitment than to suggest a view of how values are carried into action. It is true that the approach also stresses that when one acts for one's values one does so *repeatedly* and *consistently*. Nevertheless, there is little suggestion as to how one accomplishes this, whether some sort of self-training is necessary or whether there might be difficulty at times in acting in obedience to one's values (though Kirschenbaum has recently mentioned *competence* as a factor in achieving what one values).[26]

We may infer, then, that on the values clarification model the person is basically able to act on the declared values and will spontaneously do so if these can be made clear. Otherwise one would expect to see some importance given to the way in which one forms habits of repeated and consistent action, or to the development of "will power."[27] The strategies seem devoted to clarification rather than activation. Kirschenbaum does point out certain emotional conditions for good valuing,[28] and the emphasis on an atmosphere of trust and caring suggests some practical attention to this. The mere fact of having action as a separate step at all may be taken to suggest that there may be unique obstacles to executing one's decisions; but these are not specified, nor is the moral agent shown how to deal with them.

There is thus the danger that values clarification training will become a classroom exercise alone, as Kirschenbaum himself notes.[29] It may be that the movement makes assumptions similar to those of Rogerian psychology, that given a clear and undistorted ("innocent") understanding of what is valued, the healthy person will spontaneously move toward it. This would also help explain the relatively uncritical nature of values clarification methods, for such psychologists also tend to hold that one will identify "real" values if one is freed of distortions and inhibitions (often socially imposed).[30]

(5) Values clarification methods are clearly useful. Whether "value" is objective or subjective, the individual will benefit from becoming clear about it. Further, the relatively uncritical stance of the techniques helps to avoid crushing spontaneity and enforcing conformity, which may well be an important consideration at certain stages and in some circumstances. Such methods bring to the fore the fact that while factual knowledge enters into commonplace decision-making, it does not fully determine decision without the addition of value-principles of some kind.[31] Further, the methods, insofar as they stress personal prizing and cherishing, underline the importance of the affective side of the person, a more than purely cognitive involvement with the valued object. The emphasis on action in accordance with one's values suggests that they are not truly our own values until they have come to inform our actions in an enduring patterning of our choices. These are valuable contributions particularly because of the weakness of the theory's major rival, cognitive-developmentalism, in the area of translating thought into action, as we shall see.[32] All of these issues--the questions of indoctrination and autonomy, of fact and value, and of affective and cognitive factors--will require fuller examination in the following papers; but it seems clear that methods like those advocated by Raths, Simon, and Kirschenbaum will play some role in a well-constructed program of moral education.

As has been suggested above, however, values clarification also contains serious difficulties. Despite Kirschenbaum's association of the method with acts which are "personally satisfying" and "socially productive," these are treated as entirely a matter of whatever the particular individuals in question happen to prefer.[33] This reveals an underlying relativism which is insufficient as a basis for moral education.[34] It tends to result in the subtle insertion of tacit values which are unexamined.[35] Even if such values are made explicit and acknowledged, there remains the question of why these particular values (e.g., democracy, self-actualization, authenticity) are chosen, whether others should also be respected, and how any values are grounded (since the clarification process does not provide any justification at all for the acceptance of a value: "value clarification cannot solve this dilemma").[36]

On the other hand, if one fails to go beyond the clarification methods, it is impossible to criticize or change one's valuings rationally and systematically, since the methods do not clearly distinguish actual valuings from what one *ought* to value.[37] Some important "virtues" are simply built into the valuing processes themselves without examination: courage in acting on one's beliefs publicly, wisdom in "competence."[38] In addition, the emphasis on a private and individual determination of what is valued, when coupled with the humanistic psychologist's ethic of self-fulfillment, can suggest a purely self-interested moral view (although it does not necessarily do so, as Kirschenbaum stresses).[39]

From a philosophical point of view the most fundamental problem in the values clarification theory is its lack of standards for value-judgment independent of the individual's pre-existing values. It is not clear what is supposed to be left free to operate "naturally" once the field of one's valuings has been cleared and inhibitions removed, unless a pure, groundless existentialist choice is to be invoked. If one granted the existence of something really and independently valuable, such strategies might allow these things to "appear" in undistorted fashion; but proponents of the theory tend to shy away from this further step. The affective involvement stressed by values clarification is given no basis in reality; it seems no more than a set of arbitrary or accidental preferences for certain states of affairs over others. If ethics is to be objective, then some common reference for these commitments must be found.

Because there is no independent basis on which values can be criticized, it seems impossible on the values clarification model to resolve some conflicts in moral views, whether among persons or within a single person's considerations, when these conflicts are not merely results of confusions or unclarities. If I find that when utmost clarity is attained values A and B are incompatible, how can I decide which of them to give up or which is to be subordinated to the other? This weakness suggests that no systematic changes in values accepted are to be expected from the application of clarification techniques.[40] Changes may occur, but they are not likely to proceed in any particular direction (e.g., toward greater tolerance or respect for persons) if the agent has no more to go on than the demand for consistency among his various preferences; any pattern among such changes will be accidental from the viewpoint of the method. Yet, unless one embraces a relativism of values, one would expect a progressive sort of change to occur as the growing person works toward more adequate valuing. Values clarification theory has no criteria for such change, nor strategies to assist it.

Here one might make a case for adding to clarification techniques some return to the presentation of substantive moral principles to the child as well, although they need not be presented indoctrinatively. If it is not assumed in advance that values are entirely relative to the valuer, then a parallel may be drawn with education in the sciences. In science education, the current trend is to teach the student how scientific discoveries are made as well as what has actually been discovered. But one does not simply give the child the requisite methodological tools and leave her to reduplicate the work of Aristotle, Galileo, Newton and Einstein; she is expected also to profit from being taught the results of the work of generations of other discoverers. Even if values clarification provided sufficient conceptual equipment for the discovery of general and objective values, would it not make sense to assume, similarly, that the long tradition of ethical thinking might have something to contribute to the growing child's judgments, so that traditional substantive instruction might be of use?[41]

While values clarification has many good points to offer to a complete theory of moral education, it is not sufficient by itself to provide such a theory.[42]

THE COGNITIVE-DEVELOPMENTAL THEORY OF MORAL EDUCATION

Cognitive-developmental psychology had its start earlier than the values clarification movement, although it seems to have reached the height of its influence slightly later. Jean Piaget's *The Moral Judgment of the Child* set out the basic assumptions and certain results of the approach in 1937; these were both carried further and in some respects altered by Lawrence Kohlberg, who began his work in 1958. No effort will be made here to detail the history or the full theoretical framework of the approach; it will suffice to summarize its main features briefly in the same format we have employed with the values clarification theory, using Kohlberg's formulation as the starting point since it has served most often as the focal point for recent criticism and development.[43]

(1) First we shall examine the scope and limits of the notion of "morality" according to Kohlberg. He limits the range of moral questions quite strictly: moral issues are those having to do with resolving conflicts of interest in society. For this reason they may all be brought under the rubric of "justice," although this is justice more in the sense used by Rawls than in that of Plato.[44] As in values clarification, then, the basic stance of cognitive-developmental theory is one in which there are no standards for, or restrictions on, the action of an individual except the conflicting rights or desires of other individuals. Some recent developments in the approach may to some extent have modified this tendency by an emphasis on the moral development of the *group*, which provides social constraints on individual moral development and on moral action.[45] But the confinement of morality to conflicts of interest apparently remains. Choices that fall outside this area are not moral choices, and Kohlberg suggests no criteria for deciding them aside from personal preference.[46]

Moral education, then, is training in just decision-making, or proper modes of reasoning for resolving conflicts of interest. Thus its range is considerably less than that taken for granted by values clarification theory. Decisions about what vocation to pursue in life, for example, or about sexual matters (among consenting adults), would be considered by a values clarification educator to be value issues; but according to Kohlberg it would seem that they are not moral issues at all.[47]

(2) The techniques used to advance moral decision-making according to Kohlberg's scheme are straightforward and well-known. Further, since testing instruments for advance from one moral stage to another

exist, more controlled and measured experimentation has been done with them than with clarification methods. To understand their purpose, however, we must first be acquainted with the stage structure basic to the theory. Piaget's original work suggested that, after an egocentric period in which cooperative action did not occur at all, the child first adopted a heteronomous morality of constraint, in which rules were taken as absolute and authoritative; from this the child might pass to an autonomous morality of cooperation, with rules seen as self-legislated by the community of participants.[48] Kohlberg's basic theory converts these into a series of six stages, each representing a type of moral reasoning.

Level I: *Preconventional*
   Stage 1: Heteronomous or punishment-and-obedience orientation. The physical consequences of action, particularly as to punishment and reward by others, determine the moral status of an act.
   Stage 2: Instrumental relativism. Right action is what is to my benefit, although this may include reciprocal exchanges of benefit with others in a "marketplace" or trading arrangement.

Level II: *Conventional*
   Stage 3: Interpersonal conformity. Moral goodness consists in carrying out what others expect of someone in my role or position, and in the approval of these others.
   Stage 4: "Law-and-order" orientation. Obeying the fixed laws of the society or group and maintaining social order constitutes right action.

Level III: *Post-Conventional or Principled*
   Stage 5: "Social contract" orientation. Right action is action in accordance with the law as constituted by tacit or explicit agreement among agents with different values and opinions.
   Stage 6: Universalistic ethics. Moral standards are those which are self-chosen and universalizable.[49]

The stage system has been claimed to be developmentally rigid. A child must pass through the stages in an invariable order, without skipping any; one cannot regress, although one may stop temporarily or permanently at any stage. The ordering of the stages represents increasing adequacy of reasoning in solving conflicts of interest: a higher stage is better in that it successfully handles cases for which lower stages of reasoning fail.

This classical version of Kohlberg's stage system has been cast somewhat into question by recent publications in which Kohlberg retracts some of his earlier assertions about the highest stages and about the system as a whole. Kohlberg indicates that his revision of the stage system has been motivated by the failure to find a sixth stage in American and Turkish longitudinal data. The result indicated that my sixth stage was mainly a theoretical construction suggested by the writings of 'elite' figures like Martin Luther King, not an empirically confirmed developmental construct. . . . We now think the safest interpretation would be to view the construct of a sixth stage as representing an elaboration of the B (or advanced) substage of Stage 5.[50]

It is not clear where this leaves the remaining part of the stage structure, particularly in view of Kohlberg's earlier claim that only the sixth stage is fully moral, that "morality" is *defined* by Stage 6 moral reasoning.[51] Nor is it clear that this shift has been accepted by the cognitive-developmental school aside from Kohlberg; for instance, Ralph Mosher, one of Kohlberg's leading followers, was still claiming in 1980 that six stages had been "empirically described."[52] At the same time, Kohlberg himself continues to speak not only about six stages but about a stage 7 in addition.[53] It may be presumed that the basic notion of stage advance, the heart of the theory, has not been abandoned; but it is difficult to determine exactly what stages are now accepted.

From this structure of stages follows the method: moral dilemmas, actual or fictional, are presented. The learner attempts to resolve them. Where one's own level of moral reasoning is unable to solve a problem, one will be receptive to a solution proposed at a level of reasoning one stage higher than one's own, if this should be presented in discussion. Since a person can appreciate reasoning one stage higher than that person's own current stage, and since one will prefer such reasoning where it is evidently more adequate in solving problems, one will tend to "stretch" one's thinking to adopt the higher mode of thought. Thus the discussion of moral dilemmas will tend to induce children to advance more quickly through the stage sequence. This is nonetheless "natural" to them, not arbitrarily imposed by the moral instructor, since the sequence of stages is innate and invariable. In this way the charge of indoctrination is avoided.

(3) Cognitive-developmentalists stress that the concern of the moral educator is with *formal* factors in morality, with general modes of moral reasoning, not with specific content. A mode of moral reasoning is abstract and formal in the sense that it can be applied to any situation by an agent with any given set of feelings, values or interests. It is this common element which Kohlberg's tests are designed to elicit from moral discourse. Thus, again, indoctrination is said to be avoided insofar as no specific values are imposed by the instructor at any point. When constraint is placed on content or value, it is imposed primarily by the learner, in accord with the learner's own reasoning; I may refrain, for instance, from pursuing certain interests because I realize that I would not accept a condition in which everyone else pursued the same interests. Structure, not content, is essential.[54] This allows Kohlberg to em-

phasize the autonomy of the individual moral reasoner, since, according to the original formulations of the theory, no content is received from the instructor. Here also, however, Kohlberg has acknowledged a revision of the theory:

> Some years of active involvement with the practice of moral education have led me to realize . . . that the psychologist's abstract concept "moral stage" is not a sufficient basis for moral education. . . . the educator must be a socializer, teaching value content and behavior, not merely a Socratic facilitator of development. In becoming a socializer and advocate, the teacher moves into "indoctrination," a step that I originally believed to be invalid both philosophically and psychologically. . . .
>
> I no longer hold these negative views of indoctrinative moral education, and I now believe that the concepts guiding moral education must be partly "indoctrinative." . . . Education for moral action, as distinct from reasoning, always presupposes a concern about moral content for its own sake.[55]

It is clear that the underlying ethical theory of cognitive-developmental psychology is that of Kant and his modern successors, particularly Hare and Rawls, in the analytic tradition. The essence of morality is to consist of *rules* governing which actions are permissible, as with the categorical imperative of Kant. In Kant's view, goods or values were excluded as far as possible from moral decision-making, so that moral agents would not be determined in their action by factors other and less than themselves. Instead decisions were to be based on acting only according to a rule that could guide every person's action. The only unconditional good according to Kant is a will that follows this rule.[56] Modern Kantians assume that some values or goals are being pursued by moral agents, but the specifically *moral* activity is the application of rules to this pursuit to ensure that collisions of interest do not occur. Kohlberg and his associates have generally stressed the pre-eminence of rules and formal universality over content, although, again, they seem to have retreated somewhat from their earlier extreme position.[57]

(4) The moral psychology implicit in the theory also has roots in the Kantian tradition. The moral decision or judgment is made as a quasi-logical operation, which tells us that a given act is either right or wrong. This is where classical cognitive-developmentalism stops: it seems to be assumed that it is then up to the agent to act in accord with that judgment. With Kant, the role of the will is emphasized in explaining how one can act on account of the moral law. With Kohlberg, the point has generally been neglected; one gains the impression that the "will" or power to choose is to be influenced primarily through cognitive development, since a strong will can choose either rightly or wrongly, depending on the principles of thinking which direct it.[58] Until the recent revision

of the theory to treat some of the social and religious conditions affecting the agent's ability to act there have been no methods presented for helping the agent to enact moral decisions.[59]

(5) The contribution of cognitive-developmental theory in stressing the moral agent's independent reasoning ability cannot be overstated, and much of the theoretical and empirical work based on the theory will be invaluable in any adequate view of moral education. However, it is also true that the work of Kohlberg and his associates has come under considerable critical fire, and, like values clarification, it appears to have serious problems or deficiencies. Some debate has occurred over the methodology of Kohlberg's psychological research.[60] For our purposes here this is not central; it seems clear that Kohlberg is describing a kind of structure that does exist in the development of moral reasoning, although one may take issue with many aspects of the detailed description. As Kohlberg agrees, however, the philosophical justification of the notion of moral advance is not made simply by reporting the experimental findings on the issue, although it should converge with them to some degree,[61] and it is the philosophical basis with which we are concerned here.

There are significant philosophical problems with the ethical theory of cognitive-developmentalism. At the highest moral stage, it would seem that, if moral reasoning is to direct action adequately, it should tend to lead to some definite judgment about an action's rightness or wrongness.[62] Yet, it is not clear that the level of reasoning alone can produce this, as Kohlberg himself seems to have agreed in later acknowledge some sort of need for teaching of content.[63]

In fact, it can be argued that without assuming some basic valuations, or some rule of procedure other than those included in the forms of reasoning described, many conflicts of interests cannot be resolved at all; for without comparative evaluation of the content of individuals' conflicting claims, there is no way to assign them priority once universalization has placed them on an equal basis.[64] For example, if one person considers health care the most important value and wishes to commit social resources to extensive provisions for medical care, while another scorns this preoccupation and prefers using such resources to provide luxurious cities or lush national parks, there is no way for either to evaluate that decision objectively, for asking each to universalize may merely cause them to reiterate their present preferences in the name of everyone, rather than to examine them critically. Like values clarification, then, cognitive development cannot stand as a *complete* account of moral growth, at least not without some investigation into content of the sort which has only recently been admitted by Kohlberg and his followers to be at all proper as a field for moral psychology and education. Something beyond the stages of moral reasoning is needed to explain our resolution of moral dilemmas in concrete cases.[65]

It can also be argued that the Kohlbergian view (without some modifications still to be developed) cannot answer basic motivational questions concerning moral behavior--the reason why moral action should be undertaken in the first place--unless something like a notion of good or value is admitted.[66] This may be related to the fact that, as has often been remarked, the theory pays too little attention to noncognitive factors. Certainly the emotions, the will or power of choice, and perhaps character or habit, play some part in the execution of moral action, if not in decision-making as well.[67]

Further, as we have seen, many questions considered moral under other common accounts of morality tend to be ignored or rendered nonmoral in Kohlberg's treatment for lack of other standards or criteria, which he would consider "nonmoral" but which are required for moral decisions. Thus the approach seems to narrow unnecessarily the range of morality and of moral education, although the expansion of the Kohlbergian moral education to include content may to some extent return such issues to the sphere of ethics.

The research of cognitive-developmentalists has established essential points about moral reasoning which must form a central part of any comprehensive theory of moral education. Nonetheless, this theory, too, seems inadequate in its present formulation. Possibly the formalism it shares with values clarification is to some extent responsible for this. But in any case, a broader theoretical perspective seems called for.

THE COGNITIVE-ANALYTIC THEORY OF MORAL EDUCATION

In the late 1960's and early 1970's a movement with a somewhat different orientation arose in Great Britain with the publication of a number of books on moral education and related topics under the aegis of the Research Unit in Moral Education of the Farmington Trust, established in 1965, and later of the National Foundation for Educational Research in England and Wales. This approach, whose most prolific representative has been John Wilson, arises more from a philosophical basis than from the psychological orientations of Kohlberg or Piaget, and specifically from that tradition known as analytic philosophy. We shall thus refer to it as "cognitive-analytic," since, once again, its major emphasis is on moral reasoning and thought (cognition).

(1) In an early work, *Reason and Morals*, Wilson argues that the main purpose of morality is to maintain order in society; a secondary purpose is to remind us to respect persons and to regard them "holistically," not merely as tools or machines. He thus extends morality to commonplace social interactions, in line with the major focus of contemporary analytic ethics, but does not mention whether it is also to cover personal or practical decisions other than those involving conflicts of interest.[68] While he mentions the ideal of a "fuller and richer life" and argues for a certain common agreement on purposes in society, it is not clear whether these purposes are included in the social ordering and respect-evoking functions mentioned above, aside from which any respect for morality would be irrational.[69] On the other hand, in at least one

location he specifically distinguishes social-interaction applications of moral abilities from basically personal ones.[70] It would thus seem that cognitive-analytic theory admits of a wider range for morality than does the Kohlberg-Piaget account.

(2) Several sorts of methods are advocated by Wilson as appropriate for moral training. Different methods are employed for different facets or aspects of the agent that are to be trained. These Wilson refers to as "moral components," preferring to refer to them by specially coined code-words rather than by more usual names in order to avoid the accumulated connotations of more conventional terminology. Thus PHIL, from the Greek for "love," is a sort of concern; EMP, from the same root as "empathy," a capacity to identify emotions; GIG and KRAT refer to knowledge and to active use or control respectively. These are in turn specified by further abbreviations to refer to various types or phases of such achievements which are necessary in a well-developed moral agent. A fairly fixed list of these moral components is set forth in several of his works, as follows:

PHIL: An attitude of concern for people as equals. Its aspects include having the concept of a "person" (PHIL [HC]); claiming to use this concept as an overriding reason for action (PHIL [CC]); and having "rule--supporting feelings" which support rules for acting in others' interests (PHIL[RSF]). There are two sorts of PHIL:

--*PHIL (1)* Justice, respect for others
--*PHIL (2)* Benevolence, fraternity, love

EMP: The ability to identify emotions, which, of course, also presupposes having the concept of such emotions (EMP [HC]).
--*EMP(1) (Cs)* Ability to identify other people's conscious emotions.
--*EMP(1) (Ucs)* Ability to identify other people's unconscious emotions.
--*EMP (2) (Cs)* Ability to identify one's own conscious emotions.
--*EMP (2) (Ucs)* Ability to identify one's own unconscious emotions.

GIG: Knowledge relevant to moral situation. This involves:
--*GIG(1) (KF)* Knowing relevant facts.
--*GIG(1) (KS)* Knowing sources of facts, where to find out what one does not yet know.
--*GIG(2) (VC)* "Knowing how" or having the requisite skills in regard to verbal communication.
--*GIG(2) (NVC)* "Knowing how" in regard to nonverbal communication.

KRAT: Applying these in practice. This involves:
--*KRAT (1) (RA)* Relevant alertness to appropriate aspects of moral situations and seeing them under the right description.

--*KRAT (1) (TT)* Thinking thoroughly about them (using all the above).
--*KRAT (1) (OPU)* Making an overriding, prescriptive, and universalized decision on the basis of the above.
--*KRAT (2)* Carrying out the decision in practice.[71]

These have been called "virtues" by Wilson;[72] clearly they identify aspects of the moral agent which make it possible to act morally. They are occasionally summed up in terms of two other components, depending on the area in which they are to be applied: as DIK where others' interests are in question, and as PHRON where the action chiefly affects oneself.[73]

Some of these components may be taught in straightforward fashion as school subjects: GIG, perhaps EMP, and "the more cognitive or 'intellectual' aspects of PHIL."[74] These may also be communicated through the teaching of other subjects, or subtly through the very structure of institutions, as Kohlberg has also emphasized.[75] Specifically, moral education involves training in discussion aimed at clarification of one's views, from simply talking about one's ideas with a friend to establishing good formal habits of logical argumentation and clear distinction. Wilson stresses that this sort of training is directed at *clarification,* not imposition of a particular morality on the student, thus reflecting the same concern for autonomy and against indoctrination seen in Kohlberg and Simon.[76] A certain amount of rule-learning without understanding may be necessary for young children, but this is to be merely a preparation for later understanding of the purposes of these rules. It is not stated how one trains KRAT or the non-cognitive aspects of PHIL; according to Wilson any training not aiming at 'learning' would not really be education at all.[77] Thus it seems likely that ways of cultivating these other components would be different from classroom presentation.

(3) The philosophical background of the cognitive-analytic movement is, as one might expect, largely that of analytic ethics in the tradition of Hare, Baier, and Rawls. Morality is knowable and rationally defensible, although its results are not proven with absolute and indubitable certainty. In fact, Wilson holds that any appeal to "what the Church says" or to "what decent people feel" is a failure to think rationally about the issues.[78]

Nonmoral values are relative, however, and so the ethics advocated by the theory is, once again, formalistic.[79] Philosophy is not a way of gaining insight into values or goods which are otherwise undiscoverable; any appeal to "intuition" is misguided. In the end one apparently must appeal to particular actual human interests for the goals or ends of action. These are judged as "rational" insofar as they fit the *methods* of rationality; they are irrational only when equivalent to mental illness.[80]

Philosophy, then, has to do with *"meaning* and *concepts,"* and in accordance with this Wilson emphasizes clarity as the major goal and language-use as the major preoccupation of moral education. Philosophy is a method, not a doctrine.[81] Thus the main conditions set by philosophy for ethics seem to be the formal criteria which Wilson takes from R.M. Hare: universality, prescriptivity, and overridingness.[82]

Wilson's position on freedom, similarly, echoes recent analytic treatments. Morality implies responsibility for one's actions, which means that one is not entirely controlled even by the rules one accepts; non-obedience is possible. Yet Wilson is unwilling to accept a traditional philosophical account of freedom or free will, or to make definite assertions about it. The extent of one's freedom is relative because the limits of the "self" to which action is ascribed are changeable and dictated by particular purposes.[83]

(4) The psychological background of the theory places reasoning clearly in command; cognitive justification for patterns of behavior, for instance, must precede affective development or imitation of role-models.[84] Wilson does recognize the difference between *having* an ability, such as one of the components listed above, and *using* it; he even observes that the most common problem in moral action is a failure of KRAT (1), which is not subject to ordinary teaching. But he also insists that moral education must be *learning* and not simply "development" in the sense of an independent, automatic "unfolding" of the personality. Good habits must be generated by moral reasoning to be acceptable; learning by imitation of moral models must be cautious and not blind.[85] At the same time, Wilson's distinction between the intellectual and non-intellectual abilities needed, and his assertion of the need for properly developed habits and affective or motivational traits, make his theory more definite on the place of the non-cognitive than is that of Kohlberg, although it remains somewhat vague.[86]

For this reason the more traditional teaching methods described above, of which discussion is the common medium, are prescribed. Since reason gives a common method for analysis of moral questions, this method will be used at all ages, although how it is taught will vary with the maturity of the student.[87]

(5) It is clear, then, that what we have called the cognitive-analytic approach is closely related to the cognitive-developmental, insofar as both draw upon the same ethical tradition in modern philosophy. Kohlberg's view lays greatest stress on the change in patterns of reasoning as the agent grows up; Wilson's seems largely to ignore this, though such change is not necessarily incompatible with the general nature of his approach. Most noteworthy is the fact that Wilson's scheme of components clearly distinguishes a number of different factors for becoming a good moral agent; this is itself a service in view of the tendency to neglect some of them entirely in cognitive-developmental and values clarification theory. Nonetheless, Wilson's treatments seem to do little more than recognize these additional factors (such as KRAT and EMP), without elaborating their basis in the person, their precise relation to each other in moral action, or their process of development. Thus further examination of many of these factors seems still to be needed. Such

investigation will, in fact, be the burden of later articles in this and succeeding volumes.

THE TRADITIONAL THEORY OF MORAL EDUCATION

The approaches to moral education described above have appeared in response to the decline of, and the perceived inadequacy of a return to, certain earlier forms of moral training, in use from the late 19th century to the mid-20th century. Often they have defined themselves against this received "traditionalist" view in such respects as their emphasis on autonomy and their rejection of "indoctrination." Thus it seems appropriate also to consider briefly the nature of the traditional view. Further historical background will be provided in Chapter II; for the moment we may simply sketch an overall picture, simplified in many respects and combined from various individual programs and practices, of the type of moral education popular in America in the early part of this century.[88]

(1) On the traditional view, the range of morality extends to almost every field of action. Moral issues may arise in the marketplace, in social interaction, in personal life, in the conduct of individual affairs and even thoughts: justice, freedom, sexual behavior, gluttony and temperance, "sins of thought" and of action, suicide and the proper use of one's talents, thrift and industry, all are considered proper topics for moralizing. Moral excellence is still distinguished from expertise of a particular kind; while cleanliness and industry are moral virtues, no one confuses moral excellence itself with being a good carpenter or accountant. Yet moral excellence can be shown in these activities and apparently in all others; there is something morally good in certain *ways* of being a carpenter, farmer, or administrator. This suggests the notion of a standard for acting well in general, as mentioned at the beginning of this paper.

Ancient views of morality, such as those of Plato and Aristotle, suggest that we may explicate this omnipresence of morality in this way: morality is the excellence proper to us as human beings, not merely in biological or organic functions which we share with nonhuman beings, nor on the other hand in specific professions or occupations which are different in different human beings. Moral excellences or "virtues" are those qualities seen as desirable in *any* human being as such, and thrift and cleanliness are virtues in this sense just as are justice and courage.[89] Further, if the basic and overriding concern of a human being is to be a good *human being*--to be excellent as a human person--then this accounts for the fact that moral obligation is seen as overriding any other kind of reason that may be suggested for or against an action, as modern ethicists have noted.[90] Moral obligations take precedence over other achievement: honesty before profit or pleasure. They may reach into all corners of our living activities, including apparently "private" affairs, whence the possibility of "victimless crimes" and wholly internal "sins" on the traditional account.

28 *Contemporary Philosophies of Moral Education*

We find this broad scope reflected in the range of moral principles offered under traditional moral instruction. Many traditional codes include collections of rules concerning interpersonal affairs; rules for worship and religion, such as the Ten Commandments; general formal principles such as the Golden Rule; injunctions concerning manners and etiquette, or "good behavior" in human society; along with what might be called "rules for efficiency" in action, among which we might place precepts about tidiness and diligence, maxims designed to help a human being to succeed in whatever specific work one might take up. Warnings about drink and exhortations to courage might fall into the same category.[91] All of these are generally phrased as rules, imperatives or directives telling the moral agent to do, or not to do, something ("Thou shalt not . . .").

(2) Linked with this is a group of methods of instruction. The traditional method is in part *didactic*: one tells the moral learner what to do by enunciating the rule, possibly requiring students to learn it by heart. There is in addition the component of moral *stories*, "cautionary tales" with an obvious or explicit "moral" attached, or heroic tales of virtue triumphant, often in the simple and lowly, which make the rule concrete and evident in a realistic situation. Such tales were often included in textbooks. It is obvious that the formulation of moral standards in *rules* is congenial both to such methods of teaching, and also to immediate application, since the standard is framed in the imperative mood. As soon as one consults one's store of moral learning one finds an order or directive. Furthermore, it is commonly a *specific* duty which is presented by the rule: to respect and obey one's parents, to keep one's possessions in good order, to tell the truth. Presentation of moral codes in a story makes it natural to deal with such relatively concrete truths having specific content.

Bound up in the presentation of rules is a respect for authority, since the rule is given to the child or moral learner by a figure in authority, often without further explanation or argument. Thus acceptance may depend, at least in the beginning, on the authority of the teacher.[92] There is also, however, an element of direct example by peers: the moral tale represents the good or evil deeds of someone similar to the moral learner, and learners in turn may be instructed to consider themselves examples to others. This is an egalitarian or "democratic" element that offsets to some extent the authoritarian tendency more commonly remarked. It should be noted that the traditional view assumes that there is enough consensus among authorities, and among models held up for emulation, to constitute them a single voice; the child is not considered to be facing competing sets of rules among which one must choose, but more a simple choice between moral and immoral, lawful and lawless. Where conflicts exist, as with religious differences, it is generally assumed that a consensus exists at least on certain basic, common moral beliefs, which can be separated from individual religious preferences and taught as a common tradition.[93]

There is another component to the traditional mode of instruction: the notion of diligent drill or practice in obedience to moral rules. While morality may extend to any human action, moral crises tend to occur in certain typical conflict situations; the conflict is portrayed not as one between moral principles, but as a conflict between moral rules and the desires or temptations which compete with them. If one must decide whether to become intoxicated or to embezzle from one's employer when the opportunity presents itself, this is because desire may pull in one direction while the moral rule commands in the other.

It was certainly part of the traditional view that some sort of self-application to making the proper choices was required, in large or in small matters. The good Boy Scout, for example, is expected to practice his code of conduct as well as to memorize it. Thus one may fail, on the traditional account, not only by ignorance, but by weakness (cf. Wilson's component KRAT). Failure to act according to moral rules does not always imply a failure to reason properly with or about the rule; it may mean simply that the agent has not mustered the self-command necessary to act on his knowledge of the rule. In fact, moral weakness is seen as the typical mode of failure in the traditional view, for it is assumed that everyone will have been made aware of the moral rules themselves in childhood. Moral lapses, then, are more often failures of courage or determination than of wisdom or reasoning.

(3) From this account we can discover the underlying ethical theory and moral psychology of the traditional account. It is assumed that there are *rules* of right conduct which can be clearly formulated, definitely known, and verbally communicated to others. Their application to situations is taken to be normally unproblematic; there does not seem to be as much attention to difficulties in discovering what is the honest thing or the just thing to do in a given case as there is to resisting the temptation not to do it.[94]

It also seems to be assumed that the rules as accepted by contemporary society and supported by tradition are substantially correct. Not only is moral knowledge possible, and of a sort which is definite, applicable to specific situations, and formulable in rules; it is taken for granted that such knowledge has by and large already been achieved. At any given time it is probable that traditional educators would concede that some higher moral principles had not yet been adopted by society at large, as in abolitionist arguments before the Civil War. But even here the principles were concrete and had a definite content, in contrast to the formal character of the principles typically championed by values clarification or cognitive-developmental approaches. Specific institutions and practices were mentioned as right or wrong, along with the recommendation of formal principles such as the Golden Rule. In fact it seems that traditional moral education did not make a clear distinction between form and content, but incorporated both in moral precepts.

(4) Such would seem to be the ethical view underlying the general approach we have called "traditional." The corresponding moral psychol-

ogy is also revealed in the methods of that view. Good moral action appears as a function of knowing the proper rules and applying them by the exercise of pure "will-power," often in the face of counter-inclinations. Of the two the latter seems to be the more important. Once one has attained a minimum "age of reason," it is presumed that one knows and can understand the moral law, and action becomes a matter of self-discipline--or discipline from outside, if this does not suffice. Hence the emphasis on strict external training and the punishment of infractions. It is suggested, moreover, that careful and vigilant training results in a state relatively free of such temptation. Once one overcomes a bad habit, it will tend not to reassert itself. Thus there seems to be at work in the traditional view something like the classical notion of habituation, or the training of relatively fixed tendencies of character: indeed, the traditional mode of education in some cases was titled simply "character education."[95]

(5) This traditional view remains a general substratum of training in the home and hence of the implicit efforts of very many teachers. There is even talk of a resurgence of views to some extent related to them, a "new conservatism," at present. In the last fifty years, however, traditional explicit character education has been abandoned by many types of scholars in the face of general questioning of both its effectiveness and its desirability.[96] It is impossible to discuss in full detail here the reasons for this movement away from traditional methods. The breakup of what consensus there may have been in turn-of-the-century America on values and virtues; the desire to find "scientific" and often technological solutions to all problems and to minimize the role of less rigorous moral notions; the decline in the force of religious beliefs in general, which played an important role in maintaining loyalty to moral standards in earlier years; and the harsh experience of the world wars and the resulting moves toward other sorts of philosophical and psychological outlooks uncongenial to a system of fixed moral standards and individual self-control; all these have been cited as possible factors in the extensive abandonment of explicit programs of traditional moral education. Whether they rationally justify such an abandonment is, of course, another question.

What is more evident is what has replaced that system. Under the banner of opposition to any "indoctrination" of the child, the last half century, and even more the last twenty years, have seen a tendency to oppose the regimentation of strict discipline and the conformity and respect for authority that tend to accompany traditional moral education. The result has been a tendency toward experimentation and spontaneity in moral learning, and a search for a more complex description of the process of learning than that employed in traditional frameworks. In some cases this has taken the form of opposition to any fixed moral principles whatsoever. The values clarification, cognitive-developmental, and cognitive-analytic movements represent attempts to retain moral standards without falling back into what is perceived as undesirably autocratic or dogmatic. The autonomy of the individual learner, rather than the authority of the moral teacher, has been emphasized, as we have seen, and along with this the equality of moral agents. It should be noted that such a moral democracy was not really foreign to the traditional view, which, in some forms at least, tended to frown on class distinctions and prejudices and to encourage the agent's independence and self-directedness, although this was not always expressed in practice.[97] But the authority through whom the moral law was passed down was generally seen as something of an exception to this rule. The reaction against the tradition extended the "democracy of opinion" to the authoritative rule itself, and tended to promote an acceptance of pluralism and diverse opinions even on issues which heretofore had been considered part of the common ground of moral agreement.

Such criticisms of the way the traditional view was put into practice seem justified in part. On occasion the traditional programs appear to have become hidebound and mechanical, or to have degenerated into the manufacture of obedient citizens rather than the development of responsible moral agents.[98] Yet there are values in this approach which deserve retrieval, such as the admission of moral content or definite values as necessary ingredients in moral thinking, the use of stories and examples to inspire as well as to stimulate changes in reasoning, and the emphasis on self-discipline in action as well as on proper moral judgment. Such a reconsideration of both positive and negative points of the traditional view is important in the attempt to construct a more just and adequate theory of moral education.

CONCLUSION

The four approaches to moral education discussed above are not the only ones currently under discussion.[99] Humanistic psychology, for instance, while it has influenced the course of work in values clarification, has also had a certain amount of influence in other active programs of moral training. Aside from specific theories or explicit systems of thought, a certain sense that a prerequisite for moral development is trusting one's spontaneous tendencies and "getting in touch with one's feelings" can be seen throughout the practice of early education. This reflects some of the respects in which popular consciousness has absorbed the tenets of self-actualization views in psychology.[100] Psychoanalytic thinkers such as Erich Fromm and Erik Erikson have also brought into contemporary attitudes classical Freudian notions about human drives and repression, as well as more developed theoretical structures such as Erikson's scheme of developmental tasks.[101]

Marxist thinkers have attempted to digest the work of cognitive-developmental research in particular and to bring it into line with a more comprehensive system explaining the development of the moral consciousness according to a Marxian historical, economic, and sociopolitical analysis.[102] And certain behaviorist approaches to the appropriate conditioning of human beings, insofar as this may be regarded as an aspect of moral education, have contributed data on techniques of reinforcement and what earlier views might have called "habit formation."[103] Recent emphasis on the process of "socialization," while referring explicitly to the individual's adjustment to a conventional social system rather than to universal or cross-cultural moral standards, has opened avenues of investigation which should be applicable to broader aims of education as well. These will be reflected below and in the following two volumes.

The present state of moral education theory seems to reveal, on the one hand, a proliferation of alternate approaches of varying applicability and adequacy and, on the other hand, a tendency to converge in some respects among those which are most fully worked out. The recent movement of values clarification away from relativism, and of cognitive-developmentalism away from its earlier limitation to the purely cognitive and formal, suggest that each major theory or paradigm is attempting to adjust to the awareness that some broadening of perspective is necessary.[104] None of the major approaches presents a complete theory, and thus each one's practice has revealed certain limitations and shortcomings. Most notable, perhaps, is the growing realization that despite the dominant formalism of most of the currently popular approaches, one cannot in fact use or teach structure without content, or vice versa.[105]

As a result, many different stands are being taken and methods applied with respect to morality in the schools: some return to certain traditional methods, others adopt highly sophisticated innovations, while still others exhibit merely the inaction of confusion.[106] The absence of a fully adequate approach is reflected in the continuing call for some sort of renewal in moral education, in the face of a perception that many people are not becoming morally mature, and also in the lack of a general theoretical framework capable of linking and making sense of the various data and techniques now available.

Nonetheless, many themes which must be integrated in any more complete theory have been brought out in the different approaches examined. The techniques for coming to a better self-understanding prominent in values clarification and humanistic frameworks; the stage system of Kohlberg, with its associated tests and methods for accelerating stage advance; in response to these, the emphasis from many quarters upon the affective side of the person and the social environment; the resurgence of a traditional concern with specific modes of behavior and with social order; these factors should play a part in the formation of any new theory.

The work of the schools of thought discussed above has made clear certain crucial problems or issues which should be taken up in any attempt at untangling the conflicting movements now afoot and pointing out where their strengths and weaknesses lie. These include the problem of autonomy as opposed to indoctrination and to social convention; the problem of separating content from form in moral judgment and action; the question of freedom as related to fixed character, conditioning, or "habit;" and perhaps most central of all, the problem of the ultimate foundation and justification of moral principles to be used in education.

The time would seem to be ripe for attempts at theoretical synthesis which also can be made definite in practical application; such a synthesis must be sufficiently detailed to apply and test, but sufficiently flexible to be adapted to new data. The proliferation of divergent methods bears the hallmark of a "pre-paradigm period," in Kuhn's terms.[107] In order to build upon the contributions made thus far toward a philosophically and psychologically more adequate approach to moral education, it is necessary now to look for resources needed to delve more deeply into some of the problems raised in our discussion of current moral education approaches in order to work out the crucial difficulties of the extant views, and to see what positive elements can be identified and integrated for a comprehensive theory of moral development.

The Catholic University of America
Washington, D.C.

NOTES

1. Louis Raths, Merril Harmin, and Sidney B. Simon, *Values and Teaching* (Columbus, Ohio: Charles E. Merrill, 1966). See Sidney B. Simon, Leland W. Howe, and Howard Kirschenbaum, *Values Clarification: A Handbook of Practical Strategies for Teachers and Students* (New York: Hart Publishing Co., 1972). Kirschenbaum, in his *Advanced Values Clarification* (La Jolla, CA: University Associates, 1977), ch. 11 (pp. 139-43), gives a brief history of the movement to 1971.

2. Sidney B. Simon and Howard Kirschenbaum, eds., *Readings in Values Clarification* (Minneapolis: Winston Press Inc., 1973). Kirschenbaum's summary is made in his "Beyond Values Clarification," in that volume, pp. 92-109.

3. Kirschenbaum, *Advanced Values Clarification, op. cit.*

4. See Kirschenbaum, *Advanced Values Clarification*, pp. 14, 17, 140; research from 1970-1976 is summarized in ch. 3.

5. See John S. Stewart, "Problems and Contradictions of Values Clarification, " in David Purpel and Kevin Ryan, eds., *Moral Education: . . . It Comes With the Territory* (Berkeley: McCutchan Publishing Corp., 1976), pp. 146-49.

6. Kirschenbaum, *Advanced Values Clarification*, pp. 18, 43.

7. *Ibid.*, pp. 9-10, 58.

8. See Howard Kirschenbaum and Sidney B. Simon, "Values and the Futures Movement in Education," in *Readings in Values Clarification*, pp. 23-26; Kirschenbaum, "Beyond Values Clarification," pp. 95-101; Peter Scharf, "Indoctrination, Values Clarification, and Developmental Moral Education as Educational Responses to Conflict and Change in Contemporary Society," in Peter Scharf, ed., *Readings in Moral Education* (Minneapolis: Winston Press, Inc., 1978), p. 25; Kirschenbaum, *Advanced Values Clarification*, pp. 8-12.

9. Kirschenbaum, *Advanced Values Clarification*, p. 49; cf. ch. 9.
10. *Ibid.*, p. 9, and see passages cited at note 7.
11. Cf. *ibid.*, p. 11; Gary Wehlage and Alan L. Lockwood, "Moral Relativism and Values Education," in Purpel and Ryan, eds., pp. 334-35.
12. See Merrill Harmin and Sidney B. Simon, "Values," in *Readings in Values Clarification*, pp. 11-12; James Rest, "Developmental Psychology as a Guide to Values Education: A Review of 'Kohlbergian' Programs," p. 254; Wehlage and Lockwood, pp. 334-335.
13. See Kirschenbaum, Advanced Values Clarification, pp. 12-13, 46-47; though cf. p. 52.
14. Cf. Kirschenbaum, *Advanced Values Clarification*, pp. 12-13. "The conformity engendered by peer pressure is one of the primary behaviors value clarification is designed to eliminate. Our goal is for students to think for themselves and be willing to express their views" (p. 50).
15. See James W. Watkins, "Forming a Value Curriculum: Two Philosophical Issues to Consider," in Purpel and Ryan, eds., p. 15. Cf. Jean-Paul Sartre, "Existentialism Is a Humanism," in Robert Solomon, ed. *Existentialism* (New York: Modern Library, 1974), pp. 200-202.
16. Cf. Kirschenbaum, *Advanced Values Clarification*, pp. 43-44, 52.
17. See Harmin and Simon, pp. 12, 14; Kirschenbaum and Simon, pp. 22-23; Simon, Howe, and Kirschenbaum, p. 112.
18. Kirschenbaum, *Advanced Values Clarification*, p. 13.
19. Cf. *ibid.*, p. 50.
20. See Harmin and Simon, p. 11; Kirschenbaum and Simon, pp. 29-30; Kirschenbaum, "Beyond Values Clarification," pp. 100, 109.
21. Kirschenbaum, *Advanced Value Clarification*, p. 23.
22. See Watkins, p. 14. See also the discussion of Dewey in Chapter II.
23. See Kirschenbaum, "Beyond Values Clarification," p. 109; *Advanced Values Clarification*, p. 31.
24. See the treatment by Carl Rogers in "Toward a Modern Approach to Values: the Valuing Process in the Mature Person," in *Person to Person*, by Carl R. Rogers and Barry Stevens (New York: Pocket Books, 1967), pp. 4-21. Cf. Alan L. Lockwood, "A Critical View of Values Clarification," in Purpel and Ryan, eds., pp. 158-64.
25. Cf. Lockwood, pp. 154-56; Wehlage and Lockwood, p. 344. It is worth noting that some current ethical theorists hold that no complete objective rank-ordering of values is possible. Cf. John Finnis, *Natural Law and Natural Rights* (Oxford: Clarendon Press, 1980), pp. 112-115.
26. Kirschenbaum, *Advanced Values Clarification*, p. 12.
27. Cf. Lockwood, p. 155.
28. Kirschenbaum, *Advanced Values Clarification*, pp. 10-11, 48-49.
29. *Ibid.*, pp. 146-47.
30. Rogers, pp. 4-21; Irving Kristol, "Moral and Ethical Develop-

ment in a Democratic Society," in Purpel and Ryan, eds., pp. 372-73.
31. See Philip H. Phenix. "The Moral Imperative in Contemporary American Education," in Simon and Kirschenbaum, eds., pp. 42-47.
32. For some discussion of this point, see "An Exchange of Opinion Between Kohlberg and Simon," in Simon and Kirschenbaum, eds., pp. 62-64.
33. Kirschenbaum, *Advanced Values Clarification*, pp. 23, 10, 12, 17.
34. For example, see Donald B. Cochrane, "Prolegomena to Moral Education," in Donald B. Cochrane, Cornel Hamm, and Anastasios C. Kazepides, eds., *The Domain of Moral Education* (New York: Paulist Press, 1979; Toronto: Ontario Institute for Studies in Education, 1979), p. 76; Scharf, p. 27.
35. See Stewart, p. 138. Cf. the similar, but explicitly introduced, "basic values assumption" in Cornel M. Hamm and L. B. Daniels, "Moral Education in Relation to Values Education," in Cochrane, Hamm, and Kazepides, eds., pp. 21-22.
36. Kirschenbaum, *Advanced Values Clarification*, p. 13. Cf. p. 14; Lockwood, pp. 165-67.
37. See Cochrane, p. 75; Stewart, p. 139.
38. See Stewart, p. 142.
39. Kirschenbaum, *Advanced Values Clarification*, p. 9.
40. See Cochrane, p. 75; Scharf, pp. 26-27. But cf. Kirschenbaum, *Advanced Values Clarification*, ch. 3.
41. Cf. Israel Scheffler, "The Moral Content of American Public Education," in Purpel and Ryan, eds., pp. 25-28. The questions of the existence and knowledge of such values will be taken up later in this volume.
42. Kirschenbaum seems to agree; see *Advanced Values Clarification*, pp. 151-52.
43. A history of the development of the testing methods of Kohlberg's theory can be found in Anne Colby, "Evolution of a Moral-Development Theory," in William Damon, ed., *Moral Development: New Directions for Child Development*, vol. 2 (San Francisco: Jossey-Bass, Inc., 1978), 89-104.
44. See Lawrence Kohlberg, "From Is to Ought: How to Commit the Naturalistic Fallacy and Get Away With It in the Study of Moral Development," in Theodore Mischel, ed., *Cognitive Development and Epistemology* (New York: Academic Press, 1971), pp. 192, 209, 211-12, 215, 219; Lawrence Kohlberg, "Moral Education in the Schools: A Developmental View," *School Review*, 74 (1966), 41; Lawrence Kohlberg, "Education for Justice: A Modern Statement of the Platonic View," in Nancy F. Sizer and Theodore R. Sizer, eds., *Moral Education: Five Lectures* (Cambridge, Mass.: Harvard University Press, 1970), pp. 58-59; F. Clark Power and Lawrence Kohlberg, "Religion, Morality, and Ego Development," in J. Fowler and A. Vergote, eds., *Toward Moral and Religious Maturity* (Morristown, N.J.: Silver Burdett, 1980), pp. 344, 346.

45. See Lawrence Kohlberg, "Revisions in the Theory and Practice of Moral Development," in Damon, ed., *op. cit.*, p. 85; Clark Power and Joseph Reimer, "Moral Atmosphere: An Educational Bridge Between Moral Judgment and Action," in Damon, ed., pp. 106-107.

46. See, e.g., Kohlberg's conclusion in his paper "The Implications of Moral Stages for Problems in Sex Education," for The Sex Information Council of the United States Conference, December 1971, reprinted in Lawrence Kohlberg, *Collected Papers in Moral Development and Moral Education* ([Cambridge, Mass.: Harvard Center for Moral Education], 1973). In "From Is to Ought," Kohlbert contrasts moral judgments with "judgments of prudence or aesthetics" (p. 215), in that moral judgments are "universal, inclusive, consistent and grounded on objective, impersonal, or ideal grounds," while the others "lack the characteristics of moral judgments." It would seem to follow then, that only nonuniversal and nonobjective grounds such as personal preference or taste remain. Other standards for such choices also seem to be denied in Kohlberg's claim that "no philosopher ever has seriously attempted to demonstrate that an alternative substantive principle to justice could function in a universal prescriptive fashion in a satisfactory way" ("From Is to Ought," p. 222).

47. Anne Colby, "Two Approaches to Moral Education," in Purpel and Ryan, eds., pp. 280, 284.

48. Jean Piaget (with the assistance of seven collaborators), *The Moral Judgment of the Child*, trans. Marjorie Gabain (New York: Free Press, 1965); see esp. p. 335.

49. See Lawrence Kohlberg, "The Cognitive-Developmental Approach to Moral Education," in Scharf, ed., pp. 50-51; Lawrence Kohlberg, "Moral Stages and Moralization: The Cognitive-Developmental Approach," in Thomas Lickona, ed., *Moral Development and Behavior: Theory, Research, and Social Issues* (New York: Holt, Rinehart & Winston, 1976), pp. 34-35. The latter essay was published in 1976; the former, while originally published in 1975, was republished without significant change by Scharf in 1978. The table showing the standard six stages was also republished by Kohlberg in his "High School Democracy and Educating for a Just Society," in Ralph L. Mosher, ed., *Moral Education: A First Generation of Research and Development* (New York: Praeger Publishers, 1980), with the statement "We claim to have validated the stages defined in [that table]" (p. 21).

50. Kohlberg, "Revisions," p. 86. See also Kohlberg, "High School Democracy," in Mosher, ed., pp. 27-28; Colby, "Evolution of a Moral-Development Theory," pp. 89-104. Stage 6 is omitted in the discussion of religious stages in Power and Kohlberg, "Religion, Morality, and Ego Development," pp. 364-65, but is retained in a note at the end of that paper as the highest moral stage (p. 371). Cf. Lawrence Kohlberg, *The Meaning and Measurement of Moral Development*, Heinz Werner Lecture Series, 13 (1979) (Worcester, Mass.: Clark University Press, 1981), p. 34.

51. For example, "From Is to Ought," p. 216: "The individual whose

judgments are at stage 6 asks 'Is it morally right?' and means by morally right something different from punishment (stage 1), prudence (stage 2), conformity to authority (stages 3 and 4), etc. Thus, the responses of lower-stage subjects to aesthetic or other morally neutral matters fail to be moral. In this sense, we can define a higher stage judgment as 'moral,' independent of its content and of whether it agrees with our own judgments or standards." The claim is repeated in Kohlberg's version of that essay reprinted in his 1981 collection *The Philosophy of Moral Development: Essays on Moral Development*, vol. I. (San Francisco: Harper and Row, 1981), p. 172. It may be that stage 5 is to take the place of stage 6 in the revised theory, but this has not been made clear.

52. Ralph L. Mosher, "An Uncommon Cause," in Mosher, ed., p. 4.

53. Lawrence Kohlberg, *The Philosophy of Moral Development*, Essay 9, and pp. 308-309 in its introduction. See the chapter on religion in this volume for a detailed discussion.

54. Cf. Rest, p. 254; Colby, "Two Approaches," p. 279.

55. "Revisions," pp. 84-85. See also Kohlberg, "High School Democracy," in Mosher, ed., pp. 25-26.

56. See, e.g., Immanuel Kant, *Foundations of the Metaphysics of Morals*, trans. Lewis White Beck, (Library of Liberal Arts; Indianapolis: Bobbs-Merrill Co., Inc., 1959), pp. 9, 16 (pp. 392-93, 399-400 in Akademie edition). Cf. Piaget, p. 352.

57. See Kohlberg, "Revisions," pp. 84-85. See also the references to value in Kohlberg, "High School Democracy," in Mosher, ed., pp. 25-26; Power and Kohlberg, "Religion, Morality and Ego Development," p. 345.

58. See Kohlberg's comments as reported by Thomas C. Hennessy, "Interviewing Lawrence Kohlberg," *New Catholic World*, 221, no. 1324 (July/August, 1978), 152-53. Cf. Kant's treatment of the good will as the only thing "unconditionally good" (Foundations, pp. 9-10 [Akademie, pp. 392-94]).

59. See Kohlberg, "Revisions," pp. 84-85. Cf. Colby, "Two Approaches," p. 279; Mosher, "An Uncommon Cause," pp. 9-10; Kohlberg, "High School Democracy," in Mosher, ed., p. 39; Power and Kohlberg, "Religion, Morality, and Ego Development," pp. 344, 348, 350, 351, 364, 367, 368; Kohlberg, *Meaning and Measurement*, pp. 6, 34-35, 37-38, 45-46, 51. Kant has a very similar formula in his early *Lectures on Ethics*, trans. Louis Infield (Indianapolis: Hackett, 1963), p. 82.

60. See especially William Kurtines and Esther Blank Greif, "The development of Moral Thought: Review and Evaluation of Kohlberg's Approach," *Psychological Bulletin*, 81 (1974), 453-70, discussed briefly by Kohlberg in "Revisions," pp. 85-86, and at greater length in *Meaning and Measurement*, pp. 1 ff. A more recent criticism is made by John Michael Murphy and Carol Gilligan, "Moral Development in Late Adolescence and Adulthood: A Critique and Reconstruction of Kohlberg's Theory," *Human Development*, 23 (1980), 77-104. See also Colby's description of the development of the theory and the testing methodology, and Rest, *op. cit.*, along with Kohlberg's own statements in *Meaning and*

Measurement, especially pp. 1-3, 8, 17-18, 32-34, 37.

61. See Kohlberg, "From Is to Ought," pp. 181-82, 195-96, 214; *Meaning and Measurement*, p. 7.

62. See Scharf, pp. 58-59; Lawrence Kohlberg, "The Claim to Moral Adequacy of a Highest Stage of Moral Development," *Journal of Philosophy*, 70 (Oct. 25, 1973), 644.

63. Cf. also James R. Rest's examples of arguments to opposing conclusions from each stage, reproduced in Lawrence Kohlberg, "Stage and Sequence: The Cognitive-Developmental Approach to Socialization," in D. Goslin, ed., *Handbook of Socialization Theory and Research* (New York: Rand McNally, 1969), pp. 379 ff.

64. This point is developed more fully in Rick Ellrod, "Morality and Interests: A Critique of Kohlberg's Ethical Theory," *Communio*, 7 (Fall, 1980), 259-68. Cf. Kohlberg, "High School Democracy, " in Mosher, ed., p. 27.

65. See Kohlberg, "Revisions," p. 84. Cf. Kohlberg, "High School Democracy," in Mosher, ed., pp. 29, 39; Kirschenbaum, *Advanced Values Clarification*, pp. 13-14.

66. See Ellrod, *op. cit.*

67. Some comments on motivation are made in Power and Reimer. Cf. Mosher, "An Uncommon Cause," pp. 9-10; Power and Kohlberg, "Religion, Morality, and Ego Development," as cited in note 59 above.

68. John Wilson, *Reason and Morals* (Cambridge: At the University Press, 1961), pp. 82, 92, 111-12, 118-19.

69. *Ibid.*, pp. 129, 146-50; p. 131.

70. See John Wilson, *Practical Methods of Moral Education* (London: Heinemann Educational Books, 1972), pp. 27-30.

71. See Wilson, *Practical Methods*, pp. 19-28, 150; John Wilson, *Moral Thinking: A Guide for Students* (London: Heinemann Educational Books, 1970), pp. 50-65; John Wilson, "The Study of 'Moral Development,'" in Gerald Collier, Peter Tomlinson, and John Wilson, eds., *Values and Moral Development in Higher Education* (New York: John Wiley and Sons, 1974), pp. 9-10.

72. Wilson, "Study," p. 9.

73. See Wilson, *Practical Methods*, pp. 27-29. DIK would be "justice" (*dike*) in its interpersonal sense; PHRON is from *phronesis*, "practical wisdom" or "prudence," apparently taking the latter translation in its English (but not classical) sense of efficient action to fulfill one's own desires or interests.

74. *Ibid.*, p. 92. See also pp. viii, 5-7, 111, 141; Michael Scriven, "Cognitive Moral Education," in Purpel and Ryan, eds., p. 318.

75. See John Wilson's "Introduction" to Collier, Tomlinson, and Wilson, eds., p. 2; *Moral Thinking*, pp. 67-70; John Wilson, *Education and the Concept of Mental Health* (London: Routledge and Kegan Paul, 1968; New York: Humanities Press, 1968), p. 81.

76. See Wilson, *Moral Thinking*, p. 11; *Practical Methods*, pp. 42, 45, 49, 51-54; Wilson, "Study," p. 8. Cf. *Practical Methods*, p. 94; *Moral*

Thinking, p. 17; John Wilson, "Philosophy," in Collier, Tomlinson, and Wilson, eds., p. 97.
77. Wilson, *Practical Methods*, pp. 59, 103; *Moral Thinking*, pp. 21-22. Cf. *Practical Methods*, pp. 55-59, 82, 103; *Moral Thinking*, pp. 17, 19; *Reason and Morals*, pp. 129, 131; John Wilson, *Philosophy and Educational Research* (Windsor: National Foundation for Educational Research in England and Wales, 1972), pp. 2-3; Scriven, pp. 321-22. On the definition of "education," see Wilson, *Philosophy and Educational Research*, pp. 2-3; cf. John Wilson, *Preface to the Philosophy of Education* (International Library of the Philosophy of Education; London: Routledge and Kegan Paul, 1979), p. 21; "Study," p. 14.
78. Wilson, *Practical Methods*, p. 10; *Moral Thinking*, pp. 38-39; Scriven, 38; Wilson, *Moral Thinking*, pp. 4-5.
79. Scriven, pp. 326-27; Wilson, *Moral Thinking*, pp. 28-29; Wehlage and Lockwood, pp. 330-33, 343. Cf. Wilson, *Practical Methods*, pp. 28-30; though some necessary content for rational ethics seems suggested in *Reason and Morals*, pp. 31-32.
80. Wilson, *Moral Thinking*, pp. 8, 29; Wilson, *Moral Thinking*, pp. 41-42, 83-85. Cf. "Study," p. 8.
81. *Ibid.*, pp. 14-15; "Study," pp. 17-18. See Wilson, *Practical Methods*, p. 32; *Philosophy and Educational Research*, p. viii; *Reason and Morals*, p. 1; "Philosophy," pp. 96-97; *Moral Thinking*, p. 12; *Practical Methods*, pp. 33, 36-38, 40, 41, 48. Language, however, is studied not merely for its own sake, but so as to "sharpen our perception of the phenomena via awareness of the words" ("Philosophy," p. 99). On the role of philosophy, see Wilson, "Philosophy," p. 97; *Education and the Concept of Mental Health*, pp. 81, 96, 102, *Moral Thinking*, pp. 38-39, 45.
82. Wilson, *Moral Thinking*, pp. 39-40. Rules need not, however, be absolutely universal; see *Reason and Morals*, p. 93.
83. Wilson, *Practical Methods*, p. 57; *Moral Thinking*, pp. 19-20, 31, 33-34; *Reason and Morals*, pp. 124-25.
84. Scriven, pp. 315-16, 323; Wilson, *Moral Thinking*, pp. 7, 43.
85. See Wilson, *Moral Thinking*, pp. 46-47; *Practical Methods*, p. 34; "Study," p. 13; *Moral Thinking*, p. 60; see also pp. 7, 49-50.
86. See ibid., pp. 63, 76.
87. Wilson, *Practical Methods*, pp. 2-3, in *Moral Thinking* Wilson states that DIK is a *"stage"* or a *"mode of thought"* (p. 59), but this simply seems to be a global application of the other components in an interpersonal situation (see note 73 above).
88. Some background for this discussion may be found in Stephen M. Yulish, *The Search for a Civic Religion: A History of the Character Education Movement in America, 1890-1935* (Lanham, Md.: University Press of America, 1980), where a large number of "traditional" programs are described. See also Scharf, who gives a brief summary from the cognitive-developmental point of view, pp. 19-24.
89. While this view of virtue is reflected in traditional moral education, it should also be noted that programs for developing virtue often

tended to reduce it to those excellences which made one a good (and obedient) citizen alone, as will be mentioned below.

90. See, e.g., R.M. Hare, *Freedom and Reason* (London: Oxford University Press, 1965), pp. 167-69. Cf. Wilson, *Moral Thinking*, p. 40.

91. See Yulish's many lists of moral rules and virtues (*passim*).

92. See Yulish, pp. 6-9, 136.

93. Cf. Benjamin Franklin's statement of moral rules thought to be common to all religions, in his Autobiography, as quoted by Scharf, p. 20.

94. Cf. the traditional M'Naghten rules for legal responsibility, which hold that anyone who understands the nature and the illegality of an act is responsible for it (described by H. L. A. Hart in *Punishment and Responsibility: Essays in the Philosophy of Law* [New York: Oxford University Press, 1968], p. 189).

95. See Yulish, pp. 6, 17, 32, 56, 124-25, 252.

96. The well-known study of Hartshorne and May has often been taken as a watershed in regard to such methods. See Hugh Hartshorne and Mark A. May, Studies in the Nature of Character, by the Character Education Inquiry in cooperation with the Institute of Social and Religious Research: vol. I, *Studies in Deceit*, by Hugh Hartshorne and Mark A. May (New York: Macmillan, 1928); vol. II, *Studies in Service and Self-control*, by Hugh Hartshorne, Mark A. May, and Julius B. Maller (New York: Macmillan, 1929); vol. III, *Studies in the Organization of Character*, by Hugh Hartshorne, Mark A. May, and Frank K. Shuttleworth (New York: Macmillan, 1930). A summary of their results on the "situation-specificity" of character traits may be found in vol. III pp. 372-74. Some comments on the interpretation of these results will be made in the paper on character in this volume.

97. See Yulish, pp. 1, 108.

98. Yulish, pp. 46-47, 61, 65, 74, 257.

99. Cf. Wehlage and Lockwood, pp. 335-42, for some discussion of variations on the above types.

100. See, for example, Carl R. Rogers and Barry Stevens, *op. cit.*; Carl R. Rogers, *On Becoming a Person: A Therapist's View of Psychotherapy* (Boston: Houghton Mifflin, 1961); A.H. Maslow, *Motivation and Personality* (New York: Harper & Row, 1954), esp. ch. 12-13.

101. See Erik Erikson, *Childhood and Society*, 2nd ed. rev. & enl. (New York: W. W. Norton and Co., 1963), esp. ch. 7; the achievements of the various stages are called basic virtues in the note at the end of that chapter. In *Identity: Youth and Crisis* (New York: W. W. Norton and Co., 1968), chapter III, Erikson discusses them in more detail; see especially note 8 (p. 325).

102. Among the Marxist responses to cognitive-developmental theory, see: Edmund V. Sullivan, *Kohlberg's Structuralism: A Critical Appraisal*, Monograph Series, 15 (Toronto: Ontario Institute for Studies in Education, 1977), on social interests and cultural bias (pp. 2-3, 12, 22), historicity (pp. 11-13), the importance of goals or ultimate meanings

(p. 14), the dichotomy of thought and action or theory and praxis (pp. 18-19); John M. Broughton, "Dialectics and Moral Development Ideology," in Scharf, ed., pp. 298-307, and his more elaborate treatment suggesting a thorough Marxian transformation of the theory, "Development of Concepts of Self, Mind, Reality, and Knowledge," in William Damon, ed., *Social Cognition: New Directions for Child Development*, 1 (1978) (San Francisco: Jossey-Bass, Inc. 1978): 75-100; Jurgen Habermas, "Moral Development and Ego Identity," *Telos* 24 (1975): 41-55, and R. Howard, "Moral Development and Ego Identity: A Clarification," *Telos* 27 (1976): 176-82; cf. also Habermas, *Knowledge and Human Interests*, trans. Jeremy J. Shapiro (Boston: Beacon Press, 1971), ch. 12.

103. Cf. Scriven, p. 317.

104. Cf. Colby, "Two Approaches," pp. 275, 283-84.

105. Stewart, p. 138.

106. Cf. Harmin and Simon, pp. 6-14; Kirschenbaum and Simon, pp. 18-23; Phenix, pp. 40-44; Scharf, pp. 19-24.

107. See Thomas S. Kuhn, *The Structure of Scientific Revolutions*, 2nd ed., enlarged, vol. 2, no. 2, International Encyclopedia of Unified Science, (Chicago: University of Chicago Press, 1970), ch. 2, esp. pp. 12-17.

CHAPTER II

NORTH AMERICAN PHILOSOPHICAL BACKGROUND FOR MORAL EDUCATION THEORY

JESSE A. MANN

In the first chapter of this volume Dr. Ellrod has described and noted the traditional view of moral education as being didactic and rule conscious, as claiming authority for its deliverances and as bent on drill and practice of its theories. He then noted the inclinations of the modern temper toward other kinds of moral theory which would allow for autonomy on the part of the student, avoidance of indoctrination, and especially a willingness to be formal in character rather than to establish any content for ethics. It is, of course, true that any brief description of traditional moral theory has to be highly compressed and is vulnerable to being thought a caricature. Obviously not all species of traditional moral philosophy had all the characteristics described, but the general truth of the description is borne out by historical examination. Professor Ellrod analyzed two versions of contemporary moral education: values clarification theory and cognitive developmental theory. He showed their difficulties and concluded with a statement of our contemporary need for some kind of theoretical synthesis which will enable us to avoid the problems of earlier attempts.

It is the purpose of this article to examine some of the philosophical background of current moral development theory, particularly in America in the nineteenth and early twentieth century. It is hoped that such an examination of modern ethics, particularly in their American setting, will contribute toward the goal of a new synthesis of moral education theories. Clearly there has been an assumption in educational circles particularly within the last decade that the recent enthusiasm for courses in moral development reflects the American tradition. Associations of concerned parents have rightly insisted to school boards that moral education not be neglected. The newspapers are always concerned to print stories about parents who object to the poor moral influence of some of the things that their children read. Indeed American culture has long been concerned with promoting democratic values especially in the school system.

Chapter I shows clearly the problem involved. On the one hand parents are determined that the educational process at the very least not be destructive of the moral values of child and parent. On the other hand parents themselves represent different religious and sometimes even moral perspectives. How can the same educational program have content, if in fact all content is necessarily perspectival and therefore not welcome to some parents with an alternate ethnic or religious perspective? It will be the burden of this volume to show that there is a middle ground between purely formal, value-free ethics, and ethics that is so partisan that it cannot be universalized to benefit the entire student community. It is the burden of this paper to make the point that within the American tradition, especially in the works of Dewey, James and Royce, there has been an interest in ethics which is at once content-oriented and completely American in character. An example of this can be seen in the teaching of ethics in the nineteenth century American college.

ETHICS IN THE NINETEENTH CENTURY AMERICAN COLLEGE

A recent article gives an historian's analysis of the situation alluded to by Ellrod. I quote at length from the conclusion of that article.

> Two things happened during the nineteenth and twentieth centuries that were to have momentous consequences for higher education and modern society in general, as well as for the teaching of ethics in particular. Both were centuries-long developments that reached a kind of culmination in the 1890's although it was not for several decades thereafter that their full impact and implications began to become clearly manifest. One development was the splintering of the culture of learning into many different self-contained disciplines of knowledge.... The other development--essentially much more important than the first--was that one of these branches of knowledge, namely natural science, began to be regarded as the one and only valid mode of knowledge.
>
> As this conception of knowledge became increasingly dominant, it began to make extremely difficult any consideration of values other than those already embedded in natural science and its technological application. The eventual impact of this attitude on the teaching of ethics--in fact, on all attempts to determine the place of ethics in higher education was profound.... The growing conviction that science alone dealt with an objective world of knowledge meant that ... nonscientific subjects were more and more regarded, not as modes of knowing or sources of new knowledge, but as, at best, merely expressions of subjective feelings and preferences, or as repositories of folk customs and social habits, or as ideological manifestations of group interests. They even began to have difficulty finding a place within the university, except insofar as they sought to model themselves after the natural sciences. Doing this, however, meant the sacri-

fice of their own integrity and identity as independent sources of value and ethical judgment.[1]

Clearly some of the "nonscientific" subjects to suffer along with ethics have been other philosophical disciplines such as metaphysics. If Sloan is correct in his conclusions about the impact of professionally trained and separate disciplines, and the emergence of natural science as the solely respected mode of knowledge, then we may ask further how long this has been the case.

Sloan suggests that it has been since about 1930 that professionalism and scientism have made it impossible for moral philosophy to be magisterial. He further believes that from 1890 until about 1930 moral philosophy, though in trouble, was nonetheless very much viable, and that generally moral philosophers were optimistic that a needed synthesis would emerge.

For nearly all of the nineteenth century, however, moral philosophy was the central course in the American college. Quite often it was taught by the President; always it was looked to as the one course that would somehow unify the educational venture. The student had spent his previous courses on the humanities such as English and history, the study of the classical languages and mathematics. In the morality course he was to be told how to translate all of this into the world of appropriate moral action. The course soon developed into two parts. One was an analysis of the general principles of morality such as those of the Kantian school, of the Scottish Common Sense school, or the British Utilitarians. This was soon complemented by a more practical application of these principles to social life. Thus in the nineteenth century the morality course came to contain much material which today is taught in the separate courses of political theory, sociology, and parts of economics. This was the one course which was dedicated to the preparation of the student for a life of noble action.

Let us now look a little more closely at the kind of philosophical wisdom which was contained in some of these courses. First it should be made clear that during the greatest popularity of these courses the favored philosophers consulted were usually of an idealist persuasion. The influence, for instance, of the theologian-philosopher Jonathan Edwards (1703-1758) on the nineteenth century was profound. He had been president of Princeton University for a brief time. His philosophy was largely influenced by Locke and Berkeley and ultimately shaped by his view of Presbyterian theology. Central to his version of idealism is the primacy of mind and its activity in the process of knowing, and the initiatives taken by the will in the formulation of good decisions.[2]

Another frequent source of nineteenth century moral wisdom was the Scottish School of common sense realism of Reid, Stewart, and others.[3] The principal representative of this method in America was the President of Princeton, from 1868-1888, namely James McCosh,[4] (1811-1894). He held the non-inferential beliefs of man generated by man to be reliable and unable to be sensibly questioned. In particular the principle of causality and the imperative to do moral good are recognized as necessarily true.

Perhaps the most influential thinker in communicating the Puritan view of the world was Cotton Mather (1663-1728). Though born in an earlier century, this Christian philosopher[5] was a frequent source of moral influence on the nineteenth century college president.

Another influence was that of Deism. In America this was understood by Benjamin Franklin (1706-1790) whose *Autobiography* reflected the Puritan emphasis on such virtues as industry and frugality.[6] From the precepts of Poor Richard onward he was deservedly known as a moralist. In a similar vein, Thomas Jefferson (1743-1826) was deeply influenced by Locke, Bacon, and Newton, and was a lifelong representative of the British tradition in philosophy.[7]

Since both Jefferson and Franklin are often looked up to as moral ideals by American school children, the student of moral philosophy has a further reason for not overlooking their writings and moral vision as solid influences on what was to be esteemed as morality by philosophy professors in America in the nineteenth century. Both were men of the enlightenment and both were deeply read in the moral philosophy of their times. Indeed sections of the *Autobiography* of Franklin, such as those on the virtues and the examination of conscience, are common places of American literature.

While it is true that Scottish Common sense philosophy as taught by McCosh, and the religious Puritan tradition as understood by Edwards and Mather had a very large influence on the college courses of the early nineteenth century, they were not as decisive as two other movements in nineteenth century American thought. One was the influence of German Romantic Idealism[8] which began to be heavily felt in the last four decades of the century, and whose central exponent was Josiah Royce. The other was the beginning reaction to that idealism in the early philosophies of James and Dewey, which was to develop into American Pragmatism.

Of all the philosophers in the American tradition who directly influenced ethics up until at least 1940, three are most clearly magisterial, Royce, James and Dewey. Therefore I propose to examine some of their basic moral positions in order better to understand what possible contributions their philosophies could make to the needed synthesis of moral theory which Ellrod has described in Chapter I. Accordingly, I will treat the idealist position of Josiah Royce first, then follow that with an analysis of some of the voluntaristic characteristics of the pluralist ethics of William James. Finally I will attempt an analysis of some of Dewey's major writings on education, psychology, and moral philosophy.

THE IDEALISM OF JOSIAH ROYCE

Josiah Royce is the primary representative in American thought of idealism in the Kantian tradition.[9] Thus he stresses man's character as a subject, a rational being, and a person. Personal morality accordingly must be autonomous rather than heteronomous. Personal autonomy is initiated through an act of good will, a conscious rational choice of one's duty and of the moral life. Those who live their lives without autonomy, whose moral law is received from outside the agent, are considered, in Kantian terms, heteronomous. Royce, together with Kant, would insist that such a passively accepted morality imposed from without is not sufficient for true morality. It does not do justice to the really crucial fact about human nature--namely that man's most prized possession is his autonomous will. That means that man is one to whom it is given to initiate, to recognize, and to impose his duty on himself.

This Kantian theme of the autonomous will, commented upon at length by Royce is a familiar theme in contemporary moral development theory. It is most clearly seen in the writings of Piaget, especially in *The Moral Judgment of the Child*. Kohlberg also has linked the categorical imperative of Kant to some of his discussion of Stage Six, the highest of his moral stages. Both topics were discussed in Chapter I.[10]

If the first ethical theme in Royce, namely the autonomous character of moral choice as the initiating move to a moral life, is more or less a direct derivative from Kant, a second theme, the philosophy of loyalty is more creative and uniquely Roycean. By loyalty Royce means the acceptance by the moral subject of a cause to which he binds his will. Royce as an idealist considers the individual as fragmentary and fragile, unable to function metaphysically except in reference to the absolute, and unable to function morally except by dedication to a cause. The very definition of a cause for Royce initially is that it is something outside of oneself to which one must commit oneself by a vital act of allegiance or loyalty. The idiosyncratic or personal will is thus rendered lawful or loyal by freely choosing a cause. The cause must be such as to be life-giving and self-creative of the choosing individual. Hence choices of empty fame or trivial honors are excluded.

The truly qualifying attribute of a worthy cause, loyalty to which creates a self, is its character of being supra-personal--something larger than the individual--in that it requires no subordination to any material or ignoble dimension. Examples of proper causes or worthy choices to dominate a life would be the love between husband and wife, the patriotic feeling of a soldier for his fatherland, the dedication of a scholar to truth, and the devotion of a physician to health, of a religious person to God, or a jurist to justice.

In contemporary moral development there is no explicit use of Royce's theory of loyalty. There is, however, a very similar emphasis on worthy and unworthy causes. Thus both Kohlberg and Piaget stress the need of the developing child to move from self-seeking behaviors, narcissistic in character, to more community directed behavior. Thus worthy causes such as patriotism, dedication to truth, respect for law and order, and respect for persons become developmental themes to which the moral person must be "loyal."

But beyond the demand that the moral choice be autonomous and directed to a supra-personal cause such as the love uniting two spouses, there is a third theme to which Royce is driven by his idealism, the theme of community. Kant himself had seen man as a member of a community of rational persons the primary move of whose will was to act in such wise that one could universalize the maxim behind one's act in a way that would be rationally satisfactory to all men.

In his theory of the "beloved community" Royce goes beyond Kant. Where Kant talked of a community of rational persons who ought to recognize each other as persons and respect each other as moral agents, Royce wrote of a community of loving persons. He saw Christianity as especially important because its vision of loving one's neighbor as oneself was community making. Thus Christianity represented the highest realization of the autonomous person because it offered to the person the most life giving choice that could be made, namely an extension of that individual personal life by an act of loving allegiance to the universal beloved community.

Each of these themes as they are developed by Royce has an unique American setting. Community, for instance, is related to his personal experience of the growing American democratic community, both numerically and geographically. His parents had travelled west in a covered wagon during the 1840's in search of gold. He had personally witnessed the lawlessness of some of the early mining settlements and became aware of the great good that the later more lawful and moral small town brought to human beings. As a youngster studying and later teaching in California, he was deeply impressed with the great moral value of community and of community making. His theory of the Beloved Community is very cohesive with American democratic traditions and aspirations.[11]

The philosophy of Royce was an idealistic version of the American Dream. Millions were drawn to America as immigrants by the cause represented by "America." It enabled them to make a life in medicine, or law, or business, the trades or the church. Royce celebrates them and their direction of their will toward the pursuit of community making ends. In many respects the Beloved Community was America.

WILLIAM JAMES

Clearly William James, especially in his moral writings, discussed and popularized many moral ideas and ideals which later came to have impact on those who developed contemporary theory in moral development. Although not a neo-Kantian, as was his friend Royce, James agrees with the Neo-Kantians in stressing the active role of the moral agent as an existential subject. In his famous essay, "The Will to Believe," James argued that human beings in the course of their moral development frequently encountered highly problematic moral situations--something like the "dilemmas" described by Kohlberg. These moral problems sometimes are in the nature of "forced options." In these situations they are confronted with a choice they cannot escape; yet they are unable to gain the requisite knowledge for a reasoned and informed choice. James argues that in such a situation men have a right to follow their "passional" nature and to exercise risk in the spirit of a natural faith.

He gives the example of a man caught on a precipitous mountain path in the face of a blinding snow storm. As the man seeks to descend he finds his way impeded by the snow; and finds that the snow is covering the only safe trail on the mountain. If he stops in his tracks on the grounds that he does not know where the trail really is, he freezes to death. If he goes on blindly he may fall off the precipice. James argues that the best solution is to risk to venture forth, to keep walking; that the best human mode in the situation is thus to trust and to dare. James uses this kind of analogy to describe many points in the moral life of human beings.

The very essence of the moral life as it is concretely and actually lived is that we must on occasion make momentous choices without full or often even complete information. A man chooses to marry, not really knowing the consequences for him of that marriage. A couple decides to have another child which may be retarded, or criminal, or even lead to the death of the mother. James argues that the obviously right attitude is for people to risk their persons to each other in love, and in this respect he is a voluntarist. He strongly opposes any theory of ethics which would be overly rationalist to the extent of excluding faith, natural or supernatural, from any role in the process of moral choice.

In *The Will to Believe* James argues against the claims of moral scientism, particularly as expressed by his contemporary, Clifford. Followers of moral scientism argue that one is immoral if one makes a choice without the requisite pre-knowledge. It is the claim of James that such moral scientists basically assume that it is better to give up possible truth than to be involved in possible error. James insists that he does not treat knowledge lightly; he urges that we be as informed as possible. But he insists that life forces us to make many choices which for the moral scientist would be uninformed choices; these choices cannot be escaped.

James points out that in some important choices our knowledge is by nature incomplete because it concerns persons and not objects or things. Thus one who pledges his love to his wife does so with risk and with faith. Such an act of risk and faith often constitutes the love which is pledged.

One of the accomplishments of James is his awareness that language and arguments about objects in the material world can often be settled by logic whereas great moral decisions of a personal kind cannot often be so settled. He is aware of the profound differences between moral and scientific discourse. Risk in science may be unjustified; risk in morals may often be essential. Contemporary moral development theories often suppose that the only problem in the moral life is knowing what to do. James makes a point of some significance when he claims that authentic development in morals and human goodness centers, at least in part, in the capacity for faith and calls for real risk in those instances in which we do not know completely what to do.

For a more adequate understanding of James' doctrine of moral choice, one must balance "The Will to Believe" with another well known essay, "The Moral Philosopher and the Moral Life."[13] In the conclusion of the latter essay James makes his famous distinction between the strenuous and the easy-going mood. Morals, he claims, is properly a matter of "the strenuous mood." The essence of the strenuous mood is that it constitutes the response of a moral agent to the demands of another person. For believers that person is God, for whom the very essence of the moral life is seeing that God has a claim on one's life, on one's duty. Life is accordingly a serious matter, a matter of meeting demands, a matter of response to a person, indeed, to God.

In this part of the essay, James is clearly closer to orthodox religious positions on morality than either Dewey or Royce. At the end of *Human Nature and Conduct* Dewey argues that the ideal of human life is to identify one's actions as having a living connection with the entire human community, past, present, and future. Royce is more concerned with the Absolute Spirit in which all finite persons inhere. James is more Hebraic, seeing God as a person with demands on man, whose response is the most serious part of his existence. This religious aspect of his moral theory occurs at the end of his essay on the moral life.

The central part of the essay contains material directed to the good of the individual. He argues that the moral man makes a certain kind of moral or categorical imperative: so act that your choices constitute a life which is as inclusive a whole as possible. Our choices must be as inclusive as possible so that our lives will be fuller. In this he is a life philosopher in the tradition of Bergson. Both saw the influence of Darwin as a major re-discovery of life as a supreme value. Both saw rationalism with its abstract order and necessity as barren and lacking the attractiveness of a world and of a philosophy in which life and the fullness of life would be magisterial. Thus, when James asks that we so order our lives that they be 'inclusive' choices he is asking us to bring fullness into our lives.

In a sense one might interpret this in an Aristotelian fashion and say that both James and Aristotle agree that "realization" or "actualization" of some kind is essential to the good life. However, for James the best thing about life is the very exuberance of the living process, whereas for Aristotle it is more a matter of the contemplative life or the actualization of the intellectual soul.

James is a pluralist. For him there are a great many choices a rational person can make, and, so to speak, a great many orders of choices. The essential human condition, according to James, is symbolized by the stress of consciousness with its fringe and its foreground, its extraordinary variety and fullness, its overwhelming multiplicity of possibilities for human awareness and selective attention.[17] Human beings can select only a very small number of things for their attention from among the almost infinite number of possible choices. Therefore the demand is for choices that will not be life denying and negative. Since by choosing one thing we are rejecting everything that is incompatible with that choice, we must choose those which are compatible with the most good possible to us. James is thus arguing for a kind of Darwinian process of selection: we should select the "fittest" objects for giving us the "fullest" life.

James' theory can be important to moral development for stages five and six are especially concerned with the choices made by members of a pluralist society. Motives for choosing ought, in a utilitarian way, to be compatible with the greatest possible good of the individual as well as to society. Motives also ought to be inclusive and allow for a fuller life both for the individual and for the community. The highest choice is the choice that enriches life the most both for the individual and for the society.

An additional contribution of James to moral development theory can be seen in his theory of habituation. For instance, James is very stern in his chapter on habit in the *Psychology*. There he admonishes the reader that one cannot live a good or useful life without the early development of appropriate habits. This is relevant to an extent to stages two and three where children wish to gain habits that will meet with peer or parental approval. James is particularly aware of the tragedy of those undeveloped moral individuals whose lives do not have habits of industry, emotional control and mental discipline. In *Talks To Teachers*[19] he states the very serious challenges to those who are to aid the young child in the early stages of development, which he sees in some respects as a point of no return. With certain kinds of habituation those who are not properly habituated at that time will be subsequently deprived of the proper fullness and smoothness of an ordered life.

One may say that the category of "habituation" is in fact a function of his conclusions about human nature both as a physician and as a psychologist. As a physician he was deeply aware of the working of the nervous system and for years was oppressed by his mistaken belief that one's future was determined by the state of one's nervous tissue. He was convinced that incorrectly habituated persons suffer needlessly. "Get good habits early" would be his maxim for early childhood, just as "make the most inclusive choices" would be his overall category for adult life.[20]

We may conclude this section on James by listing four of his contributions to moral developmental theory. In the first place he established the legitimacy of acting on belief, even when that belief was not certified by positive science. In the second place he insisted that the motives for one's choice ought to be inclusive in character and make for the fullest actualization of the individual possible. Thirdly, he stressed, through his metaphor of the stream of consciousness and its figures of the fringe and foreground, the great variety of choices open to the developing individual and the consequent need for study and care in the options to be made. Finally he emphasized the very great importance of proper habituation, particularly in the young developing child.

JOHN DEWEY

John Dewey, of all the American philosophers, is best known for his contributions to the philosophy of education, as well as to ethics and psychology. His work has been known and appreciated by all who have followed him in this field.[21]

He wrote a number of works on ethics, perhaps best represented by the first section of *Ethics* which he did with Tufts, and by his later work, *Human Nature and Conduct*. Like James, he wrote a book on psychology early in his career. He also wrote a number of classical works on education, the best known being perhaps *Democracy and Education*.[22] His very early *Pedagogical Credo*[23] contains many principles which were later adopted by the developmental psychologists.

One may rightly claim that the Hegelian themes of process, mediation, and development are an essential part of Dewey's subject matter, though he differs importantly from Hegel. Though like Royce, he started his career as a confirmed Hegelian, the Hegelian "Spirit" was to become "Nature" in the later Dewey. Hegel made it natural for Dewey to think of the world as in a constant developmental process, though Dewey replaced the immanent Spirit of Hegel with the process of his own later naturalism.

Another thinker whose influence on Dewey was equally massive is Charles Darwin, whose *Origin of Species* was published in 1895, the year of Dewey's birth. By reason of his devotion to Darwin and to the techniques of scientific method as a mode of inquiry or discovery, Dewey replaced what he thought to be the excessive rationalism of Hegel with a spirit of "experimentalism." This contributed notions of "struggle," "coping," and the necessity of the organism to maintain essential balance with the environment.

Perhaps Dewey's greatest direct contribution to moral development comes from his early writings on education. At the University of Chicago around the turn of the century Dewey was simultaneously chairman of three departments: philosophy, psychology, and pedagogy. He was also director of the famous "Laboratory" School of the University of Chicago in which educational theory was consciously tested. At this time Dewey wrote a document, *My Pedagogical Credo*, in which he advanced a number of principles which were to remain central to his thought in the area of development for the rest of his career

One of these principles which is somewhat Hegelian in character is that of continuity, namely, that the part should be related to the whole, the individual to the *totum*. In another form it states that the totality is somehow the explanation or the ground for what is partial. In Dewey's educational theory, this means that the goals of the school must be somehow consistent with those of the larger society. Thus a democratic society will demand a school system of a special kind. In a second application, just as society demands schools consistent with the larger ends of society, so the school must truly further and perfect the family. The fragmentary individual should be mediated or reconciled to the larger society and rendered one with its goals by an education which so develops the talents of the individual that he can make the society itself better.

Dewey reached his principle of continuity, in part because of his experience, just after his graduation from the University of Vermont and before his entrance to Johns Hopkins University, as teacher in Oil City, Pennsylvania.[24] There he formed a very negative picture of traditional elementary and secondary school education. Such education, he felt, especially lacked interaction among the pupils themselves, as well as of the students with the subject matter. The material in the famed McGuffey readers was fairly stale and given to students to memorize and recite back; things went according to the schedule set by the teacher. Dewey reversed much of this. The character and significance of that reversal is closely related to further developments in his own writings on moral development.

In a somewhat surprising move Dewey claimed that the stage of development of the pupil--the interests of the pupil and not of the teacher--should be the major concern of the educational process. This change in emphasis was in accord with Dewey's principle of challenge or interest. He was convinced that students cannot "learn" in any authentic sense those things for which they have not developed an interest, that is, for which their own minds are not yet ready. Thus, the point of development at which the child actually happens to be is of the utmost importance. Children, Dewey wrote, have a way of telling teachers what the stage of their development is by the questions they ask and the topics in which they show interest.

Once a child has shown interest, for instance, in measurement, or in understanding the root system of plants, or in the making of cloth, then the child should be given considerable work in that area. By responding intelligently and seriously to the student's greatest curiosity, the student most easily grows, develops, becomes less isolated and more socialized. Whereas in traditional education students were to receive detailed education when the teacher was ready, in Dewey's theory such detailed explanation must wait until the student is ready.[25] There is much to be admired in Dewey's principle of continuity by which he clarified that the educational institutions of any community must prepare students for the larger life of the community outside the school. In a democratic society education must be for everyone not just for the brightest or a cultural elite. American education, he insisted, must be related to citizenship even though other less free societies might legitimately keep it for the few.

Dewey's insistence on development of all citizens so that they might contribute to the American democratic way of life, was further heightened by his experience with Jane Adams and Hull House, the famed settlement house for immigrants in Chicago. The millions of immigrants from other countries placed special duties on the educational establishment, in response to which American schools must not only talk about democracy but must themselves reveal and create structures which are democratic. Students, accordingly, who are to be expected to plan together later in town halls, ought early in life to be instructed in working together on projects

Dewey valued the use of projects which required the cooperation of more than one student. By offering a group of students a meaningful project, socialization and peer cooperation were encouraged. Further, there was also a gain for practicality in the learning process, since life is eminently practical and made of discreet moral situations as well as general principles.

These pedagogical principles--the project method, the use of "interest" as a key to the development of the child, the continuity principle which related the child to the school and this, in turn, to the visions of the overall democratic society--all of these are related to Dewey's moral or ethical principles of which we will now seek to examine a few that were most essential.

First, is his principle of "growth" sometimes called his "meliorism," which literally suggests that moral persons and moral communities are capable of continuously improving in important ways.[26] A second is the principle of balance and equilibrium, namely, that the human situation is one of constantly "balancing" novelties with traditional wisdom, for instance, what can we say about cloning on the basis of traditional wisdom? A third principle of his ethics is that ethical knowledge is a matter of inquiry into actual concrete situations. A fourth topic is his model for inquiry by persons with sufficient moral development.

Dewey places the capacity for growth as the key mark of a moral self in his *Ethics*. In his chapter on the moral self Dewey makes the following claim:

> All voluntary action is a remaking of self, since it creates new desires, instigates to new modes of endeavor, brings to light new conditions which institute new ends. Our personal identity is found in the thread of continuous development which binds together these changes.[27]

In the same passage Dewey argues in an almost Kierkegaardian or Jamesian way that the self can never really stay still, that it is always becoming either better or worse, that it is the quality of the becoming that counts. He further claims "the end is growth itself."

Dewey then distinguishes between what he calls a "fixed self" and a "dynamic self." Clearly, for him, it is the dynamic self that is capable of continued moral development. First, he describes the fixed, the "old" or the "habitual" self.

> The habitual self . . . is constituted by habits already for-

med. Habit gives facility, and there is always a tendency to
rest on the oars, to fall back on what we have already a-
chieved. For that is the easy course; we are at home and feel
comfortable in lines of action that run in the tracks of habits
already established and mastered. Hence the old, the habitual self, is likely to be treated as if it were *the* self.[28]

In contrast, the dynamic self is the one capable of further development and habituation.

The growing, enlarging, liberated self, on the other hand,
goes forth to meet new demands and occasions, and readapts
and remakes itself in the process. It welcomes untried situations. The necessity for choice between the interests of the
old and the forming, moving self is recurrent.

Dewey continues with the observation that the good person is one with a dynamic self, a self that is capable of growth and further moral development. It is clearly never "given" to the self to be "fully" or "finally" developed: every moment of existence is one of existential tension. Nothing in nature prevents the self from either further actualization by an enduring choice of the good or, on the other hand, from a deterioration of some kind.

Who then is the good person? Dewey writes:

For everywhere there is an opportunity and a need to go
beyond what one has been, beyond "himself" if the self is
identified with the body of desires, affections, and habits
which has been potent in the past. Indeed, we may say that
the good person is precisely the one who is most conscious
of the alternative, and is the most concerned to find openings for the newly forming or growing self; since no matter
how 'good' he has been, he becomes 'bad' (even though acting upon a relatively high plane of attainment) as soon as he
fails to respond to the demand for growth.

These concluding paragraphs of Dewey's section of the *Ethics* make it clear that his definite ideal is the dynamic self which continues to be open to further growth. In the language of the concluding section of *Human Nature and Conduct*, this is to continue to be a consciously relating member of the human community by responsible and loving action.

A second major theme of Dewey's *Ethics* is his insistence that it is a matter of inquiry whose conclusions are often tentative and experimental. A willingness to be tentative and to be able to live with less than mathematical certainty in morals is clearly as old as Aristotle. Dewey came to his approval of being tentative by reason of his attraction to the scientific method. This is a theme repeatedly stated in *Reconstruction in Philosophy*. He felt that the method of the physical sciences, especially biology, physics, and chemistry, had qualities which could well be imitated by philosophers. He did not hold that men should do ethics as they do biology, but he did think that the spirit of experimentation and of free inquiry which stimulated the biologist should be assimilated by the moralist. It was not a matter of experimenting irresponsibly with what is already known to be wise and good, but of seeking to entertain as many alternatives as possible in considering problematic moral situations.

Though one does not wisely tamper with established wisdom, in those highly problematic areas in which there are as yet no wise solutions--in which in fact solutions are notably wanting--we should not be reluctant to employ the method of the sciences with proper changes for philosophy. Thus, inquiry is, on the one hand, the capacity to be tentative, to be willing to explore, to be willing to experiment. On the other hand, it is the willingness to make philosophy a community action, to be ready to submit one's methods and results to the scrutiny of others. Indeed, it positively encourages group or community involvement in reaching moral decisions.

Thus the working out of the solution to a problem or dilemma can be a social affair. It need not be just Socrates in dialectic with one or two opponents or collaborators, but a group effort in which the philosophical dynamics may be somewhat freely structured, but a vital intellectual process nonetheless. The group can be united in its perception of a felt need, a moral perplexity, or a moral puzzle. Such small classroom groups should be encouraged to be initially tentative, to seek alternatives, to look for confirmation, to admit exceptions, and to avoid being pretentious in the sense of claiming absolute certainty too early.

A further characteristic of inquiry is that it is directed to actual concrete physical conditions, or in Dewey's term, to "unique" situations in space and time with limited scope. In addition to his conviction regarding the public character of the scientific method and his admiration for the tentative quality of its pronouncements, he was strongly influenced by the Darwinian notion that intelligence was man's best and unique way of coping with the problems and difficulties of life in a sometimes threatening environment.

Dewey's well known chapter on moral conceptions in his book *Reconstruction in Philosophy* claims that the primary role of intelligence is to keep life in balance by handling problems intelligently. In that work, intelligence is conceived as problem-oriented. Moral reasoning is a matter of man responding to situations which are unique, in some way novel, and unexpected. Further, because of the evolution which is continually taking place, man is destined continually to have problems with novelties for which traditional wisdom has no full or adequate explanation. Man is fated to have on-going problems with personal, institutional and cultural habits because these are constantly in process. When institutional, cultural, or personal solutions no longer work the person or society with the problem has to stop and think in order to rebalance and re-integrate itself with the environment, be that familial or societal. Dewey describes this process as the method of intelligence in *Reconstruction in Philosophy*:

> A moral situation is one in which judgment and choice are required antecedently to overt action. The practical meaning of the situation--that is to say the action needed to satisfy it--is not self-evident. It has to be searched for. There are conflicting desires and alternative apparent goods. What is needed is to find the right course of action, the right good. Hence inquiry is exacted; observation of the detailed make-up of the situation; analysis into its diverse factors; clarification of what is obscure; discount of the more insistent and vivid traits; tracing the consequences of the various modes of action that suggest themselves; regarding the decision reached as hypothetical and tentative until the anticipated or supposed consequences which led to its adoption have been squared with actual circumstances. This inquiry is intelligence.[30]

Dewey was himself aware that a major objection to his own theory of morality was that he had overestimated the possibilities of scientific method--more precisely, that he had incorrectly assumed that a science of objects could be useful as a model for a practical science of persons. On the one hand, this is clearly a reasonable objection. Dewey did write at a time when many persons unrealistically expected all types of wisdom to emerge from the proper use of the scientific method. Two world wars fought by nations imbued with highly scientific bureaucracies served to diminish, indeed to eliminate any hope that science was the one answer to all problems. On the other hand, there are "spiritual" aspects of the scientific method which Dewey appropriately celebrated--such as its openness, its tentativeness, its community aspect. These are rightly prized and should become a more constant feature of moral discourse.

A second, and indeed a major objection is that Dewey was so fascinated by process that he could not see the presence of "natures" really operating in the world. Thus he was unable to admit that human nature in the Neolithic age has much in common with human nature in the time of Aristotle or in the contemporary age or that it is a valuable source of moral reasoning. In contrast, Aristotle and Aquinas saw a knowledge of human nature adequately conceived in its essential relationships to other men, to other things, and to God, to be a substantial foundation for moral theory.

Further, it must be noted that Dewey was almost always unable to give proper credit to the Greek conception of man because his understanding of Greek philosophy overstressed its attribution of permanence and necessity as features of reality. Because of his own fascination with the Hegelian process and the biological model of Darwin, he exaggerated the possibilities of science for philosophy and underestimated the role of metaphysics as an aid to ethics. In defense of Dewey, it should be said that the rather rigid Platonic metaphysics he saw at Columbia was not nearly as useful to him as some modern metaphysics of the Person might have been. In addition, there is merit in his claim that moralists often presume that because there are eternal truths there can be no real or insoluble moral problems and in his question of how we are to know an eternal truth when we see one.

In conclusion to this section on Dewey it should be stated that the moral doctrines of Dewey just described are clearly relevant to the current work on moral development. Dewey's theory of the dynamic self that continues to be actualized is clearly consonant with moving from stage to stage of development. In addition his pattern of moral inquiry which stresses the role of the active use of the intelligence in morally perplexing situations has been a major influence in the considerations of moralists concerned with the proper exercise of prudential judgment. Clearly too, his insistence that the solution of moral problems should include the reasoning of the whole community is important.

It has been the major claim of this article that the moral theories of Dewey, James, and Royce provide important philosophical background for contemporary moral development theory. It is perhaps fitting to conclude with a maxim from the moral theory of William James: "So Act that your choice will lead you to the most inclusive life." This is but another way of saying, as Aristotle had centuries before, that we must actualize our potentialities if we are to be virtuous or to be happy. To a religious tradition of moral development James is clearly far more important than Dewey, for it is James who defines the strenuous mood, the ability to see life as a response to the claims of a person, which for a believer is God.

Georgetown University
Washington, D.C.

NOTES

1. Daniel Callahan and Sissela Bok, eds., *Ethics Teaching in Higher Education* (New York: Plenum Press, 1980), p. 44-55. The quotation is from the paper by Douglas Sloan, "The Teaching of Ethics in the American Undergraduate Curriculum, 1876-1976."

2. See Perry Miller, *Jonathan Edwards* (New York: 1958). See also the Pulitzer Prize winning biography by O.E. Winslow (New York: Macmillan, 1980).

3. Two principal members of the Scottish School are Thomas Reid and Sir William Hamilton. Reid's *An Inquiry into the Human Mind on the Principles of Common Sense* in *Philosophical Works* (Hildesheim: Olms, 1967 [1764]) was a defense of common sense in the face of scepticism.

4. McCosh wrote *Intuitions of the Mind, Inductively Investigated* (New York: Carter, 1860) and *The Method of the Divine Government, Physical and Moral* (Edinburgh: Carter, 1850).

5. A major purpose of his *Christian Philosopher* (Gainsville,

Fl.: Scholars Facsimilies, 1968 [1721]) is to show his movement from a strict Puritan Background to an acceptance of many of the attitudes of the natural religion so popular in the age of reason.

6. See Carl Van Doren, *Benjamin Franklin* (New York: Viking, 1938) or Carl Becker, *Benjamin Franklin* (New York: 1965).

7. The standard biography is Dumas Malone, *Jefferson and His Time*, 3 vols. (Boston: Little, Brown, 1948-1962).

8. The great trio of German Romantic Idealists were Johann Gottlieb Fichte (1762-1814), Friedrich Schelling (1776- 1854) and G.W. Hegel (1770-1831). The British and American moral thinkers were deeply influenced by this tradition. For instance, Thomas Carlyle was deeply influenced by the moral idealism of Fichte. Coleridge, who was to have an influence on American moral philosophers, was himself influenced by Schelling.

9. There has been renewed interest in Royce in the last two decades. See the excellent edition of Royce in the volumes by John J. McDermott, *The Basic Writings of Josiah Royce* (Chicago: The University of Chicago Press, 1969). There are also a number of excellent commentaries: James Harry Cotton, *Royce on the Human Self* (Cambridge, Mass.: Harvard University Press, 1954); Gabriel Marcel, *Royce's Metaphysics* (Chicago: Henry Regnery, 1956); and Peter Fuss, *The Moral Philosophy of Josiah Royce* (Cambridge, Mass.: Harvard University Press, 1965).

10. Jean Piaget, *The Moral Judgment of the Child* (New York: Macmillan, 1965).

11. A similar approach to moral theory can be seen perhaps in the work of John Rawls, who like Royce was also deeply influenced by the ethical theory of Kant. Thus Rawls would seem to insist that the very institution of a democratic society is inconsistent with practices that systematically depress any minority within the community. There has clearly been some use of Rawls by Kohlberg in his discussions of stage six.

For an account of the moral philosophy of James see John K. Roth, *The Moral Philosophy of William James* (New York: Thomas Y. Crowell, 1969). This is an anthology with a helpful introduction. Perhaps the most important single essay by James on morality is "The Moral Philosopher and the Moral Life." Other essays of importance are "The Dilemma of Determinism," "The Sentiment of Rationality," and "The Will To Believe."

12. William James, *The Will To Believe and Other Essays in Popular Philosophy* (New York: Dover, 1956). See esp. p. 11.

13. *Ibid.*, p. 184-215.

14. *Ibid.*, p. 212.

15. John Dewey, *Human Nature and Conduct (New York: Modern Library, 1930)*.

16. *Op. cit.*, p. 213.

17. See the selection on the stream of consciousness in Roth.

18. The famous chapter is to be found in Volume One of William James, *The Principles of Psychology* (New York: Henry Holt & Company, 1890).

19. See *Talks to Teachers on Psychology and to Students on Some of Life's Ideals* (New York: Henry Holt & Company, 1899).

20. This admonition to 'get the most' out of life is not really a hedonistic attitude in James. His theory of the "strenuous mood" would not allow pleasure to be the primary principle.

21. Among the more important books by Dewey on Ethics are the following: *Ethics* (Revised Edition; New York: Henry Holt & Co, 1932 [1908]), written with James H. Tufts; *Freedom and Culture* (New York: G.P. Putnam, [1939]); *Human Nature and Conduct* (New York: The Modern Library, 1930 [1922]); *Theory of Valuation* (Chicago: University of Chicago Press, 1939). Two recommended books on his moral theory are: Robert J. Roth, S.J., *John Dewey and Self-Realization* (New York: Prentice Hall, 1962); and James Gouinlock, *John Dewey's Philosophy of Value* (New York: Humanities Press, 1972).

22. *Democracy and Education* (New York: The Macmillan Co., 1916).

23. *My Pedagogic Creed* (New York: E.L. Kellog & Co., 1897).

24. See Neil Coughlin, *Young John Dewey*.

25. Kohlberg illustrates the use of this principle by the careful selection of content for his dilemmas, which differ for the very young child in comparison to the child of eleven or twelve.

26. This is discussed in detail in Dewey's *Ethics*.

27. *Theory of the Moral Life*.

28. *Ibid.*

29. *Ibid.*

30. *Reconstruction in Philosophy*, p. 163.

CHAPTER III

AFFECTIVITY:

THE POWER BASE OF MORAL BEHAVIOR

SEBASTIAN A. SAMAY, O.S.B.

EXECUTIVE KNOWLEDGE OR SOCRATIC FALLACY?

Whatever else might be said about the relationship between science and morality one thing is fairly clear: the two are aimed at different ends. Science is undertaken with a view to gaining awareness, knowledge, information about the world, while the aim of morality is to develop dispositions for right action, right behavior in the agent. To be sure, science too involves action, but only as a means of attaining its end. All the methodical probing, measuring, testing merely serve as preparatory steps toward what is really intended by the scientific enterprise. That end is knowledge. By contrast, morality makes use of knowledge and turns it into a means for its own end. As a preparatory step toward deliberate and righteous action, knowledge is undoubtedly a guide to morality, but not the whole of it; nor is knowledge the goal or final end of morality. That end is action which transmutes knowledge into concrete performance and thereby actualizes what knowledge merely represents. Through this actualization, a certain power or perfection, a surplus-being or reality accrues to the moral agent. Traditional wisdom calls this increase virtue.

One would expect from this that moral philosophies, especially theories of moral education, would have a great deal to say about how to foster virtue in people. At the very least, one would expect that, along with analyzing the sources, principles, objects and methods of moral knowledge, ethics would also explain to us the dynamics which turns our moral representations into performative skills. Besides enumerating the *reasons for which* people act or should act, ethics must call attention also to the *energies through which* people are enabled to act for those reasons. After all, the reality which moral philosophy studies can be said to exist only after people acquired the ability and disposition, not only to *think* according to a certain set of principles, but also to *act* on them. To understand morality, therefore, requires that we investigate not only the processes of moral discourse, but also the root of the dynamism of moral life.

Alas, most moral theories traditional and current alike, are rather thin on the latter score. Preoccupied with the problems of moral reasoning and moral discourse, many of them quickly gloss over the dynamics of moral action as virtually unproblematic. But there *are* problems, many of them, that cannot be resolved in terms of knowledge alone: How is it that certain moral judgments are implemented while others are not? Is it the truth or falsity of these judgments that decides their implementation or the lack of it? What initiates the action of implementation? Is the initiative causal or merely directional? What exactly is the connection between knowledge and behavior, between judgment and action, between theory and practice?

Finding few or scant answers to problems such as these slowly gives rise to the nagging impression that most moral theories, in spite of their verbal protestation to the contrary, are content with being theories about moral thinking rather than theories about moral life and moral action. Regardless of what they intend to be, they can be correctly labelled as "spectator ethics" to one degree or another.

It would be difficult to account adequately for this persistent neglect of the dynamic dimensions of morality, but one reason for it may be found in the particular kind of intellectualism which is never very far from the center of Western philosophy.[1] The kind in question is the ethical intellectualism of Socratic origin, which has the tendency of absorbing the dynamic components of moral life into knowledge by simply assuming that *agents,* when they are involved in a concrete situation,[2] will necessarily and automatically perform according to the principles which they uphold as uninvolved *spectators* of similar situations. All commentators seem to agree that Socrates credited knowledge with a kind of executive efficacy with regard to moral action: "knowing what is good is not only a necessary but also the sufficient condition of possessing goodness and hence of doing what is good."[3] This means, of course, that knowledge is not only an *informing* factor but also the *enabling* factor of moral behavior. Moreover, it also follows that, if knowledge is ability, a man with the ability of doing the good could not knowingly do what is wrong; his wrong-doing could only be inadvertent, a matter of ignorance. Based on the belief that knowledge is virtue, intellectualists of all ages could always appeal to a ready-made solution to the central problem of moral education, which is the problem of how to teach virtue. Right action in the learners of virtue says this silent creed, is best elicited by improving their knack of making the right moral judgments. Pointing out to them what is good and what is evil, or demonstrating with logical stringency the advantages of the "real" good over mere "apparent" good is the best way of turning them away from the latter and making them pursue the former.

The hope of this essay is to point out that that belief, even when better stated and accompanied by cautious qualifications, is illusory and inconsistent with the structures of human behavior. The intellectualist conception not only does not give an adequate account of the dynamic determinants of moral action, it also puts the cart before the horse when it attributes primacy to cognition among those determinants. That primacy belongs to a striving or conative force which shall be designated here by the term "affectivity." As an all-pervasive propensity of living nature, affectivity will be seen as the general power supply of all behavior, the igniting spark of all activity, the integrating force of all knowledge and valuation, the parent rapport between life and reality. The principal thrust of this essay will be to show that moral behavior is only half understood as a consequence of moral judgments. Without the executive propensity of the affective or striving impulse, such judgments would not be made in the first place, or if made, would remain forever in the domain of mere knowledge or pure representation.

Identifying affectivity rather than the intellect as the dynamic source of moral life is based on the firm conviction that the essential perfection and final end of human development is not to be an epistemic or knowing subject, but to become an autonomous person, a self-regulating agent, who not only *has* life but also freely and resolutely *leads* it. While the beginnings of this self-regulating existence may coincide with the primitive strivings of life's self-movement, its peak is reached only in that affective exchange among sovereign individuals which we call love. It is love rather than contemplation that constitutes man's ultimate relation to reality and even provides the obediential disposition into which an invitation to supernatural destiny can be projected.

This conviction is in marked contrast with some aspects of the hallowed Greek tradition, according to which the highest, most divine, element in man is his participation in the imperishable Intelligence (*Nous*), whose final perfection consists in a beatifying contemplation of the Supreme Idea or Form. Totally separated from matter, simple and incorruptible, the Intelligence was held to be the standard of excellence in being and its contemplative mirroring of spiritual reality an end in itself. The rank or worth of all other kinds of reality was measured against this ideal degree of being, and all other activities were judged by how closely they resembled the restful awareness of contemplation or how closely they contributed to it.

The irresistible pull of this intellectualistic bias is detectable even in the otherwise balanced philosophy of Saint Thomas Aquinas. It is not that he was an intellectual determinist,[4] according to whom knowledge exercised not only a guiding influence over the freedom of the will but also a causal determination, he was, nevertheless, an intellectualist when it came to evaluating the position of the will in relation to the intellect. According to Thomas, even in those cases where will and intellect cooperate, they can be distinguished by their respective objects: the object of the intellect is the abstract meaning of the good (*ratio boni*), while the object of the will is the concrete good itself (*bonum ipsum*). Ordinary readers would imply from this that, as an appetite for the concrete good, the will excels the intellect. But then came the surprising conclusion which illustrated how deeply Aquinas was committed to intellectualism. Precisely because its object is "simpler and more abstract," the intellect is, absolutely speaking, "higher and nobler" than the will.[5]

Although Thomas admitted that accidentally the will and its chief activity of love could be considered higher than the intellect, he attributed this superior ranking to the provisional imperfection under which the intellect is forced to operate in the present pilgrim state of man. That imperfection, however, was expected to be lifted in man's definitive state, heaven, where the intellectual vision of the supreme good would secure the possession of that good all by itself:

> ... Human values, identically intellectual ones in the definitive state of our final destiny, [undergo] a certain reversal in man's present state where values belong essentially to the order of the will. In heaven the perfection of the blessed is measured by the clarity of each one's Beatific Vision; but on earth the only criterion of moral rectitude we possess is to be found in each one's capacity for love.[6]

I simply do not hold with such reversals of priorities. I hold instead that on any level, experiential as well as metaphysical, natural as well as supernatural, man's primary relation to the real is always of the affective order, an order of love, *ordo amoris*, as Max Scheler called it. I coined the term *protention* to characterize this relation. The elements of this coined word for man's primary relation to the real suggest that the original thrust of affectivity includes both the energetic aspect of launching oneself toward something (a *project*) and the knowing aspect of directing one's attention toward it (an *intention*). Of the two aspects, I consider the first more basic. In other words, I hold that the real is primarily that with which living beings are affectively involved, and only secondarily that which is offered to human inspection. Knowledge, inspection, representation are merely cognitive expressions of peoples' spontaneous attachment to, and appetite for the real.[7] True, sometimes this attachment must be suspended, delayed and critically examined by reflective thought so that our allegiance may be bestowed not necessarily on the nearest good but on the greatest good available at the moment, nevertheless, the whole process of inspection is carried out for the sake of subsequent involvement. (See Chapter VIII on the objective human good). This is eminently true in the moral domain where the perennial problem is how to carry our best judgments into action. Any theory of morality or moral development that neglects this problem or deals with it but sparingly, is not very helpful.

AFFECTIVITY AS PROTENTION:
ATTENTIVE DYNAMISM OR DYNAMIC AWARENESS

The problem of how to carry our moral thoughts into action seems to be no problem at all for thinkers of the intellectualist persuasion because, as suggested above, the very tendency of intellectualism is to invest thought with a sort of causal efficacy with regards to action. This is not to say that all intellectualist theories always attribute this efficacy directly to thought itself, although some expressions of Spinoza's *Ethics*, for instance, could be interpreted in that sense. Instead, most theories hold that causal influence is exercised through a separate intellectual faculty, the will. The will is seen by them as an intermediary between pure thought and physical action. Inhabiting a sort of spiritual command post and prompted by representations of the intelligible good, the will is portrayed as dispatching summons to the other faculties to spring into action and execute the movements necessary for the attainment of that good. Sometimes thought and volition are fused, and the will is regarded merely as the energetic aspect of reason itself. Kant, for instance, defined will as the efficacy of the intellect,[8] and as such, "nothing else than practical reason."[9]

Whether operating directly or mediated through other faculties, thought is seen by most intellectualists as the ultimate force behind moral action, moving us to actualize the objects of our moral representations. For reasons already hinted at and reasons that will become clear later on, I wish to attribute that kind of motive force to affectivity instead. But in order to do so without creating a whole series of misunderstandings, it is necessary first to cut away some of the habitual connotations attached to the concept of affectivity and redefine it in a more comprehensive and radical way. It is hoped that, as a result of this severe pruning, a fresh understanding of moral development can be grafted on the stock of affectivity by the other contributors.

To begin with, affectivity, as intended by this essay, must be rigorously distinguished in many respects from the psychological constructs called "emotions," "affects" or "passions." A few maverick views apart, emotions are considered by the behavioral sciences as temporary disturbances in a person's normal state of mind and body, induced by the representation of particular situations as desirable or undesirable, and accompanied by a certain tendency either to seek or to avoid those situations through appropriate action.[10] Theories of emotion based on this general understanding differ, and differ considerably, depending on which of these component aspects are thought to constitute the defining feature of emotion. "Bodily upset" theories emphasize the agitation of the organism and consider emotions to consist in the very awareness of that agitated state, its "psychic shadow"; "motivational" theories view emotions as prompters of action based on some kind of value estimation or calculation of utility; "feeling" theories emphasize the immediacy and spontaneity of emotions; and so on. The great diversity and sometimes sharp contrast between these theories do not, however, exclude a certain convergence on several points.

Influenced by a certain organic interpretation of system balance or equilibrium (*homeostasis*), most psychological theories consider emotions to be impermanent, transient affairs, as opposed to attitudinal or dispositional states which are more stable and permanent. As a feature of living systems, equilibrium requires the maintenance of a steady state of balance between organism and environment. When this steady state is upset, some mechanism within the system itself springs into action in order to reestablish the equilibrium. According to most theories, emotions are typically human ways of responding to temporary disequilibrium and of triggering the process of return to steady state.

66 Affectivity and Moral Behavior

Secondly, most theories consider emotions to be particular and specific reactions to imbalance, even when overt behavior or physiological research can disclose no pattern that would be characteristic of, say, "embarrassment" as distinct from "shame." In other words, both ordinary language and psychology operate with many more terms designating emotional mental states than there are behavioral or bodily symptoms manifesting these (supposedly) distinct states.

Thirdly, all of them agree that emotions are conditioned, or at least triggered, by some form of perception, idea or intuition, in short, by some type of representation. Perception is seen as the cause of emotion-- "cause" being understood here in the sense that most positive sciences use the term, namely, as an "antecedent state" which strictly determines the subsequent event in question. In fact, it has been suggested by some experimenters that "the same state of physiological arousal could be labeled 'joy' or 'fury' or 'jealousy' or any of a great diversity of emotional labels depending on the cognitive aspect of the situation."[11] This, of course, would mean that knowledge or cognition not only occasions the occurrence of an emotion, but also determines its identity and meaning.

Finally, in spite of this strongly mentalistic and cognitive interpretation, the most consistent connotation attached to emotions is "irrationality," "turbulence," "frenzy."[12] This is especially true when emotion is equated with the singularly ambiguous term "passion." Emotion in this sense is a sheer liability to be avoided, or at least kept in strict control, for the sake of rational action. There are very few theories that consider emotions to be of service in revealing the real nature or real value of things. (See Chapter VII on moral sensibility.)

Without contesting the right of the positive sciences to define and elaborate their theoretical constructs in a way most suitable to their particular purposes and most in harmony with the explanatory models they have chosen, I claim that "affectivity" has very little in common with the psychological acceptation of "emotion" and other cognate terms. In fact, as referred to here, affectivity is characterizable by features that are very nearly the opposite of those applied to emotion.

First of all, the term affectivity designates that enduring orientation and universal propensity, adherence or tendency by virtue of which living individuals are bonded to their environment and interact with it, both by fitting themselves to it and rearranging it to their own advantage or to the advantage of their kind. In this sense, affectivity is immeasurably wider, older, more basic than particular human emotions. As a fundamental orientation (an ontological intentionality), affectivity is found in various forms in all sentient beings and perhaps even in some higher forms of plant life. It would be an unwarranted extrapolation, however, to conclude from this that people, beasts and vegetation are ontologically the same, just because they share in the propensity of all life for spontaneity and self-actualization. Affective intentionality is called ontological not in order to designate sameness of nature in all its bearers, but in order to indicate that affectivity is not deployed through a special faculty, but involves the individual in its totality and imparts directedness to its life as a whole. By contrast, noetic intentionality is an act mediated through conscious representation or appetite, an act of the mind by which it tends toward the object. Moreover, the global aim of affective propensity is not the mere maintenance of being, but the promotion of increase in being. In other words, affectivity is the basic dynamism of life that can reach beyond the factual towards the possible and, at a certain level of development, can even represent the possible as a "purpose to be actualized." As such, affectivity is the energy source of all growth, progress, striving, desiring, planning and willing. Simply stated, affectivity is rooted in the fact that, for life, being is not merely an object already given but also a cradle of further reality that makes the creative evolution of life possible.

Secondly, as a basic and permanent orientation of life, affectivity has no object, aim or intention other than the general one of life's self-enhancement. However, this generality implies neither invariance nor fixity on the part of affectivity. On the contrary, affectivity is the conative or dynamic matrix of the whole unsurveyable range of drives, instincts and appetites that constantly appear along the process whereby life intrudes into the domain of inertia. It is unspecific and undifferentiated only in the sense that, in itself, it represents the global impact of cumulative living on the individual's general orientation. As such, it is not the work of any particular faculty.[13] it is not tied to any particular function or organic pattern, even though it can operate through all of them and, in so doing, acquire the specificity proper to the occasion.

Thirdly, the relationship between affectivity and knowledge is in reality the inverse of the one usually posited by philosophers between the emotional and cognitive factors of experience: it is the growth, the refinement, the evolution of affectivity that makes possible and gives rise to the different kinds and degrees of cognitive representation, and not the other way around. (This point finds a more extensive development in Chapter VII.) This means that the kind of knowledge available to a subject is directly related to the kind of attitudinal posture he or she is capable of assuming; that the process of objectification required for cognitive development depends on a process of affective dissociation or diffusion.

Some aspects of this process will be indicated presently, but first a remark or two about the inversion itself. The heterodoxy of this position should not be hidden from view, on the contrary, it should be emphasized from the start in order to signal that this essay is slightly off the beaten path in the sense that it does not endorse the long-standing Greek bias of unquestioned primacy of speculative knowledge over conation in every respect, though it goes to the heart of many recent developments in the understanding of the person and of personal life. One need not be a wholesale pragmatist, in fact one need not be a pragmatist at all, to agree with Dewey's analysis that pure thought has a certain colonizing bent which tends to absorb the whole of experience into reflection. Like a typical colonial settler, reflection soon claims the whole territory of experience, so that after a while even the native occupants are believed to exist at its sufferance alone:

> What is known, what is true for cognition, is what is real in being. The objects of knowledge form the standards of measures of the reality of all other objects of experience. Are the objects of affections, of desire, effort, choice, that is to say everything to which we attach value, real? Yes, *if* they can be warranted by knowledge; if we can *know objects* having these value properties, we are justified in thinking them real. But as objects of desire and purpose they have no sure place in being until they are approached and validated through knowledge.[14]

It is against just this sort of familiar but usually unexpressed encroachment that these few pages wish to defend the rights not of action, as Dewey tried to do, but of affectivity and life in general. This wish is motivated by the firm conviction that the human world is originally and throughout a lived world of involvement rather than a spectacle provided for the dispassionate gaze of speculative thought.

Finally, if affectivity cannot be justly regarded as a ward of knowledge, neither can it be considered its rival. Knowledge is merely a later and more developed form of that affective discernment through which all living things endeavor to sort out the value and meaning of their environment. Long before the appearance or even the possibility of explicit representation of goals by individual organisms, life already has an intrinsic directedness through genotypically shaped processes, such as the instinctual acts of animals. Thanks to their value-orientation and affective interchange with the environment, living beings can feel "at home" in the world, even though they can only enact, but not yet represent, that feeling. This ability of life forms to be selective of value without the benefit of separate and antecedent representation of ends and means suggests that life as a whole cannot be regarded either as an entirely mechanical process or as a properly purposive one. On some levels at least, life seems to "know" reality by its mere attitudinal involvement with the real, and is able to accomplish its "purposes" almost automatically and unconsciously.

Even on the properly human level, it is affectivity that provides the field of force from which the initial meaning of the "lived world" (*Lebenswelt*) is progressively precipitated, drawn out. That original world is not so much a network of objects as a forge of actual goods and ideal values, and the rapport through which these values are disclosed is not so much an intellectual grasp as an affective grasp or protention. In other words, it is significant and decisive that the process through which the world is gradually invested with meaning takes its origin in valuation rather than in contemplation. Likewise, at the end of this process of meaning-production we discover love, the noblest expression of affectivity as well as a principle of knowledge *par excellence*, which alone permits us to understand others in their uniqueness, a dimension forever inaccessible to the attitude of detached spectatorship.

Therefore, the fear that granting affectivity its rightful place in human experience might somehow lead to emotionalism, irrationality or blind voluntarism is a needless fear. Affectivity does not detract from knowledge because it is the parent source of knowledge, man's dynamic attachment to being. Ideas that not only inform us but also move us derive their energy to do so from the fact that, by virtue of their affective residue, they are able to address themselves to the center of dynamic striving in our being, where goals, resolutions and actions are forged. Fact and value, knowledge and action can indeed be reconciled through the mediating role of affectivity which forms an actual bridge between the true and the good.

LIFE AND KNOWLEDGE

The altered meaning of "affectivity," its contrast to the customary psychological acceptations, necessitates a few adjustments in the understanding of the terms "knowledge" and, by extension, of "reason" as well. In order to introduce these modifications, one must first outline some salient points of the dominant view concerning knowledge in general.

By and large, most current theories recognize that knowledge is an emergent process, rooted in such precognitive and even preconscious phenomena as adaptive action, habit formation or patterned response. The recognition of this link does not mean, however, that continuity between preconscious and conscious life is admitted as a matter of course by most theories. On the contrary, conscious life is usually posited in direct opposition to mere organic reaction to stimuli. Consciousness is regarded as the sole, or at least the principal, producer and purveyor of meanings, and as such, the first of a series of qualitative breaks in the order of life forms. Similar breaks are said to exist also between the various forms of consciousness and the various degrees of knowledge. These degrees are believed to constitute a structural hierarchy of distinct forms of meaning-giving, culminating in the construction or discovery of purely abstract intelligibilities represented by conceptual symbols and expressed in assertive judgments. This is the familiar Greek ideal of speculative knowledge (*theoria*). The tendency to regard only this final degree as "real" knowledge is so addictive that even so-called genetic epistemologists, who admit a linear continuity between the various stages of knowing, end up considering this stage as normative for all the rest. In other words, all other forms and degrees of knowing are allotted intelligibility only to the extent that they approximate or somehow imitate this ideal degree.

It seldom occurs to knowledge-theorists or to genetic epistemologists to surmise that the development of consciousness ("the meaning-giver") may not be single-valued or linear at all; that, starting with some primitive datum that is both value and knowledge laden (axiological and noetic), development may fan out in several directions and tend towards not one but several ideal goals. Many theorists and philosophers simply disregard the fact that there is more than one mode of judging, more than one way of expressing and communicating the various meanings constructed or discovered by consciousness, and that there are in fact distinct forms of consciousness, many of which are not primarily cognitive. As Sartre once said, "all consciousness is not knowledge" (*toute conscience n'est pas connaissance*).[15]

What is needed, therefore, is a new theory of knowledge, one that is not boxed into a single-model explanation and can resist the pull of reductionism. *What is needed is a perspective which can reveal not only the external complementarity of life and knowledge but also their internal, genetic connection which founds that complementarity. What is needed is an explanation of the life of knowledge.* The limits of this essay, and even more the limitations of its author, make the appearance of such a theory at best a faraway possibility. The most that can be done for the time being is to propose a few theses which, when properly validated, could coalesce into a theory capable of presenting knowledge as a polyvalent and cumulative process that enables an organism to learn from its continued living, not only by storing and repeating crucial aspects of past experience, but also by inventing new and unprecedented ways of experiencing.

A. *The first thesis* about knowledge as a basic phenomenon of life in general has been suggested earlier. Here it could be recapitulated in the following manner: *Originally, knowledge is a purely symbiotic function of life's spontaneous self-differentiation and self-actualization, totally indistinguishable in scope from that spontaneous urge itself.* It is crucial that this first thesis be understood in the exact sense it was intended.

First of all, the statement refers to what knowledge is thought to be in its roots or "originally" in the double sense of the German term *urspruenglich*. In one sense, origin signifies a "primordial leap," an act of emergence and novelty, a process of departure from what was there before; in another sense, it signifies the ancestral resemblance, the permanent stamp left on the process by its parentage. Therefore, in its originality, knowledge both transcends the processes of life and is branded by them. In one sense, knowledge is an original departure from mere life, in another, it is continuous with it. This means that, no matter how far knowledge evolves "beyond" its origins, it never ceases to be recognizable as a vital function, serving some higher interest of life; inversely, no matter how primitive a life form may be, it can never lack that minimal degree of interiority (*Innesein*) through which living things are for themselves (*Fuersichsein*) and which also constitutes the embryonic meaning of consciousness.

Nevertheless, on this original level, knowledge is not yet undergirded by consciousness in the explicit sense of that word because, on that level, knowledge itself is only an operational aspect of an undifferentiated vital impulse towards self-differentation. This is the lowest form of psychic life which Max Scheler used to call a *Gefuehlsdrang*. As an original form, this "feeling-impulse" cannot be defined by reference to something more original; it can only be circumscribed:

> As the term implies, "feeling" and "impulse" are not yet separated. Impulse always has a specific direction, a goal-orientation "towards something," for example nourishment or sexual satisfaction. A bare movement "toward," as toward light, or "away from," as a state of pleasure or suffering *devoid of object*, are the only two modes of this primitive feeling. Yet this impulse is quite different from the centers and fields of energy that we associate with the images of inorganic bodies without consciousness. They do not have an inner life in *any* sense.[16]

Primitive as it may be, this impulse is not chaotic. In the first place, it already has a proto-tendency "towards" or "away from." But more importantly, as it pushes against the resistance of the environment, the vital impulse communicates to the living organism that first sense of "reality" or "objectivity" which, in the later reaches of development, becomes the guiding motivation of all search for knowledge.[17] The very same push also sets into motion the processes by means of which the primitive *Gefuehlsdrang* develops into conscious representation, knowledge, appetite, will and all the other higher functions of life. As Scheler pointed out, one of those processes is, at least in its over-all design, dissociative.[18] As we shall have occasion to show, it is through the dissociation of the representational and striving or conative elements of experience that intentional consciousness, the locus of cognition proper, begins to emerge. The other process, complementary to dissociation, is what more recently came to be called equilibration. This theoretical construct of Piaget is a sort of integrating principle, defined as "a general biological tendency to organize isolated elements into structured wholes."[19] This tendency comes into play in the interest of associative learning and practical intelligence, both of which represent further degrees of vital development through which behavior is gradually set free from the relative fixity of instinctual response and turned into a self-regulating process that is increasingly open to modification by individual invention and control.

However, the point to note in all this is that both dissociations and reintegrations are possible only because the dissociated elements are first delivered in an original unity of experience prior to knowledge proper. Cognitive development takes place as a series of polarizations in that experience. In itself, however, before the onset of polarizations, that basic experience is more of an affective adherence than a cognitive confrontation between organism and nature; it is more a matter of *eros* than of *logos*. In fact, even after the emergence of consciousness, certain initial stages of cognition derive their cognitive value from the affective side of reactive behavior to which they are linked and which they serve. To a certain extent, most animal knowledge falls into this category. Animal knowledge is economical: each animal has only as much knowledge as it needs to live by. As J.J. von Uexkull so ably pointed out, most animals are allowed to be aware only of those segments and qualities of their environment to which they can respond by adaptive behavior.[20] The rest is not merely dismissed or ignored, it simply does not exist for the animal. Only need-related qualities compose the "objects" of animal awareness; life-neutral qualities are absent. Whether the ideal of complete neutrality is ever reached at all even by man is a further question; it certainly is not an original datum of cognition.

B. *The second thesis* refers directly to knowledge as it appears on the properly human level. Without defining first what makes certain types of knowledge properly human, a summary statement could be framed in the following words: *Any effort at understanding human understanding must include a framework which is not that of a self-reflective, entirely translucent consciousness but rather that of a consciousness engaged in a multiple dialogue with the world. Such a consciousness is only partially understood as a polar relationship between a knowing subject and objects known (noesis-noema structure), and its dialogue with the world is poorly grasped as a production of speculative meanings expressible in universally valid, propositional judgments.* A great deal of explanation would be needed to elucidate adequately the precise meaning of this thesis, but the following remarks should at least help to clarify its general import.

The first remark is merely a reminder that theories about knowledge are particularly vulnerable to what Whitehead termed the "fallacy of misplaced concreteness," and that this fallacy can be committed in more ways than one. The usual way of committing it consists in first reifying the theoretical constructs of an explanatory schema and then treating them as concrete things or entities. Many of the theoretical objects of modern science, such as models of the atom and atomic particles, are accorded reality at the expense of the objects of ordinary experience on such mistaken grounds.[21] Placing concreteness where it does not belong can also be done in the paradoxical way of judging and validating the reality of existing, concrete phenomena by their approximation to an unrealizable ideal case. Here "an entity is considered merely so far as it exemplifies certain categories of thought."[22] This gives rise to the curious view that the real is really the ideal but does not exist, while concrete existence is only an imperfect illustration of reality. Finally, concreteness can be misplaced when it is sought among the constructs of explicit consciousness rather than in the operations of lived experience. Knowledge as a concrete phenomenon of human life is thus diluted every time it is measured against the imaginary standards of absolute knowledge, born of a pure and transcendental mind.

Warning against the danger of such dilution, Professor Calvin Schrag of Purdue University recently attempted to establish a sort of "archeology of knowledge" that could serve as a protophilosophical anchor point for the human sciences. In a book-length critique of traditional theories of consciousness, he is calling for a "radical reflection" that would avoid the fallacy of misplaced concreteness by refusing to identify knowledge with the work of pure consciousness.[23] Drawing on the Marxian critiques of theoretical knowledge as well as on some general lessons of phenomenology, Schrag attempted to get to the roots of knowledge by tracing it back in the direction of pre-reflective comprehension of experience, where "reflection is no longer separable from the order of things into which man is inserted and in which he moves about as perceiver, speaker, and actor."[24]

The original world of experience is not a construct of pure consciousness, but a matrix of things, facts and values offered to the use, knowledge and appreciation of people. Instead of being an object of contemplation by an all-seeing eye, the world of experience is an arena for human action of *praxis*, as Marx used to point out. Perhaps the profound philosophical meaning of the Marxian notion of *praxis* is that it "reorients the classical concept of consciousness in such a manner that it no longer simply serves the function of a theoretic-epistemological grounding of human thought."[25] The consciousness underlying human action is only secondarily a cognitive subject: in its immediacy it is an affective openness. Likewise, the world of action is only secondarily a collection of objects to be known: in its immediacy it is an object of exchange, utility and delight. Even Husserl recognized this at the beginning of his phenomenology:

> Therefore this world is not there for me as a mere *world of facts and affairs*, but, with the same immediacy, as a *world of goods*, a *practical world*. Without further effort on my part I find the things before me furnished not only with the qualities that befit their positive nature, but with value-characters such as beautiful or ugly, agreeable or disagreeable, pleasant or unpleasant, and so forth.[26]

The fact that his later philosophy, in particular, his transcendental reduction was able to recover only a diluted version of this lived world does not detract from Husserl's initial recognition of it.

The injunction against equating consciousness with the ideal of epistemic consciousness does not mean, of course, that the very idea of transcendental consciousness is without merit. As the capacity for knowledge with general, impersonal validity, the notion of transcendental consciousness correctly identifies *one* of the *ideal* goals of human knowledge. Humans and humans alone are capable of positing and approximating such an ideal. While an animal recognizes and reacts to whatever corresponds to its subjective interests, man can know *more or*

74 Affectivity and Moral Behavior

less disinterestedly. Man's advantage over the animal resides in his ability to judge and evaluate the world objectively, that is, in *relative independence* from his immediate needs. An animal does not, properly speaking, confront its environment: its organism is an integrated circuitry, where the input of environmental stimuli are immediately turned into reactive output. Here organism and environment are continuous. In man, the circuitry *can* be interrupted. What man knows and perceives need not spill over into immediate action: between external stimulation and internal leaning to action there is a *possible* break. The possibility of that interruption is what we ordinarily call thinking or reflection, and the relative distance from immediate interests we call the objectivity of human knowledge. The world for man ceases to be a mere vital correlative and becomes an object, a *Gegenstand* in German. Rather than always fading and melting into the environment, man sometimes "stands opposite" to it, and it stands opposite to him. By virtue of this confrontation, man can emerge as a "self" against the resistant "non-self" of the world. All this is quite true as long as we keep in mind that impersonal validity is only *one* possible direction in which human awareness can develop; that objectivity in the sense of complete detachment from subjective interest is more a matter of *ideal task* than actual fact;[27] and that the concrete human knower is and remains a body-consciousness and not a disembodied speculative reason.

Beside its speculative orientation, human consciousness is constantly scanning the world through a whole series of distinct intentionalities in search of a range of distinctive meanings. Not only in thought and speech, but by every act of looking, listening, molding, arranging, moving, contriving, in bustle as well as in repose man is continuously taking up positions towards the world, he is making pronouncements about himself and the environment around him. To say this is not to imply that all these ways are incipient or abortive thoughts, which, had they been given a sufficient period for gestation, would have emerged as mental propositions or would have converted into verbal assertions. Rather, the point is simply that these are nonspeculative ways of getting meaning out of our relations and exchange with the world, non-verbal appraisals and pronouncements about reality and its value, for which speculative meanings and verbal judgments are no substitutes.

> It is evident that in the experience of every individual certain actions and certain works of art are best left untranslated into statements, not because of hidden antipathy to the promotion of knowledge, but because, on the contrary, verbal translation is inadequate, irrelevant, or anticlimactic to knowledge already felt to be gained.[28]

A full-blown theory of meaning would have to inventory all the possible intentionalities by means of which meaning is generated. For our limited purposes, however, it is sufficient to refer to Buchler's theory, which distinguishes three generic classes of producing meaning out of our relations with the world: *doing, making* and *saying*. To each of these corresponds a type of judgment that is designated respectively as active judgment, exhibitive judgment and assertive judgment. The merit of Buchler's theory lies precisely in its ability to argue convincingly that active and exhibitive judgments are cognitive, but not in the sense of being inchoative assertions; they are *cognitive in different respects*, not in differing degrees.[29]

C. *A final and brief statement*, linking cognition and affectivity in the very idea of reason, could be framed in the following words: *Human consciousness is possessed of a dynamism that demands an unqualified receptivity for the presence and meaning of being, no matter how that meaning reveals itself and regardless of the road that leads to it. That passion of consciousness for openness, that global effort to confer sense on everything it encounters and to let nothing stand unrelated and meaningless, that universal appetite of the human mind is the essence of reason itself.*

This means, in the first place, that any definition of reason that does not take into account this multidimensionality and dynamic character of human consciousness is going to be defective and misleading. For example, reason defined as a timeless structure of universally valid meanings is an impoverished idea, because it limits the meaning of meaning to one of its manifestations, the one accessible to the impersonal intellect of scientific understanding. Such a constriction of reason is contrary to the most fundamental attitude of reason itself, which, as Karl Jaspers pointed out, is one of sympathy, unlimited attentiveness and accommodating receptivity.[30]

Thanks to that accommodating attitude, reason can give meaning to all human endeavors. "If it is insufficiently decisive to regard man as an animal that judges, it may be sufficient to regard him as an animal that cannot help judging in more than one mode."[31] Not only man's science, but also his industry, art, philosophy, moral life and religion are taken up in the unity and unifying recollection of reason. In other words, the unity of reason includes more than a system of ideas: it shepherds all the efforts of human life towards a harmony of meaning and action. The grotesque option that man must be engaged either in unfeeling science or drowning in the swamp of mindless feelings is unmasked as a pseudo-option (see Chapter IX on the objectivity of moral judgments) by the original living unity or symbiosis (*Mitleben*) of knowledge and affectivity in reason.

Moreover, the development of reason, the universal giver and interpreter of meaning, receives its impetus from the direction of its affective component. Degrees, stages and modes of evolving understanding result from the progressive maturation and refinement of the affective side of reason. Stimulation for the growth of knowledge comes from man's love of truth, not only because truth has "cash value" for him, but primarily because he senses that it is truth that will make him free. Knowledge for him is a means of emerging as a sovereign subject in the world, and even more as a free partner in a dialogue of love.

TOWARD A THEORY OF DYNAMIC CONSCIOUSNESS

To represent the original symbiosis of action, love and knowledge in the ancient layers of reason calls for a theory of dynamic consciousness, a theory that would enable us to understand how consciousness can be a kind of interiority as well as a project at the same time. Such a theory would avoid the twin danger of either reducing consciousness to the "nothingness" of pure intentionality (e.g., Sartre), or of inflating it into a spontaneous activity of an ideal or "transcendental ego" producing ideal or pure objects (e.g., Kant, Hegel, Husserl). Finally, as an alternative also to behaviorism, which banishes consciousness altogether by insisting that behavior is merely a set of glandular and muscular reactions to stimuli, this theory would also show that behavior as an aggregate of unit reflexes is no more intelligible than behavior as a pantomime for pure thought. Behavior is the manifestation of a *conscience engagee*, exhibiting the primarily affective character of consciousness. Presenting affectivity as the anchor point of consciousness in real life could provide the mediating link between the energetic and directional aspects of all behavior, including moral life. The building of such a theory with all the attendant laws and models belongs to psychological research.

In the meantime, however, philosophy can be of some help to psychological research by suggesting either the possible shape of such theories or the areas of research in which they are most likely to be found. The present essay wishes merely to highlight a few broad concepts from which an affectivity-based theory of consciousness in general and of moral behavior in particular could be constructed by empirical researchers.

Without prejudice to Freud and his pioneering work on the role of instinctual energy in the psychological development of the individual, the insights of three other authors Maurice Merleau-Ponty, Kurt Goldstein and Max Scheler seem particularly promising for laying the foundations of a science of affective consciousness. From different starting points and for different reasons the thoughts of all three appear to converge on the central thesis of this paper, namely, that the energetic component of any form of human behavior, including moral life, is an affective impetus which drives the mind to recognize the "worth of things" and drives the somatic and other processes to pursue that worth. A brief sketch of the relevant points of each of these thinkers is in order here.

The Pivotal Role of Body-Consciousness:
Maurice Merleau-Ponty

In the beginning of Chapter Five of his *Phenomenology of Perception*, Maurice Merleau-Ponty points out why analyzing our experience in terms of a preponderantly cognitive consciousness can never recapture the organic relationship between the living subject and its world. It cannot do so because such an analysis "is transformed by its own activity into an intercourse between the epistemological subject and the object."[33] While perfectly illuminating in other respects, this cognitive approach cannot reveal the world as value-charged, because the ideal goal of cognition is precisely value-free objectivity. If we want to see then how values are brought to birth in the exchange between subject and the world, "we must look at the area of our experience which clearly has significance and reality for us, and that is our affective life."[34]

Even more significantly, Merleau-Ponty recognized affective life not merely as "a mosaic of emotional states of pleasures and pains," but as a distinct form of consciousness through which the world is invested with values.[35] Using sexuality as a particular example, he shows that it is consciousness as affection rather than consciousness as knowledge that projects a human world around the body-subject. Although his rich analyses cannot even be outlined here, a few points must be noted in passing.

It is in the context of affectivity that Merleau-Ponty argues for the existence of an erotic mode of perception supporting objective perception but "distinct from objective perception and intellectual significance."[36] This perception is not a form of knowledge (*cogitatio*), but the protention of a body-subject towards the world. Disturbances in that affective substratum always result in disturbed behavior, even when no impairment of knowledge can be detected to accompany the affective trauma.

Certain forms of these disturbances, like the famous Schneider case,[37] are particularly instructive by their broad implications. The very structure of Schneider's mode of perceiving the world has undergone a change because that secret connivance with the world that constitutes normal affectivity is impaired: because he no longer addresses the world about certain subjective values, the objective stimuli coming from the environment no longer speak to *his* body and, consequently, confuse rather than inform him. For instance, he has difficulty pointing to his nose or the middle knuckle of his left hand on command. Similarly, he cannot carry out the movements of his trade (sewing of leather goods) in the abstract. His movements appear hesitant as though he were trying to "locate" his limbs in objective space.[38] No such hesitation occurs however, when his body is involved in a network of familiar needs, such as blowing his nose or scratching his knuckle where a mosquito is stinging him.[39] It is as if his consciousness functioned intermittently.

But how is this possible, Merleau-Ponty asks? "If I know where my nose is when it is a question of holding it, how can I not know where it is when it is a matter of pointing to it?"[40] His answer is very simple and very much to the point of this essay: for the disturbed patient the "nose-to-be-pointed-to" and the "nose-to-be-blown" are not the same value objects; they do not belong to the same phenomenal world. The former belongs to the world of knowledge as an object of abstract inquiry; the latter is not an object at all because it belongs to the integrated dynamism of a living, acting body-consciousness. As *his* nose, the latter is a functioning aspect of his subjectivity. Something can be given to this consciousness, to this subjectivity, without being given as an object of representation and *vice-versa*. Schneider's trouble consists precisely in his inability of making the transition from one to the other. Therefore his impairment could be described from either side. On the one hand, it could be said that he is "lost" and cannot "find" himself in the objective world precisely because that world is *only* objective, without subjectively meaningful qualities. "Faces for him are neither attractive nor repulsive. . . . Sun and rain are neither gay nor sad . . . and the world is emotionally neutral."[41] On the other hand, it could be said that it is his abstract attitude that is disturbed and that his "knowledge" is restricted to the comprehension of those situations which represent familiar problems to be solved by the mobilization of his body. In either case, the uncoupling of the normal link between representational and dynamic consciousness is attributed to an affective disturbance, and not the other way around. It is not the weakening of representations that causes reduction in desire or importance in action, because "absent-mindedness and inappropriate representations are not causes but effects."[42] Both action and representation are diminished in the patient because of his loss of affective attachment to the world.

That is why, according to Merleau-Ponty, the role of body is so pivotal in all this. Ideas and representations do not come first in life. They come later as "expressions" of our gathering existential momentum, as mental symbols of our concrete striving for greater life and greater values. Because ours is an incarnate existence, we do not start with "inner phenomena," which we subsequently translate into bodily pantomime, but with real *situations* or value-orientations that have to be changed into actual values. It is the "body's role to ensure this metamorphosis."[43] The body is precisely that two-way gate which can either open or bar the way of the forward project of existence. Insofar as I have a body, I have the power to withdraw from existence and "shut myself up in an anonymous life which subtends my personal one. But precisely because my body can shut itself off from the world, it is also what opens me out upon the world and places me in a situation there."[44] It is bodily existence as projective that "continually sets the prospect of living before me . . . and establishes my first consonance with the world."[45]

This consonance is the concrete "expression" of that bonding between organism and environment mentioned above as a defining element of affectivity. However, the term "expression" is not to be understood here in the ordinary sense of an arbitrary sign to which a signification is attached by conventional predication.

> Anterior to conventional means of expression, . . . we must recognize a primary process of signification in which the thing expressed does not exist apart from the expression, and

in which the signs themselves induce their significance. In this way body expresses total existence, not because it is an external accompaniment to that existence, but because existence comes into its own in the body. This incarnate significance is the central phenomenon of which body and mind, sign and significance are abstract moments.[46]

In the same way, one might say that the affective propensity which breathes life into our original world is the central phenomenon in which one can discern the germs of development both in a cognitive as well as in an axiological direction.

The Drive Toward Self-Actualization: Kurt Goldstein

An interesting side-light with regard to the nature of this development can be gained from the writings of Kurt Goldstein. In cooperation with Adhemar Gelb, a psychologist, Goldstein's initial researches were about the after-effects of brain injuries on German soldiers in the First World War. His work yielded many practical results for medicine and psychology, but it also led him to interesting theoretical concepts. Among others, Goldstein soon adopted a *holistic approach* to human nature. He believed that every human phenomenon normal as well as pathological, was the activity of the whole organism.[47] This was already evident to him from the facts gathered through studies of the nervous system. "The nervous system," he wrote, "is an apparatus which always functions as a whole. It is always in a state of excitation, never at rest."[48] All behavior is an expression of this condition of perpetual protention of the nervous system in particular and, through it, of the organism in general. Although not all points of the organism are affected the same way by this energetic state, all excitation concerns the entire system.

This is so because the organism as a whole is motivated by one drive only: *self-actualization.* Goldstein insisted that this drive was not to be confused with what is frequently regarded as "a tendency to maintain the existent state, to preserve oneself."[49] Self-preservation is characteristic of life at the stage of incipient decay: the only form of actualization that remains for a person in an impaired condition is to hang on to his existent state. "This is not the tendency of a normal person.... Under adequate conditions the tendency of normal life is toward activity and progress."[50]

The drive to actualize one's capacities as fully as possible obviously has to have a built-in cognitive component. To be successful in discovering one's possibilities one has to go beyond tried ways of reacting; one must develop what Goldstein calls an *abstract attitude.* This involves the capacity of "approaching things that are only imagined, 'possible' things, things which are not given in the concrete situation."[51] Thus abstraction is not so much an action, for all action is concrete, but an attitude and an evaluation of action before it takes place.

The ability to approach things abstractly forms an integrated part

80 *Affectivity and Moral Behavior*

of the behavioral circuitry of healthy and developed individuals. It helps them to relate to their environment creatively by leading them beyond the beckonings of the immediate situation outlined by a present perception and preparing them for new and unprecedented ways of dealing with the familiar. The break-down of this circuitry results in the most fascinating and, from certain perspectives, the most puzzling behavioral disorders. Goldstein's works[52] are replete with the study and explanation of just such disorders. The case histories of these disorders make for fascinating psychological reading. Philosophically, there are two general conclusions worth noting here.

First, Goldstein's descriptions show that abstraction is a relative late-comer on the scene of human development. Long before the appearance of this behavioral skill, and often long after its disappearance in patients suffering from amnesic aphasia, meanings are organized by the more ancient and durable scheme of affective exchange between the subject and the world. Secondly, even though Goldstein insists on the decisive advantage that comes with the ability to grasp things abstractly, he nevertheless agrees with those who claim that "the formation of abstract concepts is usually not an end deliberately sought for itself. It has always been a means to an end."[53] For Goldstein that end is self-actualization, though not in the obviously utilitarian or hedonistic sense: abstraction is an instrument of self-actualization and, as such, affectively based.

Before leaving the writings of Goldstein, there is one final point that must be made. Goldstein's persistent claim that "there is only one motive by which human activity is set going, the tendency to actualize oneself,"[54] may easily lead to the impression that his studies were merely justifications for individualism and egotism based on biology. Nothing could be further from the truth. He rarely missed an opportunity to emphasize that "*self-realization, i.e., human existence, is possible only in relation to the self-realization of the 'other'.*"[55] Moreover, the discovery of the presence of other persons takes place not in an impersonal act of object-consciousness, but in a more intimate act of bonding called "encounter." Encounter is an original mode of consciousness, signaling the affective significance of another ego. "The experience in encounter," wrote Goldstein, "brings to the fore something that is profoundly characteristic of human nature, namely, that my existence is bound to the self-realization of the 'other one'."[56]

The experience of the presence of others is in fact composed of several elements.:

1. First of all, it contains an immediate recognition that others are necessary for my self-actualization. Here others are revealed in their relative value for me: my self-actualization requires a corresponding self-restriction on their part.

2. On the other hand, the presence of others is also recognized as a limiting factor on my self-actualization. Inasmuch as their presence encroaches on my freedom, the others represent a relative disvalue for

me. Their claim to self-realization relativizes mine, and calls for self-restriction on my part.

3. This means that, while the recognition of the relative value or relative disvalue of others is an immediate datum of my experience, the reconciliation between them is not. In the words of Goldstein, "there is not a pre-established harmony between human beings . . . they must seek it in an active way."[57] Harmony can be achieved only through a deliberate adjustment of attitudes. It comes about when individuals can accept self-restriction for the sake of others without resentment, and when they can lay claim to the affection of others without self-accusation.

4. Finally, the experience of encountering the presence of others leads to the derivative awareness that self-actualization demands an active balancing of compliant and encroaching behavior.

> Only then can the individual realize himself, and assist others in their self-realization. Furthermore, the highest forms of human relationship, such as love and friendship, are dependent on the individual's ability and opportunity to realize both of these aspects of human behavior. . . . *Love* is not merely a mutual gratification and compliance; it *is a higher form of self-actualization*; a challenge to develop both oneself and another in this respect. . . . Self-restriction is experienced as inherent in human nature; it corresponds to what we call the ethical, to the norms.[58]

The Primacy of Value-Orientation: Max Scheler

An even richer source of insight into the affective substructures of consciousness can be found in the philosophy of our third author, Max Scheler. Consciousness as an axiological protention towards reality comes especially to the fore in his *Formalism in Ethics and Non-Formal Ethics of Values*,[59] which argues that value-qualities grasped by affective acts have the same objective status in nature as sensory qualities grasped by perception. *Man's Place in Nature*,[60] Scheler's last published work, goes even further to identify the deepest stratum of life with a consciousless "forward-urge" (*Drang*), which provides the "steam" (*Dampf*) for life's perpetual self-transcendence, including the ultimate sublimation of life by the "spirit."

In the introductory remarks to *Formalism*, Scheler notes that he wanted to present later on a work on philosophical ethics based on phenomenological experience, but saw as an obstacle Kant's moral philosophy, "that colossus of steel and bronze"[61] still generally accepted as valid. This meant that first he had to get around the formalism of Kant without, at the same time, lapsing into the errors of all non-formal[62] ethics of goods and purposes, the ultimate rejection of which Scheler considered "the sole merit of Kant's practical philosophy."[63] Ethics of goods and purposes (*Gueter und Zweckethik*) are all those inquiries which start with the question, What is the highest good or what is the highest purpose of all volitional conations? Scheler's acceptance of Kant's general critique of all such ethics while rejecting some presuppositions of that critique[64] resulted in a highly original value-ethics, which tries to steer a middle-course between material ethics and Kantian formalism.

From Scheler's complex theory of values, two major points are of special interest here: first, his insistence that conation plays a decisive role in the apprehension of values (Cf. Chapter VII below on the revelatory aspect of passion); and secondly, his belief that in all goal-directed action the *value-component* or affective aspect precedes and founds the *picture-component* or representational aspect. Considering these two points briefly will illustrate for us how he regarded value-feelings as "an original relation towards objects," and how he attributed categorical priority to affectivity, and ultimately to love, "as pure attraction and pure interest in the world."[65]

Scheler speaks of striving or conation (*Streben*) in the context of goals and purposes, yet his point is precisely to show that striving and purpose are not logically connected.[66] While conation "possesses its own intrinsic phenomenal differences of directedness"[67] by itself and on all levels, "it is only and exclusively at a definite level of our conation that purpose makes its appearance."[68] Conation, which begins as an impersonal and unconscious inner stirring (*Regung*), reaches the level of purposiveness when it becomes the act of a central ego. It is in purposive conation that the *value-component* and *picture-component* of striving really become distinguishable and the latter achieves prominence, because purpose, for Scheler, signifies precisely "*represented contents of goals of conation*."[69] What takes place at this level is the emergence of the consciousness of conation from conative consciousness. The confluence of the two is called the *will* in traditional terms; that is why purposes are often mentioned by Scheler as "purposes of the will."

How the value-component and picture-component of an act of will are related to each other is pivotal not only for understanding Scheler, but also for the general drift of this essay. It is a matter of quite ordinary experience that the value-control of our conations are often independent of our ability to represent those values. For instance, we may at times experience a great readiness to make sacrifices or to be kind to people without having any clear idea of the objects we are going to give up or of the benevolent deeds we are going to perform. Here, the resoluteness with regard to the value of sacrifice or kindness contrasts sharply with the irresoluteness of the *idea* or picture-content of their representation. However, the significance of such experiences for Scheler is not simply the fact that value-contents are distinct and even separable from representations, but the more radical claim that *values are in fact the foundations and first messengers of representational meaning*. To quote him: "The ontic relation between them is such that the value-component founds the picture-component; that is, the picture-component is differentiated *according* to its possible suitability to the realization of the value-component."[70]

The last part of the statement just quoted directs our attention to another work of Scheler, *Man's Place in Nature*, where he outlined the stages of differentiation, through which the picture-component or representational aspect of behavior emerges from life's basic value-orientation. From plant to person, the primary orientation of life is toward value, according to Scheler, not the same value, to be sure, but a whole hierarchy of values.[71] In fact, personhood itself is a value, in deference to which life yields up its innate direction (see Chapter XII on personhood). As a result of this yielding, personal life gains a new guiding principle: spiritual knowledge.[72]

As we shall see, this does not mean that Scheler considered the spirit an outgrowth of life's natural evolution or that he tried to reduce human knowledge to a need-related function of vital drives. Quite the contrary: if anything, he is guilty of a sort of metaphysical dualism that pitches spirit against life, presenting it as "a principle opposed to life as such, even to life in man."[73] In its origin and according to its essence, Scheler saw spirit as independent from, and even antagonistic to, life, a perpetual naysayer to life's libidinal impulses. Nevertheless, he was careful in pointing out that the autonomy of the spirit is in reality a borrowed one, for in actual operation, the spirit is completely dependent on the energies withdrawn from life, having none on its own. Scheler thought it was a "fallacy to assume that the world in which we live is so ordered that, with the superior meaning and values revealed in higher forms of being, there goes a corresponding increase in power and energy."[74] In other words, spirit is superior to life and supersedes it only as a navigational device, not as a power source: "Spirit and will never mean anything else but guidance and direction."[75]

Our point, however, is not to present Scheler's metaphysics, the acceptance or rejection of which leaves our concern relatively untouched. Our concern is to show how, through successive polarizations of its value-orientation, life can refine and redefine the goals toward which it strains, until it gives way to that non-objectifiable (but objectifying) process of self-ordered acts which we call personal life. Scheler has a great deal to teach us about the life of persons and their interpersonal exchange, independently of his ultimate metaphysical doctrines. The following outline provides a few hints about life's development towards the stage and value of emerging personhood.

1. *Vital Urge.* The first modality of life, already noted as the point of departure also for a theory of cognition, consists in a non-specific vital push (*Gefuehlsdrang*) of the organism against its environment. This primitive push is non-specific precisely because, in it, innerliness and protection are as yet undifferentiated, knowing and tending coincide. Found in all life, including plant life, this original urge lacks all means of reporting back the events that take place inside or outside the organism. Life at this level is completely consciousless, without any sensorimotor equipment and, consequently, without active purposiveness of any kind. It fulfills itself in a blind protection of nourishment, growth and

reproduction.

Vital feeling or urge is characteristic of plant life, but it is present in animal and human life also. Mixed in with more complex functions and largely subsumed by them, the vital urge nevertheless retains a certain archaic independence from them. Even when energy is withdrawn from more specific drives and functions, as in states of sleep, hibernation, fainting or coma, the vital urge burns on. On the other hand, "there is no sensation, no perception, no representation behind which is not the dark impulse burning continuously through periods of sleeping and waking. Even the simplest sensation is not merely the response to a stimulus, but always the function of a drive-motivated attention."[76]

2. *Instinct.* Life's value-orientation begins to give rise to representational content in instinctual behavior, because it is on this level that the drive-motivated attention just mentioned brings about sensation. Sensation, in turn, as a reporting back of an organ to a nerve-center, modifies the subsequent deployment of the drive. Thus begins a dialectic process within the vital urge between action and representation, leading to repeated "disintegrations" (in the non-pejorative sense) and reintegrations of the initially undifferentiated protention of life. It is in instinct that the "undifferentiated energy of growth, reaching out ecstatically into a neutral, unspecified environment, is modified by sensation and spontaneous locomotion . . . which begin to untie the living being from its vegetative level."[77]

Scheler calls behavior instinctive when it exhibits the following five characteristics: it must be meaningful for the whole of the organism or for the whole of another organism; it must have a set rhythm; it must be typical for the species; it must be innate; it must be complete rather than tentative. The first feature refers to the quasi-purposive or end-directed nature of instinct. Scheler coined the word "teleoclitic" for this kind of purposiveness which does not depend on individual representation. The second feature emphasizes the fact that instinct is not constructed by imitation or learning from others. Thirdly, instinct is typical behavior, typical of the species rather than of the individual. Fourthly, instinct is not acquired but hereditary. This does not mean, however, that "instinctive behavior must be present at the time of birth. It means only that it is coordinated with fixed stages of growth and maturation, and possibly even (in the case of polymorphism) with different developmental stages in animals."[78] Finally, instinct does not come about through the stringing together of partial movements that proved successful before. Its essential pattern is mounted ready-made, so to speak, before the processes of trial and error.

The really intriguing thing for us, however, is what Scheler has to say about the function of knowledge in relation to instinctual behavior. There is in instinct, as noted above, a beginning of the separation between sensation and drive, but there is also a very close functional connection. In a biologically shaped behavior, such as instinct, knowledge can serve only an instrumental function to action: "*What* an animal can imagine or perceive is controlled by the a priori relation of its instincts to the structure of the environment. . . . An animal sees and hears what is significant for its instinctive behavior."[79]

Moreover, the knowledge operative in instinct is not the property of individuals; it is the atavistic wit of the whole species, so to speak. That is why instinctual knowledge is as much a filter as it is a mirror with regard to the environment. It admits only as much of it as the wisdom of the species allows the individual to perceive.

Finally, Scheler indicates that instinctual knowledge is predominantly and by nature affective. "Knowledge inherent in the instinct is not a knowledge by means of representations, images or even ideas. It is rather a feeling of value-charged resistances which are differentiated as attractive or repulsive according to these value-impressions."[80]

3. *Associative Memory.* The next stage in the "disintegration" of the vital urge is the vast domain of learning, that is, the domain of behavior modification on the basis of previous experience. The possibility of learning from previous experience implies that the past has not entirely passed, but left some traces of itself behind which can be recalled and combined with a new experience. The ability of retaining the past and linking parts of it with the present is called associative memory.

The appearance of the associative principle is significant for our essay from two points of view. First, the affectivity underlying associative learning is quite manifest here. Progress in learning, fixation of habit, strength of conditionment are directly proportionate to the number of trial movements on the one hand, and to the affective meaning ("satisfying," "frustrating") or value-quality of those trials, on the other. In other words, the twin engines of behavior modification, i.e., *reinforcement* and *inhibition*, are obviously value-driven. Associative learning is significant, secondly, because it initiates the emergence of the individual *qua* individual. Insofar as an animal begins to manifest behavior learned through association, it also begins a process of emancipation from its bondage to the species. It begins to be more and more a *center* of its own behavior rather than a mere arena for it. "For only with the operation of this principle can the individual adapt himself to new situations, to situations not typical of the species. Thus the individual ceases to be no more than a point of transition in the reproductive process of the species."[81]

4. *Practical Intelligence or Cunning.* The liberation and centralization of individual behavior resulting from associative learning is counterbalanced by the attendant perils of mechanization of learned behavior. No sooner freed from the rigidity of species-bound instinct, behavior is in danger of lapsing into routine and stereotypy. As a corrective for such dangers, further differentiation brings forth cleverness or practical intelligence.

This type of intelligence is called "practical" because it deals with action and the choice of action by means of which the animal seeks to attain some goal set by its drives. This does not mean, however, that animal intelligence is a mere motor skill, for in fact it contains a great deal of independent imagination and even some hints of protoabstraction. Indeed, intelligence is the faculty of "a sudden *insight* into a connected context of facts and values within the environment that is not perceived now nor was ever perceived previously."[82]

The newness of the situation acts as an *obstacle* to the attainment of the need-determined goal. To overcome this obstacle, to master the unprecedented situation, the experiential field of the animal has to be actively restructured for possible clues. Hitherto neutral elements or elements corresponding to other needs must assume an instrumental relationship to the goal in question. This means, however, that those elements must be drawn into a relatively "abstract" and "objective" perspective by the animal. Commenting on Kohler's experiments with chimpanzees, Scheler called special attention to the degree of abstraction involved here. To reach the fruit lying outside the cage, these clever beasts used not only sticks which, after all, resemble branches on which the fruit normally hangs, but also pieces of wire, the brim of a straw hat, a blanket, anything that satisfied the abstract representation of "movable and elongated."

Nevertheless, Scheler also noted that this kind of *ad hoc* abstraction is not yet the reflective and universal abstraction usually associated with human inventiveness. Rather, "it is the dynamic energy of the drive itself that is here objectified and projected into constituents of the environment."[83] The objectivity discovered here is still only the instrumental aptness of some environmental feature to satisfy a particular end.

5. *Spirit*. Fully abstract knowledge, which can represent the qualities and values of things objectively, i.e., not just in particular circumstances but universally and independently of subjective need, is reached only by the properly human capacity called spirit. While the concept of spirit for Scheler includes the capacity for such acts as volition, love, remorse, reverence, despair and so on,[84] we shall concentrate on it exclusively as a special function of knowledge.

Whatever the ontological status of the spirit may be, the importance of its cognitive function is fairly clear. It is in spiritual knowledge that the drive toward *objectification*, which was merely begun and foreshadowed by instinct, memory and intelligence, finally succeeds. The consequences of this breakthrough are far-reaching and decisive for the understanding of the proper relationship between the cognitive and affective components of moral behavior.

Scheler correctly presents objectification as an act of emancipation of spiritual knowledge from narrow environmental pressures and interests, but he is mistaken when he perceives this emancipation as a form of detachment pure and simple. He is more correct when he emphasizes that detachment from the environment in human knowledge actually means the unlimited *expansion of man's interests* to the point of his being open to the world (*weltoffen*). "To become human is to acquire this openness to the world by virtue of the spirit."[85] Instead of being tied to a limited field of interaction, as is animal life, human interest extends to the most remote aspects of the world at large. Spirit is the ability of placing one's living space with its select centers of attraction and resistance into an extended context that objectifies that space and transforms one's "environment" into a "world."

This transformation is in reality a *transvaluation*. Objectification and objectivity is sought, first and foremost, as a value for man. It is sought as a condition for inventiveness, as a means of creative diversification of behavior. Instead of seeing things and relating to them only in the light of determined needs, man can see them and interact with them multifacetedly. Objective knowledge is so far from being a form of detachment from reality that it could be properly described as a *universalization of attachment*, for it expresses man's unbounded appetite for being that reaches beyond the points of interest given in animal knowledge.

But above all, objectification is sought as an access to *self-consciousness*, that is, "consciousness that the spiritual center of action has of itself."[86] Simultaneously with the objectification of the world, but logically consequent upon it, man's consciousness can objectify even his own inner states and vital drives and thus emerge as a substantial "self" against the "non-self" of the world.

All this is in marked contrast to animal knowledge which has no object, has no center, has no world. The animal inhabits a limited environment, "which it carries along as a snail carries its shell."[87] Its knowledge is a more or less dependent function of that environment in which things are given only as centers of resistance to attraction or repulsion. Anything that falls outside those centers is not given at all. "Animals only notice and grasp those things which fall into the secure borders of their environmental structure."[88] This environmental structure itself, forming a functional circle with the animal organism that is fitted into it,[89] guides both animal knowledge and animal behavior.

Man, on the other hand, has a new and largely independent method for guiding his behavior. *Inasmuch as he is able to objectify even his vital impulses, he can evaluate them, coordinate their several goals under an overarching representation, and rechannel their energies toward a freely chosen project.* In psychological terminology, the ability to call upon natural energy complexes to accomplish goals not necessarily native to those complexes is usually referred to as sublimation, and the agent behind sublimation as the will. Both of these terms are useful, but both are liable to be misinterpreted.

Sublimation is a useful concept if it throws light on the change that takes place in the transition from sensory striving or drive-directed behavior to voluntary striving or mind-directed behavior. The essential difference is usually and mistakenly seen by philosophers as a difference in the kind of goal or object pursued by each: the object of sensory striving is said to be some "particular" good, while the object of the will is supposed to be the "universal" good. The same difference is sometimes

88 Affectivity and Moral Behavior

expressed in terms of the contrast between the "concrete" and the "abstract." However, these distinctions confuse the *object* of striving with the *manner* of representing that object. While it is true that the object of a voluntary act is represented generally and abstractly, that does not mean that its object is a "good in general," and much less that it is an "abstract good." There might be abstract intelligibilities and general meanings, objects for pure thought, but as the object of appetition, the good can only be concrete and particular. All affective propensities love, volition, desire, even instinctual drive seek the concrete reality rather than the abstract representation of their object. To be sure, some of them, like love and volition, seek their goal *by the light of abstract representation*, but what they seek is not abstract. The theory of sublimation is a refined way of saying all this. It is a way of suggesting that some of man's goal-directed actions are indeed objective and spiritual in the sense that, in them, the basic value-orientation of life finally gives rise to a separate picture-component that can function as an independent guidance system for those actions. By virtue of this guidance, the initially stereotyped operations of libidinal energies are freed and redirected towards the accomplishment of cultural projects. Needless to say, the production of culture itself is only a means for producing the very maker of culture: man himself.

EPILOGUE: THE FORMATION OF TRENDS AND ATTITUDES

This essay began by hinting at the inadequacy of studying morality and moral education under the heading of cognition. Treating morality as one more instance of applied knowledge, it was noted, tends to overlook the problems connected precisely with the application of such knowledge in action. The tendency is to assume that the very cogency of the reasons offered by the various moral theories for acting in a certain way is sufficient to trigger the process of appropriate application. At the very least, all cognitive moral theories are haunted by the ghosts of ideomotorism, that is, the belief that the picturing of appropriate ends and means can somehow overflow into purposive action all by itself.

The thrust of this essay has been to exorcise that ghost once and for all and to argue that ideation cannot be both the informing and the enabling factor of moral action, that knowledge, while indispensable to morality as a directional device, cannot at the same time be its energetic component. That component, it was argued, derives from life's fundamental value-orientation, called affectivity. This power to act morally is furnished by a goal-directed disposition which all living beings possess, but which in man is elevated to the rank of a conscious striving toward self-realization.

But introducing affectivity as a second major component of moral behavior is liable to give rise to some unintended and potentially misleading implications. For instance, to the extent that philosophers and psychologists make use of the concept of affectivity at all, they usually take it to mean the same thing as emotion, some kind of strong visceral agitation which signals the upset of the normal balance between organism and environment, but which also initiates the process of return to that normal state. Other, more untoward acceptations equate affectivity with unruly passions and chaotic arousals, with the moods and urges of a turbulent id. In either case, affectivity is usually seen as an interloper in human affairs. Under the first perspective, it appears as a momentary departure from a preset norm which, however, soon rights itself; under the second, it is seen as a violent counterforce to reason that has to be kept in constant check by commensurate rational resistance. But even without such sinister connotations, to say that moral behavior has an affective as well as a cognitive component is liable to make morality appear a dual phenomenon, the work of two separate faculties existing side by side and working either in tandem or against one another. It could be interpreted to mean that in moral questions the "heart" too has its say, after reason has spoken. In order to preclude such a dualistic interpretation, on one hand, and to make sure that it is not taken for a cybernetic theory of behavior, on the other, this essay tried to describe affectivity as life's fundamental value-orientation from which both knowledge and the particular acts of emotion, desire, will and striving take their origin. In other words, the essay does not merely complement other, cognitive considerations, it ascribes primacy to the affective processes, because it considers these to be the actual movers of moral life.

This last point may strike one either as momentous or as trifling, depending on what one considers the goal of moral education to be. If the goal is simply to teach students how to discover higher and broader moral purposes, their affectivity need not be stimulated beyond the point of awakening in them a curiosity to learn about such topics. But if the task is to form in them a steady skill and disposition to strive toward these purposes, then something more primordial than their intellectual curiosity must be touched (see Chapter V below on character formation). Their dynamic value-orientation must be stirred up, their love of probity must be set in motion, for that alone transforms them into moral agents.

In order to intimate that purposiveness and value-orientation are indeed non-derivative dimensions of human consciousness, the essay next presented a sampling of the pertinent ideas of three authors, two philosophers and one psychologist, which point to the possibility of reconstructing the theory of consciousness on an affective basis. The actual reconstruction, should it ever be attempted, will require a great deal of programmatic research and model building on the part of educational psychologists. That is obviously no longer a philosophic task.

Before leaving the scene, however, philosophy can perform one last service for the researcher by warning him about one more fruitless attempt of representing affectivity through concepts which are unsuitable to the task. The recurrent emphasis of these pages on the importance of affectivity in moral behavior might have led to the idea that the matter must, therefore, be restated in terms of "motivation;" that the dynamic component so often mentioned is to be read as the "motivational" component of behavior; especially, that the question of moral education may now appear as a question of how to "motivate" people to act righteously. But the point of the warning is that theories of motivation, while enormously relevant in explaining other things, tell us very little about how to think and what to do about the properly affective structure of purposive behavior.

A relative late-comer on the intellectual scene, the concept of "motive" or "motivation" betrays its philosophical ancestry by the manner in which it was made to function in the behavioral sciences. The psychological and sociological usage of "motive" designates what in the older context used to be called either the "final cause" or the "efficient cause" of conduct. One set of theories identifies motives with the "reasons" for which an action is performed.[90] By "reasons" here is meant the anticipatory representation of an end-state to be brought about by means of a certain course of action. In ordinary language usage, we call that the "purpose" or "point" of an action. The representation of the end itself is thought to be the full explanation of why the action was undertaken. Here motive functions as a final cause.

However, since it is at least arguable that the "real" reason for an action was not what the agent himself "thought" it was, another set of theories dispenses with the representation of purposes altogether, and rebuts the belief that reasons are necessary at all for the understanding of regulated acts. A motive, according to this view, is not the intent for the sake of which or in view of which something is done, but a certain tropism, an unconscious drive or a tissue condition, which is already programmed to bring on self-regulatory behavior.[91] Theories which regard the underlying mechanism of motivation to reside in brain stimulation or endocrine processes, theories of drive reduction, libidinal theories, social learning theories, all belong to this second group. Their explanations are modelled on efficient causality.

Thus alternating between ideas and drives, between final and efficient causality, motivational theories lack the integrated view necessary to understand the value-orientation of moral behavior. On one hand, they can give no adequate description of the dynamics of moral pursuit, on the other, they can explain what *happens* to man, but not what he *does* (see the concept of agent causality in Chapter IV). While each of them can bring to light some valid aspect of purposive behavior, theories of motivation fall short of providing a theory of affectivity or a conceptual model for moral education. That theory and that model must be looked for along different lines of approach.

To find them, empirical research must turn from focusing on the reasons or compulsions of human behavior to exploring the deep-dynamic structures of consciousness. For it is the activation of these structures, rather than thought or duress, that underline the formation of such positive trends of character disposition as courage, persistence, trust, confidence, interest, respect, rectitude, kindness and love. It should be fairly clear that these dispositions are not motives either in the sense of reasons for which one acts or as causes that make one act. Nor are they agitations and emotions in any meaningful sense of the word. They are, instead, relatively stable modifications in the general value-orientation of affectivity. As such, their influence on action and the quality of action is undeniable. Even though their influence is not causal, their presence imparts a particular cast to the acts whereby values are actualized.

One might say that the remaining task consists essentially in answering two fundamental questions: "How is human affectivity organized"? and "What pedagogic measures are likely to promote the positive development of affectivity"? Accent here is on the word "positive," for it seems that there can also be a negative development of value-orientation. This happens whenever the natural impulse of affectivity towards self-actualization is either arrested, repressed or misdirected. It is then that the foundations of immoral or criminal behavior are laid in such negative character dispositions as fear, mistrust, isolation, diffidence, apathy, cynicism, deviousness, meanness and hatred. In other words, the goodness or badness of affectivity appears to depend on the direction of its development. Four of Scheler's value-axioms are quite pertinent here:

1. Good is the value that is attached to the realization of a positive value in the sphere of willing.
2. Evil is the value that is attached to the realization of a negative value in the sphere of willing.
3. Good is the value that is attached to the realization of a higher (or the highest) value in the sphere of willing.
4. Evil is the value that is attached to the realization of a lower (or the lowest) value in the sphere of willing.[92]

Thus, education in goodness must mean education in value-realization and not merely value-recognition. At the very least, moral education must involve the removal of all inertial obstacles which tend to block or deflect the positive direction of the affective impulse. But more than that, it also requires the strengthening of the will and the imparting of such positive attitudes to affectivity as were mentioned above. Only a person with positive moral inclinations is really a mature moral subject. How can such positive attitudes be imparted? Must they be "caught" from the teacher by way of role-modelling or merely elicited from the native powers of the student himself? What are the concrete lines of communication between the directional and energetic components of behavior? How is a commitment to recognized values made and maintained? All these problems are so many aspects of one and the same essential problem, "What is moral education"? This is the issue! *Hic labor, hic opus est!*

St. Vincent College,
  Latrobe, Penna.

NOTES

1. For the various meanings and implications of intellectualism see Andre Lalande's *Vocabulaire technique et critique de la philosophie* (Paris: Presses Universitaires de France, 1960), pp. 522-25. See also the introduction of Pierre Rousselot's book, *The Intellectualism of Saint Thomas* (London: Sheed & Ward, 1935), an apology for intellectualism.

2. Note that it is only by virtue of that involvement, and not apart from it, that a person is constituted an agent.

3. Norman Gulley, *The Philosophy of Socrates* (New York: St. Martin's Press, 1968), p. 83.

4. Even though some careless expressions of his could be so interpreted. For instance: "quia enim intellectus movet voluntatem, *velle est effectus eius*" (italics mine). In *Rom.*, 7,3.

5. Si ergo intellectus et voluntas considerentur secundum se, sic intellectus eminentior invenitur. Et hoc apparet ex comparatione obiectorum ad invicem. . . . Nam obiectum intellectus est ipsa ratio boni appetibilis; bonum autem ipsum appetibile, cuius ratio est in intellectu, est obiectum voluntatis. *Quanto autem aliquid est simplicius et abstractius, tanto secundum se est nobilius et altius* (italics mine). S.T. I, q. 82, a. 3.

6. Rousselot, *The Intellectualism of Saint Thomas*, p. 199.

7. In the classic words of M. Blondel, "au fond de mon etre, il y a un vouloir et un amour de l'etre, ou il n'y a rien." *L'Action* (Paris: Presses Universitaires de France, 1950), p. xxiii.

8. "Wirksamkeit des Verstandes," see *Grundlegung zur Metaphysik der Sitten* in *Kant's Werke*, herausgegeben von der Koeniglich Preussischen Akademie der Wissenschaften, Band IV (Berlin: Georg Reimer Verlag, 1911), p. 412.

9. *Ibid.*, p. 446. It must be noted, however, that Kant is not always consistent in fusing will with practical reason: there are times when he talks of practical reason only as a representational faculty and the will as the real source of motive force.

10. Cf. Benjamin Wolman (ed.), *Dictionary of Behavioral Sciences* (New York: Van Nostrand Reinhold, 1973), p. 118; also William P. Alston, "Emotion and Feeling" in *The Encyclopedia of Philosophy* (New York: Macmillan, 1967), vol. 2, pp. 479-486.

11. Stanley Schachter and Jerome E. Singer, "Cognitive, Social, and Physiological Determinants of Emotional State," *Psychological Review*, 69, (1962), pp. 381-82.

12. Philip L. Harriman in the *Handbook of Psychological Terms* (Totawa: Littlefields, Adams & Co., 1975), p. 57, defines "emotional" as "prone to strong reactions rather than cognitive responses." The same is repeated by the *Dictionary of Behavioral Sciences*, p. 118. In an essay "In Praise of Cognitive Emotions," *Teachers College Record*, 79, (1977), pp. 171-186, Israel Scheffler of Harvard finds it necessary to apologize for coupling these two terms, "for cognition and emotion, as everyone knows, are hostile worlds apart. Cognition is sober inspection; it is the

scientist's calm apprehension of fact after fact in his relentless pursuit of truth. Emotion, on the other hand, is commotion an unruly inner turbulence fatal to such pursuit but finding its own constructive outlets in aesthetic experience and moral or religious commitment." The rest of the essay, however, challenges this entrenched opinion by arguing that there are some emotions "in service of cognition" and some that are positively "cognitive emotions."

13. That is why the term "will" was not chosen. Will is regarded by most traditions as a separate faculty of rational appetite. It is called rational not because it is considered as a form of discernment in itself, but because--lacking any discernment--it must follow the judgments of the intellect. Whenever the will is not considered this kind of dependent function of intellectual representation, it is usually inflated into an altogether blind force of cosmic dimensions. Schopenhauer's "will-to-live" is a case in point (cf. *The World as Will and Representation*, transl. by E. F. J. Payne [Indian Hills: The Falcon's Wing Press, 1958], pp. 275ff). Neither will as an appendage of the intellect, nor will as an irrational thing-in-itself can do justice to the concept of affectivity as a cumulative directedness or protention of life.

14. John Dewey, *The Quest for Certainty: A Study of the Relation of Knowledge and Action* (New York: Minton, Black & Company, 1929), p. 21.

15. Jean-Paul Sartre, *L'Etre et le Neant* (Paris: Gallimard, 1943), p. 18.

16. Max Scheler, *Man's Place in Nature* (New York: Noonday Press, 1962), p. 9; italics added.

17. ". . . this vital feeling is also the subject of that primary experience of *resistance* which is the root of experiencing what is called 'reality,' especially the unity and the impression of 'reality' which precedes any specific representation." *Ibid.*, p. 14.

18. "This creative dissociation, not association or the synthesis of single pieces, is the basic process of psychic evolution. The same is true in physiological terms." *Ibid.*, p. 20. This may give the impression that Scheler considered the nature of intelligence purely analytical. His treatment of instinctual behavior, the second stage of psychic life, may indeed reinforce this impression. According to him, instinct can operate without previous learning because instinctual behavior does not have to construct a meaningful whole out of disjointed bits of experience (the *blosse Mannigfaltigkeit* of Kant); instinct and environment form a single organic configuration, a value-laden whole or *Gestalt* to start with. Intelligence is needed only for the "dis-integration" of such wholes into their component parts. Nevertheless, even Scheler admits that every disjunction of experience is done in order to permit new associations and creative recombinations of the dissociated elements. The twin ability to do both is at the basis of further evolution that results in associative memory (= learning), imagination, problem solving (= practical intelligence) and abstract thought.

94 *Affectivity and Moral Behavior*

19. Peter H. Wolff, "The Biology of Morals from a Psychological Perspective," in *Morality as a Biological Phenomenon*, ed. G. S. Stent (Berlin: Dahlem Konferenzen, 1978), p. 96.

20. Baron Jacob J. von Uexkull, *Streifzuege durch die Umwelten der Tieren und Menschen* (Berlin: Springer Verlag, 1934), p. 6ff. See also p. 61: "Wir werden sagen duerfen, soviel Leistungen ein Tier ausfuhren kann, soviel Gegenstaende vermag es in seiner Umwelt zu unterscheiden. Besitzt es bei wenigen Leistungen wenig Wirkbilder, so besteht auch seine Umwelt aus wenigen Gegenstaenden."

21. See Alfred North Whitehead, *Science and the Modern World* (New York: The Macmillan Company, 2954), p. 82.

22. See Alfred North Whitehead, *Process and Reality* (New York: The Free Press, 1978), pp. 7-8.

23. *Radical Reflection and the Origin of the Human Sciences* (West Lafayette: Purdue University Press, 1980), p. 35.

24. *Ibid.*, p. 72.

25. *Ibid.*, p. 36.

26. *Ideas: General Introduction to Pure Phenomenology* (London: George Allen & Unwin, 1931), p. 103.

27. That "the distinction between subjective and objective is relative" has been brilliantly argued by Thomas Nagel of Princeton in one of the essays of his recent book *Mortal Questions* (New York: Cambridge University Press, 1979). In the same essay, he has the following to say: "We flee the subjective under the pressure of an assumption that everything must be something not to any point of view, but in itself. To grasp this by detaching more and more from our own point of view is the *unreachable ideal* at which the pursuit of objectivity aims" (p. 208, italics added). The reason objectivity is said to be unattainable is that the very attainment of it requires a subjective acceptance and incorporation of it into one's personal world-view: ". . . since an agent lives his life from where he is, even if he manages to achieve an impersonal view of his situation, whatever insights result from this detachment need not be made part of a personal view before they can influence decision and action. The pursuit of what seems impersonally best may be an important aspect of individual life, but its place in that life must be determined from a personal standpoint, because life is always the life of a particular person, and cannot be lived *sub specie aeternitatis*. . . . The impersonal standpoint takes in a world that includes the individual and his personal views. The personal standpoint, on the other hand, regards the deliverance of impersonal reflection as only a part of any individual's total view of the world" (pp. 205-206).

28. Justus Buchler, *Nature and Judgment* (New York: Columbia University Press, 1955), p. 35.

29. ". . . the fact that history is more particularistic than physics does not make it less truly knowledge. And if poetry is, as Aristotle says, more universal than history, . . . that does not make it more truly knowledge. Physics, history, and poetry are cognitive in different respects, not

in different degrees. The cognitive values of the three modes of judgment are not easily comparable, and perhaps not comparable at all; and this may be a part of what has to be meant by the view that there are three modes of judgment." Ibid., p. 39.

30. There is an absolutely resonant passage in Jaspers' *Von der Wahrheit* (Muenchen: Piper Verlag, 1947), p. 115, which is here quoted in the original to show the compenetration of active and passive aspects of sympathy and assistance:"Grundhaltung der Vernunft ist universelles Mitleben. Vernunft als das staendige Vordringen zum Anderen ist die Moeglichkeit des universellen Mitlebens, Dabeiseins, des allgegenwaertigen Hoerens dessen, was spricht, und dessen, was sie selbst erst sprechen macht. Vernunft ist Vernehmen, aber das uneingeschraenkte von allem, was ist und sein kann."

31. Buchler, *Nature and Judgment*, p. 194.

32. London: Routledge & Kegan Paul, 1962; hereafter cited as *Phenomenology*.

33. *Ibid.*, p. 154. Proving the inadequacy of analyzing experience and behavior either in causal or in cognitive terms was the burden of Merleau-Ponty's earlier work, *The Structure of Behavior* (Boston: Beacon Press, 1962), cf. "Behavior is not a thing, but neither is it an idea" (p. 127).

34. *Phenomenology*, p. 154.

35. *Ibid.*

36. *Ibid.*, p. 156.

37. First analyzed in the works of Adhemar Gelb and Kurt Goldstein.

38. J. Steinfeld, "Ein Beitrag zur Analyse der Sexualfunktion" in *Zeitschrift fuer die ges. Neurologie und Psychiatrie*, 1927, p. 174: "Da er [= Schneider] keine Vorstellungen von der raumlichen Lage seiner Glieder hat, muss er . . . zunaechst das betreffende Glied 'finden'."

39. *Phenomenology*, p. 103.

40. *Ibid.*, p. 104.

41. *Ibid.*, p. 157.

42. *Ibid.*, p. 156.

43. *Ibid.*, p. 164.

44. *Ibid.*, p. 165.

45. *Ibid.*

46. *Ibid.*, p. 166.

47. Kurt Goldstein, *The Organism; A Holistic Approach Derived from Pathological Data in Man* (New York: American Book Co., 1939).

48. Kurt Goldstein, *Human Nature in the Light of Psychopathology* (Cambridge, Mass.: Harvard University Press, 1951), p. 11.

49. *Ibid.*, p. 141.

50. *Ibid.*, pp. 141-42.

51. *Ibid.*, p. 54. The same ability is sometimes referred to as "categorical attitude."

52. A complete bibliography of Goldstein's works was put together

by Joseph Meiers in *The Reach of Mind; Essays in Memory of Kurt Goldstein* (New York: Springer Publishing Co., 1968), pp. 271-295.

53. Kurt Goldstein, "Abstract and Concrete Behavior," in *Selected Papers/Ausgewaehlte Schriften* (The Hague: Martinus Nijhoff, 1971), p. 391.

54. *Human Nature*, p. 201.

55. "The Smiling of the Infant," *Selected Papers*, p. 481. (Italics are in the original).

56. *Ibid.*, p. 483.

57. *Human Nature*, pp. 203-4.

58. *Ibid.*, pp. 207-8. Italics added.

59. Evanston: Northwestern University Press, 1973, hereafter cited as *Formalism*.

60. See note 16, hereafter cited as *Man's Place*.

61. *Formalism*, p. 6.

62. This term is used here as an equivalent of "contentual" or "material."

63. *Formalism*, p. 5.

64. For a pertinent reference, consult Farrelly's distinction between teleological and deontological ethics in this volume.

65. Manfred Frings, *Max Scheler* (Pittsburgh: Duquesne University Press, 1965), p. 111.

66. E.g., the color and fragrance of flowers serve the "purpose" of attracting pollinating insects, but this does not mean that flowers are "striving" to achieve pollination by these means.

67. *Formalism*, p. 33.

68. *Ibid.*, p. 32.

69. *Ibid.*, p. 39.

70. *Ibid.*, p. 34.

71. Scheler noted four distinct ranks in that hierarchy: 1. sensible values; 2. vital values; 3. spiritual values; 4. values of holiness. Cf. *Formalism*, pp. 104-110.

72. Scheler understands by *spirit* "a term which includes the intuition of essences and a class of voluntary and emotional acts such as kindness, love, remorse, reverence, wonder, bliss, despair and free decision." *Man's Place*, p. 36.

73. *Ibid.*

74. *Ibid.*, p. 64.

75. *Ibid.*, p. 68.

76. *Man's Place*, p. 13. Italics added.

77. Frings, *Max Scheler*, p. 34.

78. *Man's Place*, p. 17.

79. *Ibid.*, p. 18. The last sentence suggests that even developmentally the receptor system, what the Germans call *Merknetz*, is tailored to the capacities of the effector system, the *Wirknetz*.

80. *Ibid.*, p. 21.

81. *Ibid.*, p. 27.

82. *Ibid.*, p. 30.
83. *Ibid.*, p. 32.
84. See note 72.
85. *Man's Place*, p. 39.
86. *Ibid.*, p. 40.
87. *Ibid.*, p. 39.
88. *Ibid.*, p. 38.
89. Cf. Ernst Cassirer, *An Essay on Man* (New Haven: Yale University Press, 1962), p. 24.
90. Cf. William McDougall, *The Energies of Men* (New York: Charles Scribner's Sons, 1933); Richard S. Peters, *The Concept of Motivation* (London: Routledge & Kegan Paul, 1958).
91. Cf. John Atkinson, *An Introduction to Motivation* (Princeton: Van Nostrand, 1964); Leonard Berkowitz, *Aggression* (New York: McGraw-Hill, 1962); Sigmund Freud, *The Psychopathology of Everyday Life* (London: Ernest Benn, 1914); Gilbert Ryle, *The Concept of Mind* (London: Hutchinson, 1969).
92. *Formalism*, p. 26.

CHAPTER IV

TRADITIONS, CULTURES AND VALUES

GEORGE F. McLEAN

This chapter concerns the appropriation and realization of values by persons living with others and in time. Optimistically, time might be seen as the opportunity to become aware of the good one has received in creation, to be attracted in turn to creative action, and therein to exercise one's freedom. More pessimistically, the history of human freedom has never been a tale simply of the good, for the human potentiality to do good is correlatively the ability to fail and do evil. Consequently, the task here is not simply to draw from history a vision of the good and of values, but to determine how to decipher these from a history of human ambiguities and to work with persons of other outlooks in applying these in new and creative ways. In a word, the task is one of interpretation, that is to say, of hermeneutics.

DIMENSIONS OF THE PROBLEM

The term 'hermeneutics' is derived from the son of Zeus, Hermes, the messenger of the Olympian gods. This etymological root with its three elements--(1) a messenger, (2) from the gods and (3) to mankind--suggests three corresponding dimensions of our problem, namely, hermeneutics, values and historicity.

Hermeneutics. The circumstances of the Greek messenger make manifest the basic dilemma of hermeneutics and interpretation, which has come to be called the hermeneutic circle. This consists in the fact that any understanding of the parts requires an understanding of the whole, while the grasp of the whole depends upon some awareness of its parts. This appears in four ways. First, the herald had not merely to pass on a written text, but to speak or proclaim it. This could be done only by reading through all the parts of the message in sequence. But grasping these as parts requires some understanding of the whole message from* the very beginning. How can a whole of meaning depend upon parts, which for their very meaning depend upon the whole? Secondly, the message had to be conveyed in a particular historical time and place, and with specific intonation and inflection. But this would convey only one particular sense from the many potentialities of the words. Thirdly, the messenger had not only to express, but also to explain the message and its ramifications or meaning. This required a certain awareness of the broader context of the issue and of the language as the repository of the culture within which the message was composed. In sum, in order to interpret, convey, or receive a message, some sense of the whole is required for assembling and interpreting its parts; but how can one know the whole before knowing its parts?

This appears also from the task of the messenger in translating or bearing the meaning of the text from the source, in its own context, to others in their distinctive set of circumstances and with their projects and preoccupations. The etymology of the term underlines this task. 'Interpret' combines *praesto*: to show, manifest or exhibit, with the prefix *inter* to indicate the distinction of the one from whom and the one to whom the message is passed.[1] This difference could be between past and present, as when an ancient text is being reread today; between one culture and another, as when a text in another language than one's own is being interpreted; or indeed, between persons, even in the same culture and time, provided full attention be paid to the uniqueness of each person. But given this difference, how is communication and its implied 'community' between the two contexts possible? And were it not to be possible we would be left with never-ending violent clashes between persons, classes and values.

Values. The term 'value' was derived from the economic sphere where it meant the amount of a commodity required in order to bring a certain price. This is reflected also in the term 'axiology,' the root of which means "weighing as much" or "worth as much." This has objective content, for the good must really "weigh in"--it must make a real difference.[2]

The term 'value' expresses this good especially as related to persons who actually acknowledge it as a good and respond to it as desirable. Thus, different individuals or groups, or possibly the same but at different periods, may have distinct sets of values as they become sensitive to, and prize, distinct sets of goods. More generally, over time a subtle shift takes place in the distinctive ranking of the degree to which they prize various goods. By so doing they delineate among objective moral goods a certain pattern of values which in a more stable fashion mirrors their corporate free choices. This constitutes the basic topology of a culture; as repeatedly reaffirmed through time, it builds a tradition or heritage.

By giving shape to the culture, values constitute the prime pattern and gradation of goods experienced from their earliest years by persons born into that heritage. In these terms they interpret and shape the development of their relations with other persons and groups. Young persons, as it were, peer out at the world through cultural lenses which were formed by their family and ancestors and which reflect the pattern of choices made by their community through its long history--often in its most trying circumstances. Like a pair of glasses, values do not create the object, but reveal and focus attention upon certain goods and patterns of goods rather than upon others.

Thus values become the basic orienting factor for one's affective and emotional life. Over time, they encourage certain patterns of action--and even of physical growth--which, in turn, reinforce the pattern of values. Through this process we constitute our universe of moral concern in terms of which we struggle to achieve, mourn our failures, and celebrate our successes.[3] This is our world of hopes and fears, in

George F. McLean 101

terms of which, as Plato wrote in the *Laches*, our lives have moral meaning and we can properly begin to speak of virtues.

The reference to the god, Hermes, in the term 'hermeneutics' suggests something of the depth of the meaning which is sought and the implication of this for the world of values. For the message borne by Hermes is not merely an abstract mathematical formula or a methodological prescription devoid of human meaning and value. Rather, it is the limitless wisdom regarding the source and hence the reality, the priorities and hence the value of all. Hesiod had appealed for this in the introduction to his *Theogony*: "Hail, children of Zeus! Grant lovely song and celebrate the holy race of the deathless gods who are forever. . . . Tell how at the first gods and earth came to be."[4]

Aristotle indicated this concern for values in describing his science of wisdom as "knowing to what end each thing must be done . . . ; and this end is the good of that thing, and in general the supreme good in the whole of nature." Such a science will be most divine, for: "(1) God is thought to be among the causes of all things and to be a first principle, and (2) such a science either God alone can have, or God above all others. All the sciences, indeed, are more necessary than this, but none is better."[5] Hence, rather than considering things in a perspective that is only temporal and totally changing--with an implied total relativization of all--hermeneutics or interpretation is essentially open to a vision of what is most real in itself and most lasting through time, that is, to the perennial in the realm of being and values.

Historicity. In undertaking his search for unchanging and permanent guides for human action Socrates had directed the attention of the Western mind away from the temporal and changing. In redirecting attention back to this changing universe, the modern mind still echoed Socrates by searching for the permanent structures of complex entities and the stable laws of change. Nevertheless, its attention to the essentially temporal character of mankind and hence to the uniqueness of each decision, individual and corporate, opened important new horizons.

In the term hermeneutics, the element of translation or interpretation stresses the presentation to the one who receives the message. In this their historical situation, and hence the historical character of human life, becomes essential. This brings into consideration not merely the pursuit of general truth, but those to whom truth is expressed, namely, persons in the concrete circumstances of their cultures as these have developed through the history of human interaction with nature, with other human beings and with God.

This human history sets the circumstances in which one perceives the values presented in the tradition and then mobilizes his or her own project toward the future. Given the admixture of good and evil in human action the process of realizing the good in human history always has been compromised with evil. Consequently, the past as well as the present must always be deciphered or interpreted in order to identify both its value content and the contradictions of that content; and projections towards the realization of values in the future must provide also for encountering and overcoming evil.

THE CHALLENGE

In working upon these three themes: hermeneutics, values and historicity, there are two major problems. One concerns truth; it is the rationalist/enlightenment ideal of clarity for all knowledge worthy of the name. The other concerns the good as the object of our will; it is our penchant for considering either only what is good or of value, or only what is evil.

Truth

The enlightenment ideal focuses upon ideas which are clear and distinct both in themselves and in their interconnection. As such they are divorced--often intentionally--from existential or temporal significance. Such an ideal of human knowledge, it is proposed, would be achieved either through an intellect working by itself from an Archimedean principle or through the senses drawing their ideas from experience and combining them in myriad tautological transformations.[6] In either case the result is an a-temporal and consequently non-historical ideal of knowledge. This revolutionary view was adhered to even by the romantics who appeared to oppose it, for in turning to the past and to myths they too sought clear and distinct knowledge of human reality. Thinking that this could be attained if all was understood in its historical context and sequence, they placed historicity ultimately at the service of the rationalist ideal.

In the rationalist view any meaning not clearly and distinctly perceived was an idol to be smashed, an idea to be bracketed by doubt, or something to be wiped clean from the slate of the mind as irrational and coercive. Any type of judgment--even if provisional--made before all had been examined and its clarity and distinctness established would be essentially a pre-judgment or prejudice, and therefore a dangerous imposition by the will.

This raises a number of problems. First, absolute knowledge of oneself or of others, simply and without condition, is not possible, for the knower is always conditioned according to his or her position in time and space and in relation to others. But neither is such knowledge of ultimate interest for the reality of human knowledge, as of being, develops in time and with others. This does not exclude the more limited projects of scientific knowledge, but it does identify these precisely as limited and specialized views: they make specific and important--but not all-controlling--contributions.

Secondly, as reason is had completely by everyone according to Descartes,[7] authority could be only an entitlement of some to decide issues by an application of their will rather than according to an authentic understanding of the truth or justice of an issue. Further, the limited number of people in authority means that the vision of which they disposed would be limited by restricted individual interests. Finally, as one decision constitutes a precedent for those to follow, authority must become fundamentally bankrupt and hence corruptive.[8]

Hermeneutics will need to relocate knowledge in the ongoing process of human discovery as taking place within a still broader project of human interaction.

Good

A second problem area for hermeneutics concerns the good, for it is important to avoid the danger of attempting to take either the good or the bad--values or their negations--in isolation one from another. In considering only the good, or values, there is danger of abstracting from human life; one loses the sense of the struggle to realize values and tends to supplant this with an idealistic simplicity and inhumane rigor. Ultimately this can only discourage and then destroy authentic human efforts toward the realization of values. Further, by considering only its values we are in danger of taking as an absolute norm a tradition which, being in human history, can only be ambiguous. This would result in our continuing its disvalues as well or, upon recognizing evil therein, rejecting the tradition as a whole.

Finally, it is sometimes observed that the tendency to turn to tradition gives a priority to conservatism in personal ethos or public politics. Those who by privileged education have been able to become familiar with that tradition are constituted thereby as an elite, while others, rather than being encouraged in their freedom, are pressed into a state of dependency.

Other problems derive from treating the negation of value without the broader context of the good--that is, of making evil the context for the consideration of the good. The meaning of evil is dependent upon the good and cannot be understood without some notion thereof. On the one hand, one might surreptitiously suppose a pattern of values which, being unarticulated and uncriticized, is in danger of being partial or false--and later disastrously misleading in our effort to realize a society worthy of mankind. On the other hand, and still worse, one might have no notion of the human good and thus reduce the description of evil to the simply factual. In that case, it would be no more than a structure described by a value-free theory, without relation to the area of human freedom or responsibility. The antithesis, evil, without its thesis, good, is either blind to, or devoid of, value concern.

Finally, where all, including evil, is a mere state of affairs, one cannot hope to generate a sense of the good or of value. When the horizon becomes one of mere psychological manipulation of the ego, the response can be only through further manipulation. This allows the ego to dominate the self and thereby excludes human freedom. Politically, for lack of an horizon adequate for the appreciation of freedom no progressive liberation can occur. Instead socio-political changes become mere substitutions of one manipulator for another until there arrives one whose permanence is due to his or her success in repressing others.

The problem then is how to understand or interpret human values in a tradition, which, in its human ambiguity, contains not only its classical ideals, but its historical contradictions. This enables one, in the words of John Dewey, to discover

> in thoughtful observation and experiment the method of administering the unfinished processes of existence so that frail goods shall be substantiated, secure goods be extended and the precarious promises of good that haunt experienced things be more liberally fulfilled.[9]

The response here will follow a dialectical pattern. The thesis will concern the hermeneutics of value discovery in history and tradition. The critique or antithesis will look at the way contradictions of value also are integral to the dynamics of human social structures and the problems this generates for deciphering the values in one's tradition, for sharing in the vision of other people and for working together toward a future which more fully realizes human values. The final step will look for the ways in which tradition and critique are mutually interdependent, working as thesis and antithesis toward the elaboration of a synthesis in which each person can make his or her full and proper contribution to life in our times.

TRADITION

This section will attend: first to tradition as the normative locus and summation of the ambiguous human experience of values; second, to the notion of application as the progressive revelation of meaning and of value in the concrete circumstances of history; and third to hermeneutics as a method for making positive use of the distinctiveness of one's own point in history in order more broadly to appreciate this content of human experience.

To situate and emphasize the relation of meaning to tradition John Caputo, in *Act and Agent: Foundations for Moral Education and Character Development*,[10] notes that from its very beginnings, even before birth, one's experience is lived in and with the biological rhythms of one's mother. Upon birth there follows a progressively broader sharing in the life of parents and siblings; this is the context in which one is fully at peace, and hence most open to personal growth and social development. In a word, from its beginning one's life has been historical: it has been lived in time and with other persons. In the family one's life and learning is realized in relation to the prior life and learning of family members upon which it depends for development and orientation. This is the universal condition of each person, and consequently of the development of human awareness and knowledge.

In terms of this phenomenological understanding interpersonal dependence is not unnatural--quite the contrary. We depend for our being upon our creator, we are conceived in dependence upon our parents, and we are nurtured by them with care and concern. Through the years we depend continually upon our family and peers, school and community. Beyond our personal and social group we turn eagerly to other persons whom we recognize as superior, not basically in terms of their will, but in terms of their insight and judgment precisely in those matters where truth, reason and balanced judgment are required. The preeminence or authority of wise persons in the community is not something they usurp or with which they are arbitrarily endowed, but is based upon their capabilities and acknowledged in our free and reasoned response. Thus, the burden of Plato's *Republic* is precisely the education of the future leader to be able to exercise authority, for while the leader who is wise but indecisive may be ineffective, the one who is decisive but foolish is bound upon destruction.

From this notion of authority it is possible to construct that of tradition by adding to present interchange additional generations with their accumulation of human insight predicated upon the wealth of their human experience through time. As a process of trial and error, of continual correction and addition, history constitutes a type of learning and testing laboratory in which the strengths of various insights can be identified and reinforced, while their deficiencies are corrected and complemented. The cumulative results of the extended process of learning and testing constitute tradition. The historical and prophetical books of the Bible constitute just such an extended concrete account of one's people's process of discovery carried out in interaction with the divine.

The content of a tradition serves as a model and exemplar, not because of personal inertia, but because of the corporate character of the learning by which it was built out of experience and the free and wise acts of succeeding generations in reevaluating, reaffirming, preserving and passing on what has been learned. The content of a long tradition has passed the test of countless generations. Standing, as it were, on the shoulders of our forebears, we are able to discover and evaluate situations with the help of their vision because of the sensitivity they developed and communicated to us. Without this we could not even choose topics to be investigated or awaken within ourselves the desire to study those problems.[11]

Tradition, then, is not simply everything that ever happened, but only what appears significant in the light of those who have appreciated and described it. Indeed, this presentation by different voices draws out its many aspects. Thus tradition is not an object in itself, but a rich source from which multiple themes can be drawn according to the motivation and interest of the inquirer. It needs to be accepted and embraced, affirmed and cultivated. Here the emphasis is neither upon the past or the present, but upon mankind living through time.

But neither is tradition a passive storehouse of materials to be drawn upon and shaped at the arbitrary will of the present inquirer; rather, it presents insight and wisdom that is normative for life in the present and future. Just as prudence (*phronesis*) without law (*nomos*) would be as relativistic and ineffectual as muscular action without a skeletal substructure, so law built simply upon transcendental or abstract vision, without taking account of historicity, would be irrelevant idealism. Hence, there is need to look into historicity to see if human action in time can engender a vision which sufficiently transcends its own time to be normative for the present and directive for the future.

This would consist of a set of values and goals which each person should seek to realize. Its harmony of measure and fullness would suggest a way for the mature and perfect formation of persons and of mankind.[12] Such a vision would be both historical and normative: historical because arising in time and presenting an appropriate way to preserve and promote human life through time; normative because presenting a basis upon which to judge past ages, present actions and options for the future. The fact of human striving manifests that every humanism, far from being indifferent, is committed to the realization of some such classical and perduring model of perfection.

It would be erroneous, however, to consider this merely a matter of knowledge, for then it would engage, not entire peoples, but only a few whom it would divide into opposing schools. The project of a tradition is much broader and can be described only in terms of the more inclusive existential and phenomenological horizon as described Samay and Caputo in *Act and Agent*[13], namely, as including both body and spirit, knowledge and love. It is, in fact, the whole human dynamism of reaching out to others in striving toward ever more complete personal and social fulfillment through the realization of understanding and love, and thereby of justice and peace.

Finally, the classical model is not drawn forward artificially by overcoming chronological distance; rather, it acts as inspiration of, and judgment upon, man's best efforts. Through time it is the timeless mode of history. We do not construct it, but belong to it, just as it belongs to us--for it is the ultimate community of human striving. Hence, historical and cultural self-criticism is not simply an individual act of subjectivity, but our situatedness in a tradition as this fuses in us past, present and future.[14]

As mentioned in the introduction, the sense of the good or of value which constitutes tradition is required also in order to appreciate the real impact of the achievements and deformations of the present. Without tradition, present events become simply facts of the moment, succeeded by counter-facts in ever succeeding waves of contradiction. This would constitute a history written in terms of violence in which human despair would turn to a Utopian abstraction of merely human origin--a kind of *1984* designed according to the reductive limitations of a modern rationalism.

This stands in brutal contrast to the cumulative richness of vision acquired by peoples through the ages and embodied in the figure of a Bolivar or Lincoln, a Gandhi or Mother Theresa, or a Martin Luther

King. Not mere matters of fact, but eminently free and unique as concrete universals they exemplified the above-mentioned harmony of measure and fullness which is at once classical and historical, ideal and personal, normative and free. Living in their own times, they emerge out of history to judge and inspire peoples of all times and places.

APPLICATION

In considering application we turn, as it were, from the whole to its parts, from tradition to its particular meaning for each new time, to ordering the present and constructing the future. This is a matter, first of all, of taking time seriously, that is, of recognizing that reality includes authentic novelty. This contrasts to the perspective of Plato for whom the real is the ideal, the forms or ideas transcending matter and time, of which physical things and temporal events are but shadows. It also goes beyond rationalism's search for clear and distinct knowledge of eternal and simple natures and their relations. A fortiori, it goes beyond method alone without content.

In contrast to all these, Gadamer's notion of application[15] means that tradition, with its inherent authority or normative force, achieves its perfection in the temporal unfolding of reality. Secondly, it shows human persons, not as detached intellects, but as inextricably enabled by, and formative of, their changing physical and social universe. Thirdly, in the area of moral values and human action it expresses directly the striving of persons to realize their lives, the orientation of this striving and its development into a fixed attitude (*hexis*). Hence, as distinct from the physical order *ethos* is a situation neither of law or of lawlessness, but of human and therefore developing institutions and attitudes which regulate, but do not determine.[16]

There are certain broad guidelines for the area of ethical knowledge which can serve in the application of tradition as a guide for historical practice. The concrete and unique reality of human freedom when lived with others through time constitutes a distinctive and ever-changing process. This is historicity and means that our responses to the good are made always in concrete and ever changing circumstances. Hence, the general principles of ethics as a philosophic science of action must not be purely theoretical knowledge or a simple accounting from the past. Instead, they must help people exercise their conscious freedom in concrete historical circumstances which as ever changing are ever new

Here an important distinction must be made between techné and ethics. In techné action is governed by an idea as an exemplary cause which is fully determined and known by objective theoretical knowledge (epistéme). Skill consists in knowing how to act according to that idea or plan; and when it cannot be carried out perfectly some parts of it are simply omitted in the execution.

In ethics the situation, though similar in the possession of a practical guide and its application to a particular task, differs in important ways. First, in action as moral the subject constitutes oneself, as much as one makes the object, for agents are differentiated by their action. Hence, moral knowledge as an understanding of the appropriateness of human action cannot be fully determined independently of the subjects in their situation.

Secondly, adaptation by moral agents in their application of the law does not diminish, but rather corrects and perfects the law. In a world which is only partially and generally ordered, the law cannot contain in any explicit manner the concrete possibilities which arise in history. It is precisely here that the freedom and creativity of the person is located. This does not consist in an arbitrary response, for Kant is right in saying that without law freedom has no meaning. Nor does it consist simply in an automatic response determined by the historical situation, for then determinism and relativism would compete for the crown in undermining human freedom. Human freedom consists rather in shaping the present according to a sense of what is just and good, and in a way which manifests and indeed creates for the first time more of what justice and goodness mean.

Hence, the law is perfected by its application in the circumstances. Epoché and equity do not diminish, but perfect the law. Without them the law would be simply a mechanical replication doing the work not of justice, but of injustice. Ethics is not only knowledge of what is right in general, but the search for what is right in the situation and the choice of the right means for this situation. Knowledge regarding the means is not then a matter of mere expediency; it is the essence of the search for a more perfect application of the law in the given situation. This is the fulfillment of moral knowledge.[17]

It will be important to note here that the rule of the concrete (of what the situation is asking of us) is known not by sense knowledge which simply registers a set of concrete facts. In order to know what is morally required, the situation must be understood in the light of what is right, that is, in the light of what has been discovered about appropriate human action through the tradition with its normative character. Only in this light can moral consciousness as the work of intellect, (*nous*) rather than of sensation, go about its job of choosing the right means.

Hence, to proceed simply in reaction to concrete injustices as present negations of the good, rather than in the light of one's tradition, is ultimately destructive. It inverts the order just mentioned and results in manipulation of our hopes for the good. Destructive or repressive structures would lead us to the use of correspondingly evil means, truly suited only to producing evil results. The true response to evil can be worked out only in terms of the good as discovered by our people, passed on in tradition and applied by us in our times.

The importance of application manifests the central role played by the virtue of prudence (*phronesis*) or thoughtful reflection which enables one to discover the appropriate means for the circumstances. This must include also the virtue of sagacity (*sunesis*), that is, of understanding or concern for the other. For what is required as a guide for the agent is not only technical knowledge of an abstract ideal, but knowledge that takes account of the agent in relation to other persons. One can assess the situation adequately only inasmuch as one, in a sense, undergoes the situation with the affected parties. Thus, Aristotle rightly describes as "terrible" the one who can make the most of the situation, but without orientation towards moral ends, that is, without concern for the good of others in their situations.

In sum, application is not a subsequent or accidental part of understanding, but co-determines this understanding from the beginning. Moral consciousness must seek to understand the good, not as an ideal to be known and then applied, but rather through discerning the good for concrete persons in their relations with others.

This can contribute to sorting out the human dilemma between an absolutism insensitive to persons in their concrete circumstances and a relativism which leaves the person subject to expediency in public and private life. Indeed, the very statement of the dilemma reflects the deleterious aspect of the Platonic view of ideas. He was right to ground changing and historical being in the unchanging and eternal. This had been Parmenides' first insight in metaphysics and was richly developed in relation to human action through the medievals' notion of an eternal law in the divine mind. But it seems inappropriate to speak directly in these terms regarding human life. In all things individual human persons and humankind as a whole are subject to time, growth and development. As we become increasingly conscious of this the human character of even our abstract ideals becomes manifest and their adapted application in time can be seen, not as their rejection, but as their perfection. In this, justice loses none of its force as an absolute requirement of human action. Rather, the concrete modes of its application in particular circumstances add to what can be articulated in merely abstract and universal terms. A hermeneutic approach directs attention precisely to these unfoldings of the meaning of abstract principles through time. This is not an abandonment of absolutes, but a recognition of the human condition and of the way in which this enriches our knowledge of the principles of human life.

What then should we conclude regarding this sense of the good which mankind has discovered, in which we have been raised, which gives us dominion over our actions, and which enables us to be free and creative? Does it come from God or from man, from eternity or from history? Chakravarti Rajagopalachari of Madras answered:

> Whether the epics and songs of a nation spring from the faith and ideas of the common folk, or whether a nation's faith and ideas are produced by its literature is a question which one is free to answer as one likes. . . . Did clouds rise from the sea or was the sea filled by waters from the sky? All such inquiries take us to the feet of God transcending speech and thought.[18]

THE INTERPRETATION OF TRADITION: HERMENEUTICS

Thus far we have treated the character and importance of tradition. This bears the long experience of persons interacting with this world, with other persons and with God. It is made up not only of chronological facts, but of insights regarding human perfection which have been forged by human efforts in concrete circumstances, e.g., the Greek notion of democracy and the enlightenment notions of equality and freedom. By their internal value these stand as normative of the aspirations of a people.

Secondly, we have seen the implications of historicity for novelty in the context of tradition, the continually unfolding circumstances of historical development, and the way in which these not merely extend or repeat what went before but constitute an emerging manifestation of the dynamic character of the vision articulated by the art, religion, literature and political structures of a cultural tradition.

It remains for us now to treat the third element in this study of tradition, namely, hermeneutics. How can earlier sources which express the great achievements of human awareness be understood in a way that is relevant, indicative, and directive of our life in present circumstances? In a word, how can we draw out the significance of tradition for present action?

First of all it is necessary to note that only a unity of meaning, that is, an identity, is intelligible.[19] Just as it is not possible to understand a number three if we include but two units rather than three, no act of understanding is possible unless it is directed to an identity or whole of meaning. This brings us to the classic issue, described above as the hermeneutic circle, in which knowledge of the whole depends upon knowledge of the parts, and vice versa. How can we make this work for, rather than against us?

The experience of reading a text might help. As we read we construe the meaning of a sentence before grasping all its individual parts. What we construe is dependent upon our expectation of the meaning of the sentence which we derived from its first words, the prior context, or more likely a combination of the two. In turn, our expectation or construal of the meaning of the text is adjusted according to the requirements of its various parts as we proceed to read through the parts of the sentence, the paragraph, etc., continually reassessing the whole in terms of the parts and the parts in terms of the whole. This basically circular movement continues until all appears to fit and to be clear.

Similarly, as we begin to look into our tradition we develop a prior conception of its content. This anticipation of meaning is not simply of the tradition as an objective or fixed content to which we come; it is rather what we produce as we participate in the evolution of the tradition, and thereby further determine ourselves. This is a creative stance reflecting the content, not only of the past, but of the time in which I stand and of the life project in which I am engaged. It is a creative unveiling of the content of the tradition as this comes progressively and historically into the present and, through the present, passes into the future.

In this light, time is not a barrier, a separation or an abyss, but rather a bridge and opportunity for the process of understanding, a fertile ground filled with experience, custom and tradition. The importance of the historical distance it provides is not that this enables the subjective reality of persons to disappear so that the objectivity of the situation can emerge. On the contrary, it makes possible a more complete meaning of the tradition, less by removing falsifying factors, than by opening new sources of self-understanding which reveal in the tradition unsuspected implications and even new dimensions of meaning.[20]

Of course, not all our acts of understanding are correct, whether they be about the meaning of a text from another culture, a dimension of a shared tradition, a set of goals or a plan for future action. Hence, it becomes particularly important that they not be adhered to fixedly, but be put at risk in dialogue with others.

In this the basic elements of meaning remains the substances which Aristotle described in terms of autonomy and, by implication, of identity. Hermeneutics would expand this to reflect as well the historical and hermeneutic situation of each person in the dialogue, that is, their horizon or particular possibility for understanding: an horizon is all that can be seen from one's vantage point(s). In reading a text or in a dialoguing with others it is necessary to be aware of our horizon as well as of that of others. It is precisely when our initial projection of the meaning of a text (another's words or the content of a tradition) will not bear up under the progressive dialogue that we are required to adjust our projection of their meaning.

This enables us to adjust not only our prior understanding of the horizon of the other with whom we are in dialogue, but especially our own horizon. Hence, one need not fear being trapped in one's horizons. They are vantage points of a mind which in principle is open and mobile, capable of being aware of its own horizon and of transcending it through acknowledging the horizons of others. The flow of history implies that we are not bound by our horizons, but move in and out of them. It is in making us aware of our horizons that hermeneutic consciousness accomplishes our liberation.[21]

In this process it is important that we retain a questioning attitude. We must not simply follow through with our previous ideas until a change is forced upon us, but be sensitive to new meanings in true openness. This is neither neutrality as regards the meaning of the tradition, nor an extinction of passionate concern for actions towards the future. Rather, being aware of our own biases or prejudices and adjusting them in dialogue with others implies rejecting what impedes our understanding of others, of texts or of traditions. Our attitude in approaching dialogue must be one of willingness continually to revise our initial projection or expectation of meaning.

There is then a way out of the hermeneutic cycle. It is not by ignoring or denying our horizons and prejudices, but by recognizing them as inevitable and making them work for us. To do so we must direct our attention to the objective meaning of the text in order to draw out, not its meaning for the author, but its application for the present. Through this process of application we serve as midwife for the historicity of a text, tradition or culture and enable it to give birth to the future.[22]

Method of Question and Answer

The effort to draw upon a text or a tradition and in dialogue to discover its meaning for the present supposes authentic openness. The logical structure of this openness is to be found in the exchange of question and answer. The question is required in order to determine just what issue we are engaging in order to direct our attention. Without this no meaningful answer can be given or received. As a question, however, it requires that the answer not be settled or determined. In sum, progress or discovery requires an openness which is not simply indeterminacy, but a question which gives specific direction to our attention and enables us to consider significant evidence. (Note that we can proceed not only by means of positive evidence for one of two possible responses, but also through dissolving counter arguments).

If discovery depends upon the question, then the art of discovery is the art of questioning. Consequently, whether working alone or in conjunction with others, our effort to find the answer should be directed less towards suppressing, than toward reinforcing and unfolding the question. To the degree that its probabilities are built up and intensified it can serve as a searchlight. This is the opposite of both opinion which tends to suppress questions, and of arguing which searches out the weakness in the other's argument. Instead, in conversation as dialogue one enters upon a mutual search to maximize the possibilities of the question, even by speaking at cross purposes. By mutually eliminating errors and working out a common meaning we discover truth.[23]

Further, it should not be presupposed that the text holds the answer to but one question or horizon which must be identified by the reader. On the contrary, the full horizon of the author is never available to the reader, nor can it be expected that there is but one question to which the text or tradition holds an answer. The sense of the text reaches beyond what the author intended; because of the dynamic character of being as it emerges in time, the horizon is never fixed but continually opens. This constitutes the effective historical element in understanding a text or a tradition. At each step new dimensions of its potentialities open to understanding; the meaning of a text or tradition lives with the consciousness and hence the horizons--not of its author--but of persons in history. It is the broadening of their horizons, resulting from their fusion with the horizon of a text or a partner in dialogue, that makes it possible to receive answers which are ever new.[24]

In this one's personal attitudes and interests are, once again, most important. If our interest in developing new horizons is simply the promotion of our own understanding then we could be interested solely in achieving knowledge, and thereby domination over others. This would lock one into an absoluteness of one's prejudices, for being fixed or closed in the past they would disallow new life in the present. In this manner powerful new insights can become with time deadening prejudgments which suppress freedom.

In contrast, an attitude of authentic openness appreciates the nature of one's own finiteness. On this basis it both respects the past and is open to discerning the future. Such openness is a matter, not merely of new information, but of recognizing the historical nature of man. It enables us to escape from what had deceived us and held us captive, and enables us to learn from new experiences. For example, recognition of the limitations of our finite planning enables us to see that the future is still open.[25]

This suggests that openness consists not so much in surveying others objectively or obeying them in a slavish and unquestioning manner, but is directed primarily to ourselves. It is an extension of our ability to listen to others, and to assimilate the implications of their answers for changes in our own positions. In other words, it is an acknowledgment that the cultural heritage has something new to say to us. The characteristic hermeneutic attitude of effective historical consciousness is then not methodological sureness, but readiness for experience.[26] Seen in these terms our heritage is not closed, but the basis for a life that is ever new, more inclusive, and more rich.

SOCIAL CRITIQUE AND TRADITIONAL VALUES

As was noted above one major fear arises regarding the hermeneutic project as described by Gadamer, namely, that recognition of the authority of tradition might undermine the freedom of those to whom the tradition is mediated. This could be the result of a romantic attitude towards the past as having been in possession of the complete meaning of human life and of the structures for its realization. In that case the past would rule the present: text would become dogma.

H.G. Gadamer's response focuses rather upon new and unique applications of the tradition for the present and future. It is neither desirable, nor even possible, to attempt simply to reconstruct the text objectively according to its original horizon. Instead, from its perspective the text challenges us to live up to its insights and values in our own circumstances, while from our perspective we question it in order to draw from it new implications for our life. Gadamer considers this questioning to be a matter of understanding, and its implied fore- or preunderstanding to be an essentially contemplative act, the task of the human sciences (*Geisteswissenshaften*) here is to correct any misunderstanding.

In contrast, critical hermeneutics focuses upon the material conditions which causally shape our awareness. It is concerned, not with understanding and hence judgments and prejudices, but with interests and ideologies, and with their correction through the social sciences. Its task is to identify the material causes and thereby to make possible action to remove or adjust those material factors which by impeding the proper flow of dialogue and communication give rise to misunderstanding and conflict.[27]

There is real continuity between the hermeneutic efforts of Gadamer and critical hermeneutics. Both are directed ultimately towards understanding, both search for theoretical truth, and both oppose dogmatic acceptance of the "text." However, where Gadamer seeks this through understanding, critical hermeneutics seeks it through an explanation of the conditions for misunderstanding and their correction. Yet, even in this, the positions are still not as far apart as at first they might seem for, if today's interests lie less in the materials of production than in the techniques thereof, it is not so much material possessions as knowledge and its implementation that hold the keys to power.

Hence, the roots of critical concern lie deep within the development of modern vision, and indeed within the nature of intellectual knowledge. As reflexive, the person had been understood classically to be self-aware and hence capable of reasoning, language and self-responsibility. As long as, with Aristotle, in the act of knowledge the subject was understood to become the object and all was received according to the mode of the receiver self-consciousness was not undermined by the distinction between subject and object.

With Descartes, however, the object of knowledge came to be seen as ideas rather than things. As the conditions of knowledge, which previously had been within consciousness but were not distinctly attended to, did not figure in his clear and distinct ideas of natures, it became crucial to know these conditions of knowledge, that is, to have critical knowledge. Kant thematized as categories the factors which actually, but only implicitly had been in knowledge. Hegel articulated them in a developmental pattern through which the subject is progressively realized in and for itself and for us. He saw this as taking place, not through pure theoretical reason or practical reason acting in separation, but in the lived process of the socialization of the person in the universal history of mankind.

In search of a real, rather than an ideal, basis for his dialectic, Marx turned to labor in interaction with others--social labor--as the mechanism for the evolution of the human species through history. This works by creating the conditions for the reproduction of social life. Indeed the very identity of the social subject is altered with the scope of his or her power of technical control. This, in turn, determines the epistemological order by constituting the conditions for apprehending the world.[28]

In this way Marx was able to integrate much in his understanding of history. By adding to the forces of production the institutional framework or relations of production his analysis encompassed both material activity and a critique of ideologies, both instrumental action and revolutionary practice, both labor and reflection.

Unfortunately, in increasingly focusing upon work alone as the self-generative act of the species, he lost the ability to understand his own mode of procedure. Though he did not eliminate the structure of symbolic interaction and the role of cultural tradition, they were not part of his philosophical frame of reference for they did not coincide with instrumental action. Yet, it is only in these terms that power and ideology can be comprehended and dissolved by a mode of reflection to which Marx applied the Kantian term "critique."[29]

Since instrumental action by the forces of production responds only to external stimuli, communicative action is required for liberation from the suppression of man's nature by the institutional framework of socially imposed labor and socially determined rewards. For when due to progress this labor is no longer objectively necessary for the common good, in continuing to demand it, the state reflects only the private interests of the class in power.[30]

THE SYNTHESIS OF TRADITION AND CRITIQUE

We are then in an essentially dialectical situation which reflects the hermeneutic circle. On the one hand, the pattern of interests can be evaluated only in the context of a tradition and its sense of human life and meaning. On the other hand, tradition must be critically examined continually in order to avoid, by mechanical repetition, becoming an instrument of repression rather than of liberation. As both tradition and critique are required and both are interrelated, it becomes important to look more closely into this dialectic. There are two ways in which tradition must draw upon critique if it is to respond to what Habermas refers to as an "interest in emancipation" which surpasses technical or instrumental and practical interests. First, Gadamer's hermeneutics concerns the application of our cultural heritage in the present by a renewal and reinterpretation of tradition in order to draw out its new implications. The means for this are especially the humanities in which the tradition--through texts in their literary form, and as values and ideals--is articulated. Here, the emphasis is upon appropriating the tradition, identifying with it, and acknowledging its presence as fore-understanding in our every question.

In social critique the sciences must not only describe regularities as do the merely empirical sciences, but also identify the controlling relations of dependence at a deeper level which have become fixed ideologically. Self-reflection, governed by an interest in emancipation, subjects these to a critique which, in turn, allows the real implications of the tradition to emerge.

There are roots in Gadamer's thought for recognition of the importance of this critical element, for he sees historical distance and a consequent new horizon for questioning as a prerequisite for drawing out new implications of the meaning of the text or tradition. This, in turn, reflects the importance of distinguishing the text from the intention of its author(s), for the text transcends the author's psychological and sociological context. This emancipation of the text--its psycho- and sociocultural decontextualization--is a fundamental condition for hermeneutic interpretation: "distanciation now belongs to the mediation itself."[31]

This is reflected both on the essential or structural level and on the existential level. In the former it becomes necessary to go beyond Gadamer's description of discourse as a spontaneous conversation of question and answer and to begin to consider discourse as a product of praxis by which it is crafted from smaller units. Here meaning takes place in structures: "the *matter* of the text is not what naive reading of the text reveals, but what the formal arrangement of the text mediates."[32] Hence, structural analysis is required in order to understand the *depth semantics* of the text as a condition for grasping its matter.

If the sense of the work is its internal organization, the reference of the text is the way in which being unfolds *in front*, as it were, of the text. This is the existential reality of being emerging as temporal and historical--as the power to be. In sharp contrast to a deadening repetition of the past, frozen in a fixed ideology, the creative space opened by reference to the "power to be" constitutes a critique of ideology.

This implies not merely a liberation from the structures of our environment, but a liberation of the self as well. Hermeneutic understanding is not an imposition of the reader upon the text; rather, the text provides an interlocutor which enables the reader consciously to examine his or her own subjectivity. By making possible imaginative variations of one's ego, one can achieve the distance required for a first critique of his/her own illusions and false consciousness, and of the ideology in which he/she has been reared.[33]

Critical distance is then an essential element for hermeneutics. It requires an analysis by the social sciences of the historical social structures as a basis for liberation from internal determination by, and dependence upon, unjust interests. The concrete pyscho- and socio-pathology deriving from such dependencies and the corresponding steps toward liberation therefrom are the subject of studies by J. Loiacono and H. Ferrand de Piazza *The Social Context of Values: Perspectives of the Americas*.[34] Critical distance also has an existential dimension which is made possible by the temporality of being and man's projection toward the historical future (see the studies of O. Pegoraro and M. Dy in the same volume.) Together these open up the possibility of liberation of the subject.

Dependence of Critique upon Tradition

The relation between hermeneutics and social critique being dialectical, just as the distancing characteristic of the critical social sciences can make possible some dimensions of awareness essential for emancipation in a world of increasingly technical and convoluted structures, so also tradition provides other dimensions of awareness essential for the critique to which these sciences contribute. Paul Ricoeur has attempted to codify these contributions in his article, "Hermeneutics and the Critique of Ideology."[35]

First, a critique must recognize that it is carried out in the context of interests which establish a frame of meaning. The sequence of technical, practical and emancipating interests reflect the emergence of man out of nature and correspond to the developmental phases of moral sensitivity. Habermas studies Kohlberg closely on this and employs his work. But to the question of the basis of these interests no adequate answer is provided. They are not empirically justifiable or they would be found only at the level of technical interests. Neither do they constitute a theory as a network of working hypotheses for then they would be justified at most by the interest in emancipation, which in turn would fall into a vicious circle.

The only proper description of these interests as truly all-embracing must lie in Heidegger's existentials, which are hidden only in being so present as to be in need of being unveiled by a hermeneutic method. Thus Gadamer's hermeneutic project on the clarification of prejudices and Habermas's suggestion of critical work on interests through the social sciences--though not identical--share common ground.

Secondly, critiques of ideologies appear in the end to share characteristics common to those of the historical hermeneutic sciences. Both focus upon the ability to develop the communicative action of free persons. Their common effort is against a reduction of all human communication to instrumental action and institutionalization, for it is here that manipulation takes place. Hence, success or failure in extending the critique of interests beyond instrumental action determines whether the community will promote or destroy its members.

Ricoeur moves from this concern regarding the general horizon of social critique to the observation that it is unlikely ever to be successful if we have no experience of communication with our own cultural heritage. This can be required in a dialogue, for the effective basis of any real consensus must lie not in an empty ideal or regulative idea, but in life that has been experienced and shared. "He who is unable to interpret his past may also be incapable of projecting concretely his interest in emancipation."[36]

Thirdly, today communicative action needs more than a model to suggest what might otherwise not occur to our minds, for the rationalization of human life has become such that all of its aspects are controlled pervasively in terms of instrumental action. Whereas Marx could refer in his day to surplus value as the motive of production, this is true no longer. Instead, the system itself of technology has become the key to productivity and all is coordinated toward the support and promotion of this system; this is the ideology of our day. As a result the distinction between communicative action and instrumental action has been overridden so that control no longer can be expected from communicative action.

This raises a new type of question, namely, how can the interest in emancipation be kept alive. Undoubtedly, communicative action must be reawakened and made to live if we are not to be simply subjects--indeed 'slaves'--of the technological machine. But how is this to be done; whence can this life be derived if the present situation is pervasively occupied and shaped by science and technology as the new, and now all-encompassing, master? The answer of Ricoeur and Gadamer is that it can be done only by drawing upon our heritage in the manner suggested by Heidegger. We need--now as never before--to reach back into our heritage in order to retrieve contents which were present seminally, but never developed. These are the resources of our tradition, which can give rise to the radically new visions needed for the emancipation of mankind living in an age of increasing domination and manipulation--and this not primarily of economy and politics, but of minds and hearts.

Finally, there is a still more fundamental sense in which critique, rather than being opposed to tradition or taking a questioning attitude thereto, is itself an appeal to tradition. Criticism appeals unabashedly to the heritage of emancipation as an ideal inherited from the Enlightenment. But this tradition has longer roots which reach back to the liberating acts of the Exodus and the Resurrection. "Perhaps" writes Ricoeur "there would be no more interest in emancipation, no more anticipation of freedom, if the Exodus and the Resurrection were effaced from the memory of mankind."[37]

According to the proper norms of communicative action, these historical acts should be taken also in their symbolic sense according to which liberation and emancipation express the root interest basic to traditional cultures. In this manner they point to fundamental dimensions of being, indeed to Being Itself as the unique existence in whom the alienated can be reunited, to the logos which founds subjectivity without an estranging selfishness, and to the spirit through whom human freedom can be creative in history. Remembrance and celebration of this heritage provides needed inspiration and direction both for any in power who might be indifferent to the needs of the poor and alienated and for the alienated poor themselves. It enables both to reach out in mutual comprehension, reconciliation and concern to form social unity marked by emancipation and peace.

The Catholic University of America
Washington, D.C.

NOTES

1. Richard E. Palmer, *Hermeneutics* (Evanston: Northwestern Univ. Press, 1969), pp. 12-29.

2. Ivor Leclerc, "The Metaphysics of the Good," *Review of Meta-*

physics, 35 (1981), 3-5. See also *Vocabulaire technique et critique de la philosophie*, ed. André Lalande (Paris: PUF, 1956), pp. 1182-1186.

3. J. Mehta, *Martin Heidegger: The Way and the Vision* (Honolulu: Univ. of Hawaii Press, 1967), pp. 90-91.

4. Hesiod, *Theogony* trans. H.G. Everland-White (Loeb Classical Library; Cambridge, Mass.: Harvard Univ. Press, 1964), p. 85.

5. Aristotle, *Metaphysics*,I, 2.

6. R. Carnap, *Vienna Manifesto*, trans. A. Blumberg in G. Kreyche and J. Mann, *Perspectives on Reality* (New York: Harcourt, Brace and World, 1966), p. 485.

7. R. Descartes, *Discourse on Method*, I.

8. H.G. Gadamer, *Truth and Method* (New York: Crossroads, 1975), pp. 240, 246-247, 305-310.

9. John Dewey, *Existence as Precarious and Stable,* see J. Mann & G. Kreyche, *Perspectives on Reality* (New York: Harcourt, Brace and World, 1966), p. 379.

10. G. McLean *et al.* eds. (Washington: The Council for Research in Values and Philosophy and The University Press of America, 1986).

11. Gadamer, pp. 248, 250-251.

12. *Ibid.*, pp. 252-253.

13. See n. 4 above along with Ch. III by S. Samay, "Affectivity: The Power Base of Moral Behavior," pp. 71-114.

14. Gadamer, p. 258.

15. *Ibid.*, pp. 281-286.

16. *Ibid.*, pp. 278-279.

17. *Ibid.*, pp. 281-286.

18. *Ramayana* (Bombay: Bharatiya Vidya Bhavan, 1976), p. 312.

19. Gadamer, p. 262.

20. *Ibid.*, pp. 263-264.

21. *Ibid.*, pp. 235-242, 267-271.

22. *Ibid.*, pp. 235-332.

23. *Ibid.*, pp. 225-332.

24. *Ibid.*, pp. 336-340.

25. *Ibid.*, pp. 327-324.

26. *Ibid.*, pp. 324-325.

27. J. Bleiker, *Contemporary Hermeneutics: Hermeneutics as Method, Philosophy and Critique* (London: Routledge & Kegan Paul, 1980), pp. 143-151.

28. J. Habermas, *Knowledge and Human Interests* (Boston: Beacon, 1971), pp. 28-35.

29. *Ibid.*, p. 42.

30. For a more extended treatment of the character of the critical hermeneutics of J. Habermas, see G. McLean, "Cultural Heritage, Social Critique and Future Construction" in R. Molina, T. Ready and G. McLean, eds., *Culture, Human Rights and Peace in Central America* (Washington: Council for Research in Values and Philosophy and The University Press of America, 1988), pp. 1-24.

31. "Hermeneutics as the Critique of Ideology," *Hermeneutics and the Human Sciences*, ed., J.B. Thompson (New York: Cambridge, 1981), pp. 81.
32. *Ibid.*, pp. 93.
33. *Ibid.*, pp. 93-95.
34. G. McLean and O. Pegoraro, eds. (Washington: The Council for Research in Values and Philosophy and The University Press of America, 1989).
35. *Hermeneutics and the Human Sciences*, J.B. Thompson, ed. (New York: Cambridge, 1981), pp. 82-91
36. *Ibid.*, pp. 97.
37. *Ibid..* pp. 99-100.

PART II

ASPECTS OF AN INTEGRATED THEORY

OF THE MORAL AGENT

CHAPTER V

FREEDOM AND MORAL CHOICE

FREDERICK E. ELLROD III

INTRODUCTION

In dealing with moral education we necessarily encounter the philosophical problems concerning freedom of choice. Action involves not only thinking out dilemmas, but doing something about them--executing the decision. Most theories of moral development merely take for granted some interpretation of freedom or the means of enacting one's wishes, without examining in detail how moral thought becomes moral action.But it is necessary to understand how the moral agent comes to put moral beliefs into action if we are to understand how one may become a better moral agent.

Some aspects of this problem will be discussed later in this volume in considering the moral roles of emotion and of character. Here I will concentrate on the question of the fundamental power to choose, the ability which philosophers have sometimes called "will" (without, however, implying that "the will" should be considered a separate entity within the person). Our goal is to present only those contentions central to an adequate theory of moral development.

One of the most pressing problems having to do with choice is that of its freedom or unfreedom. In this chapter I shall argue that a power of free choice, interpreted as "agent causality," must exist in human beings to sustain morality as generally understood, and that the evidence for such a power is sufficient to justify accepting it. The next chapter will argue that the notion of a relatively fixed and determined character is not incompatible with this, but, on the contrary, serves to complement such a theory and make it more consonant with the facts of moral experience.

ARGUMENTS FOR FREEDOM

Many arguments have been made to establish "freedom" or "liberty" in some sense. Here I will concentrate on those most important to morality.

The first datum to consider is the fact that persons, in at least some of their actions, seem to themselves to act freely, determining what will occur with control over the results. Whether or not this experience should be considered illusory, the fact of the experience is indisputable. This does not by itself prove that moral agents actually are free; but it provides evidence that must be taken into account.[1]

We also find that in very many cases persons are taken to be legitimately held responsible for their actions. In the absence of special excusing conditions, people may be called to account for what they have done, praised or blamed for having done it, rewarded or punished where appropriate. Certainly we normally hold that a person cannot be morally evaluated unless responsible for the act in question. If someone is wholly lacking in responsibility for a deed, we may evaluate the deed, but we consider the individual blameless (or praiseless, as the case may be). Thus responsibility is an integral part of common-sense moral experience. Without it, although we might still be able to remark on the goodness or badness of events, we could not bring these into any important moral relationship with people.[2]

It is possible to claim that all attributions of responsibility are wrong and harmful, as is sometimes done in the name of humanitarianism. While adopting such a view might remove guilt and remorse, it would also eliminate most of ordinary human action, *as* human, and most of what we consider the unique importance of persons. For responsibility is also one of the characteristics that defines human beings as persons against a world of things. We hold persons accountable for what they do, good or evil; to deny accountability is to say that the agent is to that extent not regarded as a fully functioning person. We prosecute and punish human beings, not inanimate objects; we regard humans as heroes or saints, and do not confer this status upon things, regardless of the events the things have made possible or the stresses they have borne. The girder which supports a crumbling bridge while the last drivers scramble off may be referred to loosely as "responsible for" their safety; but the girder will never receive a ticker-tape parade or even a word of thanks.[3]

What does this responsibility which characterizes human beings imply about them? What is its ground? By inductively examining those cases where we assert or deny responsibility for an action, we may gather that responsibility is in some sense a function of *control*. A person is held to account for an act exactly insofar as its doing was under that person's control. Such a criterion is visible in Aristotle's well-known discussion of voluntariness, for example: ignorance and coercion, which remove voluntariness and excuse from responsibility, are factors which prevent agents from exercising control over events, for they either are unaware of crucial aspects of the situation which might lead them to alter their actions, or are compelled to perform certain deeds by force.[4] Traditional accounts in moral theology of factors which limit accountability refer to things which deprive us of essential information, compel us to act unwillingly, or limit our choices in such a way as to lead us to act in ways that are otherwise undesirable.[5] Even those modern treatments which deny responsibility due to psychological factors do so because the agent's psychology was such that no real choice was open at that time, precluding effective control over events.

We are led, then, from the notion of responsibility to that of control or choice, the exercise of some discretionary power by the agent which enables one to decide which events will occur and which will not.[6] Further, the sorts of cases just cited allow us to discover two criteria for responsible choice, which will be of use to us in defining the sort of freedom which must be attributed to human beings if the ordinary no-

Frederick E. Ellrod III 125

tion of morality is to be accepted.

In the first place, a free or responsible choice must be one which allows at least two possible outcomes. Before the choice is made, there must be more than one result which can occur, within the agent's power. If it were not so, then there would be no choice to be made: any internal process leading to action could have only one result, and thus the agent cannot be held responsible for producing one rather than another. It may be that infinitely many results are open to the agent, or it may be that events have so constricted the possible choices that only two alternatives are available; but as long as alternatives exist, the agent may be responsible for choosing among them. (Note that this makes clear our feeling that conditions may force a good agent to a difficult choice: one is responsible *only* for choice among possible alternatives, not for things one could not possibly have done.)

In the second place, it must be under the agent's control *which* of the possible alternatives is realized. At some point the decision must be made, and some alternatives rejected, another accepted. At this point, it must be up to the agent which alternative is enacted. If some other factor were to intervene at this point and determine what happens, then clearly the agent would not be responsible for the result. In order for us to say that the agent controlled what happened, we must be able to say both that more than one thing might have happened, and that the agent was the one who made one happen rather than the other. If this is not the case, then we do not have an *agent*, but merely an "innocent bystander" to the event.

The force of this stipulation will become more apparent later. At this point, let us accept these two conditions or criteria as defining - "freedom" in the sense in which we will use the term (see ch. XII for a further sense of freedom based on self-determination rather than on alternate objects; see also section III of this article). If the action could have happened in no other way, then the agent is not responsible for it, even if the motivating force or cause of the act was somewhere "within" the agent; yet the cause must indeed be "within the agent," under the agent's control, if one is to be held accountable. The conditions are each necessary, and are jointly sufficient, to define "free choice" or "freedom of the will."

It should be noted here that in using the term "will" I do not mean to suggest that this denotes a separate entity inhabiting the person, a small inner person or voice, as satirized many times in recent philosophy. Rather, the term functions as do "intellect," or "emotion," to refer to whatever it is in the individual which enables one to carry out certain activities: choosing, thinking, feeling. To say that "the will" causes an alternative to become actual may simply stress the fact that choice need not be thought of as depending on having certain thoughts or feelings, or solely on the neural and muscular responses which are involved in carrying out most human actions. There is surely a sense in which we can differentiate one who would act in a certain way, and one who would not, even if both are helpless to effect their choices, and we might reasonably express this by saying that one wills the result and the other does not. "The will" is simply that in us which allows us to choose freely.

I have dealt with the argument from responsibility at some length because it is crucial to the matter of moral education and because its requirements considerably illuminate the concept of free choice. A closely related argument begins from our experience of moral obligation, once again taking common moral experience as the datum, but concentrating on our sense (at times) that we are called upon or commanded to act in a certain way, without at the same time being forced to act in that way; that is, of finding one course of action obligatory while two or more in fact remain open to our choice. Such experiences presuppose that the one obliged can in fact act in accord with the obligation, or otherwise, insofar as obligation is different (and is experienced differently) from either compulsion or impulse. It may, of course, be argued that the experiences are illusory; that is, they do not by themselves prove that the agent actually *is* free. Nonetheless, they present data that must be taken into account, and in the absence of convincing reasons to the contrary should be taken as evidence of the freedom of the agent.[7]

Finally, if one accepts a certain characterization of the norms of rational discussion as imposing a similar sort of obligation upon the thinker, then an argument may be made that the denial of freedom is self-referentially impossible: even to deny freedom one must freely choose to follow these rational norms.[8] While all these arguments may be debated at great length, it is reasonable here to conclude that the evidence for admitting free choice justifies us in doing so, and that available counter-evidence or alternative explanations do not alter this.[9] Some ways in which apparent difficulties in the assertion of human freedom can be overcome will become apparent in the discussion to follow; others must be left to the relevant philosophical literature on the topic for a full exposition.

The person with the power of free choice, then, or the moral agent, is a source of actions, a producer of results. The will is a sort of causal power: it gives rise to effects. We may define more closely the freedom of the will, which we have held to be necessary to affirm its responsibility, by considering the sort of causality it exercises. What kind of cause would satisfy the two criteria which have been specified above? A clarification of this assertion, in view of the practical use to which it is to be put in succeeding volumes, is worth a digression on this topic.

MODELS OF CAUSALITY

The fact that we have two criteria, each of which may or may not be satisfied, suggests that we may identify four possible patterns for causal activity, or causal models. We will begin by examining determinism, indeterminism or chance, and what will here be called "internal determinism." The fourth model, "agent causality," will be discussed in the following section.[10]

A. *Determinism.* The most common theory of causation is the one referred to as "determinism," which can be found as far back as the Greek atomists, who held that all Being was ruled by unswerving necessity. Plato and Aristotle, and indeed most cosmological thinkers at any time, have held that in at least some areas of the universe effects are strictly determined by their causes and that causes are invariable in their action. Epicurus and his successors held explicitly that the motion of atoms in the void depended in a determinate fashion on their previous conditions of weight, velocity, and relation to other atoms (with one important exception, to be discussed later on). Various other philosophical versions of determinism joined with the new classical mechanics in Newton's time to produce a widespread affirmation of universal determinism, determinism without exceptions, which has remained influential throughout the modern period. The classic statement of this view is that of Pierre Laplace: "We ought to regard the present state of the universe as the effect of its antecedent state and as the cause of the state that is to follow."[11] Each state in the series determines a *unique* next state, without possibility of variation.

What are the significant characteristics of determinism for our purposes? First, given an initial state of a universe with certain sorts of laws, a number of succeeding states may be possible in an abstract logical sense. For example, given a Newtonian universe of moving atoms and such laws as that of conservation of mass, a number of states are logically possible, where the atoms have different locations or move with different velocities. The causal influence of an initial state, however, as described by causal laws, serves to "pick out" from these the one and only one state which actually will follow the initial state. Given the causal relation of the first state to the second, there is no actual possibility that any other alternative will occur.

Second, we may ask precisely what element or elements of the universe in its initial state may be involved in determining the state of any given object (or the occurrence of any given event) in the succeeding state. We may focus on one item, say atom A, and ask whether all elements of the universe at the earlier time participate in determining the fate of atom A at the later time, or whether some elements of the universe might have been different while resulting in the same state for atom A at the later time. In most cases of deterministic causation, not all elements of the universe will play a significant role; if snow begins to fall in Washington, for instance, we look to relatively local events for the explanation, rather than to events in the Magellanic Clouds. But in principle it would seem that any element in the universe may be involved in exerting deterministic causal influence on any object; in fact, it is part of the role of "laws of nature" to specify which elements may do so, more or less directly, in a given system. No factor is necessarily excluded in principle. Thus we may say that generally the state of some element of the universe at a given time is uniquely determined by the whole of the universe at the preceding moment, for we do not know in advance which elements of the preceding state may turn out to be relevant. (In fact, of course, in a Newtonian or relativistic universe all elements are connected at least gravitationally.)

In any case where an agent is affected only by deterministic causes, then, a given initial state of the universe, including the agent, may be followed by exactly one next state of the agent. Similarly, an action controlled entirely by deterministic causes could not have been otherwise than it was. Only the next state or action is "causally possible," that is, possible given the initial state and its causal influence on the next state. Which state that will be is selected in principle from the range of logical possibilities by the initial state of the entire universe.

From this characterization we can see at once why determinism cannot provide a causal model for free action, why there is a conflict between determinism and freedom. Determinism fails both tests for a free cause: it leaves only one alternative causally possible, and that alternative is selected not by the agent, but by anything in the universe which may happen to exert an influence. Further, since the agent will presumably have an earliest state (unless it exists eternally) and since that state will also have causal antecedents, every causal condition for an action will ultimately be found outside the agent. Determinism is the case in which both of our criteria are unsatisfied. Thus if the person is conceived only as a network of deterministic causes, there is no freedom, and no responsibility. Morality, then, requires the existence of causes other than deterministic ones.

B. Indeterminism. The second causal model to be considered is the one often identified with "chance" or "randomness." Here the meaning of "chance" is not, for instance, that of Aristotle's example in Book II of the Physics,[12] where two relatively independent events happen to meet in an unexpected way. Nor is it any other sense which makes the indeterminacy epistemological, that is, a matter of our limited knowledge rather than a real possibility of multiple alternatives. These sorts of "chance" are compatible with strict determinism. For a new causal model we must seek a real or ontological sense of "indeterminism," where the initial state does not give rise to a unique succeeding state. This is a mode of causation distinctly different from the deterministic pattern described above.

The Epicurean theory of atoms may serve as one example of such a causal model. As we have seen, this rain of atoms falling through the void generally follows deterministic laws of motion; but every now and then an uncaused and unpredictable "swerve" in the atomic motion occurs. In the words of Lucretius, "particles, while they are borne straight downwards by their own weights through the void, at quite uncertain times and in uncertain places push a little from their track."[13] In Epicurean theory this random deflection is linked explicitly to freedom.

The indeterminist model became particularly popular in the wake of the discoveries of quantum physics in the first third of this century. A certain indeterminism among very small particles seemed to be required by the very physics that had previously demanded universal determinism, and reactions of physicists and philosophers were mixed. At least three distinct interpretations of these results have been proposed, but only one of them is important for our purposes. Under this interpretation an electron, for instance, has a specific and definite position and momentum at any given instant, but its position and momentum at the next instant are not completely determined by the prior position and momentum, or by any causal conditions in the universe at the prior moment. It has a specific probability of appearing in any given state, but no one of these states is certain to occur. As with Epicurean atoms, given one initial state, more than one subsequent state is possible. It is, of course, debated whether this interpretation of quantum theory is correct, but it is not necessary here to decide that point. The interpretation described serves simply as an example to make clearer the notion of indeterministic causation, and to lead us to see its crucial features.

Determinism demands a one-to-one relation of cause to possible effect; indeterminism maintains a one-to-many relation. One initial state provides adequate causal grounds for two or more possible results. Only one, of course, is realized; but that one is realized not because the state of the universe compels its realization, but by chance, by accident. The selection of the actual outcome from the causal possibilities is random.

To define such "random selection" precisely is difficult. The openness to alternatives is not absolute, for it may be that only a limited range of possibilities exists; not any logical possibility may occur. Presumably only certain degrees of "swerve," for instance, are available to Epicurean atoms. Further, over a long period of time the realization of alternatives may not be equal, that is, some alternatives may be more probable than others; randomness may have a "probability structure" of a sort, although there are well-known methods of reducing such structures (analytically at least) to equiprobable randomness. In any case, admitting a certain indeterminism would not necessarily lead to absolute chaos, as some criticisms have implied.[14] But our purpose here is not to decide whether any such causality does exist, but rather to examine it with respect to our two criteria.

Can this causal model, assuming it to be worked out in detail, explain freedom of choice? Indeterminism satisfies the first condition, providing multiple causally possible alternatives for a given initial state; but it fails to satisfy the second, that the *agent* must decide which outcome is realized, for here there is no decision of any kind, but rather a chance result comparable to the common-sense notion of flipping a coin. If the agent were an indeterministic cause, individual choices would follow no rule, but would occur randomly, while the long-term series of choices would presumably follow some statistical pattern. Yet this does not seem to be what is meant by a free choice which lends responsibility to an action: the deterministic plea "I couldn't help it," is an excuse from accountability, but so is "it just happened, it was a matter of chance." As long as the agent does not control the outcome, the causation involved is not what we normally mean by "free."

It may be briefly noted here that mixed models might be possible, but would bring us no nearer to a solution of our problem. An indeterminism restricted to a small class of possibilities, with its limits set by determinism, can be exemplified by an idealized six-sided random die. When it is rolled, only six results are possible (it will not stand on edge, or crumble into dust, this condition being imposed by the state of the universe as a whole), but which of the six sides turns up will be "decided" randomly. This, however, is not freedom: insofar as the possibilities are delimited deterministically the agent is compelled and thus unfree, while insofar as the resolution occurs by chance, the agent lacks all control and thus is unfree.

Indeterminism is distinct from determinism, for it satisfies one of our two conditions where determinism satisfies neither; but it is not a suitable model for a free person's power of choice. At best, it may serve as an example suggesting that determinism, though present to a large degree in the universe, need not be regarded as absolutely universal.

C. *Internal Determinism.* A third causal model, which we shall inspect only very briefly, may be suggested by the formulations, often heard in arguments for freedom, that the free agent must be independent of any coercion or compulsion from outside. Kant, at one point, calls freedom the property of a cause "by which it can be effective independently of foreign causes determining it."[15] With determinism, an agent about to act is open potentially to determination by the whole state of the universe or by any part of it. But causes determining a being from within itself are not "foreign causes," and thus seem to escape the charge of determinism. Does it make any difference for the problem of freedom if the causal ancestry of an act lies wholly inside the acting being?

Although many theorists, especially in the field of developmental psychology, employ the metaphor of an entity "unfolding" from within itself in a determinate way without the influence (in some respects at least) of other entities, most of these theories can be reduced without detailed examination to the first model by the observation that human agents, at least, have a beginning in time.[16] If the "unfolding" of their actions is derived, following the third model, from a necessity inherent in them from their beginnings, then insofar as those beginnings themselves are conditioned by other factors, those conditions will also control the later actions of the agents. The only cases in which such "internal determinism" might truly hold as a model distinct from simple determinism would be those in which the agent was originally produced by some random event (in which case, however, the lifelong pattern of action would seem to be due ultimately to chance), or perhaps those in which the agent was in some sense self-caused or uncaused, a prerogative usually reserved to God. Thus for practical purposes in explaining human freedom, internal determinism is of limited applicability.

Aside from this, however, internal determinism fails to meet our first condition, the provision of multiple possibilities. In the third model, succeeding states of a being have only one causal possibility at each moment, and that one is determined by causes inside the being: it is predetermined by a pattern or "program" embedded in the being. The agent is not coerced from outside; but nonetheless, only one course of action is open at any time. One's acts may be ascribed to fate or one's history, but not to choice. In Kant's phrase, such freedom "would in essence be no better than the freedom of a turnspit, which when once wound up also carries out its motions of itself."[17]

We have seen that a suitable causal model must satisfy two criteria if freedom is to be preserved. Of the logically possible caused states, which of the possibilities is realized must depend on the choosing agent; and this requirement may perhaps be said to be satisfied by internal determinism. But in addition, at least two alternative states must be causally possible given the same antecedent state of the choosing agent. This condition is not satisfied by internal determinism. Once again, mixed types of causality will not help: if a partially internally determined agent is also partially influenced by outside causes, or affected by random variations in action, then one merely distinguishes those respects in which the seminal necessity is at work from those in which other factors are controlling, without generating freedom in our sense at any point. Internal determinism may be distinguished from the first two models, for it fulfills the second and not the first criterion, just as determinism fulfilled neither criterion and indeterminism fulfilled only the first. But it does not answer to the concept of freedom in the sense we are investigating.

AGENT CAUSALITY

A number of modern thinkers have directed our attention to a richer notion of the agent as a cause, and have suggested that an agent may be a different kind of cause than an object, exerting a causal power of a kind distinct from that of moving billiard balls or developing plants. John MacMurray, for instance, in the Gifford Lectures of 1953-54, developed a theory in which human beings act to determine events in a way in which they are not themselves determined; from this it follows necessarily, according to Macmurray, that agents must be free.[18] The central notion is that I am able to act to determine future events in more than one way, and, since I am acting and not merely having something happen to me, the event actualized depends not on chance but on my own decision. C. A. Campbell, in a well-known article entitled "Is 'Freewill' A Pseudo-Problem?" and in a number of other essays, suggested that a similar description of free action might enable the defender of freedom, as a *self*-determinist, to escape the charge of *in*determinism.[19] Similarly, J.N. Findlay, in his 1961 book *Values and Intentions*, also proposes a sort of selfdetermination by agents which need not be restricted to a single possibility.[20] Freedom here would be not a violation of causality, as is sometimes suggested by the term "contra-causal freedom," but a species of it, a special sort of causality.[21] Findlay stresses that such a self-determination would account for the familiar phenomenon of moral effort and choice among alternatives *by the power of the agent*. In difficult decisions, he suggests,

> the course chosen or persevered in is in some sense *not* the easiest or most natural continuation of the states it grows out of, ... it is difficult ... as involving the putting forth of an unearmarked power or virtue ... .[22]

In such cases the alternative that occurs depends on the exerting of some effort or power that was within the agent's control, and that the agent might not have put forth, but did. This is why the resulting action depends on that agent. Such a description can then be generalized to apply to free action in cases where there is no severe resistance to be met and overcome, yet the resulting action in fact depends on the agent's putting forth effort, although it is not then felt as difficult.

One of the most fully developed agency theories is that of Richard Taylor. While he claims that his theory of agent causality is open to either deterministic or non-deterministic development,[23] he holds clearly that an agent is a cause, but a cause in a different way from that of other objects. This causation is the expression of a power or efficacy by a subject, and that notion, he states, is a basic notion, not further analyzable.[24] While we cannot here examine this theory in detail, it is clear that the exercise of power by an agent, if it is different from the mere transmission of "power" by a moving billiard ball, must involve a causal chain that in some way starts or originates in the agent, and thus is not wholly conditioned from outside. Yet the agent may exercise this power in various ways, and is thus self-determining.[25]

This very brief look at some ideas of agent causality may serve as a basis for describing this fourth model and its salient features. Let us assume that an agent is in a certain initial state, faced with a choice. Determinism holds that only one outcome is possible, that one which is causally necessitated by the various forces of the universe at the initial time. Indeterminism maintains that several outcomes may occur, but that it is a matter of chance which one comes to pass. Using the model of internal determinism for the agent would involve holding that the result depends entirely or largely upon the agent, but that the agent can in fact act in only one way. But agent causality suggests that the agent may have the power to act in several ways, and that the result will depend on which way one exercises one's power or agency. From the range of logically and causally possible alternatives, it is the agent who determines which one is realized.

Such a description may be clarified by considering our second and third models. With indeterminism, as we saw, several alternatives remain open, even given the same initial state; in agent causality the same multiplicity of possibilities exists, although it is not resolved randomly. With internal determinism, although only one possibility existed, it was a function of the agent's own causal potential, of a cause "within" the agent in at least some sense. In agent causality the agent is seen as having a power--what we have called the "will"--through which the agent determines alternatives, which selects causal possibilities and enacts them or renders them real. In agent causality the decision of the acting person is not itself determined from outside; the person is self-determining.

It might well be objected that such a solution would only push the problem back a step. The determinist might immediately reply: The action is said to be determined by a "decision of the will." What, then, determines that decision? Either it is determined entirely by some previous event, in which case we are left with determinism again; or it is merely a causeless, random event, undermined by previous events, an example of indeterminism. Yet certainly, as already admitted, chance events cannot be attributed to the agent as the one responsible for them; thus the only viable choice is to accept determinism.

But the crucial point to note here is the assumption behind the question: a happening must be either determined by previous events, or produced by mere chance. Only these two possibilities are given, thus apparently trapping the anti-determinist in a dilemma. But the determinist has not proven, only assumed, that there is no third or fourth way out of the dilemma. The distinction of four causal models offered here suggests that other possibilities exist, and that the burden of proof thus shifts to the determinist to argue that agent causality is in some way impossible or unintelligible. In particular, the elucidation of agent causality by reference to the characteristics it has in common with the second and third models (multiple possibilities and determination by the agent, respectively) seems to make clear that it is not an entirely new or indescribable notion, but rather one with certain qualities like those of other sorts of causation which, if not uncontroversial, are commonly accepted as intelligible.

A positive characterization of the power of free choice, or "will," may now be given. A man, let us say, is faced with two or more alternatives, of which only one may be realized. Which one is realized depends entirely on him, insofar as he is free. To determine which will occur, he acts (in the sense of Aristotle's category of action): he puts forth the causal efficacy available to him and makes things happen in one way rather than another. This does not mean he is not subject to influences of various kinds, either external forces or internal motives. Rather, it means that insofar as he is free, those factors leave some room, some open range of possibilities, within which his act alone determines the result. The agent is here a determiner who is not altogether determined until his own action "fixes" the result, and thereby decides and "rounds off" the congeries of competing influences using this executive power.

Given inclinations and possibilities are disorganized; in choosing freely, a person endorses some and gives them high priority, while consigning others to a subordinate place in his life. Thus a person organizes himself, pulls himself together, and becomes a mature person.[26]

If the notion of agent causality seems strange and at times opaque, it is important to see why this is. In seeking an example from which to abstract a causal pattern or model, we tend, particularly in modern philosophy, to turn first to the world of nature, eschewing anthropomorphism: the free agent must act like a billiard ball (idealized) or a tree, or even an electron. But if the proponents of agent causality are correct, it may be that the only models to be found in nonhuman nature are those of the first three types. A fourth model may be discoverable only among human beings. And this is, of course, exactly where we do discover it, at least in our commonplace experience and thinking about choice and responsibility, as many of the thinkers mentioned above have observed. It is in human action that we find exhibited the mystery of a new beginning, an act not entirely fixed by the past, something unknown in the world of nature and peculiarly characteristic of the acting person.[27]

Unless some argument proving universal determinism should be offered, there seems no *a priori* reason to assume that only one type of causality may exist in the universe (whether electrons, for instance actually offer a second type of causation must be decided by the physicists). But if more than one type may exist, then if we are justified in retaining the concept of freedom as we normally consider it, we must conclude that the fourth model may apply to free agents in those respects in which they are free. Anthropomorphism in the study of human beings should be a virtue, not a fault.

It is clear that the model of agent causality is the fourth possibility indicated by our original two criteria. Several alternatives are available to the choosing agent, among which may be virtuous or vicious acts, good or evil ends; all of these may be within the agent's power. But which possible deed becomes actual depends on the agent, not on outside forces or on random selection, or even on the agent's own past states, for those are not completely determinant of the present decision.

We have seen that morality as normally understood requires the notion of responsibility for action, and that this in turn requires some notion of freedom. However, the two criteria set up for models of free causation suggested that four alternatives might exist. In describing them and distinguishing them from each other, it was made clear that the most plausible candidate for a causal explication of freedom is the fourth model, which we may call agent causality, since it is the causal mode of the agent as an agent. We may now make more precise what was said in the first section of this article: the power of free choice, or "will," is whatever enables us to act according to the model of agent causality. The following chapter will distinguish this ability from certain other aspects of the moral agent.

FURTHER ASPECTS OF AGENT CAUSALITY

If we hold that the moral agent can choose freely among alternatives, then of what importance is this to morality? First of all we must recall that the claim for freedom made above is by no means one of absolute freedom or of independence from all constraining conditions. One may retain free choice within a limited range of alternatives even though that range has been restricted very stringently by other factors. If, as often happens, one has no alternatives at all, one still retains the *power* to choose freely, should options again become available. If I fall from a window, for instance, I have little freedom until I reach the ground; but if I survive, I will be able to act freely from then on.

Thus the assertion of freedom in the sense described above does not deny that our responsibility may be limited by factors beyond our control; much less does it discourage attempts to extend the range of that control by liberating the individual from restraining conditions, or by providing enabling conditions for extending the efficacy of one's choices. On the contrary, it makes clear why we are concerned to extend the range of possibilities for human beings and not that of rocks or trees: human beings have the fundamental freedom to make use of such an expanded range, others do not. The causal model to be applied to the acting person is not that of a pure, abstract agent cause, but a "mixed model" in which agent causality is exercised within the limits imposed by deterministic conditions.

This also explains why and when responsibility is limited or reduced. Insofar as one's alternatives are circumscribed, one's freedom is only partial; one can be held responsible for choice within the possibilities, but not for the given possibilities themselves--unless, of course, these can be traced back to prior acts of choice on the agent's part.

There are thus various extended senses of "freedom" which apply to the conditions around us insofar as they obstruct and frustrate, or support and enable, our choices. Social and political institutions may be called free or unfree when they promote or suppress our ability to put free choices into action. Methods of psychological conditioning, such as the operant conditioning used in some psychiatry, are objectionable if they prevent us from exercising our ability to select among possible choices. On the other hand, insofar as they are used to remove psychological traits that obstruct our choices, they serve to make greater freedom possible and thus are praiseworthy. Drug addictions and similar factors may also limit the range within which free choice can be exercised, or perhaps prevent its action altogether.

It should also be noted that freedom as it has been described here does not eliminate the network of urges, inclinations, and motivating forces also active within the agent. Rather, it represents an ability to select among them and thus to avoid merely falling victim to the strongest motive. But these retain their force even if free choice may be exerted against them; the stronger the impelling forces, the harder one must try, the more one must exert oneself to alter the direction of their impulse. Thus some choices require greater "moral effort" than others, and this is taken into account in evaluating responsibility. We may say that an individual could have resisted torture, or overcome a hot temper; but to the extent to which this is difficult to achieve, we ameliorate the stricture. Though the person can be blamed, the blame is reduced. The more powerful the incitements, the more the agent's causal power must be exercised to divert them. That this is not an easy thing to do is part of our ordinary moral experience: some temptations are harder to resist than others.

A related point to be noted is that free choice does not create the alternatives of which it takes advantage, although it may influence them. Our ability to get a purchase in the world is a gift; its extent, given that fundamental ability, depends on the surrounding conditions of life. In this light it may be pointed out that often choice may be a matter of accepting or rejecting an offered possibility, rather than one of comparable or coequal options. For example one may already have a strong inclination to see a movie, to snub an acquaintance, or to take up the study of medicine; one's "decision" to do so may be simply allowing the pre-existing tendency to have its head, permitting the inertia of that tendency to carry one along. Such a "yes or no" choice still fits our general description of agent causality, since it requires at least the possibility of exerting or withholding one's causal power and practical assent, which is still a selection among logical alternatives, a controlling by the agent.

This highlights the fact that the agent is responsible not necessarily for the alternatives presented, but only for the choice among them. We do not create the world in its entirety, as existentialist descriptions sometimes suggest;[28] rather, in large part it is presented to us for rejection or endorsement, for proud denial or loving acceptance, and for acting upon to bring it closer to what we judge it should be. It will thus depend upon our moral judgments which parts of the world we should accept and which parts we should reject. Thus the moral agent may be credited with a certain sort of autonomy and spontaneity, but not the absolute spontaneity of a Kantian self-legislating will or the absolute creation of a Sartrean "for-itself" (*pour soi*).[29] One's executive power may consist in a power to obey or not to obey the law, and thus to affect within the limits of one's powers the course of events; the agent need not at the same time be taken as the legislator. In every human situation freedom is the ability to choose a response to a given situation.

Just as the exercise of free choice proceeds outward to shape the world, but is not omnipotent in it, so choice has effects also within the agent. Each action necessarily affects the developing tendencies and habituations of the one who acts (as will be discussed in the following chapter). Good or bad action not only has effects in the outside world, it also reshapes the fixed aspects of the self well or badly. Such "self-constitution," while not unlimited by any means, is an inherent property of choice; a free choice is no mere abstract volition, but is transitive in its effects both outside and within the person who acts.

It may also be noted that insofar as the alternatives facing me are the same, I can still exercise my option to enact one or the other, but there will be no point in doing so. Agent causality is not primarily a "liberty of indifference" if by that is meant the selection of one among identical alternatives. Such a choice is free, but meaningless, since the same result would occur no matter what the choice (or if we have no way of knowing which result will follow which choice). If I am offered a "choice" between death by poison and death by electrocution, then there is very little reason to choose between them. I can choose, but it is a "choice" only in a degenerate sense; choice is possible, but it is now meaningless or "absurd." Such a situation of absurdity is precisely that described by such writers as Sartre and Camus, where the moral agent has the power to choose but no objective values as reference points to steer by. Our account of freedom, however, does not require that this be the case, for it is perfectly compatible with the existence of objective values, laws, or norms, as long as these do not *compel* (though they may *command*, and even involve sanctions).

The agent cause, then, does not lose freedom by acting according to reasons or motives. Rather, one's freedom consists in the fact that despite the obligatory force of moral reasons, one is able to choose which reasons one will follow or obey, and be judged according to that choice.[30] At the same time, one has by no means produced the obligatory force of the reasons or standards one accepts. It is perfectly possible for the moral law to stand over against us as a demand by another, yet we remain free insofar as we may respond or not respond to that demand. The reasons for choice are not provided by the choice itself; if it is to be intelligent the choice must be made in the light of those reasons, as evaluated by thoughtful consideration (as discussed below). Thus freedom is a necessary, but not a sufficient, condition for responsibility.[31] Freedom is the subject-most pole of the act of choice; but it requires an object or guiding principle if it is to have any importance.

From this it may be seen that freedom is not necessarily good in itself. A free act is not by its freedom alone good or evil; it is the chosen act itself, the content of the choice, which makes it good or evil--whether this is evaluated according to ends, universal laws, virtues, or other principles--as will be discussed below. Freedom is primarily an instrumental good, a power which is good insofar as it allows us to attain something else which is good in itself, and this is why it must guide itself by reference to some independent standard. Thus the goal of some action may itself be freedom, as when I resign from a committee in order to free my time for other possible dispositions. But this is by no means always the case, and in fact such a goal is laudable only insofar as it leads to some further good: if I resigned to enable me to rob banks more often, it would not be a good act. The real goal of our activity is almost

138 Freedom and Moral Choice

never freedom itself. This is a weakness in the Kantian and Sartrean views of freedom, insofar as they suggest freedom as its own standard or its own end.

That claim does not follow from the view of freedom as agent causality which we have adopted here. There is no need to think that the "good will" must be defined by some internal characteristics of its freedom in willing. Yet this does not imply that a good will is controlled by some outside force, for it has chosen its course freely in accord with an external standard.

The will is in control of the steering, but it steers by something external to itself. In fact, "wilfulness," choosing simply in opposition to any external call or demand and with no other end but one's own independence, is a recognized moral vice. Taking one's own willing as an end is pointless, insofar as it seeks no true good, and harmful, insofar as it blinds us to any true goods or reasons for action which may obtain.[32] Feebleness of will is a crucial weakness for the moral agent, but an exclusive preoccupation with willing for its own sake is a distortion of its real role. It is thus misleading to treat self-direction as the sole component of human goodness and autonomous choice as necessarily healthy. For example, Carl Rogers' tendency to assume that therapy need only return one's valuation to a primordial innocence of self-choice, and the tendency of values-clarification treatments at times to speak as if making the individual an autonomous valuer were all that is needed for moral education, both distort the importance of free choice in this way.[33]

It remains true that some choices tend to enable, others to disable, further freedom of choice. This is a factor to be taken into account in making one's decision; a high-school student's decision whether or not to go to college, for instance, should involve a consideration of what further possibilities would be opened up by gaining a degree (or closed off by doing so). But it is not the only such factor, and it is dependent on what further goods aside from freedom itself follow from those possibilities. Thus our theory of agent causality does not prohibit or discourage the making of commitments which limit future choices. Their circumscription of my freedom of action must be weighed against their other advantages, and particularly against the fact that some great goods may be unattainable without such a commitment. To choose any definite act is at the same time to foreclose any alternatives; this is merely the nature of choice, and whether it is a good choice or not will depend on which alternative is preferred. Marriage will remove the possibility of certain actions which I might have taken without it; but it may make possible a stability of interaction and depth of friendship which could not have been achieved without that permanence.

It is clear, therefore, that the well-constituted moral agent needs much besides freedom in order to act well. Without the powers of the body to execute action, for instance, the agent might make virtuous resolves, but could not complete the moral act by carrying them out. Insofar as the body can plausibly be construed as a deterministic system, the perfection of the moral agent requires certain fixed properties of a deterministic sort as well as the unfixedness characteristic of free choice. Similarly, the ability to understand and to integrate the reasons for action described elsewhere in this volume will be required if an act is not to be blind and pointless. Certain relatively fixed qualities of character (discussed in Chapter V below) may be needed as well for the proper enabling, reinforcing, and implementing of free choices, for propagating the particular choices of agent causality, and for making them firm and enduring. Thus the perfection of the agent and, in that sense, of freedom as a human good, is not to be found in agent causality alone. Freedom is *intentional* in the sense that it is directed toward a certain perfection of use; it is there to be actualized into right acts, well-formed character, and sound commitments, not merely to preserve itself as a miser does his gold. So important is this that some would even reserve the name of "*true* freedom" only for the well-formed and freely *determined* self insofar as it has been shaped by the primordial freedom of agent causality (see Chapter XII). The relationship between free agent causality and its extension in determined character, however, will be treated at length in the following chapter.

Though we must not exaggerate freedom as if it were the only good or the only important aspect of the agent, it is also true that we must not attempt to "capture" or delimit it as the exclusive property of any particular view of the good or of goodness itself, as we may be tempted to do in such rhetorical phrases as "*true* freedom." Such rhetoric may serve to point out that some choices enable further freedom, while others narrow one's options and "enslave" one to some form of dominance; thus we might speak loosely of wrongdoing as a mere slavery to one's passions, as does Kant.[34] Nevertheless, we must hold that one who acts wrongly does so freely in the fundamental sense of agent causality, for otherwise one could not be held responsible for one's actions. Both good and evil persons may act freely; if we give to one way of life the honorific "true freedom," it must be in recognition of its agreement with correct standards of action or of its being a precondition for further freedom in other acts. Free agent causality is not itself the standard of choice, for by definition it is the ability to accept or reject other tendencies without predetermination, and so it cannot itself be a tendency toward a specific end.[35] But freedom is neither the only principle within the person, nor the one most apt to set such standards; it finds them in knowledge of and reasoning about the good (see below).

If freedom is not, then, the standard for evaluation of actions, what role does it play in morality? The answer is that it makes the agent responsible for choices. The action could be evaluated on other grounds even if it were not free, as we evaluate the beauty of a landscape or the worth of a keen mind. But we can attribute the act to the agent and thus make its worth moral only insofar as it is under the agent's control. It is by freely choosing the good that the moral agent appropriates it, as it were. It is because the act was performed freely by an agent that we can evaluate the agent on the basis of that action, and so give the evaluation of the act the title "moral" as relating to *mores* or to patterns of human action.

In this sense we can speak of freedom as something essential to being a *person*. A person is a source of actions, a locus of responsibility, a player in the game, not merely a puppet or a pawn. More precisely, a person is someone who has the *capacity* to be such a player, and it is for this reason that "oppression" as the systematic deprivation of the opportunity to exercise freedom is wrong.[36] As far as we know, only human beings on earth possess this sort of capacity, and it is by having it that they qualify as members of a moral community. This fundamental power of freedom is the basis for all other meaningful freedom. Yet by that very token it is in itself only a beginning; the full development of human freedom involves other components as well, which are discussed in the following chapter.

The Catholic University of America
Washington, D.C.

NOTES

1. Joseph M. Boyle, Jr., Germain Grisez, and Olaf Tollefsen, *Free Choice: A Self-Referential Argument* (Notre Dame: University of Notre Dame Press, 1976), pp. 26-30. This book includes an extremely concise and comprehensive discussion of the major arguments for and against the thesis of free choice.

2. Cf. Boyle *et al.*, pp. 10-36.

3. There may be reason to think that the realization of this distinction is itself a developmental achievement; the point is that it is clearly an advance over a view that would assign responsibility to inanimate objects.

4. See Aristotle, *Nicomachean Ethics*, III, 1-5. But "control" involves more than voluntariness alone; it seems to include rational knowledge and not just the immediate perception sufficient for voluntariness according to Aristotle, and it requires that the agent not be internally fixed on a certain path in such a way that all further determinations are specified in advance.

5. See, for example, Austin Fagothey, S.J., *Right and Reason*, 6th edition (St. Louis: C.V. Mosby Co., 1976), pp. 25-31.

6. Our usage of the term "choice" is not identical to that of Aristotle, which refers to any voluntary action after deliberation, but without definitely asserting what we will call agent causality; it is essentially that of Boyle et al.

7. Cf. Boyle et al., pp. 172-74. They do not deal with the argument from obligation in exactly this form; but the principle used on pp. 172--74 to justify acceptance of the experience of freedom as veridical should apply to the experience of obligation as well.

8. See Boyle et al., especially pp. 162-68, 171-77.

9. Cf. Noam Chomsky, "A Naturalistic Approach to Language and Cognition," *Cognition and Brain Theory,* 4 (Winter 1981), 14: "It seems to me that the power of willing and the sentiment of this power lie as far beyond the scope of inquiry today as they always have been in the past."

10. The description of the four models here is based upon the more complete investigation carried out in another connection in Frederick Edward Ellrod III, *Four Models of Causality: A Study of Freedom, Agency and Causation in Kant* (Ann Arbor: University Microfilms International, 1979), a Ph.D. dissertation submitted to Boston University in 1979.

11. Pierre Laplace, quoted in Ernest Nagel, *The Structure of Science* (New York: Harcourt, Brace, World, Inc., 1961), p. 281, note.

12. Aristotle, *Physics*, 196b33-38, 197a2-3. Cf. also *Metaphysics* 1025a14.

13. Lucretius, *De Natura Rerum*, in Gordon H. Clark, ed., *Selections from Hellenistic Philosophy* (New York: Meredith Publishing Co., Appleton-Century-Crofts, 1940), Book II, 216- 60, 284-93 (pp. 15, 17).

14. Cf. Nagel, pp. 333-34, 326, 344.

15. Immanuel Kant, *Foundations of the Metaphysics of Morals*, trans. by Lewis White Beck (Library of Liberal Arts; Indianapolis: Bobbs-Merrill Co., Inc., 1959), pp. 445-46.

16. If the notion of causal dependence were developed without reference to temporal sequence, then this observation would refer to the condition of such dependence alone, or "causal ancestry."

17. Immanuel Kant, *Critique of Practical Reason*, trans. by Lewis White Beck (Library of Liberal Arts; Indianapolis: Bobbs-Merrill Co., Inc., 1956), p. 97.

18. John Macmurray, *The Self as Agent* (London: Faber and Faber Limited, 1957), p. 134.

19. C.A. Campbell, "Is 'Freewill' A Pseudo-Problem?", *Mind* 60 (October 1951), 441-65; see also his *In Defence of Free Will, with Other Philosophical Essays* (Muirhead Library of Philosophy; London: George Allen and Unwin Ltd., 1967; New York: Humanities Press, Inc., 1967), and *On Selfhood and Godhood* (Muirhead Library of Philosophy; London: George Allen and Unwin Ltd., 1957; New York: The Macmillan Company, 1957).

20. J.N. Findlay, *Values and Intentions* (Muirhead Library of Philosophy; London: George Allen and Unwin Ltd., 1961; New York: Humanities Press, Inc., 1961), p. 192.

21. Findlay, p. 200.

22. Findlay, p. 197.

23. Richard Taylor, *Action and Purpose* (Englewood Cliffs, N.J.: Prentice-Hall, Inc., 1966), pp. 114-15, 127, 140, 198, 200, 263. It may be argued, however, that a deterministic development would in fact eliminate the characteristic features of agent causality.

24. Taylor, pp. 13-14, 59, 111, 154; pp. 8, 16, 39, 99, 216.

25. Taylor, pp. 53-55, 183.

26. Boyle et al., p. 83. See also pp. 81-85. A detailed analysis of the ontological conditions of such freedom, generally compatible with the account given here, is to be found in Edward Pols, *The Acts of Our Being: A Reflection on Agency and Responsibility* (Amherst, Mass.: Univ. of Mass. Press, 1982), and "The Conditions of Ontic Responsibility," *Review of Metaphysics* 35 (December 1981), 297-319; note especially p. 312.

27. On this point cf. Hannah Arendt, *The Human Condition* (Chicago: University of Chicago Press, 1958), sec. 24, 26, 34.

28. Cf. Jean-Paul Sartre, "Existentialism is a Humanism," in Robert C. Solomon, ed., *Existentialism* (New York: Modern Library, 1974), pp. 200-202.

29. Cf. Kant, *Foundations of the Metaphysics of Morals*, pp. 431-33, 440-41, 446-47.

30. Cf. Thomas Aquinas, *Summa Theologica*, trans. Fathers of the English Dominican Province, 3 vols. (New York: Benziger Bros., 1947-- 48), I-II, q. 19, a. 3: "the goodness of the will depends on its being subject to reason." Cf. also Fagothey, 137. Agent causality may thus be taken as a more precise analysis of at least part of what is meant in cognitive-analytic theories of moral education by KRAT, particularly KRAT(2). See the opening chapter of this volume for a description of this component.

31. Cf. Aristotle's requirement of both initiative and knowledge for voluntary action (*Nicomachean Ethics*, III, 1), and Pols's reference to "*rational* agency" (italics added), p. 297.

32. ". . . in moral matters the end is of greater importance than the active principle." Aquinas, II-II, q. 98, a. 1, ad 2.

33. Cf. Carl R. Rogers, "Toward a Modern Approach to Values: the Valuing Process in the Mature Person," in Carl R. Rogers and Barry Stevens, ed., *Person to Person* (New York: Pocket Books, 1967), pp. 7-8, 15, 18; Philip H. Phenix, "The Moral Imperative in Contemporary American Education," in Simon and Kirschenbaum, eds., *Readings in Values Clarification*, pp. 40-41.

34. Cf. Josef Pieper, *About Love*, trans. Richard and Clara Winston (Chicago: Franciscan Herald Press, 1974), p. 20.

36. Cf. Pieper, p. 21. It may be noted, for the sake of strict accuracy, that the *power* of free choice seems itself to be an innate characteristic of the person; every person has it as long as one remains that person, and in fact free choice is part of what defines personhood (as will be discussed in a later article). It is the *exercise* of that power, the action, which is not predetermined except by the agent's own choice.

CHAPTER VI

MORAL CHARACTER

WALTER NICGORSKI AND FREDERICK E. ELLROD III

It follows then, Glaucon, ... that education in music and the fine arts is most potent, because by this chiefly rhythm and harmony sink into the inmost part of the soul and fasten most firmly upon it, bringing gracefulness and making it graceful if one is well trained, but otherwise just the opposite; and again, because if any things are defective or badly made or badly grown, one trained as he should be in that way would perceive it at once and would be pleased or pained with true taste. He would praise the beautiful things, and eagerly receive them into his soul, and feed on them, and become himself beautiful and good; but the ugly things he would blame with true taste, while still too young to have reason by which to understand about them, and when reason came to him he would gladly welcome her as a friend whom he recognized by a sense of affinity. Don't you think so? (Plato, *Republic*[1])

INTRODUCTION

The introductory papers by Ellrod and Mann in this volume described the traditional concern with character in moral education, and the reaction, supported by Hartshorne and May's study in the thirties, which has tended to remove this aspect of the human agent from the center of interest. We wish now to examine in more detail the contemporary critique of the notion of character development as a part of moral development, focusing primarily on Lawrence Kohlberg as the most vocal critic. In addition we shall outline what seems to be the proper place of character in an integrated theory of moral growth, particularly in relation to the free choice attributed to the agent in the preceding chapter.

To do this effectively we must define briefly the terms we will use to refer to different aspects of the human agent. The power of free choice, or "agent causality," described in the last paper is that in us which enables us to select among alternatives, including the alternatives of accepting or rejecting some impulse or tendency, when no pre-existing factor either within or outside us is sufficient to necessitate our action. This power of free choice is probably related to the "ego-strength" of modern psychology and is assumed by the virtues of self, such as willing, discussed in *Psychological Foundations of Moral Education*, the next volume in this series. "Character," as we will use the term here, is that in us which patterns our actions in a relatively fixed way. It is made up of dispositions or "habits" which can be changed, but which, while they last, cause us to tend toward certain goals or to act in certain ways. A third factor may be distinguished: that in us which is fixed permanently and is normally unchangeable by our own actions, such as a resting metabolic level, perhaps, or "native intelligence." Whatever there is of the innate and unalterable in us we may call "temperament." Character and temperament, then, both differ from agent causality in being determined toward certain ends in advance; but character can be restructured, while temperament cannot.

THE IMPACT OF HARTSHORNE AND MAY

Kohlberg has generally stood by his 1969 observation that "no findings have been reported suggesting fundamental revisions of Hartshorne and May's (1928-30) conclusions as to the situational specificity and longitudinal instability of moral character . . . ."[2] The Hartshorne and May study looked at character traits of honesty, service and self-control which had been established through traditional modes of moral education, namely, example, exhortation and opportunities for practice such as those emphasized in the Boy Scouts. The significant conclusions regarding the situational specificity and longitudinal instability of moral character are explained by Kohlberg as follows:

> If a person cheats in one situation, it does not mean he will or will not in another. . . . In other words, it is not a character trait of dishonesty which makes a child cheat in a given situation.
>
> People's verbal moral values about honesty have nothing to do with how they act. People who cheat express as much or more moral disapproval of cheating as those who don't cheat. More recently than Hartshorne and May psychologists have studied moral character using psychoanalytically inspired words like "resistance to temptation," "conscience strength," "superego strength," and "moral internalization." However, they have essentially used Hartshorne and May's tests and obtain [sic] similar results of situational specificity.[3]

This report of Kohlberg suggests that such notions of "character," "conscience strength" and "moral internalization" in the literature are rather shallow. Even so, some low correlations were found by Hartshorne and May between cheating in different situations. Kohlberg explains that "these correlations are largely due to non-moral 'ego strength' factors of IQ and attention, and the correlations between cheating tests disappear when these ego factors are controlled (Grim et al., 1968)."[4] Thus for Kohlberg, character, identified by certain habits and an accompanying verbal profession of appropriate values, is not a reliable predictor of action or behavior in accord with those values. The way is then open for Kohlberg's emphasis on the cognitive development of values or moral judgment and appropriate modes of stimulating it. Habit training in the ways of virtue is displaced, except possibly for its bearing on the category of "ego strength" which is said in some, not very significant, way to bear on moral action or behavior.[5]

In rejecting character development as a significant part of moral development Kohlberg sees himself as rejecting the dominant American approach to moral education. In Kohlberg's less than respectful description, this is termed the "bag of virtues" approach; it is the popular American version of the cultural transmission theory of moral education, which has been called the "traditional" approach earlier in these essays. "Deweyite thinking," writes Kohlberg, "has lent itself to the Boy Scout approach to moral education which has dominated American practices in this field and which has its most direct affinities with Aristotle's views."[6] This "common sense" approach to moral education that is explicitly defended in the *Nicomachean Ethics* is, in Kohlberg's analysis, at least partly and wrongly accepted by Dewey. Kohlberg specifically objects to Aristotle's paradoxical statement that one comes to possess moral virtue by practicing moral virtue.[7] It seems that it is Dewey's openness to society-induced habituation as playing an explicit role in the interaction between the "fixed" and "dynamic" selves which provides what basis there is in Dewey for the traditional approach and the source of Kohlberg's difficulties with Dewey.[8]

THE ARGUMENT WITH ARISTOTLE

Kohlberg identifies what he regards as the critical error in Aristotle as the distinguishing of the intellectual and moral spheres.[9] Dewey, on the other hand, is said to involve the intellect more centrally in moral development. This is evident in the first and third of three assumptions of Dewey which the Deweyites in progressive education have often ignored:

> (1) that intelligent thought about the education of social traits and values [sic] required a philosophic concept of morality and moral development which is a very different concept from "social adjustment" or "mental health";
>
> (2) that moral development passed through invariant qualitative stages; and
>
> (3) that the stimulation of moral development, like other forms of development, rested on the stimulation of thinking and problem-solving by the child.[10]

Aristotle's alleged separation of the moral from the intellectual is said, however, to have prevailed so that "American educational psychology, like Aristotle, divides the personality up into cognitive abilities, passions or motives and traits of character."[11]

Aristotle's error is seen as critical because by allegedly supposing that virtue is simply gained by practicing virtue it opens the door for a variety of forms of attempting to induce moral practices or virtues free from any real intellectual or cognitive engagement. Aristotle's approach, the cultural transmission theory, the traditional American way, and the behavior modification movement are all one in Kohlberg's eyes in ignoring or diminishing the role of intellect in moral development. In his important article with Rochelle Mayer on "Development as the Aim of Education" Kohlberg describes traditional educators, including the academic humanistic tradition of Western education, as understanding the "educator's job" to be "direct instruction" that results in "transmitting knowledge, skills, and social and moral rules of the culture."[12] The approach of behavior modification is thereafter presented as one variant of the cultural transmission view. All these approaches are seen to be doomed to failure as modes of moral education. Insofar as they succeed, they are dangerous and unsatisfying, for they "rest on the value premise of social relativism--the doctrine that values are relative to, and based upon, the standards of the particular culture and cannot be questioned or further justified."[13] In Kohlberg's more colorful way of stating the point, whose "bag of virtues" is to be passed on, isn't each society arbitrarily filling it? Rather, the aims of education must be defined by "rational ethical principles" or "ethical universals" and not by "the values of parent or culture."[14]

The authors are not alone in believing that Kohlberg has inadequately understood Aristotle.[15] Furthermore, one suspects that he reduces some rather sophisticated and rational approaches to moral education along with Aristotle to species of cultural transmission, associates them with the patent defects of Skinnerian behavior-modification, and dismisses them from consideration. Even in the American tradition, one suspects that a rather uncritical lumping or mixing has gone into what he refers to as the "bag of virtues." It is to be especially regretted that by such blanket dismissals he has cut himself off from sources that his theory of moral development could use to build a more complete view of moral development around the cognitive core which he stresses. Here it is possible and perhaps sufficient to emphasize Kohlberg's misunderstanding of Aristotle.

It is wrong to read the cognitive or intellectual element out of Aristotle's understanding of moral virtue. His distinction between the moral and intellectual virtues does not entail the view that moral virtue is devoid of a significant intellectual dimension. When he introduces the distinction at the end of Book I of the *Nicomachean Ethics*, moral virtue is seen to consist in an irrational element of the soul sharing in a rational principle.[16] Later in the *Ethics* Aristotle makes clear that choice, which involves "deliberation" or reasoning, is integral to virtue. When writing in Book VI of "virtues" or natural dispositions to such qualities as self-control or courage, he says:

> For both children and brutes have the natural disposition to these qualities, but without reason these are evidently hurtful. Only we seem to see this much, that, while one may be

led astray by them, as a strong body which moves without sight may stumble badly because of its lack of sight, still, if a man once acquires reason, that makes a difference in action; and his state, while still like what it was, will *then be virtue in the strict sense.*[17]

Natural dispositions or a blind habituation induced by traditional methods or behavior modification do not constitute virtue in the strict sense. Virtue proper, for Aristotle, must be chosen. But such chosen virtue will necessarily involve practice and habituation if it is to be virtue in the strict sense, that is, a characteristic excellence of the soul rather than a single good act.

It appears that Kohlberg's procedure is not that of having worked through Aristotle's writings and concluding that he is wrong; his procedure is more experiential and inductive with respect to the tradition Aristotle is thought to lead. It is a case of Kohlberg's finding the common practices of moral education deficient, of being impressed with the evidence for their deficiency, especially Hartshorne and May's study, and of seeing Aristotle, perhaps because he is cited at times by common practitioners, as the head of this long tradition of "misdirected" effort. Both the ground of popular morality and its mode of perpetuation or socialization are deficient for Kohlberg. Its assumption "that any adult of middle-class respectability or virtue knows what virtue is and is qualified to teach it by dint of being adult and respectable"[18] is uncongenial to Kohlberg's Socratic thrust noted above.[19] Further, his incorrect interpretation of Aristotle seems to grow out of a somewhat understandable reaction to a certain way of teaching popular morality. Paul J. Philibert puts this concern very well:

> Possibly Kohlberg is correct in interpreting most actual experiences of the discourse of virtue in the classroom as morally crippling. In our present categories, what he speaks of would be the imposition of arbitrarily chosen exterior acts upon students in the name of virtue. Such procedure is indeed morally crippling, for it does not engage the moral awareness which is the source of authentic ethical understanding. But despite its being named "virtue," the "bag of virtues" had virtually nothing in common with the classical tradition of the discourse of virtue.[20]

THE ROLE OF HABIT

The important consideration finally is not primarily whether an overreaction to common practices and to Hartshorne and May's study led to misinterpreting Aristotle, but whether this overreaction leads Kohlberg to neglect the habitual while emphasizing the cognitive in moral education. One is hard pressed to find any use of the word "habit" or "habitual" in his constructive work. He has argued that habit training is not directly relevant to moral action or behavior, and that there is no positive relationship but, in fact, some negative relationship between childhood habit training and the development of moral judgment. Alston correctly concludes that Kohlberg "feels such concepts have no place in moral psychology."[21] He goes on to argue that this is to overgeneralize the Hartshorne and May results from applicability to some habits to the entire habit-category, and that Kohlberg's overall theory cannot withstand the consequent loss of the entire category.

The role of habit seems ineluctable in human development and, though neglected, appears to some degree under another guise in Kohlberg's theory of moral development. There are, first of all, the patterns of reasoning at the various stages of moral development, which appear to be mental habits.[22] In addition and seemingly more significant in the long run is the indication that behavior induced by reward and punishment or by example is welcomed by Kohlberg as socially necessary with respect to people at certain stages of development. He accepts the relevance of stimulus-response patterns to human development, but draws attention to the cognitive processes as critical in the mediation of such events (stimulus, mediation or cognitive processing of the stimulus in the framework of the stage of moral reasoning, human response following moral judgment).[23] Understanding of those cognitive processes is necessary not only to immediately effective "habit" training strategies but also and above all to strategies of training that are consistent with development to the highest moral stages.   Three openings in Kohlberg's work are, therefore, apparent as possible points of reconciliation and integration with the tradition of character training in moral education. They point to the need to explore: (1) habits as developers of "ego strength," (2) mental habits as involved in cognitive stages, and (3) cognitive factors implied in the operation of a habit and the process of coming to possess habits of different kinds. These openings to some integration of his work with the notion of habit training are not utilized or even mentioned by Kohlberg. Alston writes discerningly about the difficulty of dispensing with habit in a theory of moral development.

> ... if we knew enough about the deeper sources--cognitive, emotional, etc.--on which situation-response regularities depend, we would probably not need to conceptualize the person, even partly, in habit terms. But until that millenium arrives, talking about one's capacities and proclivities for moral reasoning will not do the whole job.[24]

Habits might, of course, work with or against cognitive moral development; assuming them to be part of being human, they must be utilized positively in moral development. In a full theory of personal development, it is likely that habits operate prior to, during, and after any particular set of cognitive operations, at whatever level. Moral action or behavior will be aided or retarded by habits no matter what the level of moral judgment. Much attention in theories of traditional socialization has been paid to habit training as a preparation and aid for the rational moral life. This was Plato's concern in wanting the soul disposed to welcome reason "as a friend." Peters has highlighted this issue with respect to Aristotle and Kohlberg. It is the key point for the reconciliation of socialization and autonomy (as will be developed in Chapter X below).

> Kohlberg, like Plato, emphasizes that the most important features of moral education are cognitive. The individual has to come to the grasp of principles and to connect particular rules like that of honesty with these instead of with extrinsic reinforcements such as praise and blame, reward and punishment. A grasp of principles, he maintains, cannot be directly taught; it can only develop with appropriate environmental stimulation, like the grasp of the causal principle or of the conservation of material things. This confirms Aristotle's point that children cannot, in the early stages of their lives, behave like the just man. . . .
>
> What, then, is to be said about early moral education? Must children first of all become habituated to following certain rules, as Aristotle suggested, and can we conceive of a form of behavior which is learned in this way, developing into the rational form of behavior of Aristotle's just man or into Kohlberg's principled type of morality?[25]

Thus there is no reason to think that the entire category of character or "habit" should be eliminated from consideration in moral education. The experimental evidence in hand, to be discussed in more detail in the *The Psychological Foundations of Moral Education*, the second volume of this project, shows clearly that character (relatively fixed dispositions and patterns of action) is related to moral action. Some studies specifically point to the limitations of the concepts and methods of Hartshorne and May's studies and defend the common-sense awareness that some people are more dependable in moral respects than others.[26] Kohlberg's tendency to object to searching for the basis of such dependability in any place other than cognitive structures seems, on examination, to be based on little more than a hasty generalization from Hartshorne and May's studies, coupled with a dislike of any method which to him smacks of indoctrination or authoritarianism. Furthermore, Kohlberg's own work seems to call for an elucidation of the concept of character in several respects.

We must therefore undertake a positive consideration of moral character to see whether that notion can be developed in such a way as to be fitted fruitfully into an adequate conception of the moral agent. What sort of notion of "character" might be worth reintroducing? How would such a notion be made compatible with a commitment to moral autonomy, and with the notion of free choice described in the preceding paper?

CHARACTER AND FREEDOM

The notion of freedom of choice described in Chapter IV above may seem at first glance to be directly opposed to any assertion of fixed character or personality in the agent, or even to action based on reason or consciousness of moral norms. After all, a free action is by definition not determined by previous factors, whether rational or irrational, inside or outside the agent. Does this mean that it must be a pure, absolutely unconditioned choice, as described by Sartre and some other existentialist theorists of freedom? Is this the only sort of behavior which would be autonomous and responsible?

We have seen that "mixed" models may also be considered: that is, causes which are, for instance, confined by determinism to a narrow range of possibilities, but free to choose within that range. Further, no restrictions have been placed on the factors on which a free agent may base a decision, as long as they do not *determine* the decision, that is, compel the agent to choose one or the other alternative. It is essential here to remember that the "agent cause" in question is not an event, but a person, an individual who possesses knowledge as well as will. If one is aware of various reasons for action, moral or otherwise, one is free to act in accordance with them or against them. This means that reasons of various sorts are presented to the agent to be taken into account, with their various sorts of demands or obligations; but the agent is free to attend to or disregard them. This is, in fact, moral choice as commonly understood: the decision is before us, with the different factors on either side, but it is we who must decide which factors will move us to act.

Free choice, then, is not incompatible with choice according to reasons or motives, including those generated by moral reasoning, as long as these do not condition it absolutely. It may be appropriate here to note one consequence of this fact for moral education: a program of moral education cannot be expected to be "effective" in the sense of infallibly turning out virtuous people or good moral agents. One may make as convincing a case as possible for right and justice, but the presentation of this case does not make it necessarily true that the agent will choose in accordance with it. The "force" of the right information and best reasons is such as to call for or encourage right choice, but a person who chooses to rebel or to disregard those reasons is free to do so. Even Kohlberg with his emphasis on the critical role of judgment in moral development has noted that it is a necessary but not sufficient condition for right moral behavior. Thus even the best moral education system could not guarantee that its alumni would be good men and women, only that they could be. To insist on achieving absolute and unfailing results, if that is what is meant by "character education," would lead only to attempts to suppress altogether what we have argued to be the centrally moral nature of the agent, to render one a mere automaton.

Does this compel us to admit that moral education may not act to form character or to develop good "moral habits"? We shall see that this, too, is only an apparent paradox. Moral education as character development is not only compatible with, but closely related to, the notion of a free and rational agent cause.

In the first place, the possibility of a mixed causal model for the human person means that both will and character may be at work without contradiction. As mentioned above, it is possible that certain aspects of the agent are in fact determined by causes, either outside the self or stemming from earlier states of the self. Thus a genetic predisposition to a quick temper might exist prior to all choice; strict punishment and control in early childhood might produce a strong tendency to suppress this anger, acting in the person independent of choice; and given this matrix of traits, a given situation, perhaps reminiscent of some traumatic past event, might "touch off" a reaction which occurs automatically, without possibility of control by the agent's free decision. These are precisely those respects in which the agent is generally excused from responsibility, treated as helpless to act otherwise and perhaps, in extreme cases, as "mentally ill," rather than as a moral agent.

But it is quite possible for a person to be conditioned in many ways, and yet exercise agent causality in other ways, as long as the aforementioned determinism is not considered to include the whole person. If some of my responses and tendencies are beyond my control, but others are open to my decision and command, then I am free and responsible insofar as the latter is true.

Free choice does not mean, then, that the agent is absolutely unconditioned, or that character and history can have no influence whatever on one's actions. Many conditions of the acts decided on may have been preset by deterministic causes or even by random factors, as discussed in the preceding chapter. Clearly, for instance, the actions physically possible in a given situation will generally be delimited by constraints other than the agent's choice. One may not have chosen which alternatives are now presented for selection. Given the alternatives, it may be that in some cases established tendencies strongly incline one toward, or even require, a particular course of action. In the former case we say one is "strongly tempted"; in the latter, "not responsible" or "temporarily insane." What is necessary to call the person a free agent is only that at least some choices be left open for the agent to decide; if all logical possibilities were available at all times, action would be difficult if not impossible. One is, then, free only with respect to those choices left open.

RESPONSIBILITY AND CHARACTER

The interaction of past character and present choice accounts effectively for many aspects of normal moral growth. Inherited and unalterable factors, such as hormonal balance, which we have above called "temperament," are usually considered out of the agent's control; thus the person is not responsible for them but is "just naturally that kind of person." One can hold the agent responsible only to the extent to

152 Moral Character

which such a built-in tendency could be controlled in practice. Thus, a naturally irritable person might be expected to restrain the expression of the chronic irritation.

On the other hand, "character" usually refers to facets of the person due not to nature, but to nurture: tendencies or reactions built up over the course of the person's life, either through one's own action or through the actions of others. It seems appropriate to gather such tendencies under the name of "habits" or "dispositions," as did Aristotle.[27] For much of this side of the person seems to be built up by practice, by repeated exercise of a power in certain ways until it becomes "second nature" to use it in that fashion.

By "habit" we mean only a tendency in the person which causes one to act or to react in certain relatively consistent and fixed ways, without the connotation of routine or unintelligent activity which characterizes the English term. One could speak, for instance, of a skill such as driving, tennis-playing, or speaking truthfully as a "habit" in this sense, although each involves considerable flexibility in exercising one's abilities appropriately in different situations, including the employment of theoretical knowledge and practical judgment. One skilled in driving, for example, knows how to handle a car in normal weather, in rain, or in snow, the disposition giving rise to a related but different set of actions in each case. The tennis player, similarly, must be able to respond suitably to any number of possible situations; and the truthful person must speak the truth appropriately in different situations, as honesty, tact, and courtesy advise. Even habits of action, then, are anything but blind impulses. It is in this sense that we spoke of Kohlberg's stages of moral reasoning as themselves habits, patterns of reasoning to the use of which the agent is accustomed. Such a relatively fixed pattern of response may clearly be reasonable and may be consciously accepted or established, a "discipline" or skill rather than a mere conditioned reflex.[28]

The exact process by which habits or character traits are formed is a subject for more detailed investigation in a later part of this project. For the moment it suffices to recall that there may be at least three possible segments of the personality: that which is simply given at birth and unalterable (temperament); that which is acquired and, once acquired, relatively fixed and persistent (character); and the power to act freely and to alter that character in ways not entirely fixed by any background, innate or acquired (the agent causality of free will). Since we have summarized the person's agent causality as "the will," we may assume that the traits and tendencies summarized as character and temperament, taken alone and in themselves, are related to actions deterministically (perhaps with some admixture of randomness or indeterminism). It is not necessary for us at this point to determine whether all characteristics of the person are due to heredity or to environment, or to a combination of the two. In order to consider all possibilities, and because it seems more likely in fact, we will operate on the assumption that people have both inherited and acquired traits, that both character and temperament exist.[29]

Now if temperament is generally considered unalterable in a person, character is generally taken to be changeable: acquired characteristics may be erased in the same way as they were built up. It may be that certain tendencies are merely buried or "overwritten" by attempts at suppression, not erased, and remain within the person in some sense, able to influence later action and experience. This is the essential nature of the *unconscious* as introduced by Freud and his successors. But others clearly can be changed by later action: one "breaks the habit" of smoking, improves one's golf game by reforming a tendency to hook, or accustoms oneself to greater tolerance of a loved one's foibles. The detailed account of which traits fall into which categories we leave to later psychological examination.

Here it is necessary only to point out that I am held responsible only for those results which are within my power to achieve. If my bad habit is one that could be, or could have been, overcome by my own efforts, directed by my free choice, then I can be taken to task for it. If not, it is merely an unfortunate disability, a misfortune rather than a fault. Thus a person may be held responsible for character traits exactly insofar as they fall, now or in the past, within one's own control. Moreover, we give consideration in such judgments to how much they are under one's control, in the sense of how much effort would be needed to overcome them. If a habit is breakable at all, it is under the control of my will; but if it is so strong that I would have to exert enormous moral effort to break it, my responsibility is diminished, and I am held "hardly to blame" or less culpable because of the difficulty of the task.[30]

It may be noted parenthetically here that this point also has implications for moral education. If the choice exercised by the will is not simply an on-and-off proposition, but admits of degrees of effort and difficulty, then it makes sense to speak of training in making choices, training of the will. Such training might be by "exercise," by actually making such decisions, as one trains or conditions one's muscles by using them in appropriate ways. But it is important to note that such training would not be in using the will in *particular* ways, for that would merely build up habituation (which, as we will see below, can substitute for direct free choice); rather, training in "will power" itself would consist in exercises designed to build up a general self-command or self-control and an ability to exert moral effort, if necessary, against external influences or even against one's own impulses and developed habits.[31] Such a program of development would look much like the systematic exercises of self-denial emphasized in some character education programs and particularly in religious moral education, where one is asked to "give up" certain pleasures or undergo certain hardships as part of one's moral or spiritual development. It would go a long way toward clarifying this practice if it were made clear that what is at issue is not the specific pleasure or hardship; the ascetic who fasts is not denying the goodness of food. It is, rather, the denial itself which is important, the fact that one is strengthening one's capacity in general to make free decisions by testing it against counter-inclinations.

In any case, it is evident that free will and fixed character can coexist in a person, and that they can interact at least insofar as choice may be called upon to modify the expression of established habits, to override their action-directing tendencies in certain cases, or even to change the habits themselves and alter one's own character. Similarly, the fixity of character is compatible with and even necessary for cognitive capabilities. Traits of character may beneficially "fix" cognitive patterns, so that one may develop habits of thinking clearly about situations, listening open-mindedly, or searching for relevant information.[32] But in fact the relation of choice and character is still closer than this.

While responsibility for action must rest ultimately upon a free decision to carry out that action rather than some other, a certain communication or contagion of responsibility is forwarded from such a decision along a causal chain. For example, if an assassin substitutes a package of poison for one of sugar, causing a servant unknowingly to serve an eminent person a poisoned drink, it is clear that the assassin is the one responsible for the death, not the servant, or the victim, who took the drink willingly. Even though the assassin's immediate action of switching one package for another was itself innocuous, the effects of that action, insofar as they are foreseen and intended, are also attributed to the agent who caused them "at a distance."[33] Thus an individual may become responsible for things which happen as a remote consequence of free choices, as well as for these choices themselves.

Now we have suggested above that free choices may build up habits, or remove or modify those already in place in the personality. If this is true, then the agent becomes responsible for the long-range results of this habituation insofar as one is aware of and intends them, even if we suppose that those results are such as to compel the person absolutely at a later time. For example, if I now allow myself to build up the tendency to snap harshly at interruptions and resent interference, then a time might come when it would become extremely difficult, or even impossible, for me to overcome that tendency and avoid harmful and impolite actions. Yet it would be my own fault that I had come to be in that state; thus I could rightly be held to account for my own character and the actions that flow from it. As we hold someone responsible for actions committed while intoxicated when the state of intoxication is deliberately entered, we may hold someone responsible for character traits which were freely developed. The same obtains for negligence in failing to free oneself from character traits which may have arisen from outside causes, but might have been removed if effort had been exerted.

Thus the fixity of character is often not a factor diminishing responsibility, self-directedness and autonomy, but rather a repository of the effects of past responsible actions and thus a factor in "carrying forward" responsibility and forethought to future acts. The person's character, insofar as it has been formed by one's own choices, or tacitly approved by inaction to change it, may be considered the instrument of the will. A long-practiced habit of politeness may save me from discourtesy, for instance, even when I am tired and virtually unable to make new moral efforts. I may legitimately be given moral credit for this "merely automatic and mechanical" response, because I was the one who, with prudent foresight, ingrained it in myself in the first place. Character, acting with a sort of "delegated authority" from the seat of free choice, may in fact be the normal immediate source of action in the person, yet without depriving one of moral credit or discredit for such acts. For even if the immediate cause of action is in fact deterministic, that "mechanism" of decision itself has been formed and arranged by agent causality. Character, when self-formed, is a solidification, as it were, of freedom, not its opposite.[34]

Thus we may consistently say, for instance, that a person makes most everyday decisions without going through the existential agonies of ultimate decision, because the personality which the person has developed freely makes these as a matter of routine. Yet this is not "inauthentic" or merely "conventional"; the person is still basically free and responsible for these actions. Further, we may wish to stress the fact that since free choice in the face of counter-inclinations may be exceedingly difficult and require heroic moral effort, it may be important for people to develop a strong fixed character as a support or instrumentality for the will itself in cases of temptation. The direction of the "drift" of one's established habits is a part of the deterministic causal framework within which agent causality must exert its effortful choice. A person can choose the right far less painfully and perilously if character has already, by its initial resistance to the suggestion of wrong action, sapped the strength of the temptation, which might otherwise be far harder to resist. One cannot be constantly making radically free decisions; neither personal life nor social affairs could be carried on without some stability as well as responsibility.[35]

Indeed, it might even be said with some justice that the fully human act must be rooted in a well-established character, and that the purpose of freedom is to transmute itself into intelligently formed dispositions for which the agent is responsible. A character so thoroughly formed as to ensure that the person would do only right actions (if there could be such a thing) would not be unfree in every sense. It would lack what we have called agent causality but, as a "representative" of the free choice by which it was formed or approved, it would carry forward that freedom to determine future choices. The fulfillment of free choice would thus be to solidify the character. Indeed, the most significant choices at any given point must be built upon a certain character, for the alternatives open even to agent causation are determined in part by one's prior character. Thus good character both enables and perpetuates freedom, although it is not in its own mode of action free in the same sense as agent causality.[36]

One final point should be noted. While we have just stressed the self-formation of one's own character, it is of course true that socialization also plays a major role in the formation of habits or dispositions. Nor is this trivial; the "self-forming" of character is in fact largely a ratification and adjustment of the results of one's early social upbringing, which occurred before one could critically examine it. This point will be further discussed in Chapter X on the social dimension of moral development. We may note, however, that the relation between freedom, habit, and action explains why moral education must involve both (a) the formation of the best habits we know how to instill, beginning before the time at which children can possibly make intelligent free choices to form themselves, and (b) training so that as soon as possible children will become able to make their own decisions, even to the point of revising those habits if need be. We should provide the best basis we can, yet also make possible the amendment of that basis by the autonomous moral agent into which the child will grow.

Character training is a gift from society, and one seemingly necessary for the full development of the agent. The social heritage of character must be personally appropriated by the individual if it is to enable rather than inhibit autonomy, for ingrained habits which were never accepted even tacitly would lie outside the agent's field of responsibility. But that heritage is not merely a dispensable luxury, for if agents were to grow up without at least some degree of social aid in character formation, it is unlikely that they could ever fully make up for that deficiency, being handicapped by a set of character traits formed by the inevitable random childhood influences. The cultivation of a reasonably well-formed character before this can be consciously controlled by the subject is a prerequisite for effective, conscious reshaping of that character in later years.

CONCLUSION

The interaction of will and character as we have described it suggests that a well-rounded program of moral education may require several sorts of training against what Aristotle terms "moral weakness," *akrasia.* This problem is left aside almost entirely, as we have seen, in both values-clarification and cognitive-developmental approaches to moral growth, although, as noted in Jesse Mann's essay earlier, such training received a strong endorsement in William James's classic chapter on habits. Guidance in habits of good conduct may be expected to form a reasonable part of such training. The fact that such habits are not mere automatic routines, and their control and supervision by the free choice of the agent, allow them a greater flexibility and adaptability to cases. This makes it possible for habits or dispositions to escape the charge of constraining action to "situation-specificity" cited above. In addition, there seems to be a place for training not devoted to reinforcing any particular type of tendency, but rather to exercising the free agent's ability to overcome obstacles of many sorts, be they physical opposition, opposed desires and impulses, or prior habits, and strengthening what we may perhaps call "ego-strength" or, at the risk of cliche, "will power."

We have not attempted to give a detailed account of specific virtues, partly because this is less important in the current context than clarifying their general nature and relation to freedom, and partly because many other sources have provided catalogues of good traits of character or "virtues." A complete listing would no doubt include the classical "cardinal virtues": practical wisdom, courage, moderation, and justice--understood not simply with Kohlberg as the rule of justice, but as the disposition to act according to that rule.[37] Under these may be found other traits: generosity or liberality, "magnificence" in arranging important works, proper pride, good temper, truthfulness, wittiness, friendliness, modesty, and righteous indignation where appropriate.[38] Still others might include piety, gratitude, patience, perseverance, all patterns for responding well to various situations in human affairs.[39]

The qualities of the person picked out by John Wilson's cognitive-analytic theory as "moral components," insofar as they represent trainable characteristics--particularly PHIL, EMP, and KRAT, but perhaps also GIG--can be seen as virtues.[40] Dispositions to act according to the "modes of responsibility," namely impartiality and concern for the good, to be discussed in the following chapter by Joseph M. Boyle, Jr., might also be called virtues.[41] It might be possible to identify still more human traits conducive to good action: compassion, enthusiasm, candor, and tact. We will not attempt here to survey exhaustively or to arrange systematically the full range of habits. Generally, virtues are traits which enable us to put into action the impassioned moral reasoning toward objective goods that is described elsewhere in this volume. A good habit is a crystallization of both rational knowledge and passionate commitment; it is neither blind nor routine.[42]

One further point may be made at this time concerning the importance of character in moral development. It is possible that it may play a key role, not only in the execution of moral judgments made on independent grounds, but even in the enabling of those moral judgments themselves. Clearly to hold that one's judgments were simply a function of one's previous training would reduce moral judgment to relativism, as Kohlberg observes, and as will be discussed in Chapter X. Different conditionings would then enforce different judgments on different individuals, with no way to correct or to arbitrate among them. However, it is still possible, in denying this extreme position, to hold that one's character may be instrumental in attaining moral knowledge. This would be the case if certain character developments, although they do not themselves create or compel moral judgments of a certain sort, were nonetheless necessary preconditions of such judgments. As a certain development of the eye is necessary for correct vision, although correct vision is more than simply a function of the structure of the eye, so correct moral insight is possible only through the "lens" of a personality well habituated to virtue. One's character may determine one's sensitivity to certain values, as well as to the reactions of others in the form of empathy or compassion, a necessary step toward making such judgments universal. Such a position is suggested by Aristotle, who does not espouse relativism in ethics, yet tells us that the first principles of the field cannot be grasped by one who is not already (in some degree, we might add) virtuous.[43]

A similar conclusion also is indicated by the discussion elsewhere in these volumes of the role of affectivity in value-knowledge. If one's tendencies in affective response form part of one's character, and if certain tendencies in affective response reveal to us certain goods and evils, then a certain proper development of character is necessary even to understand the fundamental principles upon which more complex ethical decisions are based.

This conclusion would support the long tradition of thought holding that mere abstract knowledge is not sufficient for practical wisdom and right judgment in moral issues, as well as providing some explanation for the empirical fact of the "amoral" person who seems unconcerned with moral matters altogether and inaccessible to any reasoning on the subject. If the data required by such reasoning must be acquired through a certain sort of character, then education in character may assume an importance in moral development at least equal to that of logical and more purely cognitive growth.

Walter Nicgorski
University of Notre Dame
Notre Dame, Indiana

Frederick E. Ellrod III
The Catholic University of America
Washington, D.C.

NOTES

1. The epigraph is from the translation of W.H.D. Rouse in *Great Dialogues of Plato* (New York: New American Library, 1956), 401e-402a.

2. Lawrence Kohlberg, "Stage and Sequence: the Cognitive-Developmental Approach to Socialization," in D. Goslin, ed., *Handbook of Socialization Theory and Research* (Chicago: Rand McNally, 1969), p. 367; see also Lawrence Kohlberg, "Moral Development and the Education of Adolescents," in Richard F. Purnell, ed., *Adolescents and the American High School* (New York: Holt, Rinehart and Winston, 1970), p. 145. More recently the basic direction of Kohlberg's revisions is reflected in statements which do not take issue with Hartshorne and May's findings about stable character traits, but dispute their approach to the study of moral conduct. "We believe," writes Kohlberg in 1978, "the behavioristic approach to studying individual moral conduct first taken by Hartshorne and May . . . to have failed, and we have chosen instead the group approach. Thus we examine behavior not in terms of individu-

al moral character but in terms of the character or 'moral atmosphere' of a group or community." "Revisions in the Theory and Practice of Moral Development," in William Damon, ed., *Moral Development, New Directions for Child Development*, no. 2 (San Francisco: Jossey-Bass, Inc., Publishers, 1978), p. 85. For more on these revisions, see also Clark Power and Joseph Reimer, "Moral Atmosphere: An Educational Bridge Between Moral Judgment and Action," in Damon, ed., and Joseph Reimer, "Moral Education: The Just Community Approach," *Phi Delta Kappan* (March, 1981). Cf. also the mention of "character" in Lawrence Kohlberg and F. Clark Power, "Religion, Morality, and Ego Development," in J. Fowler and A. Vergote, eds., *Toward Moral and Religious Maturity* (Morristown, N.J.: Silver Burdett, 1980), p. 350; and Lawrence Kohlberg, *The Meaning and Measurement of Moral Development*, Heinz Werner Lecture Series, vol. XIII (1979) (Worcester: Clark University Press, 1981), p. 4.

3. Kohlberg, "Moral Development and the Education of Adolescents," p. 146.

4. Kohlberg, "Stage and Sequence," p. 394.

5. If this factor is identical or related to the ability for free choice discussed in the preceding essay, however, it may be of considerable moral significance.

6. Lawrence Kohlberg, "Education for Justice: A Modern Statement of the Platonic View," in N. F. Sizer and T. R. Sizer, eds., *Moral Education* (Cambridge: Harvard University Press, 1970), p. 59.

7. Lawrence Kohlberg, "Indoctrination Versus Relativity in Value Education," *Zygon* 6 (December, 1971), p. 288; "Education for Justice," p. 59.

8. Dewey's concern is, above all, for the democratic habits that are conducive to personal and community development. This is the point of interaction between the "fixed" and "dynamic" selves. For his basic statement on those selves, see Chapter III above.

9. Kohlberg, "Indoctrination Versus Relativity," p. 288; "Education for Justice," p. 59.

10. Lawrence Kohlberg, "A Cognitive-Developmental Approach to Moral Education," *The Humanist*, 32 (November/December, 1972), p. 14.

11. Kohlberg, "Education for Justice," p. 59.

12. Lawrence Kohlberg and Rochelle Mayer, "Development as the Aim of Education," *Harvard Education Review*, 42 (November, 1972), p. 453.

13. *Ibid.*, p. 468.

14. *Ibid.*, p. 473.

15. R. S. Peters and Paul Philibert among the critics of Kohlberg have both called attention to his misinterpretation of Aristotle and to the potential benefit to his theory from the classical tradition. Peters argues that both Aristotle and Kohlberg direct attention to the "relationship between virtue and habit in the moral life" and to the related problem "of the development of a rational morality out of a basis provided by early

habit formation." William Alston is also aware that Kohlberg might be said to "direct attention" to these problems only by his seeming neglect of the role of habit in moral development. Philibert, though very positive on the significance of Kohlberg's work and critical of the understanding of virtue which Peters himself develops, has directly and rightly focused attention on Kohlberg's misunderstanding of Aristotle and the tradition that follows from him. Philibert argues "that Kohlberg's characterization of virtue is unfair to the Western philosophical tradition" and "that some traditional teachings about the nature of virtue provide better resources for organizing the data of Kohlberg's research into a comprehensive theory of moral education than he himself has done yet." What Kohlberg has done, in Philibert's view as well as ours, is to reject "out of hand an important instrument of philosophical reflection, viz., the Aristotelian characterization of virtue." See R. S. Peters, "Moral Development: A Plea for Pluralism," in Theodore Mischel, ed., *Cognitive Development and Epistemology* (New York: Academic Press, 1971), p. 254; William P. Alston, "Comments on Kohlberg's 'From Is to Ought,'" in Mischel, ed.; Paul J. Philibert, "Lawrence Kohlberg's Use of Virtue in His Theory of Moral Development," *International Philosophical Quarterly* 15 (December 1975), p. 459.

16. Aristotle, *Nicomachean Ethics*, 1102b13-28.

17. *Ibid.*; trans. by W. D. Ross, in Richard McKeon, ed., *The Basic Works of Aristotle* (New York: Random House, 1941), 1144b8-14 (italics added).

18. Kohlberg, "Education for Justice," pp. 64-65.

19. The passage quoted at the beginning of this paper suggests, however, that Socrates himself may have been less hostile to cultural transmission than Kohlberg leads one to believe. Socrates, like Dewey later, is concerned with the proper disposition of the student and adjusts his teaching to the state of readiness of the student before him. See Mann's earlier statement on Dewey (Chapter II) and Walter Nicgorski's subsequent chapter on "Environment: The Social Dimension of the Moral Development."

20. Philibert, p. 471.

21. Alston, p. 281.

22. This point is made in an unpublished doctoral dissertation by Thomas Atherton, *A Critique of Lawrence Kohlberg's Theories of Moral Development and Moral Education* (Boston University, 1979), in which habit generally is defended, and it is pointed out that Kohlberg's own cognitive stages can be seen as "habitual modes of deliberating about moral dilemmas" (p. 241).

23. Kohlberg, "Indoctrination," p. 295. See also R. P. Craig, "Lawrence Kohlberg and Moral Development: Some Reflections," *Educational Theory*, 24 (Spring, 1974), p. 129.

24. Alston, p. 283.

25. Peters, pp. 254-55.

26. See, for instance, William Damon, "Structural-Developmental

Theory and the Study of Moral Development," in M. Windmiller, J. Lambert, and E. Turiel, eds., *Moral Development and Socialization* (Boston: Allyn and Bacon, 1980), pp. 47-50; Roger V. Burton, "Honesty and Dishonesty," in Thomas Lickona, ed., *Moral Development and Behavior: Theory, Research, and Social Issues* (New York: Holt, Rinehart and Winston, 1976), pp. 173-97. In fact, Hartshorne and May regard "character education" as possible and desirable if approached properly. Their view is that ideals and standards cannot simply be preached but must be integrated within the developing self as that self becomes integrated with the groups within which it is interacting. See William E. Chapman, *Roots of Character Education* (Schenectady, New York: Character Research Press, 1977), pp. 54-64. Here the observation of Edward A. Wynne should be noted. "An intriguing irony," he writes, "is that the research findings of Hartshorne and May were not actually in conflict with the major intellectual themes of the great tradition. The tradition always emphasized that moral education needed to be incremental, pervasive, persistent and rigorous. Given these principles, it is logical that the measured long-term effect of any limited form of 'moral instruction' would be minute. The findings primarily demonstrated that American educators had exaggerated expectations about the effects of formal systems of character education. But any historian of American education would take as given the proposition that Americans usually have exaggerated expectations about what can be produced by education." "The Major Models of Moral Education: Evaluating the Research," unpublished paper, p. 13.

27. See Aristotle, *Nicomachean Ethics*, II, 1-6.

28. See the chapter by Samay, above; see also Robert Sokolowski, *Presence and Absence: A Philosophical Investigation of Language and Being* (Studies in Phenomenological and Existential Philosophy; Bloomington: Indiana University Press, 1978), pp. 134-35.

29. It may be noted, for the sake of strict accuracy, that it is the *action* that is not predetermined; the *power* of free action belongs to a person as long as one remains that person. See Chapters IV and XII for further discussion.

30. Cf. the discussion in Chapter IV.

31. Cf. the discussion of courage in Chapter II.

32. Character would, then, in part be the locus of the component KRAT in cognitive-analytic descriptions of the moral agent, particularly of KRAT(1).

33. The exact status of results which are, for example, foreseen but *not* intended is a matter for more extended investigation. Cf. Austin Fagothey, S.J., *Right and Reason*, (6th edition; St. Louis: C. V. Mosby Co., 1976), pp. 31-34, on this topic. This complication need not be considered here, though it is highly important in a complete theory of normative ethics. See the following chapter by Boyle in this volume.

34. Cf. Erik H. Erikson, *Identity: Youth and Crisis* (New York: W. W. Norton and Co., 1968), p. 112: "The question is always whether we remain the masters of the modalities by which things become more man-

ageable or whether the rules master the ruler."

35. See the paper by Sebastian Samay above, and the discussion of Dewey's opposition between the "fixed" and "dynamic" selves in Chapter II above.

36. Cf. William James, *Psychology: Briefer Course* (New York: Collier, 1962), p. 187: "What he shall *become* is fixed by the conduct of this moment."

37. For a recent discussion, see Josef Pieper, *The Four Cardinal Virtues* (Notre Dame: University of Notre Dame Press, 1966).

38. These may be found in the list given by Aristotle, *Nicomachean Ethics*, Book II, chapter 7.

39. For these and others, see Thomas Aquinas, *Summa Theologica*, II-II.

40. See Chapter I.

41. See Chapter VI.

42. Thus Aquinas advises that moral virtue cannot exist without practical wisdom, i.e., the rational formation and governance of those habits; see *Summa Theologica*, I-II, q. 58, a. 4; II-II, q. 47, a. 7, and q. 57, a. 5.

43. Aristotle, *Nicomachean Ethics*, I, 4; II, 3; and X, 5. See also Israel Scheffler, "The Moral Content of American Public Education," in David Purpel and Kevin Ryan, eds., *Moral Education: It Comes With the Territory* (Berkeley: McCutchan Publishing Corp., 1976), p. 23.

CHAPTER VII

MORAL REASONING

JOSEPH M. BOYLE, JR.

The set of phenomena called morality is very complex. It includes both social and personal ingredients of very different kinds; for example, feelings of righteousness, admiration, shame and guilt, choices and commitments of various kinds, and convictions, conscientious judgments and decisions along with the reasons and thinking which back up these convictions and judgments. In this dynamically and reflexively related mix there is much that requires philosophical analysis. This volume undertakes this analysis with respect to many of these ingredients of morality. The purpose of this chapter is to clarify moral reasoning: the considerations and thinking which people make use of to back up, defend or explain their moral judgments.

The importance of moral reasoning is suggested by the extent of the attention paid to it by moral philosophers over the centuries. Its contemporary significance is suggested by the central role it plays in the work of recent, practically-oriented empirical studies of morality. Kohlberg, for example, relies heavily on moral reasoning, or at least what people are able to articulate of their moral reasoning in responding to standardized moral dilemmas, as an index of their stage of moral-cognitive development.[1]

The practical, educational importance of moral reasoning is easy to see. For moral reasoning seems to be an aspect of morality in which education is possible without either indoctrination or unreasonable imposition of values.[2] Moral reasoning seems to be primarily a cognitive activity, and as such seems susceptible of development and improvement. Thus, while it may seem utopian for educators to take as their goal the formation of morally good people, it does not seem unrealistic to hope for the more limited achievement of improving moral thinking. Moreover, such improvement seems to avoid any suspicion of indoctrination since helping people to develop their own thinking ability seems to be nothing more than the Socratic appeal to the individual's own intelligence.

Of course, these high hopes for moral education depend on a number of controversial assumptions about moral reasoning, in particular, that it is possible to identify moral reasoning that is correct and mature, and that it is possible to disengage an objective cognitive procedure from one's private moral convictions. These assumptions are philosophical, as the disagreements among philosophers concerning them make clear. The specific task of this chapter is to enter into this philosophical controversy with a view towards elaborating a theory of moral reasoning sufficient to provide a reasonable judgment about these assumptions and the use made

164 *Moral Reasoning*

of them in the various practical proposals about moral education. To this end, the chapter will be divided into five sections: 1) a consideration of the nature and function of moral reasoning; 2) a critique of mistaken philosophical accounts of moral reasoning; 3) an attempt to show why the Golden Rule is a central principle of moral reasoning, but is not the sole or basic principle; 4) an articulation of a more complete theory of moral reasoning; and 5) an application of this theory to the problem of overriding moral norms.

THE NATURE AND FUNCTION OF MORAL REASONING

To develop a clear focus for the analysis that will follow, it is necessary to note that the phrase "moral reasoning" has a number of distinct but related meanings, as do its cognates and near relatives. Words and phrases like "conscience," "moral judgment," "moral decision," and so on, are used to refer to importantly different realities. These expressions refer to various aspects of the internalized demands of authority--roughly to the judgments, reasoning and reactions at what Kohlberg calls the preconventional level of morality.[3] These demands, of course, are often unreasonable and can sometimes rightly be called immoral. Similarly, the requirements of getting along with others and protecting one's place in the social order--the demands, roughly, of Kohlberg's conventional level of morality--[4] are appropriately called moral requirements. Indeed, such requirements make up a good deal of the going morality of most societies. But these standards too are susceptible of moral criticism; thus, they are not part of "morality" in the focal sense of the term,[5] but fall among the things morality in the most proper sense evaluates.

Moral reasoning in its focal sense is the subject of this chapter. For this is the moral reasoning that provides the standard for good, mature moral reasoning, and thus provides the measure of cognitive moral development and the goal of moral education.

In this focal sense moral reasoning is also the subject of the controversies of moral philosophers. For example, Kohlberg holds that his sixth stage of moral development, defined in explicitly Kantian terms, "is what it means to judge morally."[6] But this claim is by no means obvious, and would be disputed by consequentialists, natural lawyers and intuitionists alike. What these moralists would dispute is precisely the adequacy of Kohlberg's Kantianism as an account of correct moral reasoning. What is needed, therefore, is a philosophical justification of one's account of moral reasoning at its highest level. It will simply not do to assume one's own view as correct and relegate other normative theories to lower levels of moral development. The philosophical argument must be joined, and as a first step the reality which the opposed theories seek to clarify must be delineated.

Moral reasoning is a species of practical reasoning. As a form of reasoning, practical reasoning is a mental activity; it deals with such things as propositions and inferences. As a mental activity it cannot be simply identified with the language which embodies and expresses it, for we may know more than we can articulate. Practical reasoning is thinking directed towards action--thinking whose result is judgments about what to do. Moral thinking is thinking directed towards determining the morally right thing to do--thinking about what to do if one is to be a good person. Thus, the result of moral thinking is a judgment about what in the circumstances is the right thing to do.

The normative force of such judgments is that of norms for free choices. Human beings face practical options; sometimes a person faces a situation in which he or she can do one or another of the possible actions available, but not all of them. This is the situation in which deliberation and choice arise. In some such situations what one will do is settled only by one's choice to do one thing rather than another: such is a free choice.[7] Moral norms are the judgments as to which choices are consistent with, required by, or inconsistent with being a good person. Moral reasoning, therefore, is reasoning which seeks to justify judgments having this kind of normative force.

Moral reasoning as the process of justifying concrete moral judgments is an essential part of the common human experience of morality. Moral claims and judgments--even when these are rationalizations or the imperfectly moral judgments of the morally immature--are supported in some way by reasons. Theoretically, this is denied only by those who hold that each moral judgment is known immediately by some sort of intuition or moral sense. H. A. Prichard is perhaps the best known proponent of this view, and even he admits a kind of "moral thinking" which reveals the true moral character of one's acts.[8] Practically, the denial of reasons for moral judgments, or even the radical incapacity to provide such reasons, leads to treating moral judgments as taboos. As Alasdair MacIntyre has shown, taboos cannot have the force of moral judgments, and can be repealed as easily as laws which have become a dead letter.[9] Moral reasoning, in the sense delineated above, is, therefore, an irreducible part of moral experience--a part which, unless justifiable, leads to skepticism about morality as a rational enterprise.

Moral reasoning emerges clearly in a number of situations which contain features which can obscure its essential character. Thus, it is important to consider these, and to set aside what is not essential. The disagreements between people about social and interpersonal matters provide common and clear examples of moral reasoning. Differences in the conscientious judgments of citizens about public policy matters like abortion, capital punishment, private sexual activity, economic activity, and international policies often involve extensive moral reasoning. The controversial context of such arguments, however, often leads to argumentation that is passionate and rhetorical, and frequently unpersuasive. But interpersonal moral disagreements are not limited to these seemingly interminable, controversial public policy issues. People cooperating with one another in a family, business, or other joint enterprise can find themselves in fundamental disagreement about what morally ought to be done. These disagreements often involve moral reasoning, and here perhaps the efforts of persuasion are more often rational and satisfactory.

It seems to be a mistake, however, to define moral reasoning as a means of settling social disputes, as Kohlberg and others sometimes suggest.[10] For many of the moral conflicts people face--even when they have to do with fairness in dealings with others--are conflicts within the person himself, and not with other people. In fact, given that moral norms are guidelines for free choices, it is moral dilemmas of this sort which challenge moral reasoning in the most direct way. For when one faces options for choice all of which seem wrong, one is required to think clearly if one is to discover what one should do.

It is important to recognize, however, that even in these fundamentally personal moral dilemmas there is a significant interpersonal dimension. For when a person is perplexed about what to do, he or she quite reasonably relies on the advice of others. Such reliance is particularly appropriate when one relies on those who share one's basic values and commitments and have reflectively studied their implications. This reliance must be limited, however, because another person, however sympathetic, cannot fully understand one's practical situation in all its richness.

Thus, the thinking of a morally mature person who is seeking to resolve his or her own moral perplexities provides the simplest and least complicated example of moral reasoning. Rhetorical questions connected with persuading others can be set aside, as can the questions about evaluating others' advice. But even in this least complicated case of moral reasoning, there are certain limitations on what moral reasoning can achieve. One such limitation arises from the fact that people often accept inconsistent moral principles which if consistently applied give contradictory results in the same situation. One who holds, for example, that human life is sacred and also that quality of life considerations are the basis for decisions to withhold life saving treatments simply cannot think himself or herself out of some of the dilemmas which arise in cases of seriously defective newborns. One principle will direct treatment and the other non-treatment in many cases. As in other inconsistencies, one must abandon one of the inconsistent propositions.

Another limitation on even the most competent moral reasoning arises from the fact that the moral norms with which moral reasoning deals are universal propositions, whereas the final judgment about what to do is a singular judgment. Even the most fully specified moral norm is a universal statement--applicable to any choice having the intelligible features it takes into account. By contrast, the judgment of what one ought concretely to do, the judgment of conscience, is singular; one must judge that one should do or not do this individual act. To close the gap between norm and singular judgment one must determine that all the morally relevant features of the proposed act have been considered. This determination is, of course, not settled in a decisive way by moral reasoning. It involves the use of reasonable presumptions about when one has reflected enough. These presumptions are in many cases hard to establish and apply. They require the classical virtue of prudence which, in turn, presupposes an integration of one's feelings and moral thinking around sound moral commitments. However, this limitation on moral reasoning does not mean that moral reasoning is not an essential part of arriving at moral judgments, nor that it cannot enable one to decisively reject some proposed actions as morally unacceptable.

The issue, therefore, is to develop an adequate theory of moral reasoning. The attempt to develop such a theory cannot, however, operate from neutral ground above the fray of competing moral theories and judgments. There may be some common ingredients in all moral perspectives--a common pattern of deductive reasoning, perhaps, or some use of a version of the Golden Rule. But the issues which divide people on moral matters and which lead individuals to distrust the credibility of even their own moral judgments are not formal issues which could be settled by purely logical analysis or by the clarification of common moral notions. Nor are they issues that could be settled by appeal to a moral principle so general that every moral perspective would embody it. The issues are substantive moral questions which, however formal their answers may be with respect to particular moral judgments, are precisely the locus of moral controversy.

For example, the question of how generally stated moral norms can be overridden by other moral considerations cannot be answered by appeal to the logical structure of a moral system, nor by noting such formal characteristics of judgments as universalizability. Substantive questions about the justification and priority of general moral norms must be considered.

Likewise, at the very heart of moral analysis there is the question of justifying the connection between a given human action and a morally relevant predicate. Within any moral system one must be able to justify the statements which claim that acts of a certain describable kind are in fact acts permitted, forbidden or mandated by one's normative principles. More concretely, one must determine that an act, say, of killing oneself or failing to keep a promise is, in fact, an act which fails to respect rational nature, or brings about the greater good, or is contrary to right reason. The reasoning involved here is not deductive but a mix of conceptual analysis, projection of consequences, and so on. Clearly such reasoning involves taking stands on the controverted questions of moral theory.

Thus, there seem no way out of the morass of conflicting moral opinions and opposed moral viewpoints--no way except, perhaps, to think one's way through it. If there is an Olympian perspective on contemporary morality, it can be reached only by taking up the disputed issues and arguing them through. This option, unattractive as it may seem, is not doomed to failure; the differences between moral theories are not so radical that the best one can do is take one's pick of moral theories, and proceed, question-beggingly, on one's way. There are some common data and a set of conceptual problems with which any moral theory must deal. Moral theories which cannot handle the data or resolve the problems can be reasonably rejected, and conditions necessary for an adequate moral theory can thus be formulated.

Among the data for which any adequate moral theory must account are the results of the empirical studies of morality. These results cannot by themselves be used to establish the standard for proper moral thinking. As David Schindler has shown elsewhere in this volume, such a use of empirical data would be a peculiar form of fallaciously inferring what should be from what is.[11] It simply does not follow from that fact that most of those judged to be mature moral thinkers reason in certain ways that these are the proper ways to reason about moral matters. Nevertheless, most moral theories--whether natural law, or Kantian, or consequentialist or intuitionist--involve the claim that the principles and patterns of reasoning they purported to establish are the principles and patterns of reasoning which morally mature people actually make use of in arriving at moral judgments. For example, since the principles of the natural law are said by natural lawyers to be written in the human heart in such a way that every normal person can know them, even if obscurely, the results of empirical studies would be most disconcerting for natural law theory if they showed that people shared no common moral principles or that these principles had no connection to the perfection or flourishing of human beings.

Among the conceptual problems which any moral theory, and thus any theory of moral reasoning, must deal with are the two already noted above: how to explain the defeasibility of generally stated moral norms, and how to rationally justify the specificatory premises of moral arguments. There are certainly other problems with which a successful moral theory must deal, for example, questions about the relation between moral considerations and other human interests, but these two are especially central for the theory of moral reasoning. I hope to show that the dominant moral theories cannot deal with them in a plausible way.

SOME INADEQUATE ACCOUNTS OF MORAL REASONING

W. D. Ross's intuitionism is a paradigmatic example of an ethical theory designed to explain the defeasibility of generally stated moral principles. According to Ross, there are a number of self-evident moral principles. There are irreducible duties of fidelity, reparation, gratitude, justice, beneficence, self-improvement and not harming others.[12] These duties are all defeasible--Ross calls them *prima facie* duties--because any concrete act can have features such that more than one of the basic duties bear on the act. A given act might be the keeping of a promise and also a failure to provide important help to a person in need. Thus, the act is required by the obligation of fidelity, but forbidden by the duty of beneficence. One of these duties must, therefore, be overridden by the other. On Ross's account there is no ordering principle for ranking the basic duties in terms of their stringency. Depending upon the situation, any of the relevant prima facie duties might be determined to be one's actual duty and any of them might be overridden by another.

This determination of one's actual duty is not reached by a process of logical inference from the self-evident principles, nor is it reached by a further intuition like that of the moral principles; rather, it is a more or less probable opinion formed in the light of the *prima facia* duties. His position seems to be that the judgment as to one's actual duty is little more than a guess. The right act is, in this sense, the "fortunate act."[13] It is, of course, a guess made in light of the self-evident moral principle, and about one of the courses of action mandated by these principles.

Ross and others who hold similar views give various accounts of how this second stage of moral judgment or the movement from general principle to specific judgment is to be understood. Ross compares it to the judgment of the overall merit of a poem; Broad compares it to "perceptual judgments on very complex situations which we have constantly to make in playing games of skill."[14] Other suggestions are hinted at by Ross and Broad, namely, that there is a kind of weighing or balancing going on.[15] Other moralists appeal to a hypothetical decision maker--a disinterested, well informed observer, or God--as a help in deciding on what to do in cases where general norms conflict.

It seems to me that all such attempts to resolve the opposed implications of different moral principles are bound to fail. To talk about a probable opinion or guess or perception made in the context of the relevant moral principles which give contrary directions is to admit that none of these norms in fact justifies the concrete judgment. One or more of the principles may justify one line of action, and others may prohibit this line of action or require another. Which of these lines of action is to be done is simply not justified; only the disjunctive statement is justified and this statement cannot tell us what to do since the disjuncts give contrary directions.

To call the concrete judgment a "probable opinion" is something of a misnomer because this suggests some rules, however indefinite, according to which one judgment is more reasonable than others; and no such rules are available. To call such a judgment a perception suggests an intuition. Ross quite rightly rejects this possibility; concrete moral judgments are not intuitions but in some way follow from more general moral considerations. Appeal to intuitions which can be evaluated by no standards gives rise to such troubling epistemological difficulties as, for example, how intuitions are to be distinguished from feelings, prejudices or the reports of super-ego.

To appeal to weighing or balancing moral considerations in such a framework also fails to provide a rational basis for arriving at concrete judgments. This would presuppose a procedure for determining the weight of each consideration, whereas intuitionist systems of the kind in question here deny that moral considerations have any fixed serial order.[16] Likewise appeal to what God or a disinterested, intelligent observer might decide is no help, given that we have no information about how the intelligent observer would arrive at a decision.

Intuitionism of the sort exhibited by Ross' theory, therefore, is not able to account *rationally* for the defeasibility of general moral norms. Although designed to handle the fact that moral norms are defeasible, such theories provide no rational grounds for judging which norms are to be overridden in a given circumstance. The difficulty lies not in the fact that these theories require a basic intuition but in the unordered plurality of basic principles. This weakness suggests a necessary condition for a more adequate moral theory: the existence of a single basic moral principle sufficient at least for providing some order of stringency among general moral norms. A second condition is also suggested: a theory of human action which enables one to determine how central to one's action are its various morally relevant features. Without the first, contrary directions will bear equally on the same action; without the second, relatively insignificant features of one's acts will count just as much as those more central to one's act.

Act-consequentialism is a theory of moral reasoning which seems to meet these conditions, and which thereby seems to provide an account of how moral norms can be rationally overridden by other moral considerations. This characteristic is, no doubt, one of the things which accounts for its wide appeal.

Act-consequentialism is a teleological theory: moral norms are justified in terms of the human good. Thus, it presupposes a theory of the good. With this assumption in place, consequentialism proposes that the basic moral principle is that one should choose so as to bring about the greater preponderance of good over evil, or the lesser evil, in the situation. In other words, a person faced with a moral choice faces alternatives for action all of which involve some good and some evil. If the person is to determine which of these he or she morally ought to do, the person must consider the good and bad involved in each and make a comparative judgment that one of them is better, over all, or at least that one is less bad, over all. This alternative is the one a person morally should choose.[17]

Clearly, this conception of moral judgment avoids the difficulties caused by having a plurality of basic moral principles. Every moral norm is justified by the principle of the greater good. Normative opposition between the implications of general principles is thus obviated. Moreover, there is a way of determining what is essential and accidental in human action, namely, whatever affects the human good, either positively or negatively, whether this be in the action itself, or in its consequences, or in any other concomitant features of the action. The precise moral importance of any feature of the act is determined by the reasoning which determines the greater good. If a given feature of one's act contributes in a significant way to the overall good or evil of one's action, then it is a correspondingly central feature of the act as a moral undertaking.

It is obvious that act-consequentialism can easily explain the defeasibility of general moral norms. Since these norms are themselves justified by the principle of the greater good, situations in which following them fails to promote the greater good are situations in which they lack their normal moral force. The possibility of overriding general norms on consequentialist grounds need not involve a disregard or denial of the importance of general norms, since the utility of accepting the general norms and the disutility of setting them aside are among the factors which should be taken into account in judging that a given act is, in the situation, likely to promote greater good or lesser evil.

For all its plausibility as a rational means for arriving at moral judgments, consequentialism has a number of serious flaws. The catalogue of these flaws has been spelled out in great detail in the recent literature on consequentialism. Here it is necessary to develop only two of these arguments which have special bearing on consequentialism as a theory of moral reasoning.

The first of these focuses on the adequacy of consequentialism as precisely an account of moral reasoning. This line of criticism leaves untouched the claim of consequentialism to be a workable form of practical reasoning and calls into question the moral significance of its results. The objection is suggested by Ross's remark about G. E. Moore's version of consequentialism, to the effect that it "ignores, or at least fails to do full justice to, the highly personal character of duty."[18] Ross goes on to explain that if our only duty is to produce the maximum of good it makes no difference who is to be the beneficiary, and yet it surely does make a moral difference. Nor, it would seem, should it make any difference morally who does the act in question, if the good and bad consequences are not affected, and just as surely as in Ross's case, it does make a difference. Consider Plato's statement that it is worse to do evil than to undergo it, and imagine a situation in which one is either unjustly harmed by another or one unjustly inflicts the very same harm on another. For example, one is faced with a situation in which the only way in which one can prevent oneself from being killed unjustly is to kill an innocent person. Given this information, it is a toss up consequentially; there is no moral difference between killing or being killed. Plato's statement must, therefore, be false on consequentialist terms.[19] And yet it seems to be true--or at least defensible.

This line of criticism is not a decisive criticism of consequentialism, but it does highlight an important difference between consequentialist and other more traditional views of morality. It highlights the fact that morality seems to be concerned with being a good person, and so, what the person voluntarily does and refuses to do is essentially important from the moral point of view, even when the good and bad consequences are not affected. The emphasis of consequentialism, therefore, seems misplaced. It is on good and bad states of affairs as realized by our actions.[20] But morality seems to focus primarily on personal identity and character as established by correct choices, and to be concerned only derivatively with states of affairs brought about by choice. As Kant says: nothing is unconditionally good except the good will.

This difference in understanding the focus of morality is a very important one: for when the consequentialist justifies a moral judgment, he supposes that justified moral judgments reflect as well as possible what the consequentialist takes to be morally central, and this appears to be something quite other than what the Kantian or intuitionist takes to be the point of morality. If this is so, it is not surprising that moral controversies between those holding these perspectives seem to go nowhere. For the argument is not simply about how to correctly arrive at correct judgments which all would agree to be "moral judgments" in the same sense of the phrase, but it is a disagreement about what morality is. Given disagreements about this, it is not surprising that there should be disagreements about particular moral judgments and the procedures for justifying them

Of course, the mere fact that the consequentialist view of morality is significantly at odds with even the most mature and philosophically articulated versions of traditional morality does not show consequentialism to be mistaken. If consequentialism is to be dismissed, without begging fundamental questions, it must be on the basis of its inherent difficulties and not because it proposes a new understanding of the nature of morality.

The second anti-consequentialist argument I will develop focuses on just such a difficulty. It is directed towards the very workability of consequentialism as a method capable of arriving at objective, practical judgments. More precisely, it is the claim that there are difficulties in principle in justifying the specificatory premises in consequentialist arguments. These premises take the form of predicating of some kind of act in some specifiable circumstances that doing this act is the greater good or the lesser evil as compared with the available alternatives. The predicate in such judgments involves a comparison of values, and this is where the basic difficulty lies. There are, of course, other difficulties, regarding, for example, articulating the alternatives, knowing the relevant consequences, and determining who is to be affected by them.[21] These difficulties are very serious and suggest that consequentialism may not be practicable in many complex situations. But these difficulties do not show that consequentialism is unworkable in principle.

Other objections might be made to the consequentialist assumption that it is possible to arrive at correct value judgments. But this assumption can be vindicated.[22] However, a closely related assumption is not so easily vindicated--namely, that it is possible to make correct *comparative* judgments of value. This assumption is not vindicated simply by the fact that it is possible to justify non-comparative value judgments. Knowledge that one thing is good or another bad is not sufficient for knowledge that one good is better than another or one bad worse than another. To know this there must be some principle, some standard of good or bad, which is more adequately realized in some goods and bads than in others. There seems to be no evidence that such a principle exists, as well as considerable evidence that it does not.

It might appear counter-intuitive to deny that there is such a thing as a "hierarchy of values." The point here, however, is more precise: there is no hierarchy of values in the sense required for making comparative judgments of value of the sort consequentialism must make. This claim is consistent with the admission that a person can establish *by choice* a ranking of human goods for his or her own life; a community might do this as well. For the issue at hand is whether such comparative value judgments can be objective. If they are not, it is difficult to see how consequentialism could be used to justify moral judgments in any way other than by showing them consistent with prior value preference.

Nor is the denial of the consequentialist assumption that there is a standard for determining greater and lesser goods and bads inconsistent with the admission that instrumental values are not as good as the basic goods of human persons. The question concerns the order of these goods among themselves. And this denial is compatible with a ranking of goods as in some ways qualitatively better and worse. For it is not sufficient to know, for example, that the values of friendship are somehow better than those of mere bodily sustenance, in order to determine that acts embodying instances of these values and others, as well as instances of harms to these values and others are on balance better or worse than the available alternatives. This requires a rather precise and nuanced standard.

The failure of consequentialist theorists to plausibly provide such a standard is notorious. Bentham's effort is instructive. He provided the needed standard by articulating a monumentally contrary-to-fact value theory. His value theory was hedonistic; the good was defined in terms of pleasure. And pleasure was treated as a unitary sort of thing; all pleasures were qualitatively the same--differing only in measurable quantities of intensity, duration and so on.[23] Such a definition of the good provides the standard needed for the comparative judgments of value consequentialism supposes, but it is plainly incompatible with the common experience of pleasure. Pleasure, especially if it is to include all that is humanly good, cannot be a qualitatively singular type of sense impression.

More attached to experience than to the requirements of consequentialist theorizing, Mill saw this difficulty and tried to provide a more nuanced theory of the human good.[24] His attempt to rank pleasures as higher and lower is plausible as a common sense proposition, but it does not provide the resources for careful and precise ordering of values and disvalues. For example, all would agree that a dissatisfied Socrates is better off than a satisfied pig. Yet, there must be some amount of porcine satisfaction which is better than some level of Socratic dissatisfaction. Otherwise, we have given up consequentialism altogether. But if there is such a point, Mill gives us no way to discover it, particularly given his emphasis on the qualitative differences of the things compared.

This short discussion of Bentham's and Mill's attempts to deal with the standard for comparing values suggests the basic difficulty: no such standard is revealed in the common human experience of deliberating, coming to a moral decision, and choosing. Quite the contrary, choices are revealed as necessary precisely when persons face alternatives for action which are good and bad in diverse and seemingly incommensurable ways. Whether the choice is between morally good options, or between morally good and morally bad options, it seems that the alternatives each have their own attractions and merits which do not disappear when compared with the attractions of the alternatives--even the morally required alternatives. If a person were thoroughly convinced that one alternative was *definitely* better than the others, then the attraction of the others would evaporate since the better alternative would promise all the good they promise and more besides. That is, the better good would include all of the good of the other option and some further good as well.[25]

In short, we are asked to believe that there is a standard which has not been articulated by those who are committed to its reality, and which finds no place in common moral experience. In fact, its reality would seem to contradict an important component of that experience, namely, that the conditions for morally correct judgments are distinct from the conditions of motivation which make it possible to choose contrary to what one judges to be right.

An important proviso is necessary at this point: the moral judgments of many people who are not committed to consequentialism involve use of the notions of greater good and lesser evil, and of phrases which are roughly synonymous with them. For example, the phrases "proportionate reason" or "grave reason" have played an important part in the tradition of natural law, especially in its application to difficult moral problems. The argument against the consequentialist notion of the greater good does not affect these uses, since the phrase "greater good" and its cognates and synonyms have a number of distinct meanings, and this argument is directed towards only one of them. For example, a morally good person could very well regard any evil action as the greater evil since such an act simply is incompatible with being a good person. More generally, if the greater good is morally defined, if, that is, the greater good is such because it involves conformity to moral norms, then it is not the greater good in the consequentialist sense: in this sense the greater good is the basis for moral norms and not morally defined.[26]

The implication of this argument for the general uses of the phrase "greater good," therefore, is not that they are all misguided but rather that the precise meaning of such uses needs to be determined so that the precise moral import of statements using them can be understood.

To sum up: the consequentialist method of moral reasoning cannot rationally establish the specificatory premises needed to apply its basic normative conception to concrete actions. This internal difficulty strengthens the more fundamental point that consequentialism mistakenly directs the attention of moral reasoning away from what is morally central.

THE GOLDEN RULE: ESSENTIAL BUT NOT SUFFICIENT

What is morally central--being a morally good person--has been more adequately accounted for from within the perspective of Kantian ethics. We have already noted that Kant's emphasis is on the good will and not on the achievement of good states of affairs. His basic moral principle reflects this emphasis. The categorical imperative in its various formulations seems very close in content and spirit to the Golden Rule: do unto others as you would have them to unto you. One who acts in accord with the Golden Rule acts in a way consistent with the recognition of "the highly personal character of morality." What a person might reasonably be willing that someone should do to him can vary while the overall good or bad of alternatives does not. Thus it makes a difference in terms of the Golden Rule who does the evil deed even if there will be an evil deed of the same magnitude in any case.

Now, it seems that the Golden Rule is a moral truth if there are any moral truths. In some form it seems to be an ingredient in almost all moral systems,[27] and it has some analogue in all stages of moral development.[28] Moreover, it seems essential to the impartiality involved in the conception of justice as fairness; and it is hard to imagine any society totally lacking this conception. It would seem, therefore, that any satisfactory conception of moral reasoning would have to include the Golden Rule. What is distinctive about Kantian ethics is that the Golden Rule is regarded as the single fundamental principle of morality and, therefore, as the basis for all moral judgments. The question raised by the Kantian approach, therefore, is whether the Golden Rule *by itself* is capable of justifying moral judgments. The standard objections to Kantian formalism suggest that the answer to this question must be a negative one.

Kant calls the basic moral principle "the categorical imperative" and formulates it in several ways, all of which he plausibly claims, are logically equivalent.[29] The first of these is the nearest to the Golden Rule in its obvious sense: "act only according to that maxim by which you can at the same time will that it should become a universal law."[30] A maxim is one's reason for action; it includes reference to one's end and to the action which one undertakes to realize the end. A maxim is universalized when the singular terms are removed and replaced by universal terms. If the universal proposition is not self-contradictory or can be willed without contradiction, then one's maxim is a universal law and the action is morally permissible. If either of these conditions is not met the maxim cannot be universalized and the action is immoral.

The similarity of this procedure to the Golden Rule lies in the removal of the singular terms. This guarantees a kind of impartiality very similar to that achieved by imaginatively putting oneself in the position of those affected by one's action. By requiring that the reason for one's action be stated in non-singular terms, the categorical imperative excludes a kind of arbitrary self-preference. This can be seen by considering the difference between acting on a reason which can be stated in general terms and on one that cannot be so stated. In the former case, even if the action is in various ways ill-considered or is done out of self-interest, it is reasonable or rationally explicable in the sense that one could explain how any member of a describable class of persons would have grounds for doing the action. In the latter case, however, the action cannot be rationalized in this way; the mere fact that one wants to do the act is the only "justification"--which, of course, is no justification at all. In this sense, acts which cannot meet the standard of the categorical imperative are based on arbitrary self-preference. Thus, the categorical imperative does not exclude all actions based on self-interest, nor actions for unsuitable purposes. What it requires is impartiality--not playing favorites. The exclusion of impartiality does not seem sufficient for a complete moral system.

More than this formulation of the categorical imperative is needed, therefore, if a Golden Rule based morality is to plausibly claim to be a complete moral system. Another of Kant's formulations of the categorical imperative seems a likely candidate to fill this role, for on the face of it, this formulation has a far richer content than the first formulation-- namely, "act so that you treat humanity, whether in your own person or in that of another, always as an end and never as a means only."[31] It is not necessary to settle the question whether this formulation is logically equivalent to the first formulation of the categorical imperative or to the Golden Rule. For it has difficulties of application that are strictly analogous to those of the first formulation.

These difficulties are basically problems with the specificatory premises in Kantian arguments. The Kantian principle in its various formulations lacks the conceptual resources for determining in a rational way which acts are prohibited and which are permitted. The first formulation of the categorical imperative is applied to maxims which before universalizing contain singular terms. Yet these maxims can be universalized in a variety of ways, not all of which yield the same moral result. One need not, to take Kant's example of lying, replace the singular terms in the maxim by terms of such broad extension as "any one;" a highly constricted term taking into account the morally relevant features of the agent's situation would do as well. Such a term is logically completely general; for example, "anyone in circumstances such that telling the truth will cause disastrous harm to his family or community" might well replace the subject term in the maxim. The goal in the maxim could also be narrowly, but generally described. The resulting universalized maxim, unlike the universalization in the most general terms, contains no suggestion of self-contradiction. One who would will lying as a general rule for anyone in any distressful situation may indeed be attempting to will a contradiction since such a general rule would be inconsistent with the presumption of honesty on which the very possibility of lying depends.[32] But no such contradiction arises if the goals which justify lying are narrowly described and the class of persons who may lie are equally narrowly described. Which of these universalized maxims--or the other possible ones that are conceivable--should be taken as the correct one is impossible to say. As Anscombe points out, some specification of allowable descriptions of action is needed here,[33] and Kant's procedure provides none.

The attempt to work with the formulation of the categorical imperative which enjoins acting only in ways that respect persons as ends in themselves fares no better. It is no easier to determine which acts respect persons as routinely creatures than it is to tell the appropriate universalized maxim. This can be seen by considering Donagan's attempt to derive precepts from this formulation of the categorical imperative.[34] Donagan's precepts are somewhat at odds with those Kant himself thought his principle justified. For example, Kant believed that suicide always violated the categorical imperative.[35] Donagan thinks there are situations in which suicide is compatible with respect for rational nature.[36] Which of these Kantian positions is the correct one? On the face of it, there is no way to decide. The key concept "respecting rational nature" or "treating rational nature always as end and never as a mere means" is simply too vague to be decisively predicated of a describable kind of human act, except, perhaps, in a few uncontroversial cases like slavery or rape. Disagreements about what kinds of acts should be described as acts of respecting or failing to respect human nature can be settled in the end only by decision, or compromise or intuition--acts hardly sufficient to justify the correct sense of a predicate.

Thus, the Kantian attempt to found moral reasoning on the Golden Rule alone must be judged a failure. This is not because the Golden Rule or its Kantian formulations are false or confused, but because conceptual resources not found in the Golden Rule and its near relations are needed if it is to be used precisely in moral arguments. We need a moral predicate which has a rational, decidable connection to describable kinds of acts. The predicate in these statements must have some conceptual connection to the act descriptions which function as the subjects. The Kantian moral predicates--"respecting persons as ends in themselves" or "being a universal law" lack this kind of connection. In the next section I will try to sketch such a normative framework in which the basic moral predicates can be decisively related to human actions.

A MORE COMPLETE THEORY OF MORAL REASONING

Teleological theories--moral theories in which some sort of concern for the human good is the basic normative principle--seem to provide the needed connection between the basic norm and the human actions governed by the norm. For human actions as voluntary undertakings are reasonably defined by their relationship to the human goods sought, chosen, intended, and otherwise affected. Consequentialism seems to have such a connection because the basic norm prescribes doing the greater good and actions are morally defined in terms of the goods and bads predictably affected by one's undertaking. The difficulty, as we have seen, is that consequentialism supposes that one can determine the greater good, and this cannot be done. But this difficulty is not essential to teleological theories as such.

Nor, Kantian protestations notwithstanding, is it necessary for a teleological theory as such to mislocate the point of moral judgments by focusing on states of affairs produced by human activity. Human action as voluntary--as consisting of choices, intentions and their executions--can be understood teleologically. Being a good person is, on the face of it, part of living a good human life; and any plausible standard for right choice must include concern for human flourishing as a whole, including those parts of it that are not themselves morally defined.[37]

So, if there is a normative view that is teleological but not consequentialist, it might well provide what is needed for a defensible theory of moral reasoning. Some elements of such a view are suggested by Aquinas' version of natural law. Aquinas holds that there is a basic, self-evident moral principle. On one interpretation it is something like: "One ought to choose only those possibilities compatible with the entire human good."[38]

This principle is clearly teleological in that, like the basic consequentialist principle, it defines the basic moral norm in terms of the human good. But unlike the consequentialist principle there is no supposition that the components of the total human good are sufficiently homogeneous to allow the determination of the greater good or lesser evil. Nor is there the consequentialist emphasis on results. Choices compatible with the total good must respect all the elements in the ensemble of goods which comprise the total human good. This respecting of all the human goods is what brings the spirit of a morality conceived in accord with this principle close to that of Kantian ethics with its emphasis on the importance of one's personal stance and the character of one's will.

The total human good to which this principle refers is the full perfection of human potentiality--the full flourishing of all human beings. Thus, it is roughly the same as that to which John Farrelly refers as the "constitutive human good" in Chapter VIII below.[39] The source of the normative force of the principle is the fact that the good is the principle of willing and choosing, and that the total human good is not a single good or single activity. We recognize that something is good because it either is conducive to or constitutive of the perfection of one or more of our potentialities. But the perfection of any of our potentialities is not sufficient to perfect us as persons. There are other potentialities to fulfill, other goods to realize. Our capacity to choose is itself one of these potentialities, and moral norms are, in effect, the standards for perfection in choosing. But choice bears on the fulfillment of other capacities, and is possible only because of the recognition of the distinct goodness of all of them. Choices will be good and, in the relevant sense, rational, therefore, only if they recognize the distinct contribution to human fulfillment of each of the components of the human good.

This, of course, is not intended as a proof of the basic moral principle. As basic, it cannot be directly proved. That is not to say that it cannot be known to be true. Rather, it is to say that it is a self-evident proposition--what the medievals called "known of itself" (*per se nota*), known to be necessarily true once the meaning of its terms are grasped. So, this principle is not simply adopted by a decision of principle but is recognized to be true. Nor is this recognition an intuition in which one can say no more than that one *sees* the principle to be true. The focus here is on the character of the proposition and not on the subjective perceiving of it. Furthermore, it does not follow from the fact that as a basic principle this proposition cannot be proved to be true, that it cannot be defended in various ways.[40] First principles can be defended dialectically--not least by their capacity to account for the subject matter they allegedly control and their ability to avoid the difficulties encountered by alternative principles.

On the face of it, this principle has the strengths and avoids the weaknesses of the theories so far discussed. It has whatever intuitive plausibility consequentialism has in being based on human goods, but avoids the disputable assumption about the commensurability of human goods. Like Kantian ethics, this morality focuses on choice and good will. But by being based on concern for human goods it seems more able to account for aspects of morality not reducible to impartiality, and promises a way of rationally determining the specificatory premises in moral arguments. Like Ross' intuitionism this principle is proposed as a self-evident principle, but since it is the sole basic principle, the conflict between principles is avoided.

However, these hints of dialectical superiority cannot be developed without a closer look at how this principle actually works. For this principle is very general, so general, in fact, that without specification it would have little more prescriptive significance than pious generalities like "be open to other people." Non-arbitrary specification of this principle is needed for it to have any real normative utility. Such specification can be developed along the following lines. Many of the greatest moralists--including both Kant and Aquinas--have thought that rationality was of the very essence of morality. Aquinas, for example, believes that an act is moral if it is in accord with human nature, and it is in accord with human nature if and only if it is in accord with right reason.[41] It seems to me that right reason is not only reason which functions correctly or without error; it is also reason operating on the basis of thoroughly intelligible principles. I think that reason can operate on the basis of such principles only if it follows the first principle of morality.

If one makes a choice in accord with the first principle of morality then one has a completely intelligible basis for one's action--one chooses to act in pursuit of a human good because the pursuit of this human good contributes to human flourishing or to the fullness of human being. If, however, one chooses in a way that is inconsistent with this principle, then one can give no intelligible ground for the choice beyond the goodness of the particular good one pursues; one cannot be choosing this good because of its contribution to the complete human good, because, by definition, one is choosing in a way inconsistent with this ideal. Why then pick this good when one can just as well pick another which is seen to be just as good in its own way, as the one selected? Any principle one can use to answer this question necessarily fails to have the complete intelligibility of good. In other words it is, from the point of view of intelligent human action, non-rational and arbitrary. The principle used is usually some form of personal desire. One's wants are established as the principle of choices which do not conform to the first principle. One's wants are related to human goods and especially to the good of self-integration so they do provide *reasons* for action. But they are reasons which involve reference to a particular fact--namely the fact that *I want something*--and this particular fact does not have the through and through intelligibility of a good. One's interest in choosing in a way that violates the first or basic principle cannot be the simple goodness of what one chooses, for if it were, one would choose in a way open to human flourishing. Hence in choosing against the first principle one's interest must be in the good--not as such--but as realized by me or by my friends. The introduction of this egocentric reference cannot be justified by reference to goodness itself. It is just a brute fact determined by my wants.

The first or basic principle of morality is violated whenever an arbitrary principle of the sort we have been discussing is allowed to be the basis for one's choice; moreover, the first principle of morality is violated only when such a principle is followed. For example, a violation of the Golden Rule would violate the first principle of morality, for reasons suggested by Kant. Such a violation involves a kind of partiality that is not rationally grounded. But there are other ways in which one can be determined by non-rational principles than that excluded by the Golden Rule. This is what Kant failed to notice.

Thus, if we can locate the various ways in which arbitrary principles can determine our actions, we can formulate more precise principles for specific moral norms which will make the implications of the first principle somewhat clearer and more operational. These more specific moral principles will be called "modes of responsibility." This language is chosen because these general principles are not specific moral norms since they do not make reference to specific goods or to specific human actions, but refer only to the basic moral notion of full human perfection and the ways its realization can be blocked.

The modes of responsibility have their normative force entirely from the first principle of morality. But they are not themselves equivalent to it, for they introduce consideration of the various factors which can motivate a person to choose in a way that is inconsistent with the first principle of morality. In other words, the modes of responsibility exclude the various ways of being blocked from being reasonable in acting.

A number of modes of responsibility can be justified by such a process of specification. For example, we should not be deterred from acting for intelligible goods by emotional inertia; this would be to fail without good reason to act for human goods. Similarly, we should not be pressed by enthusiasm or impatience to act individualistically for human goods; this would be to fail to respect the social conditions for realizing the full human good.[42] Similar modes of responsibility exclude acting from motives opposed to the courage and fidelity required by a love of the human good.[43]

Several especially important modes of responsibility deserve special comment. The Golden Rule is, as already suggested, one of them: one should not be moved to act or deterred from acting by differences in feeling towards different persons in a way other than is in accord with a deliberate choice among intelligible goods. To violate this mode of responsibility is to sacrifice a distribution of goods in accord with integral human fulfillment to a subjectively pleasing distribution of goods. This way of understanding the Golden Rule excludes partiality for which one can give no reason except one's given preference for one person over another. It requires that differences in the way we treat people be based on considerations that are intelligible in terms of human goods. This principle is especially important for dealing with concrete moral dilemmas, especially for understanding both the moral obligation of the duties of one's social roles and the resolution of conflicts between these duties.

This understanding of the Golden Rule differs from the Kantian understanding in several important ways. First, it is not the only moral principle or the most basic one. Thus, the Kantian project of deriving the whole of morality from the Golden Rule is not undertaken. There are other ways to be practically unreasonable than by violating the demands of impartiality.

Second, the Golden Rule as here understood, is articulated within the teleological framework of concern for the human good. Thus, the factors which in the Kantian understanding are important only because of their possibly generating contradictions have moral significance because of their relation to the human good. For example, the values of trust and mutuality become important because of their connection to the good of friendship, and not simply because in a universalized maxim of a person considering the possibility of lying, they generate a contradiction. This difference allows some non-Kantian questions to arise: are the values that are ordinarily at stake in, for example, a decision to lie, *always* at stake in such decisions? If not, then there will be cases when the moral meaning of the act will be different. In these cases, one need not be "playing favorites" or making an unjustified exception in one's favor. Many lies--perhaps most--do violate the Golden Rule, because they harm the good of human community in a way no one would want their own participation in this good to be harmed. It is not clear, however, that all lies have this impact on the good of community; nor even that all lies that are immoral involve the partiality of playing favorites.

THE DEFEASIBILITY OF MORAL NORMS

In short, the theory proposed here has the resources for getting at what is morally going on in the human action which the formalist, Kantian approach lacks. This does not mean, however, that all moral norms are defeasible. For the basic principle requires that actions undertaken to harm one or another human good--whether out of hostility or for the sake of some other human good--are excluded. Such actions are inconsistent with the integral human good since they are directed against one of its components. For example, a choice to end a person's life out of retribution or some further purpose, however worthy, is a choice contrary to a basic good and, thus, always excluded. What the theory does imply is that a given act described up to a certain point may affect various human goods in one way, but that a further, more circumstantial description, may show that the act in fact affects them differently. This difference can and sometimes does affect the bearing which normative principles have on the act. Thus, there is a basis in the normative theory itself for certain "exceptions."

This account of exceptions--in other words the defeasibility of generally stated moral norms--can be developed as follows. The theory of moral reasoning proposed here involves a basic normative principle specified into a number of general norms--the modes of responsibility--which taken as a set prescribe respect and concern for the entire ensemble of human goods. These general norms all make reference to the human good, and are the functional, prescriptive premises in moral argument. The specificatory premises in moral arguments are propositions which describe actions in terms of human goods. Actions as voluntary undertakings can be thus described, since as such they are pursuits of what is recognized to be good. As noted above, it is in virtue of fuller descriptions of actions in these terms that generally stated norms can be rationally overridden.

This raises the question of how one can determine the relationship between human acts and goods. How can act descriptions be known to be true, and disputes about them rationally decided? How can we tell, for example, whether a decision not to treat a defective newborn is an unfair attack on the good of the child's life or a refusal of treatment that is really unwarranted? Or whether a misleading statement in a difficult situation is really an unfair refusal to apply to oneself the reasonable requirements of trust and openness needed for social interaction?

Questions of this sort could be multiplied indefinitely and sometimes, at least, are exceedingly difficult to answer. This is especially the case when the action's relationship to the human goods and to other people is mediated by complex institutions like marriage, civil society and so on. Nevertheless, careful reflection upon what one is doing and why one is doing it can go a long way to clarify the moral meaning of one's action. This reflection can lead to a redescription of one's act in morally more precise terms--that is, the voluntary relationship one is establishing to human goods can be more fully articulated. This redescription can enable one to see that the norm which governed the act less fully described does not really apply. Thus, it is usually unfair to break one's promises, but in some cases it is not only not unfair but something any reasonable person would agree to, even if he or she were negatively affected. Similarly with some acts which would commonly be called lying or stealing.[44] Generally stated norms prohibiting these acts are in the repertoire of most morally serious people. But even if the grounds for those general norms are only dimly perceived, one can see that in some circumstances they do not function as they normally do.

The redescription of acts proposed here is not arbitrary; it is controlled by the fact that one can uncover further the morally relevant features of a proposed human act--namely, the goods at stake in the act and the voluntary relationship a person establishes toward them. Thus, a redescription of an act in such a way as to obscure either of these features of acts is not legitimate. One way of doing so is by redescribing acts in terms of their good effects. This procedure is perfectly harmless on consequentialist grounds but inappropriate on the theory proposed here. For example, one might describe the nuclear deterrence strategy as keeping the peace, or a decision to kill a terminal patient as a painless relief of suffering, or a decision to bribe a foreign official as a cost of doing business in the country in question. All these redescriptions of the acts in question obscure what is morally central. They submerge instead of highlighting the fact that those who make the choices in question establish definite voluntary relationships to human goods. By focusing wholly on the ends to be realized, they fail to mention the actual choices made: the readiness to kill innocents involved in the threat, the choice to end the patient's life, and the choice to deal unfairly in a foreign country.

Furthermore, the redescription of actions proposed here is a method for overturning general moral norms quite distinct from consequentialism. This difference is suggested by the examples just discussed. It might be decisive for a consequentialist that the nuclear deterrence is the only way to preserve peace. Noting this good effect does not, however, change the fact that it seems to involve the willingness to kill innocent civilians. If this willingness to kill the innocent is sufficient to render the policy immoral, the good purpose of preserving peace does not change the evaluation of the act. The choice to kill someone to relieve the person's pain can be justified on consequentialist grounds; but no further consideration of morally relevant features can change the decisive fact that it involves the choice to end a person's life. A choice to give surreptitious payments to a foreign official might well be more fully described so as to throw into doubt whether in fact it is a case of unfair competition or corruption of a public official. Perhaps such behavior is established as a requirement for doing business in the locale, and all prospective businesses know it. Perhaps also, given the custom, there is no question of corrupting the official. Nevertheless, it is not clear that these considerations are in fact sufficient to show that the payment is really not unfair. There are the consumers to consider as well as other people in the country who may be unfairly treated by the official's advantage. The important point is that these are all matters of fairness, not of greater or lesser net good. Thus, even if the consequentialist judgment on the case were the same as that of the method of redescription proposed here, the judgment would reflect a different approach to moral reasoning.

In short, a more precise description of an action already described in morally relevant terms (that is, as a voluntary action, thereby related to human goods) can make clear that the action is not related to the goods in the way one originally supposed and, thus, the mode of responsibility apparently forbidding or requiring the act does not really do so.

There is a second way in which actions can be redescribed so as to make clearer the precise moral norm which should govern the act. Actions can be described in a variety of ways and many of these descriptions simply do not include the morally relevant features of actions. For example, many acts are described only in terms of the behavior involved in the act, or in terms of the behavior and some one or more of its consequences without any reference to the choice or intention involved. "Killing" is such a term; likewise "letting a person die" and "withholding treatment." Sometimes moral norms are formulated using such terms--for example, *killing is wrong*. Clearly such norms are defeasible and must be made precise if they are to be of any real use in resolving moral dilemmas.

Unless the voluntary character of the acts in question and the goods at stake in decisions involving such acts are clarified, there will be no way to distinguish, for example, between suicide and martyrdom, or between passive euthanasia and reasonable withholding of life saving treatment. For in both of these pairs of acts, there is no necessary difference in the behavior involved, but only a difference in the way death is willed.

In cases like these it is essential that one distinguish what is precisely chosen in the action from the other features of the act. Not all that is voluntary relates the person to the human goods in the same way; free choices do this in the most central way. One is responsible for one's choices because it is in them that one determines oneself. It is by one's free choices that one makes oneself to be a certain kind of person in the moral domain. Thus, since choices are free they are voluntary in the strongest sense of that term, and they are the center of moral responsibility because it is in choosing that one constitutes his moral self.

Furthermore, it is in choosing that one establishes a definite relation between oneself and the human goods. One's choices are made on the basis of the recognition that some action or omission is in some way good or evil. The evils one chooses to avoid are themselves deprivations of some good. So, in choosing one persues one good rather than another; one orders the goods in relation to oneself. Thus, it would seem that, if one's basic moral obligation is action consistent with the total human good, and if one's basic relation to human fulfillment is in choosing, then one's responsibility for one's choices is primary. Other voluntary behavior is more or less morally significant insofar as it is related to one's choices. Thus, if the foreseen consequences of a person's actions are not part of what he or she chooses, they will have a different moral significance than what one chooses.

It seems clear, both in terms of the relevant experience and on theoretical grounds, that one does not choose all that one knows will follow from one's choice. Certainly, one would not ordinarily say that one chose the unpleasant but unavoidable consequences which often accompany one's actions and which one would avoid if one could. One does not choose or intend--ordinarily at least--the pain of the dentist's chair or the hangover consequent upon a party.

Examples of this kind can be multiplied, but this multiplication serves little theoretical purpose. For the issue is really the extent and nature of a person's moral responsibility, and not the extent to which ordinary language confirms one or another view of what one must intend or choose in acting. The view proposed here is that one is primarily responsible for what one chooses or intends, and that one chooses and intends one's ends and one's means--that is, precisely the states of affairs one is committed to realizing in acting and not their even causally necessary consequences.

This is not to say that one does not voluntarily bring about the foreseen, but not-intended and not-chosen consequences of one's acts. One accepts these consequences or, to use the language of the scholastics, "permits" them to come about. But accepting is a voluntary act; one could, after all, forego the choice whose execution brings these consequences into being. The point is that the voluntariness of accepting consequences is not determinative of one's moral self in the way one's free choices are.

These differences are at the root of the principle of double effect, which turns on the difference between what one precisely intends or chooses in action and what one accepts as a side effect. In many difficult moral decisions the former is governed by the mode of responsibility which proscribes acting contrary to human goods, whereas voluntarily accepted side effects are not excluded by this mode, though they may be prohibited by other modes like fairness.[45]

Using these distinctions, it is possible to determine that the central norm contained in the generally stated behavioral norm prohibiting killing is that one must not choose to end a person's life. Moreover, these distinctions provide the resources needed to determine which deadly acts fall under this prohibition and which do not. Suicide clearly does, since the purpose of the suicide requires precisely that the person realize the state of affairs of his being dead; not so with martyrs since their purpose of maintaining their moral or religious conviction might predictably lead to death but is not furthered by the death. Similarly, with various death causing acts of self-defense or acts whereby one uses oneself as a barrier to defend others. Likewise in the case of various omissions that predictably lead to death or shorten life. Sometimes life saving treatment is withheld so that a person will die; this is equivalent to intentionally killing the person. But often the choice to withhold treatment involves no such intention; one chooses not to treat a person because one judges the treatment too costly in various ways or because the benefits are such that most people would forego them to avoid the burdens of treatment.

In short, the theory of moral reasoning sketched out here has considerable resources for rationally resolving moral dilemmas. A teleological but non-consequentialist approach to moral reasoning has the resources for describing the specificatory premises in moral arguments in a way that is rationally determinable. One can criticize and revise these descriptions in the light of what can in principle be known--by the moral agent, at least--to be morally going on.

Moral reasoning, therefore, can be carried out successfully; judgments of conscience can be rationally defended. But unless the principles for moral judgments are understood in somewhat the way suggested here, it is difficult to see how the educational effort to improve moral thinking can progress beyond the recognition of general principles like the Golden Rule, which neither cover the entire area of moral concern nor contain the resources for the careful reasoning needed to untangle difficult moral dilemmas.

University of St. Thomas
Houston, Texas

NOTES

1. See Lawrence Kohlberg, "Indoctrination Versus Relativity in Value Education," in *The Philosophy of Moral Development: Moral Stages and the Idea of Justice* (Cambridge, Hagerstown, New York: Harper and Row, Publishers, 1981), pp. 12-22. This entire volume shows Kohlberg's reliance on moral reasoning in his research on moral development.
2. See Daniel Callahan "Goals in the Teaching of Ethics," in Daniel Callahan and Sissela Bok, eds. *The Teaching of Ethics in Higher Education* (New York and London: Plenum Press, 1980), pp. 61-74.
3. See Kohlberg, "Indoctrination Versus Relativity," pp. 17-18.
4. *Ibid.*, p. 18.
5. See John Finnis, *Natural Law and Natural Rights* (Oxford, New York: Oxford University Press, 1980), pp. 9-11 on the importance of determining the focal meaning of terms in the analysis of human affairs.
6. Kohlberg, "Justice as Reversibility: The Claim to Moral Adequacy of a Highest Stage of Moral Judgment," in *The Philosophy of Moral Development*, p. 172.
7. See Rick Ellrod, "Freedom and Moral Choice," Chapter IV above.
8. H. A. Prichard, "Does Moral Philosophy Rest on a Mistake"?

Moral Obligation (London, Oxford, New York: Oxford University Press, 1968), pp. 7-8.

9. Alasdair MacIntyre, *After Virtue* (Notre Dame: University of Notre Dame Press, 1981), pp. 5-34, 105-107.

10. See Kohlberg, "Justice as Reversibility," p. 172; for a further development of this point see Rick Ellrod, "Contemporary Philosophies of Moral Education," Chapter I above.

11. See Chapter IX below.

12. W. D. Ross, *The Right and the Good*, ch. 2; cited from O. Johnson, editor, *Ethics: Selections From Classical and Contemporary Writers* (4th edition; New York: Holt Rinehart and Winston, 1978), p. 460.

13. *Ibid.*, p. 468.

14. C. D. Broad, *Five Types of Ethical Theory* (London: Kegan & Paul, 1930), pp. 222-223.

15. See Alan Donagan, *The Theory of Morality* (Chicago: University of Chicago Press, 1977), p. 23.

16. *Ibid.*, pp. 23-24.

17. See W. K. Frankena, *Ethics* (2nd edition; Englewood Cliffs: Prentice Hall, 1973), pp. 34-36.

18. Ross, *The Right and the Good*, p. 461.

19. This is a variation on an argument made orally by G.E.M. Anscombe.

20. See Charles Fried, *Right and Wrong* (Cambridge and London: Harvard University Press, 1978), pp. 7-9 for a clear account of consequentialism.

21. For a compelling development of this line of argument, see Donagan, *The Theory of Morality*, pp. 199-209.

22. See John Farrelly's "The Human Good and Moral Choice," Chapter VIII below; and Germain Grisez and Joseph M. Boyle, Jr., *Life and Death with Liberty and Justice; A Contribution to the Euthanasia Debate* (Notre Dame, London: University of Notre Dame Press, 1979), pp. 358-361; John Finnis, *Natural Law and Natural Rights*, pp. 59-95.

23. See Jeremy Bentham, *An Introduction to the Principles of Morals and Legislation*, ch. 4.

24. See J. S. Mill, *Utilitarianism*, ch. 2, "What Utilitarianism Is"?

25. This line of argument is based on Germain Grisez, "Choice and Consequentialism," *Proceedings of the ACPA*, 51 (1977), pp. 144-152.

26. See Grisez and Boyle, *Life and Death*, pp. 355-358 for more on this and on other non-consequentialist senses of "greater good." Clearly, this conclusion is not based completely on value theory, but includes premises about the relation between choices and human goods. Thus, even those who hold for a nuanced theory of the human good (like John Farrelly's account of the constitutive human good in "The Human Good and Moral Choice," Chapter VIII below), might reject these premises in the form I use them.

27. See Donagan, *op. cit.*, pp. 57-58.

28. See Kohlberg, "Justice as Reversibility," pp. 201-205; "From Is

to Ought: How to Commit the Naturalistic Fallacy and Get Away with It in the Study of Moral Philosophy," *The Philosophy of Moral Development*, pp. 147-168.

29. See Warner Wick, "Introduction: Kant's Moral Philosophy," in *The Metaphysical Principles of Virtue*, tr. by James Ellington (Indianapolis: Bobbs-Merrill, 1964), pp. xvii-xx.

30. Immanuel Kant, *Foundations of the Metaphysics of Morals*, tr. by L. W. Beck (Indianapolis: Bobbs-Merrill, 1959), p. 39.

31. *Ibid.*, p. 47.

32. See *ibid.*, pp. 18-19 for Kant's argument that lying is always wrong.

33. See G.E.M. Anscombe, "Modern Moral Philosophy," *Philosophy*, 33 (1958), 3.

34. See Donagan, *The Theory of Morality*, pp. 75-111.

35. Kant, *Foundations of the Metaphysics of Morals*, pp. 39-40, 47; see *The Metaphysical Principles of Virtue*, p. 84 for Kant's opening in the direction of allowing suicide in difficult cases.

36. Donagan, *The Theory of Morality*, pp. 76-79.

37. Some of the components of the human good are not morally defined, and can rightly be called pre-moral goods--for example, life, health, truth, and aesthetic appreciation are basic human values but do not include moral norms in their definition. Other goods, like justice and authenticity include moral norms in their definition. Hence they are moral goods: being morally defined they are moral; being components of the integral human good they are goods. Pre-moral goods clearly constitute part of the integral human good; see John Farrelly, "The Human Good and Moral Choice," Chapter VIII below.

38. Aquinas formulates the basic principle of morality in several ways: the twofold love commandment is identified as the fundamental, self-evident principle of natural law (*Summa Theologiae*, I-II, q. 100, a. 3, ad 1); in this same article he also refers to "*A human being should do harm (maleficere) to no one*" as among the primary, common, self-evident principles of the natural law. Elsewhere he refers to the basic principle more procedurally as the requirement to act in accord with right reason (*Summa Theologiae*, I-II, q. 94, a. 4). Donagan, *The Theory of Morality*, pp. 59-65, gives an account of Aquinas's moral theory which provides some of the grounds for interpreting Aquinas as suggesting a first principle along the lines developed here.

39. See Farrelly, "The Human Good and Moral Choice," Chapter VIII; Farrelly's footnote 32 explains some differences between his view of the good and mine; see Grisez and Boyle, *Life and Death*, pp. 361-371, for an account of human values and the basic principle of morality in terms very close to those used here. The entire human good is understood as a systematic whole which is an ideal. It is systematic and not just a random collection because the full realization of the human good by all persons demands a structure required by the goods themselves--related as they are in various ways.

40. See Germain Grisez and Russell Shaw, *Beyond the New Morality: The Responsibilities of Freedom* (2nd edition; Notre Dame and London" University of Notre Dame Press: 1980), pp. 97-100 for an account of how this principle accords with ordinary language about morality and common moral experience.

41. See *Summa Theologiae* I-II, q. 71, a. 3, ad 2.

42. The full human good is not defined individualistically; it is the full perfection of all human beings; see Grisez and Shaw, *Beyond the New Morality*, pp. 115-116.

43. On this mode of responsibility, see *ibid.*, pp. 116-118.

44. See St. Thomas Aquinas, *Summa Theologiae*, I-II, q. 94, a. 4 for an account of the defeasibility of a moral norm similar to the one given here. He holds that right reason requires that one return a person's goods upon request, but that this same basic standard requires that one not return the goods if one knows that they will be used for seditious purposes. Similarly in II-II, q. 66, a. 7, he holds that stealing is always wrong, but that some acts that might be considered stealing are not really such. The prohibition of stealing depends upon a normative conception of private property which, he holds, is justified only by reference to the common good. And in some cases a person's possession of something harms the common good--e.g., when it causes one who needs it to starve. Hence, in those cases it is not, morally speaking that person's property, and taking it is not stealing.

45. For a more complete account of the double effect principle, see my "Toward Understanding the Principle of Double Effect," *Ethics*, 90 (July 1980), 527-538.

CHAPTER VIII

A PHENOMENOLOGY

of

MORAL SENSIBILITY

JOHN D. CAPUTO

The fully moral act has often been located in the purely rational element--in clear knowledge and unimpeded willing. Passion, moods and feelings are taken to be somehow *external* to the inner workings of the true man. Passion is at best a matter over which the rational principle rules, and its proper role is to be submissive to the leadership of the rational principle. At worst, the impulses of our so-called sensible nature are taken as a positive threat to reason, threatening to usurp its free, rational direction of human life and to turn life over to whim, caprice, and self-seeking--in a word to "feeling."

The position which I will defend in this paper, however, is predicated upon a unitary conception of man, a conception which was best defended in the classical world by Aristotle, and which receives its sharpest contemporary formulation in the writings of the phenomenologists. Phenomenologists, and foremost among them Heidegger himself, have always recognized in Aristotle a precedent and antecedent, for it was he who wanted to return to the "things themselves," to hew the work of reflection as closely as possible to concrete experience. Whence the direction of the present inquiry is at once Aristotelian, phenomenological, and experiential. In such a view man is understood to be an essentially embodied agent so that feeling and affectivity enter into the very structure of the moral act. Hence, moral life is not conceived as a battle waged between warring metaphysical principles.

The pages which follow strive to set forth the positive role of feelings in a sound moral theory.[1] I shall do this in the name of what is termed here "moral sensibility," by which is meant the harmony between our sensible nature and moral values. The chapter will unfold in the following sequence: (1) I will show that, far from being external to the moral act, passion enters into its very fabric, so that failing passion no act is of any moral worth at all. This point will be established by following the Kierkegaardian analysis of passion. (2) Next I will show that, far from "blinding reason," passion or mood plays an essential role in the *disclosure* of our world, and that means the world of moral values. That point will be established in connection with a study of Heidegger's notion of mood and disposition. (3) Having secured our ontological bearings in the opening sections of the paper, I shall then shift to the specifics of a properly moral sensibility. The point of departure for this argument will be found in Kant's analysis of the "feeling of respect," a theory whose phenomenological implications have to be disengaged from its dualist moorings in Kant's metaphysics. (4) The feeling of respect will lead into a concrete phenomenology of the human person as the place of value or, one can say, as incarnate value. (5) And this will make it possible to formulate what is in fact the principal thesis of this paper, which is that our bodily and affective relationship to the other constitutes a "proto-ethics" upon which all moral reflection is based. Whence, instead of excluding the affective from moral life, it shall be argued that it is the spring by which all ethics is nourished.

KIERKEGAARD'S CONCEPT OF PATHOS

It was Kierkegaard more than anyone else who broke through the heavily encrusted structures of dualist ontology--who "deconstructed" them, to use a word whose day has come--and who cleared the way for a new ontology of the emotions. Kierkegaard saw that the fundamental distinction in human affairs is not between reason and the passions, but between the committed and the uncommitted, the engaged and the detached.

He considered the distinction between the rational and the emotive, soul and body, to be pagan and Platonic. Christianity was to draw a line between those whose faith is living, a vital and operative commitment permeating their whole lives, and those whom the Scriptures call "lukewarm" (CUP, 206).[2] In the New Testament, Kierkegaard thinks, the crucial distinction which emerges is that between those who are fully involved or "engaged" and the apathetic, between the *pathos* of a living faith and the apathy or non-pathos, of those who drift along in a comfortable, bourgeois Christianity. "I do not deny," he writes in bitter satire, "that it is comfortable to be a Christian, and at the same time be exempted from the martyrdom which is always present . . . ."[3] The essential distinction is thus between passion or pathos and a-pathos. This discrimination flies in the face of the Greek distinction between the rational principle and the irrational principle which has dominated the history of metaphysics from Plato to Husserl.

On Kierkegaard's terms a genuine Christian is one who is passionately committed to his faith, whose passion so informs his actions that, lacking passion, they are lifeless and rote.[4] Everything thereby is reversed: the informing principle is the pathos, which Kierkegaard also calls the "how," whereas the "what," the belief or creed or article (proposition) of faith, is but the content or matter. The creed is just a list of propositions, an external and lifeless content which comes to life only in the passion of an existing and believing Christian faith. To know that I am going to die and that I am promised in faith a life after death, is not a thought, Kierkegaard says, but a deed. It is not accomplished by pronouncing the words, but by an act of faith that sends a shock throughout our entire being.

If Kierkegaard does not distinguish passion and reason, he does distinguish a merely aesthetic pathos or passion from true, ethico-religious pathos.[5] In aesthetic pathos or aesthetic sensibility we are only partially transformed, and the transformation issues only in words, perhaps in verse. Our "taste" is struck by a thing of beauty, but our lives are not changed. Aesthetic pathos remains disinterested, looking on from afar.[6] But ethico-religious pathos means a total transformation of our whole life so that we are made over into a new man, reborn in the image of God. It issues not in words but in deeds, and it signifies that one has entered into an absolute relationship to the absolute goal or telos. One is wholly committed to the absolute, committed even unto the end, unto death.

This is not to say that Kierkegaard's religious man is continually heaving and sighing with religious fervor, or that he is uninterrupted in the performance of great and heroic deeds: continually exposed to the lion, always on the verge of martyrdom. On the contrary, he tends to keep his absolute commitment under wraps and to bear it unseen (incognito). He hides it under the mask of humor and irony [7] so that outwardly, as he says in *Fear and Trembling*, the knight of faith may lead so uneventful a life that if we met him we would find that he looks like a tax collector. The real meaning of this absolute religious pathos is that it is an abiding, constant passion:

> To relate oneself with existential pathos to an eternal happiness is never expressed by once in a while making a great effort, but by persistence in the relationship. . . . What holy vows a man knows how to make at the instant of mortal danger! But when that is passed, the vow is so promptly and so completely forgotten.[8]

Hence, the distinction between the resolute and the irresolute, which is often mistaken as a distinction between a pure, steadfast "will" and transitory passions, is rearticulated by Kierkegaard in a revolutionary way. Instead of opposing the pure will to the passion of the moment, Kierkegaard distinguishes a deep and abiding existential pathos--a totally self-transforming pathos--from a fleeting, transient pathos.

There is thus a difference in temporality between these two forms of pathos. The one is abiding, constant, sustained from day to day even under the most undramatic circumstances. The other is momentary and awakened only on great occasions:

> When the earth quakes . . . how swiftly then and how thoroughly does even the dullest scholar . . . comprehend the uncertainty of everything.[9]

When the great occasion passes this pathos slips back into its customary complacency. Some men are moved by the thought of God only on solemn occasions, at weddings and funerals, say, or at official oath-takings; but others know how to bring the thought of God together with the task of taking a trip to the park. It is all a matter of the abiding *depth* of one's passion. Kierkegaard does not oppose pure will to bodily impulse, but deep passion to shallow passion, abiding, transforming passion to transient, momentary passions which merely result in occasional disturbances on a mostly placid surface. There is no question of getting outside or above passion, no question of standing on a higher, supersensible ground from which to control passion. That is the framework of Platonism and Greek metaphysics, of "recollection," not of "repetition."[10] In the categories of Christianity, it is a question of separating the wheat from the chaff, the fervent from the lukewarm, those who are with Christ from those who are against, the total pathos from the occasional and transient one, the deep from the shallow passion.

There is, I might add, a good deal of confirmation for what Kierkegaard says in the sorts of distinctions we habitually make in ordinary language without falling into Platonism. We speak of a "cold anger," which is not the passing anger of the moment, an angry outburst, but a deep, even, life-long anger such as the patriot's profound, implacable anger against the colonial power. The same can be said of a "mortal" hatred, revenge, envy, or any other destructive passion which is deep-seated and abiding; it is too cunning and deadly serious to give itself over to mercurial and passing expressions. By the same token the love of a man and a woman, of a country doctor for his patients, of the farmer for the soil, has the same quality of quiet depth and surface calm. Still water runs deep, we say, meaning that the essential thing is the depth of a passion and not its surface stirrings.

By taking his point of departure in the categories of religious and Christian life, Kierkegaard redrew the map that Platonic metaphysics had given us: contrary to the Platonic view, there is no moral action at all outside of passion. The lack of passion in moral life means the perfunctory performance of acts which lack conviction and dedication. Indeed it is passion which brings the agent into the moral sphere, which makes his actions committed and decisive. The lack of pathos does not mean that the way has been cleared for the pure rational will. It means that we are not acting at all, but merely thinking about acting, or else that our actions are performed by rote, that they lack the moral quality of decisiveness, that they are neither heartfelt nor committed.

HEIDEGGER'S ONTOLOGY OF MOODS

But if Kierkegaard placed Platonic ontology into question, the task fell to Heidegger to formalize Kierkegaard's revolution. Heidegger proposed an ontological account of man in which affectivity was considered to be a primordial and irreducible structure of human existence.[11] Existence, he held, is constituted of three co-equal and equally radical structures which he called projection, disposition and fallenness. Inasmuch as he is "projected" man is always ahead of himself, cast forth into one course of action or another; by "disposition," the being which is cast forth is at the same time already situated within pre-given circumstances; and inasmuch as he is "fallen," the being which projects himself ahead, from out of a given situation, is ever liable to give up his project and to sink back into complacency with present actuality. The three structures are transparently temporal in character, describing the way in which man runs forth into future possibilities in the midst of an oppressing actuality into which he has already been delivered (having been) which tempts him to remain content with the present. The ontology or understanding of reality which Heidegger developed in *Being and Time* completed the revolution which Kierkegaard had set in motion. For here was an ontology which drew the decisive distinction in human nature, not between "reason" and "feelings," but between the various temporal structures of man so that the problem of an act which is "free" of feeling, or "above" feeling does not arise.

To describe affectivity Heidegger used the word "*Befindlichkeit*", whose sense for him is drawn from the colloquial expression "how are you?" ("*Wie befinden-Sie sich?*"), "how are you found?", "how do things sit with you?" "how are you situated?"[12] It is probably best translated as "disposition." If disposition represents an ontological structure, then moods are the particular entities (or "ontic" structures) through which the basic ontological structure is *disclosed*. In contrast, the intellectualist tradition speaks of the "light of reason," but regards moods as blind and subjective. Brooks do not brood; we do. Grey afternoons are not sombre, we are. But Heidegger rejects the idea that there is a subject here and an object there and focuses instead upon the interaction "between" subject and object. In that case, moods play an essential role in disclosing the structure of our world and of our experience.

Heidegger thus puts forward two basic theses about affectivity: the first concerns its *necessity*, and the second concerns its *disclosive* power. Let us examine each in turn.

The tradition treats moods as transient, mutable states which come and go and which do not enter into the stable, permanent essence of man. In contrast, Heidegger, following Kierkegaard, gives moods an ontological role and makes them essential structures of our Being. That means that everything in man is, as it were, "mooded." Moods are the way man is "tuned" to the world, and he is always in one state of attunement or another;[13] it is a mistake to think that we are or can ever get free of moods. It is indeed necessary at times not to be disturbed, but that means simply that at times we require undisturbing moods such as peace and tranquility. When Descartes speaks of getting free of his passions in order to undertake his meditations, he is mistaking the mood of tranquility with being in a mood-free state. And when Kant speaks of countering inclinations with pure will, that can only mean countering bad inclinations with good ones.

Secondly, Heidegger assigns to moods a disclosive role; this is a phenomenological point not brought out explicitly by Kierkegaard. On the phenomenological account, a feeling is not some kind of "subjective response" to an "objective stimulus," but is possessed instead of an *in-*

196 *A Phenomenology of Moral Sensibility*

tentional structure,[14] that is, it is a way of intending or turning to the world, of disclosing its make-up and the structure of our experience. It is nothing "inner" and subjective, but rather an intentional transcendence, a stepping outside (or ek-stasis), which reaches out to the world. According to Heidegger moods have a three-fold power of disclosure.

To begin with, and this is their most important function, moods disclose what Heidegger calls the "facticity," the givenness, of our Being. For Heidegger man finds himself situated within the world--within a society, a tradition, a family, etc.--prior to any possible consent on his part: that is, he is always "delivered over" (*ueberantwortet*) to his Being. Moods disclose how that being-delivered-over is experienced, whether as a burden or a weight pushing us down (de-pression), or as the lifting of a burden (e-lation). Whence they disclose the naked "fact" of being-in-the-world, which is what Heidegger means by "facticity," the naked "that-he-is-there" of man. Facticity is thus not a mere "matter of fact" in the manner of seventeenth- and eighteenth- century philosophy; it is rather a lived or existential fact, a disclosed or phenomenological fact: it is the lived through experience of being factically situated in the world.

Thus, it is not to be confused with the standard idea of "contingency," which is an objectivistic notion, referring to something which a disinterested speculative gaze observes to be there rather than not. Because facticity is something lived-through, it can be apprehended or disclosed only by mood. One can consider matters of fact with what the tradition calls intellect (*nous*) for as long as one wishes and never experience facticity. Facticity is disclosed only in that "tuning" which belongs to a being who is "thrown." Contingency is at best a distillate of lived facticity, its objectivistic correlate. One may thus give theoretical assent to the contingency of one's being without ever opening one's eyes moodfully to facticity. It would take an earthquake, Kierkegaard said, to bring some sleepy scholars to admit the uncertainty of things![15]

Moods also disclose the world as a "totality." This is explained in *What is Metaphysics?* which treats of the disclosure of the world in anxiety.[16] Through anxiety the world as a totality fades into meaninglessness, even as in joy it glows with charm. One is exposed to this anxiety even if one has an optimistic, theoretical account of things; contrariwise, one can experience Being in positive tones even if one has a pessimistic metaphysics (as seems to have been the case with Eduard von Hartmann, a Schopenhauerian pessimist who was happily married and professionally successful).

Finally, moods not only disclose the facticity of our Being and the Being of the world as a whole, they also disclose particular entities within the world in such a way as to let these entities "matter" to us, to let them be of concern to us (*angegangen werden sein*). Whence it is only in the mood of fear that something can matter to man as threatening:

> Pure beholding, even if it were to penetrate to the innermost core of the Being of something present-at-hand could never

discover anything like that which is threatening. . . . By looking at the world theoretically, we have already dimmed it down to the uniformity of what is purely present-at-hand.[17]

The fearsomeness of a fearsome object cannot be disclosed by pure beholding; fear indeed *is* this disclosure of the fearsome object as such. The mood of fear, like every other mood, discloses the world in a way which cannot be substituted for or improved upon. Thus, moods are not "blind," but insightful and disclosive. They tell us about ourselves and others in a way to which we otherwise have no access. They tell us long before reason has noticed that we are on the wrong track, that we have no business here, that so and so is not to be trusted, that we are being untrue to what we have all along believed. Socrates' celebrated "voice" was precisely such a preconceptual, moodful power of insight, a way of disclosing things long before his dialectic could summon up arguments one way or the other. If this be so then in Socrates, at the very birth of philosophy, we find moral affectivity or the mooded disclosure of value. This is the point we want to make in the following pages.

But before taking up this issue let us summarize briefly the results achieved thus far. From Kierkegaard we learned that, far from being something external or outside the properly human, passion is precisely what renders an act decisive, committed and authentic: outside of passion there is only the lukewarm, the apathetic. In terms of morality this means that it is passion which makes a moral agent an agent, someone who truly *does* something, who acts and who stands by his action. From Heidegger, we learned that the ontological structure of passion and mood is to disclose; and that moods, far from being blind or subjective, reveal the world to us in a way to which reason has no access. This means that they play a disclosive role in moral matters as well. In the same way that fear discloses the fearsome object, moral affectivity discloses moral value, or what the tradition would call the "good." We are thus at an extreme removed from the dualism of is and ought, a point which is made also by David Schindler in Chapter X below. On this account value belongs integrally to the structure of what "is," so long as "is" is understood in all its amplitude as a self-manifesting or self-revealing phenomenon, (*phainomenon*), rather than being reduced to a mere matter of fact in the manner of seventeenth-century philosophy. The task now is to show how that is possible.

THE FEELING OF RESPECT IN KANT'S ETHICS

To carry on Heidegger's metaphor, moral sensibility is the attunement of the moral agent to moral value, his sensitivity and responsiveness to value: moral sensibility is affective moral life. In search of help for a theory of moral sensibility, I shall turn to Kant, although he represents an extreme case of moral and metaphysical dualism. Kant wrestled with the question of moral feeling throughout his writings, and it is worth noting that in his earlier, pre-critical writings, he actually defended a theory of "moral sense."[18] His mature ethical position was, in fact, a reaction against a view that he himself once defended. Indeed, even after he had formulated his rigorous separation of pure will and empirical inclination, Kant himself concluded that the view as it stood was dualistic and needed to be reconciled with the sensibility.[19]

The metaphysical setting of this moral feeling in Kant is, in my view, beyond redemption. In Kant's theory this feeling is the sole feeling which arises, not from antecedent phenomenal causes, but from the will itself, pure noumenal will.[20] It is in a sense the inscription left by pure reason upon our sensible nature. But Kant can hardly defend such a view if the moral feeling is indeed a feeling and not a metaphor. For if it truly belongs to our sensible nature then it is as rigidly predictable as the movements of the heavenly bodies and has nothing to do with the freedom of the will; Kant could deny this only by denying the uniformity of nature. Moreover, on Kant's own terms, it must be fully explicable in terms of our neuro-physiological make-up and the physical stimuli which cause one neuro-physiological reaction rather than another; it can have no more to do with moral value than does feeling pain in the presence of excessive heat. It is a piece of nature which has nothing to do with the intelligible world; it has to do with facts and not values. The whole notion of moral feeling is a futile attempt to back out of the worst implications of his own theory. What he needed was a wholly new theory of experience and affectivity, one which would break with the fundamental presuppositions of eighteenth century philosophy.

Although this was not possible for Kant himself, the importance of Kant's analysis did not go unnoticed by Heidegger a century and a half later when he wrote: "Kant's interpretation of the phenomenon of respect is probably the most brilliant phenomenological analysis of the phenomenon of morality that we have from him."[21] This suggests that, with the help of phenomenology, we can rescue Kant's theory from its dualist moorings and achieve thereby precisely what our argument requires, viz., a phenomenological analysis of the moral phenomenon which centers on an affective moral intentionality.

Kant was grappling with the notion which Kierkegaard would later make abundantly clear, that the will is not moved except through passion. The purely "impassive" will is motionless and never achieves the status of being an agent at all. But Kant's metaphysics makes it strictly impossible that anything other than the moral law itself should be the "incentive" or driving force (*Triebfeder*) of the will, lest the will be moved to act by non-moral motives. As the law alone must be the sole incentive, the cause of our action could not be the moral feeling of respect, but rather the effect upon our sensible nature which the law brings about. We do not obey the law because of the feeling of respect, but we feel respect because we are subject to the law. We are moved to act by the law, and insofar as the law is moving as an incentive it effects

John D. Caputo 199

in us this moral feeling.

Now there are two moments to the feeling of respect. In the first place, the effect of the law upon our pathological nature is to thwart our inclinations which tend away from the law. The law checks the feeling of pleasure in something forbidden:

> Thus far, the effect of the moral law as an incentive is only negative, and as such this incentive can be known a priori. For all inclination and every sensuous impulse is based on feeling, and the negative effect on feeling (through the check on the inclinations) is itself a feeling. Consequently we can see a priori that the moral law as a ground of determination of the will, by thwarting all our inclinations, must produce a feeling which can be called pain.[22]

The law holds in check self-love, our selfish urge for self-gratification, and self-conceit, our misled tendency to think ourselves of worth independently of our conformity to the law.

But the law is not merely negative, it does not merely forbid, it is also a positive, an ideal of freedom and moral excellence. Accordingly the feeling it induces cannot be merely negative; its positive grandeur is thus a function of its negative power to humble our sensible nature.[23] The law subdues our pathological nature; it brings us into submission to reason; it asserts its priority over us and implants in us a sense of being a "subject" of the law. The law itself then emerges in its positive power, in its majesty, kingship and regal authority and overpowers us. The law has a power and might like the starry heavens above, a majestic sweep, a show not of physical but of moral force.

Heidegger recasts the analysis in phenomenological terms.[24] Respect is always "respect for," that is, it has an intentional structure in virtue of which it intends the moral law. For Kant the law is the ground of the feeling, not the feeling of the law; the feeling is simply the way in which the law is disclosed or made manifest to me as intentional object. For Heidegger the feeling of respect is not only a feeling for the law, but also a certain self-feeling in which I am disclosed to myself. For I experience myself as subject to the law and so as free and responsible before the law. Hence I experience myself as a being of worth or dignity (*Wuerde*). If I feel subordination or subjection to the law, the law also raises me up by disclosing my true dignity as a moral personality (*personalitas moralis*), a member of the intelligible world.

The feeling of respect is at the same time both an inclination or tendency towards it as the source of our true dignity. The feeling of respect thus resembles anxiety, which Heidegger explains elsewhere. Anxiety, too, is a shrinking back before the nullity which it discloses and at the same time a being drawn towards, inasmuch as anxiety breaks the spell in which we are held by beings and enables us to experience the upsurge of Being itself as against this nothingness.[25]

The moral feeling of respect is then precisely this affective attunement of feeling and the law whose possibility we projected in the first two sections of this paper. We are attuned to the majesty of the law the way our aesthetic sensibility is attuned to the majesty of the starry heavens; we respond as deeply to the worth of a moral deed as to the beauty of a work of art. Kant's metaphysics made it impossible for him to defend his theory of the moral feeling, but the soundness of his phenomenological account of this feeling belied the metaphysics it was meant to defend.

I have not yet discussed, however, the most important feature of Kant's analysis. "Respect," Kant says, "always applies to persons only, never to things.[26] That is a decisive qualification, for Kant's rationalist metaphysics often leads him to speak in terms of a hypostasized law or reason. But now Kant adds that respect is directed not at material objects, and by extension not at an abstract law, but always at a concrete person who embodies the law. I respect a person, not a thing, and I respect a person not insofar as he holds high office or exerts great power, but precisely inasmuch as he embodies the law. Whence Kant writes:

> Fontanelle says, 'I bow to a great man, but my mind does not bow.' I can add: to a humble plain man in whom I perceive righteousness in a higher degree than I am conscious of in myself, my mind bows whether I choose or not, however high I carry my head that he may not forget my superior position. Why? His example holds before me a law which strikes down my self-conceit when I compare my own conduct with it. . .[27]

When we witness an example of virtue which surpasses our own, our own shortcomings are exposed and our self-love and self-conceit are struck down.

Now the person bears a two-fold relation to the law. The person is both the alpha and the omega of the law, the origin and the sphere in which it is applied. The dignity of a man of concrete virtue is not only that he holds his sensuous impulses in check and responds to a supersensible principle. It is found also--and even more primordially--in that he is the author of this law, that the law arises autonomously from his own rationality and is not imposed upon him from without. Hence the *law* as a purely formal principle is convertible with the *person* as the bearer of the law (as subject and legislator). This, of course, is the basis of the alternate formulations which Kant gives of categorical imperative in his *Foundations of the Metaphysics of Morals*: the first expressing the law as a purely formal principle, the second addressing its content or matter, and the last announcing the kingdom of ends as the synthesis of the first two. Without the person, the law would be a nonexistent abstraction. It would not "hold" because it would have no one to hold *for* and no one to be held *by*. But without the law the person would lack all dignity and would remain a piece of nature, a merely phenomenal being no better than a Cartesian automaton. Whence the law insures the dignity of the person inasmuch as it is in virtue of the law that the person rises above the sphere of nature; while the person gives substance to the law, rendering it real and effective.

Now I maintain that Kant gives expression here, in the categories of a dualistic metaphysics, to a profound and genuine experience. In my view it is possible to rid this theory of its sensible-supersensible dualism and to give it the stamp of genuine phenomenological coin. This I would do in two steps. In the first place the categorical imperative is no dictum of "pure reason" over and above our "sensible" nature. As an "imperative" it is a mode of discourse, a linguistic formation in the form of a command. It takes shape in, and is possible only within the framework of, language and grammar. Hence it belongs to the sphere of "discourse" or the Being of man insofar as man speaks, what Heidegger calls *Rede*, in Greek *logos*. As a mode of discourse it is a call, indeed a call which issues from man himself, from the depths of his Being, and bids him to be the being which it is up to him to be. The categorical imperative is no supersensible law, but a call which only a being who speaks can utter-- and hear. It belongs to the Being of man as incarnate, as speaking, as calling and hearing.[28]

The same result is even more forcibly visited upon us when we turn from the "form" to the "content" of the laws, from the mere form of an imperative to the moral person (an issue which is also discussed in Chapter IX below). What is the moral person? As Heidegger asks: "What is the ontological concept of the moral person, which is thus revealed in respect, of the *personalitas moralis*?"[29] The answer is found in what Kant's *Foundations* calls the person as an end-in-himself and not merely as a means.[30] Man is not good because he is good *for* something--he is not merely a commodity in the labor force, a purveyor of services--but a good *in* himself, *for* himself. He is not good because of what he can *do*--for himself or for others--but because of what he *is*, in his Being. The Being of this being is to be of worth, and the worth of this being is ontologically secured against anything which may be ontically disagreeable about him.

Now Kant expressed the dignity of man in the dualistic terms of the ability of our supersensible will to subdue our sensible appetites. I see this as an alienated formulation of a more profound phenomenological experience of the dignity of the person. Let us listen again to Kant's adaptation of Fontanelle's words:

> "I can bow to a great man, but my mind does not bow." I can add: to a humble plain man in whom I perceive righteousness in a higher degree than I am conscious of in myself, my mind bows whether I choose or not, however high I carry my head that he may not forget my superior position.

That, I suggest, is the phenomenological origin of Kant's moral philosophy. What animated Kant's thought from the start was his experience of the dignity of the person, his concrete encounter with men and women of simple nature who understood better than generations of philosophers Socrates' statement that it is better to suffer injustice than to commit it. Kant was moved to deny reason in order to make room for faith because of a profound and animating experience of the dignity of the human person, an experience so deep and heartfelt that it has all the characteristics of the "passionate inwardness" of which Kierkegaard spoke. It was no shallow passion brought on by a great occasion, but a deep and lasting reverence which animated the whole critical philosophy.

We are thus led by Kant to a formulation of the fundamental principle of moral sensibility: that the person is given to us in the feeling of respect as a being of intrinsic worth and dignity. The moral feeling of respect discloses the concretely given person as an object of moral worth. The person is disclosed in moral affectivity as a being of dignity and worthy of respect. Lack of this moral sensibility, failure in this moral affectivity, would render us morally monstrous, coldly indifferent to the worth of others, perhaps even pathologically ill. One imagines the cold executioners of whom history provides an unfortunate list of examples precisely in these terms--as moral monsters, repugnant, repulsive, sickening. Here all the chords of our moral attunement are in discord. Our moral sensibility is in sensible, not mere metaphoric pain.

THE PHENOMENOLOGY OF THE PERSON AS A PRIMORDIAL DISCLOSURE OF VALUE

I have claimed that the Kantian thesis of the person as an end-in-himself is a metaphysical theory which can be converted directly into phenomenological coin. I want now to make good on that claim and to offer a phenomenological account of our experience of the person, the point of which will be to show that value is disclosed to us prereflectively, in the sphere of affectivity, long "before" reflective reason has a chance to put in a word of its own. There is a prepredicative moral experience which lies at the base of moral reflection, even as there is a prepredicative perceptual experience which lies at the base of theoretical assertions. We are claiming thus that the life of the moral agent is prepredicatively shaped and formed, and that the reflection of the moral philosopher must be directed at unpacking or explicating this prepredicative experience. In the present section I wish to unfold this prepredicative experience of the person as an affective disclosure of value, and then in the concluding section to discuss how this constitutes a "protoethics."

Phenomenologists like Heidegger and Merleau-Ponty have argued long and persuasively that the "world" is not *my* world but a shared world, a world with others ("with-world"); and hence that the other is not only an object on my screen, a being-for-me which can be situated on my horizons, but a being-for-himself, irreducible to me. Such a phenomenologically construed world is at the far remove from the Cartesian illusion of an *ego cogito* on the one side and a totality of objects outside me. For I am from the start "outside," drawn into the world and subject to its innumerable influences. I am from the start in a world which is not of my own making, but shaped and formed by historical and linguistic structures which are thousands of years old, which were created with imperceptible slowness by long forgotten generations. These structures are not, as in Sartre's neo-Cartesianism, threats to my freedom; rather they nourish and give shape to my world (see Chapter XI below). My world is filled with others, shaped by their contributions. I am indebted to their generosity and filled with their presence. My family, friends and colleagues, my tradition at large, is a constellation of benefactors who hand over to me the possibilities of my Being.

Now I want to show how my debt to the others reaches down to the depths of my Being, of my prereflective relationship to them. Long before I reach the stage of reflective thought I am already in a relationship to others; my Being is from the start Being-with. I owe my origin to others, my nurturing and growth. From its first moments my life develops in rhythm with others, at first in tune with the rhythm of the maternal heart-beat, and then in tune with the rhythm of the home with its cluster of smiling faces and noises and lights and aromas. The world to which I belong from the start is not a world of material objects with various sizes, shapes, and velocities. It is a profoundly personal world focussed on other persons as on radiant points of energy or light, the way the evening sky is filled with stars. From these centers of energy are radiated influences which surround and envelope me so that, when they are present I am filled with them, and when they withdraw I feel their absence. Their very absence testifies to their presence. This enveloping personal world is constantly given to us, always and already pre-given. So true is this that Heidegger says that the so called "problem of other persons" is not the Cartesian pseudo-problem of proving that others are there--that we are not alone in the universe, as Descartes puts it so astonishingly--but rather of finding ourselves in the midst of their encompassing presence. Others, Heidegger argues, are not those whom I am *not*, as if the ego came first and others afterwards as the negation of the ego, but rather those among whom I *too* am.[31] And this relationship to others, which could not be more profound, is borne witness to throughout the length and breadth of our intentional life. The whole range of our intentional acts stands under the influence of the presence of others.

Here I am concerned chiefly with the bodily and affective resonance of this relationship to others, with that affective intentionality which discloses the other to us as a being worthy of respect, and which is already at work before the *ego cogito* arrives on the scene. I wish to argue that bodily intentionality is already ec-static, that is, already extended beyond itself, stretched out to others, responsive to others. Long before the child enters the universe of words he already intends the parents' look and touch. He has already grown accustomed to the cadence of their voices, the style of their gestures, the feel of their grip, the aroma of their bodies; to the colors and patterns of the nursery, the home; to the bustle and noise of his siblings.

Long before reflective life intervenes we are tied by our bodies and bodily life and the network of its passions, feelings and moods, to the personal world around us. As intentional life matures, as the intentional moves I make become more refined and differentiated, I learn to sort out the persons themselves from the array of objects over which their influence spreads. I learn to lead a distinctively different intentional life towards other persons than I lead toward things, that is, the objects which we together share and use, accumulate and discard. Such things lead out from, and then back to others. They are made by others, sold by others, given to us by others, belong to others or to us: they are there for others or for us. I can grasp, push, pull and otherwise manipulate material objects, but my actions towards others are inscribed with caution, care and courtesy. When they are not, this is understood immediately and by everyone as offensive in the highest degree.

I can stare steadfastly at a material object in order to determine what it is, but it would be unspeakably rude to treat a person likewise. I lean against walls and furniture, but I keep a careful distance between myself and others, and an inner alarm sounds as soon as someone without an invitation approaches too close to us or touches us. I can feel a material object with curiosity about its texture, listen to a noise to discern exactly what it is, sniff about to isolate an aroma, but my bodily intentionality towards others is held strictly in check. I do not stare, poke, or sniff. I am aware, in a prereflective, bodily way, of the life which streams out from the other, of the subjectivity which makes its seat there, of the horizons which the other is constantly throwing out around himself. I do not lightly intrude into that circle. My bodily life takes heed of the autonomy which is exercised there, that the other is no being-for-me, no object reducible to my proportions and locatable on my horizon. I have from the start a bodily recognition that the other is something in itself and not merely for me.

Here then is the phenomenological equivalent of the beings which populate Kant's metaphysical world. Long before philosophical reflection arrives, there is a bodily disclosure of the other as worthy of respect, an end in himself, as a being not to be reduced to the sphere of objects available for my use. Long before philosophical reflection erects a distinction between subject and object, I am already tied to others, and they to me: together we carry out our mutual duties towards one another. Our bodily and affective life already apprehends the eye and hand of the other as the mediation of a personal life which commands our respect.

We have now been brought, I believe, to the point for which we have been striving. The world in which we live does not decompose into real facts on the one side and ideal objects on the other. What is primarily given is instead the inter-personal world, the world of other persons, their words and deeds and the things which they have made. In this world everything centers on the bodily presence of the incarnate other. The incarnate other is value incarnate, the concretely given embodiment of worth and value. The centers of energy, as we described other persons, are centers of value, commanding our respect.

Long before the debates of moral philosophers arise it is already clear that we are all, always and already, tied into a life of moral interaction and that we intend others--pre-reflectively--in a profoundly different way than we intend objects. The value of the other is not discovered by reflective thought, but only articulated in the language of concepts and judgments, for it is already prereflectively manifest in a more primordial way to our bodily affectivity. We are always and all along mooded and tuned to the other, whether in harmony (syn-pathos), or in discord (anti-pathos), or even when we treat him with callous disregard (a-pathos) which is not mood-lessness but the mood of indifference. We live all along in a charged environment of affective being-with, a field of affective impulses, a field of pathos. Were the life of pathos to give out on us, were the energy of our passionate involvement with one another to go dead on us, were we indeed ever to attain a pure reason free of the affective substructure which sustains our life, then moral reflection would become as meaningless as a treatise on the psychological effects of colors to a person born blind.

The task of reflection is to articulate a moral life in which we are already enmeshed, to which we are all pre-committed, not to hold court over it. Moral life and moral values are primordially disclosed to us prereflectively, affectively. Our prereflective attunement with one another is the spring by which moral reflection is nourished. Moral reflection simply gives conceptual shape to the prereflective moral life in which we are all along caught up.[32]

CONCLUSION: AFFECTIVITY AS PROTO-ETHICS

I have argued throughout this chapter that the moral struggle is misconceived as a struggle of reason with inclinations, of the rational principle with the irrational principle. I have said in effect that moral strife must be reconceived as a discord within a single nature. It is a dissonance within our affectivity which is reflected in a tossing to and fro between competing reasons on the reflective level: we are affectively drawn in opposite directions, and we can give reasons on either side. By the same token, moral reform does not take the form of bringing the passions back into subjection to reason, but rather of reestablishing harmony and consonance. As moral strife is not a tug of war between opposing metaphysical principles but a discord within a single nature, we should reorganize the totality of our existential forces, both reflective and prereflective, and redirect them to new and fruitful ends. It is a matter of "retuning," of a tune-up of our affective life.

In my view acquiring moral character is not unlike acquiring aesthetic taste, and I do not reject the proximity of morals and aesthetics which the expression "moral sensibility" suggests. Moral life seems to me a matter of being properly sensitized morally, and moral education a matter of seeing to it that our children grow up properly sensitized in moral matters. That means that we want them to feel for the poor and the oppressed--and that is no metaphor: they must in fact feel for the poor. If they do not, they lack moral sensibility as surely as their taste for the standard fare offered on television represents a failure in aesthetic sensibility. We want them to feel more strongly for justice than for acquisitiveness or the amassing of more and more material possessions of their own; we want them to be truly repulsed by brutality, to be horrified by war and inhumanity; we want them to feel a sense of reverence for the physical world and to abhor the technological desecration of the environment and of biological life; we want them to feel pain at violence and injustice. In short we want them to feel the right things: to take pleasure in the right things, and to feel pain at the sight of evil, as Plato and Aristotle both insist.[33] If they are taught to feel well, if they are morally sensitized, then the reasons will come of their own, just as when they are taught to feel the wrong things they do not lack for reasons to rationalize their ill-feeling and ill-will. If they do not feel these things in their marrow, then they are merely paying lip service to what we teach and will throw it over at the first opportunity, for the rationales we make them learn will be a veneer over a hollow, a shell without a kernel. If they do not respond to virtue and vice from the marrow of their bones, if they do not resonate from the depths of their sensibility to these values, if they have not been affectively turned to moral matters, then our words of moral wisdom will be to them only so many tinkling cymbals.

But by reinstating affectivity to a central role in moral life, by insisting upon the centrality of moral affectivity, do we not turn everything over to whim and fancy and make everything a matter of taste? Do we not reduce the choice between justice and injustice to the level of the choice of our favorite color? That at least is the rejoinder of those who make everything turn on the old dichotomy between fact and value, is and ought, real and ideal, sensible and supersensible. The senses tell us what is, but reason must decide what ought to be. Our tastes tell us what we like, but reason tells us what we ought to choose. The old dualism does not give up easily; its death is painfully slow. Such an objection proceeds from a grossly inadequate analysis of the nature of human experience, one whose roots are in Platonism but which extend well into modern philosophy. The one lasting achievement of phenomenology, in my view, is to have corrected this abstract and contrived idea of experience, and to have replaced it with a sound and holistic account of experience as it is really *lived*. That is what I have attempted by means of my presentation of a phenomenology of the person.[34]

I have argued that experience is value-laden from the start, that we meet up with value from the first moments of waking life, and even before that. Human experience, properly conceived in all its amplitude, is from the start an experience of value, in particular of the value of the human person. Values are not something which reason discerns while the senses stand about, stupefied, awaiting its deliberations, though metaphysics has always favored such juridical metaphors. On the contrary, human affectivity is already sensitive to the value of the other, already discloses it, long before reason can set up court. We are always and from the start attuned to the other. We do not need to reach the age of reason, to achieve the *cogito*, or to undertake transcendental reflection, to know that: it is already inscribed in our prereflective being. We have already learned it, have all along been learning it, from the first moments of our life. Our being is a being-with, and our being-with is an attunement to the other. The other's presence is an omnipresence to which our whole affective life is attuned.

Hence, by turning things over to affective and prereflective life, we have not turned everything over to whim and caprice; we have not surrendered "reason" to "feeling." On the contrary we have found there the prereflective moorings of the principle to which Kant gave a famous conceptual formulation when he told us always to treat humanity, whether in our person or that of another, as an end and never merely as a means.[35] Here is a principle which is already inscribed in our prereflective and affective intentionality, a principle which makes its presence felt from the start.

Now everything depends upon seeing that the relationship between affectivity and thought is not, as in dualist philosophers, a matter of having a blind feeling on the one side and pure reason on the other, the former lacking insight as the latter lacks incentive. On the contrary, in our scheme, affectivity and thought are related as the implicit to the explicit, so that the work of thought always consists in unpacking our prereflective life, explicating it, and giving it explicit formulation.[36] Hence when Kant announced this principle, it is not as if this were something he had devised, a theory of his, some construction which he wanted to test out. As he himself argues, this law is exceedingly well known to the simplest man and the task of the moral philosopher is to say and to defend what everybody already knows. Kant misconceived this task when he took it to mean that the philosopher must "purify" this principle of any empirical origin. I have argued in the opposite direction, viz., to show as clearly as possible the experiential-affective *base* of any such principle, to show its birth certificate in experience adequately conceived.

This means that we must set aside the wooden and atomistic counterfeit for experience which empiricism offers us. For the texture of experience is complex, rich with meaning, a ripe fruit about to burst. The philosopher is one who stations himself at that critical juncture where this explosion of experience into meaning, of the prereflective into thought, will take place, so that he will be sure to be there. He must be ready, on the spot, and hence able to report everything just as it happens. This work of reporting the most intimate movements of our prereflective life is precisely what philosophy is.

Hence, when we turn to the prereflective, the affective, we do not turn to chaos and the irrational, but rather to that origin by which any principle is nourished. *Our moral affectivity is already a proto-ethics.* It

is already possessed of proto-principles which are there, waiting to become explicit sense and meaning under the hand of reflective thought.
The moral agent is not a being of reason whose inclinations have been subdued, but a being of delicate moral sensibility who is attuned to the right things. Moral philosophy is not a metaphysics of morals which wants to preserve the rational purity of moral principles, but rather a phenomenology of moral sensibility which gives conceptual expression to that proto-ethics which is always and all along at work in affective life.

Villanova University
Villanova, Pennsylvania

NOTES

1. I have found Robert Solomon, *The Passions* (Garden City: Doubleday Anchor, 1977) to be especially helpful in formulating the present argument.

2. Kierkegaard's *"Concluding Unscientific Postscript"* (hereafter referred to as CUP), trans. D. Swenson and W. Lowrie (Princeton: University Press, 1941), p. 206.

3. Ibid., p. 208.

4. Because of his Ockhamistic metaphysics, according to which each moment is absolutely contingent, Kierkegaard rejected the Aristotelian notion of a habit (*hexis*). See George Stack, *Kierkegaard's Existential Ethics* (University, Alabama: University of Alabama Press, 1977), pp. 133-34.

5. CUP, pp. 347-50.

6. Soren Kierkegaard, *The Concept of Dread*, trans. W. Lowrie (Princeton: University Press, 1957), pp. 16-17, note. Kierkegaard is referring to the disinterestedness of the aesthetic judgment in Kant's *Critique*.

7. *Ibid.*, 446.

8. *Ibid.*, 476.

9. *Ibid.*

10. Soren Kierkegaard, *Repetition*, trans. W. Lowrie (Princeton: University Press, 1946), pp. 3-7.

11. In Ch. 3 above Sebastian Samay uses the term "affectivity" in the same ontological sense in which Heidegger uses the term "Befindlichkeit."

12. Martin Heidegger, *Being and Time* (hereafter referred to as BT), trans. J. MacQuarrie and E. Robinson (New York: Harper & Row, 1962), p. 29.

13. The word that Heidegger uses for mood is "*Stimmung*," which means the way we are "tuned," *gestimmt*, to things.

14. Husserl already established this point in *Logical Investigations*, vol. 2, trans. John Findlay (New York: Humanities Press, 1970), Inv .V, 15, where he develops the position first put forward by Brentano.

15. CUP, 476.

16. See "What is Metaphysics?" in *Martin Heidegger: Basic Writings*, ed. David Krell (New York: Harper & Row, 1977), pp. 91-112.
17. BT, 177.
18. Lewis White Beck, *A Commentary on Kant's Critique of Practical Reason* (Chicago: University of Chicago Press, 1960), pp. 213-14.
19. Hence the second Critique contained an "incentive" of practical reason whose function was architectonically parallel to the "Transcendental Aesthetic" in the first Critique, namely to provide the element of sensibility in transcendental synthesis. And it was for this reason that Kant proposed what he called the moral feeling of "respect" (Achtung).
20. Immanuel Kant, *Critique of Practical Reason* (hereafter referred to as CPrR), trans. Lewis White Beck, (Library of Liberal Arts; Indianapolis: Bobbs-Merrill, 1956, 77.
21. Martin Heidegger, *Basic Problems of Phenomenology*, trans. A. Hofstadter (Bloomington: Indiana University Press, 1982), p. 133.
22. CPrR, 75.
23. The moral law . . . completely excludes the influence of self-love from the highest practical principle and forever checks self-conceit, which decrees the subjective conditions of self-love as laws. If anything checks our self-conceit in our own judgment, it humiliates. Therefore the moral law inevitably humbles every man when he compares the sensuous propensity of his nature with the law. Now if the idea of something as the determining ground of the will humiliates us in our self-consciousness, it awakens respect for itself so far as it is positive and the ground of determination. (CPrR, 77)
24. *Ibid.*, pp. 133-7.
25. Heidegger, "What is Metaphysics?" p. 106.
26. CPrP, 79.
27. *Ibid.*, 79-80.
28. Cf. BT para. 34, 55-56.
29. Heidegger, *Basic Problems of Phenomenology*, p. 137.
30. Immanuel Kant, *Foundation of the Metaphysics of Morals; Text and Critical Essays*, ed. Robert P. Wolff (Indianapolis: Bobbs Merrill, 1969), pp. 52-60.
31. BT paras. 25-26.
32. Accordingly, one can ask how critical reflection is possible in such a standpoint. For if reason is bound to explicating a prereflective given, how is it ever possible for it to disengage itself sufficiently to put into question a particular pre-reflective structure in which it may have grown up? The answer to this is provided, I think, by Gadamer's notion of the fusion of horizons, which belongs to the heart of what he calls hermeneutics. In that view, critical reflection is awakened by the collision of my horizon, within which I have been nurtured and whose validity I have always assumed, with the horizon of the other. The collision awakens me to my horizon, which prior to this collision may well have been at work on me without my knowing it, and furthermore puts it into question by exposing its contingency. The ensuing dialogue between

diverse horizonal understandings is thus at the same time a process of critical reflection upon the relative merits of each. It is our view that it would always be possible for such a dialogue to reach agreement about the principle of the worth of the person which we have expounded here, given the appropriate conditions of a dialogue. See Hans Georg Gadamer, *Truth and Method*, trans. Garrett Barden and John Cumming (New York: Seabury Press, 1975), pp. 258-74.

33. Aristotle, *Nicomachean Ethics*, II, 3 (1104b10-15); and Plato, *Republic*, 401 E-402A.

34. For more on this question, see my "The Presence of Others: A Phenomenology of the Human Person," *Proceedings of the American Catholic Philosophical Association*, 53 (1979), pp. 45-58; and Emmanuel Levinas, *Totality and Infinity*, trans. A. Lingis (Pittsburgh: Duquesne University Press, 1969).

35. Kant, *Foundations*, p. 54.

36. The prereflective is not reducible to the affective, for there is also a cognitive pre-reflective--as when I am buried in the complexities of a mathematical problem without adverting to the fact that now I am doing mathematical work. Whence there is both a cognitive and an affective pre-reflective which it is the task of reflective thought to explicate.

CHAPTER IX

THE HUMAN GOOD

and

MORAL CHOICE

JOHN FARRELLY, O.S.B.

One basic issue that contemporary reflection on moral development and moral education raises is that of form versus content in morality. Is morality primarily a kind of human judgment that has formal criteria such as universality and prescriptiveness (e.g., principles of justice should be impartially applied to all)? If so, then moral education is a movement toward such judgments. Or is morality a matter primarily of creative life decisions guided by intelligence for certain goals such as self-actualization, usefulness, efficiency or beneficial consequences for the individual and society? If so, then moral education is a matter of helping young people toward this kind of action and decision. The division between a view of morality that can be called formalist and deontological (from the Greek word *deon*, duty) and a view that can be called content oriented and teleological (from the Greek word *telos*, goal) is perhaps the basic division among influential normative ethicists today. The view that one takes on this question affects one's interpretation of moral development and moral education.

The present chapter examines this question within the context of our whole project and the limits of the space available here. The question itself has in part been clarified by previous chapters of this book that examined contrasting views on moral education, and it will be further clarified as we proceed in this chapter. Some of the implications of these diverse viewpoints for an interpretation of moral development and of moral education will be apparent as we proceed; others will be analyzed at length in later chapters and volumes of this project. We shall examine this question through contrasting Kohlberg's interpretation of morality, which he himself and others say is formalist, with Brenda Munsey's and Israela Aron's interpretations that are teleological and claim support from John Dewey. At this point of the chapter our purpose is not to adjudicate the critiques each interpreter makes of the other or to explain the differences thoroughly--this can be found in the references that I will cite--but rather to give a rough sense of the contrast. Secondly, we will present a third interpretation of morality which, we suggest, brings us beyond the impasse in which the first two are mired while preserving the valid insights of each of them. Thirdly, we shall discuss briefly different types of values to fill out at least part of the content of the view we propose.

CONTRAST BETWEEN FORMALIST AND TELEOLOGICAL INTERPRETATIONS OF MORALITY

As Kohlberg's philosophical position has been outlined in the first chapter of this book by Frederick Ellrod, we need not repeat that here. To recall briefly what is most relevant to the concerns of this chapter, we may begin by noting that Kohlberg takes a method somewhat similar to that of Jean Piaget.[1] He saw the cognitive structure basic to modern scientific thinking as consisting in the formation and testing of hypotheses. Hence, in his study of the development of knowledge or genetic epistemology he examined the stages of interaction between the epistemological or knowing subject and the environment through which this structure emerged in the subject in early adolescence.[2] Similarly, Kohlberg has a view on what constitutes the moral judgment as such, and he examines the stages of interaction between the growing person and his or her social environment through which this structure emerges. Thus what is basic for Kohlberg is the moral judgment rather than moral action. This judgment is not so much an assertion about what is or is not, but rather a way of structuring human behavior. As he writes:

> In our view the basic referent of the term "moral" is a type of *judgment* or a type of *decision-making process*, not a type of behavior, emotion or social institution. Second, note that stage 6 is a *deontological* theory of morality. The three primary *modes* of moral judgment, and the corresponding types of ethical theory, deal with (a) duties and rights (deontological), (b) ultimate aims or ends (teleological), and (c) personal worth or virtue (theory of approbation). Our claims of superiority, then, are claims for the superiority of stage 6 judgments of duties and rights (or of justice) over other systems of judgments of duties and rights. We make no direct claim about the ultimate aims of men, about the good life, or about other problems which a teleological theory must handle. These are problems beyond the scope of the sphere of morality or moral principles, which we define as principles of choice for resolving conflicts of obligations.[3]

Kohlberg then is defining "morality in terms of the formal character of a moral judgment, method, or point of view, rather than in terms of its content."[4]

A moral judgment is distinct from an aesthetic or a prudential judgment. It is a prescriptive judgment, for it involves a structuring of human behavior that is not simply hypothetical but has a note of obligation or "oughtness" to it. It also has a universality and reciprocity, for it is a judgment such that all persons should make in similar circumstances. These characteristics are found particularly in judgments about rights and duties, or about justice:

In one sense, justice is itself content-free; that is, it merely prescribes that principles should be impartially applied to all. However, we have also argued that the stage 6 form implies justice as equity, that is, as a treatment of persons as morally equal. . . . Second, we have argued that it also implies commutative justice as reciprocity, contract, and trust . . . no principle other than justice has been shown to meet the formal conception of a universal prescriptive principle.[5]

Note that while Kohlberg as moral theoretician adopts a formalist interpretation, as practitioner of moral education he searches for ways of structuring the social environment of the growing child and the child's participation in that environment so that moral judgments will generate content.[6]

The only alternative interpretations of morality of which Kohlberg is aware are those which equate morality with the particular system of the interpreter or those which say that morality is relative. Neither of these seems to him philosophically justified, while his own empirical findings support his view that children's growth is toward that precise kind of moral judgment that he considers as constituting morality.

As a contrasting philosophical interpretation of moral development and moral education, we may call upon two recent critics of Kohlberg who claim Dewey as the source of their own views. Brenda Munsey studies the metaethical issues raised by moral development.[7] While Kohlberg holds an ethical rule theory, she proposes an ethical act theory. Ethical rule theory presupposes that moral rules are necessary to justify individual moral judgments, and so it holds that one cannot even identify the morally relevant facts without moral rules. Ethical act theory holds that one can identify the relevant particular facts without such rules. For the latter view, ethical rules have an importance as summaries of inherited wisdom, but they are subject to exceptions. They are not, as ethical rule theory holds, constitutive of what it means to reason morally, for on such a basis they cannot admit of exception. Such exception then would not be moral reasoning but some other type of reasoning. Kohlberg's "stage 6 justice defines moral justification. The stage 6 structure is taken to be as an a priori criterion for distinguishing *justified* moral judgments from *unjustified* moral judgments--there are no exceptions."[8]

For act theorists such as Dewey, particular moral disputes are based on particular factual disputes; and particular moral claims are justified by appeal to particular factual considerations. A pragmatic metaethics would suggest that we begin by showing the first stage of moral judgment that researchers are able to identify, and then map the changes that occur in reference to this structure. This approach assumes that a definition of morality is in principle a posteriori, while Kohlberg's "hypothesis about the a priori structure of sound moral judgment is treated as an a priori hypothesis, defended in terms of merely formal criteria and presumably subject to merely formal counterarguments."[9]

Israela Aron, another critic of Kohlberg,[10] acknowledges that there are advantages to Kohlberg's formalist position in that he claims to be stimulating moral growth rather than indoctrinating or inculcating particular values. Formalist philosophers, however, restrict themselves largely to metaethics and thus do not deal effectively with substantive issues, while in moral education the teacher is trying to help young people face complex experience and learn how to make creative moral decisions among the alternatives available. Kohlberg's dilemmas, Aron holds, are too pat and have too little data to be of much service here. For example, in the question whether Heinz should steal the drug necessary for his wife's recovery or allow his wife to die, other alternatives (e.g., taking out a loan, seeking public assistance, organizing a protest against the druggist, etc.) are not considered. Such dilemmas, abstracted from life and oversimplified, may contribute to the formalists' desire to preserve the autonomy of moral discourse, but they are not a tool to help students think creatively or explore new possibilities. Kohlberg's approach is more concerned with the justification of decisions than with the process of decision making itself, while the educator seeks to help the student toward making decisions in real life.

Thus there is need for supplementing Kohlberg's approach with one that deals primarily with the process of ethical decision making. Specifically, Aron suggests that Dewey's work is helpful here. For Dewey, it is the interaction of organism and environment that is the context both for experience and for decision making. The need for decision usually occurs when the habitual response is no longer adequate, perhaps because it no longer fulfills a person's desires or because there are conflicting desires. This situation leads to a suspension of action and to reflection and deliberation. Practical deliberation in this condition of felt conflict in a concrete situation begins with the formulation of the issue; it involves "a dramatic rehearsal (in imagination) of various competing lines of action."[11]

> The competing lines of action cannot, according to Dewey, be evaluated by an a priori or abstract standard (such as an ultimate principle), but must be assessed in terms of their consequences. These consequences must be construed broadly .... Moreover, the consequences of an act include the effects it will have on the character of the deliberator as well as its effects on the physical and social environment.[12]

Principles of the past are indeed important here, although not as absolutes but as summaries of wisdom that are themselves subject to modification. When a final decision is made, it is made not so much by the deliberator knowing intellectually the correctness of his decision as by his feeling the appropriateness of a particular choice from the harmony and unity that it brings along with it. In applying this method for the moral education of children, what is important is giving them practice in deliberation. They may be given actual situations or situations based on fictional or hypothetical case materials, but with sufficient data that they can envisage alternatives.

While there is much help in this approach, Aron acknowledges limitations in Dewey's ethical theory. This theory, for example, seems to endorse a highly individualistic morality because it deals with issues that are concrete and it makes moral choice depend, not simply or perhaps primarily on rational considerations, but "on direct emotional perception."[13] Secondly there is a degree of relativism in Dewey's position, but he holds that values are not simply a matter of opinion and that there are rational ways of evaluating them through the consideration of consequences (on this see Chapter VI above). Thirdly, "Dewey's denial of the prescriptive power of moral judgments seems to be the most troublesome aspect of his ethical theory."[14] But Aron asks, in defense of Dewey's viewpoint, the following question. If one presents the consequences of a line of action that a friend is contemplating and shows that they are harmful, then what can be added by saying that the line of action is immoral? This may add persuasion, but it is essentially a rhetorical addition and not an additional argument. Aron concludes by encouraging educators to adopt an eclectic approach that would include even Plato, Aristotle, and the existentialists, along with Dewey and Kohlberg.

Kohlberg and his associates are not without response to the above critiques.[15] However, for our purposes here it is not necessary to pursue this debate further. We have wished to present the opposition between an ethical theory that is formalist and deontological and an ethical theory that is teleological and content-oriented: Kohlberg, Munsey and Aron have shown us just such an opposition. This takes us to the core of this chapter and its question: Is there some valid way in which we can move beyond this opposition?

TOWARD AN INTEGRATION OF FORM AND CONTENT IN MORAL THEORY

We can see that each of the proponents of the moral theories outlined above is defending something of importance in moral activity. Kohlberg is defending the prescriptive and universal character of moral judgments in a way that is, he hopes, beyond relativism. Munsey and Aron are defending the character of moral judgments as creative decisions for some self-defined human good in a complex human and changing environment. What each is defending seems to be part of our moral experience. And yet prescriptiveness and universality seem to be defended in a way that abstains from assertion about the human good or goal, and creative decision making seems to be defended in a way that excludes the prescriptiveness characteristic of moral judgments. The defense of one aspect of our moral experience seems to put in jeopardy the defense of another aspect of that same experience. And so part of the appeal of each position lies in the weakness of the other or in the human experience that the other position does not account for; in that sense, they feed off one another.

Why should it be necessary that one aspect of our moral experience be defended at the expense of the other? Is it due to the nature of the case, or is it due to something possibly faulty in each of these positions, some premise that they have in common from which a dilemma arises that results in a parting of the ways? I suggest that the latter is the case, and in defending such a position I am in accord with the hopes expressed by Kohlberg, Munsey and Aron that their dialogue will lead beyond their present impasse.[16] To support another viewpoint, I would like to present (1) an hypothesis about the basis of morality that helps to integrate the above views and account for the divergence between them (2) a brief phenomenology that supports this interpretation of morality and of the moral judgment (e.g., that I should respect certain values or that in these circumstances I should concretely do this or that), and (3) an objection to this position that is common today and a suggested answer to it. I should note that this articulation of the position I am suggesting and my defense of it will be apparent only at the end of these three sections. In the first section, I am primarily sketching this viewpoint as an hypothesis. It is particularly in the second section that an elaboration of this position and argument for it is offered. But these sections must be completed by a consideration of, and answer to, objections some moralists base on human creativity and diversity.

It may forestall certain misunderstandings if I first make several notes on the character of the argument I am presenting. Initially in the hypothesis and later in the brief phenomenology I present the view that the context in which people act and judge morally is not only the consequences of the act being considered or an equilibration process of moral judgments progressively more universal, but what can be called the constitutive human good and the subject's orientation to this. The subject acknowledges that the act at stake is morally incumbent upon him or her because what is involved is an integral dimension of the constitutive human good and the subject's orientation to this as integral to his or her identity.

Some philosophers may consider this argument as an instance of the naturalistic fallacy, since I may appear to be drawing moral ought from what empirically is. I would see the argument as different from this. Moral theory--and viewpoints on the naturalistic fallacy are elements of moral theory--is secondary to moral experience: to be good theory it must explain the moral experience. Thus if we can agree on a phenomenology of moral experience, then there is some basis for us to evaluate moral theories--namely, on their ability to explain what is happening in moral experience. Moral theory is not prescriptive in the sense that it stipulates antecedent to moral experience what will be accepted as such.

As a matter of fact, there is a sense in which people generally do deduce moral obligations from facts. As Clifford Geertz, a cultural anthropologist, notes:

What all sacred symbols assert is that the good for man is to live realistically; where they differ is in the vision of reality they construct. Probably the overwhelming majority of mankind are continually drawing normative conclusions from factual premises (and factual conclusions from normative premises, for the relation between ethos and world view is circular) despite refined, and in their own terms impeccable, reflection by professional philosophers on the 'naturalistic fallacy.'[17]

The reason many contemporary philosophers have difficulty in accepting this may be that they attempt to explain it within the context of either an empiricist or a Kantian epistemology (or some descendent therefrom), both of which are too restrictive to be able to explain this moral experience adequately. The present book's treatment of how we establish the moral "ought" is found in Chapter X to which I would refer the reader.[18]

A final preliminary clarification concerns the use of the terms "good" and "value." By common dictionary definition "value" designates

> an amount considered to be a suitable equivalent for something else (e.g., fair price or return for goods or services) . . . monetary or material worth . . . worth in usefulness or importance to the possessor; utility or merit . . . a principle, standard, or quality considered worthwhile or desirable.[19]

Thus the word initially reflects the estimate of the one who values something. By extension we speak of his values, her values, our values, and their values. The word "good" today seems to have a more objective meaning initially. It signifies:

> having positive or desirable qualities; not bad or poor . . . serving the end desired; suitable; serviceable: *a good outdoor paint* . . . not spoiled or ruined; able to be used: *The milk is still good* . . . in excellent condition; whole; sound: *a good tooth* . . . superior to the average: *a good student*.[20]

Our view is that we can critically reflect upon and evaluate what we actually desire or value so that we have sufficient grounds to say, e.g., that education or health or religion or beauty is a real value for the child's development. These terms "value" and "good" overlap. One current author acknowledges this overlap, because while he opts to restrict the word "value" to designate "a general form of good that can be participated in or realized in indefinitely many ways on indefinitely many occasions,"[21] he uses "good" to designate both a particular objective or goal considered desirable and a general form of good. Our main concern here is not the distinction between value and good, but the critical grounding of value or good.

An Hypothesis

Our hypothesis can be presented in three steps. First, we do show in our actions and desires that we value other persons, certain objectives, attitudes, relationships, goods. We experience something in these that attracts us, and we act in a positive manner in their regard. We show great diversity in what we value, in the goals we pursue, and in what we experience as of value. This is antecedent to moral judgment; it is the context in which moral judgments arise. Secondly, we reflect upon our action and our desires or upon the values we are seeking in these actions and desires to ask whether what we are valuing is really valuable, whether there is some basis other than our actually valuing them that is the basis justifying our valuing them. After reflection what we estimate as a value appropriate for us may, of course, not be the same as what we pre-reflectively accept as a value. An answer here that consequences justify our valuing something does not seem to go deeply enough since we can always ask at this level why some consequences are thought to be fulfilling and others not, and what justifies this viewpoint. An answer that we are structuring our behavior in terms of these values does not seem to be adequate even though a whole society may agree among themselves to so structure their behavior. For example, a society of sadomasochists may agree to inflict and receive certain sufferings from each other equitably, but we cannot help but ask further whether this is a true human value by which they are structuring their behavior.

Thirdly, then, our experience of acting for a value or a good and our reflection upon this good and our experience may give us access to an insight that gets us beyond the simply factual character of this situation for ourselves or our particular society. We may have the insight that as human beings we orient our action to values or goods and that we become more fully human if we value certain goods, such as respect for the worth of another, and reject others that appear pre-reflectively as values or goods, such as subordinating others wholly to our own private desires. It may be revealed to a sadomasochist, for example, through reflection that, while inflicting pain appears good, tenderness is better or genuinely good, i.e., in accord with rather than contrary to the way human beings should relate to each other as human beings. If, on the other hand, we self-define our values as a sadomasochist community may well do and are willing to prescribe universal action in accord with this, we are perverting something constitutive of us as human beings which precedes us as experiencers and choosers of value and which is a criterion or norm for self-definitions of value that enhance our humanity. We can call this a *constitutive human good*, namely, both the human attitude (e.g., respect for truth, for others, for self) and the term of such an attitude, that is a norm or criterion for us as we define our values, because having the structure of being we have as human, certain attitudes and goals fulfill us and certain attitudes and goals diminish us or are regressive.

There is a whole class of actions that are oriented primarily not to the development of the one who acts but to some product outside the agent--such as a house to be built by a carpenter; here the immediate criterion of the value of the act is the product rather than the development of the agent. Considering the agent superior in value to such products of human activity, however, would be one of the elements of a constitutive human good; and so engagement in such action should itself redound to the development of the agent as well as of the society which he serves. What we have said about the constitutive human good has more immediate reference to actions or attitudes described by the traditional moral virtues and interaction with others in accord with them than to actions oriented to external products; but it embraces these latter as well. There is then, we suggest, a constitutive human good as horizon for and deeper meaning and criterion of our human actions, and as the basis on which we can communicate with one another about issues in this area. Most basically, we are more fully human if we self-define our goals and values in a way that enhances this than if we seek to arbitrarily create or define such a good in accord with our present choices or values. It is what we as human persons (see Chapter XIII below) can be or become at our best as this relates as horizon and meaning to our present choices, actions and experiences of value.

We can take as an example here the injunction that is basic to Kohlberg's sixth stage, namely that we should treat others in a way that is just and fair. Such a judgment can be looked at from different perspectives. From the hypothesis offered here, the value realized by this injunction is part of the constitutive human good. There is a worth in every human being as human that is distinctively greater than that which belongs to a plant or an animal as such. The worth that others have as human beings has a claim upon our acknowledgement and upon our action and attitude toward them. The worth of others entails certain consequences about how I should act toward them and how I should not act. This claim that others' worth as human has upon me is not contradictory to my own basic inclination as a human being, since in part I am constituted as human through being a social being, that is, through being oriented not simply toward my own fulfillment but also toward that of others and toward a community that embraces us both. Thus I am not fully human or mature if I consider others only from the viewpoint of my own advantage or the advantage or disadvantage of my society. There is something constitutive of the human person in virtue of which adopting an attitude of respect for others accords with his or her development, maturation or perfection.

This is contrary to an individualism that interprets social living simply as a means toward the realization of individualized goals or interests. It is also opposed to a collectivism that so exalts the good of the collectivity as to reduce individuals within it simply to the status of instruments for this good. Rather the position we offer recognizes that the good of society is the development of the individuals within it. The institutions of the political community are to serve a common good that redounds to the good of individuals.

Neither Kohlberg nor Munsey and Aron acknowledge such a basis for the moral order, or so it seems. Kohlberg makes no claim to say anything substantive about what the goals of human living are or what constitutes the good life. In fact, he equates statements about goals and the good life with relativism and indoctrination, and avoids such statements because he wants to avoid moral education that is relativistic and indoctrinative. On the other hand, while Munsey and Aron do make the good or fulfillment of the moral agent and even society the context of decisions in life, they deny anything in moral judgment such as a categorical imperative. Moral norms are only summary statements of the wisdom of experience, and always subject to exception. These authors reject anything like a constitutive human good, unless this is to guide one's life by self-defined goals. The "good" for them ends up meaning only what individuals or societies judge to be good through an examination of consequences of the proposed action. The denial of a constitutive human good as the foundation of the moral order is common to these positions.

This common refusal to adopt such a basis for the moral order leads to weaknesses in the position of each. The universalizing that Kohlberg as theoretician of morality sees as a formal criterion of the moral judgment is the result of a process of equilibration through which a young person passes in successive stages of moral judgment, each of them giving way to one that more adequately structures human behavior. Without denying the reality of such equilibration, we can ask what the good is that provokes this continual restructuring of the moral judgment toward the stage six judgment. For him, as for Rawls, it is not (as we shall note at greater length below) the constitutive human good, that is, the fulfillment appropriate for us as human beings before we judge or choose that encompasses the worth of another as human and my orientation as a human being to respect that worth. Such a basis would legitimate both universalizing the moral judgment of the sixth stage and the prescriptive force of such an injunction, since this is what it means to be human. But without an acknowledgement of this human good, the prescriptive force to which Kohlberg concludes is simply hypothetical rather than absolute. If one wants a social order that is equilibrated, then one should act and judge equitably, treating all as equals. Further, Kohlberg lacks sufficient justification for his definition of what constitutes the moral judgment if he is unwilling to make a statement about what constitutes the human good or humanity in this area of human living. Similarly, the universalizing that he wishes to preserve as a criterion of moral judgment lacks foundation if he is unwilling to judge how it is appropriate for human beings as such to act toward one another. Only if it is a constitutive human good that provokes the equilibration process and if it is acknowledged to have this significance can Kohlberg defend the universality and prescriptiveness of the moral judgment.

Munsey and Aron begin with the agent making creative life decisions in a way that is self-defined, but the context for decision that they present seems to lack the universality and prescriptive force that humans generally acknowledge is present in moral judgments. Once more, since they deny that there is some good that is constitutive for human choice, the kind of necessity they reach is hypothetical. That is, if people value such and such a goal, then they should take certain kinds of action and avoid others. It is not their rejection of a formalism that is the source of the limitation of their position, but rather their rejection of a constitutive human good. They highly esteem openness to contingencies and varying circumstances, and they want to leave any moral norm or goal open for possible exceptions. But the effect is that for them "good" ends up meaning only what individuals or societies judge or choose to value; it is no deeper than that. They are open to any human choice, but not open to the view that to be human entails that one define one's values in a way that promotes a constitutive human good. There seems then in this case to be no sacredness or necessity, importance or obligatoriness to the moral order--nothing that differentiates it from consumerism in a market economy or choices among interest groups in a democratic society. We shall show later that the proper defense of the scope and creativity of human choice does not depend upon the denial of a constitutive humanity or human good.

Perhaps it is the desire to preserve human autonomy that leads both these positions to the foundations they offer for moral decision or judgment. If so, they may be asserting that there is at least one constitutive factor in the human subject, namely, to be autonomous. We for our part are suggesting that this autonomy or self-definition that we see in human decision and moral judgment has its setting in a human person or subject who has certain potentialities, structures or orientations as a human being that cannot be denied, overlooked or rejected if one wishes to define one's goals in a way that will lead to fulfillment. Thus human autonomy is not absolute, nor is it the only constitutive factor of being human (see Chapter IV on freedom and moral choice). If it is given priority over every other aspect of being human, what results is not simply an alternative way of being human but a diminishment of the agent's human being and of the humanity of the society in which he lives.

The dichotomy between a formalism and a kind of teleology represented by consequentialism would appear to stem from a denial that there is a constitutive humanity in the moral agent and a good that completes the agent as presiding over the moral life. If this good or constitutive humanity is acknowledged, then formalism and consequentialism are transcended and given their proper context. An acceptance of this is an enlargement, not a denial, of the foundations that Kohlberg on the one hand and Aron and Munsey on the other offer for the moral order. Since such acceptance is more properly philosophical than psychological, psychology as a contemporary empirical discipline cannot as such defend this position. But it need not deny it, and in any case the psychologists

222 The Human Good and Moral Choice

we are studying acknowledge the need for philosophical judgments in their psychological work.

A Phenomenology

In support of the hypothesis we have presented, we may ask what is really happening when we acknowledge the rights of another person to be treated with respect and fairness and when such acknowledgement affects our attitudes and actions. This would be recognized both by Kohlberg and by Munsey and Aron as an occasion for moral judgment and decision. The question is whether their interpretations of what is happening here are adequate or whether they are to some extent reductionist. Kohlberg would rightly point out, of course, that different things are happening at different stages of the child's, adolescent's or adult's moral development. But as a moral philosopher he does recognize a mature stage in this development, and it is of that stage that we are asking our question. What actually happens when we make a judgment acknowledging the rights of others at this point? A brief phenomenology can help us here toward seeing whether a formalist, a consequentialist, or a view such as we have offered above best interprets this experience.

Let us take the instance of someone in the United States facing a decision whether to discriminate against blacks in hiring for a job or in regard to voting rights. In circumstances where he has the physical power to discriminate he may decide not to because the law is now opposed to this, or because he would lose economically through such discrimination or because he would be subject to violence in revenge for his action. Or he may decide not to because through role-taking, that is, putting himself imaginatively in the place of the other and through universalizing the resultant judgment, he may opt for a social order that treats all with equity when it comes to such matters; after all, he would not like to be on the receiving end of such discrimination. This latter approach is the result of an equilibration process that results in a moral judgment with the formal characteristics of universality and prescriptiveness, whereas the former approach was a consequentialist one. However, in addition to these reasons and even as his primary reason he may judge that he ought not to discriminate against others due to their color because he thinks that they have a *right* to be respected and treated equally with others in such matters simply by the fact that they are human beings. As persons they, like the agent, are masters of their own actions and lives, with their own human dignity and the essential worth that goes with this, and with their own human fulfillment toward which they are moving. This calls for respect that precludes subjecting them to discrimination with all the indignities that this involves. The necessity or prescriptiveness present in a judgment to this effect is not simply physical, economic, aesthetic, conventional, of a civil contract, utilitarian or consequentialist, or resulting from role-taking and universalization. It is properly a moral necessity, that is, one that comes from the recognition of the right the other has as a human person and a correlative duty that I have to respect this. Unlike the other bases given above, it has more than a hypothetical prescriptive force, namely, that I should act in a certain way if I want certain consequences or a certain kind of society.

To judge in this fashion is not to abstract my being a human person from all the other dimensions of my existence or to abstract the humanity of the person whose rights I am considering from other aspects of his existence. It is rather to judge the situation on grounds that both include more than the secondary considerations and that are rooted more deeply. This judgment is rooted in the essential worth of the other as a human being and how I should act if I am to come up to the standard appropriate for a human being. If I so judge, I am neither judging in a way that is separated from the values to be realized, nor selecting those values for realization because of certain desirable consequences, role-taking, or universalizing a judgment through a process of equilibration. Rather they are values or an order of good that the other has a right to, and which I as a human being have a duty to respect. If I act contrary to this (e.g., through rape, torture, slavery, manipulation, or discrimination on the basis of color in distributing voting rights or job opportunities), I am acting contrary to what constitutes human worth and human fulfillment, both mine and that of the one whose rights I reject.

Language is supportive of this interpretation of what is happening. For if a person so respecting another is challenged to justify his action, he speaks of the natural or the human rights of the other based on his human dignity or worth, thus indicating that the basis of the injunction is more than consequences, law and order, or role-taking and universalization. (The process of moral reasoning involved in such cases is treated in Chapter VII above). It is a constitutive human good of the other that must be acknowledged and respected, and it is a constitutive human good of the moral agent to accept the claims that others have upon him since he is a social being.

Of course, there can be other phenomenologies offered to interpret what is happening here, and presumably both Kohlberg and Munsey and Aron would offer alternative interpretations. As Kohlberg holds that his own view of stage 6 finds support in the philosophical position of John Rawls's, *A Theory of Justice*,[22] it may be relevant to reflect briefly here on that position. Rawls seeks to defend a social order that is fair in the distribution both of civil and of socio-economic goods and rights. He seeks to induce people to accept a foundation for such an order by inviting them to assume an original position in which they would choose the basic principles that are to govern the distribution of goods in their society. What basic principles would they set up if they did not know their own talents and where they as individuals would fit in the socio-economic scale? They would have a concern that the principles would be in their favor through being in favor of the least advantaged. Rawls considers that there are two principles such a group would establish in the original condition. First, "Each person is to have an equal right to the most extensive total system of equal basic liberties compatible with a similar system of liberty for all." And secondly, "Social and economic inequalities are to be arranged so that they are both: a) to the greatest benefit of the least advantaged, consistent with the just savings principle, and b) attached to offices and positions open to all under conditions of fair equality of opportunity."[23]

Without analyzing these principles further, we should note that the original choosers are operating out of their own interests. As D. F. Scheltens comments:

> It is important to keep in mind that the dialogue partners do not yet hold any moral principles. The latter too are suspended. On what basis then will the partners of the original position determine the choice of the principles of justice? They are led only by their own interest: "In choosing between principles each tries as best as he can to advance his interests" (p. 142); ". . . the parties are severally disinterested, and are not willing to have their interests sacrificed to the others. . ." (p. 129); ". . . they are not bound by prior moral ties to each other" (p. 128). Thus the original position is a pre-moral one, in which the parties in question still have to decide their principles of justice or their ethical principles.[24]

Rawls actually recognizes that when all in a society try to live by these principles of equity "then individually and collectively their nature is most fully realized and within it their individual and collective good."[25] However, it is not from the fulfillment of their human nature that he derives his principles:

> On p. 585 he asks whether the principles of justice should not be deduced "from the notion of respect for persons, for a recognition of their inherent worth and dignity." Yet Rawls answers this question negatively: "The notion of respect for the inherent worth of persons is not a suitable basis for arriving at these principles" (p. 586).[26]

While Rawls' formulation of the original condition may be persuasive and helpful for encouraging people to take an impartial stance, if it is presented as a phenomenology of what is actually happening when people acknowledge the rights of others it is rather unhistorical and artificial. It is true that it may represent the basis for such acknowledgement on the part of those who have not gotten beyond individual interests as a basis for social life. In this way, according to Edmund Sullivan, it defends the ideology of liberalism: "The essence of liberalism is a vision of society made up of independent autonomous units who cooperate only when the terms of cooperation are such as to make it further the ends of each of the parties."[27] Of course a society built on this principle would entail no more than hypothetical necessity in its recognition of the rights of others; that is, they should be respected insofar as this respect furthers my self-defined interests or goals.

We suggested, on the contrary, that the dynamism at the root of the equilibration process leading to the acknowledgement of human rights is a specifically human orientation at the core of our being that includes the acknowledgement of the worth of others and a concern for their fulfillment as part of its horizon. This dynamism and the affectivity (treated in Chapter III above) and activity in accord with it include these elements because as humans we are social beings and other persons have both intrinsic worth and worth for us. A dynamism of this character is part of our constitutive humanity, and thus a social order based on the dignity of all human persons is part of the constitutive human good. There is a basis beyond our individual interests or the interests of our society for a social order, namely the basis of the worth and dignity of human persons. Indeed, it seems evident that some of our institutions in the United States and in other countries are based on the inherent worth and rights of the human person rather than on the foundations that Rawls and Kohlberg provide. As T. A. Spragens writes:

> It seems fairly clear that the idea of natural rights has had a very profound operational significance in the context of limitation on governmental power, civil liberties, and so on which American courts have imposed and guaranteed. It also has had operational significance in the nation's political culture. Any empirical theory of democracy which does not incorporate such realities would strike many of us as rather inadequate.[28]

It is recognized by an increasing number of contemporary philosophers that the real basis for justice is indeed the intrinsic worth of the human person. For example, Ernest Barker holds:

> The idea of Justice, which is the impersonal source of law, is the value and worth of individual personality. . . . The intrinsic value of each personality is the basis of political thought just as (and just because) it is the basis of moral thought; and worth of persons--individual persons, all individual persons--is the supreme worth of the State.[29]

David Norton agrees:

> Each person *qua* person possesses natural entitlements in virtue of his worth, a worth that is (for actual persons) both potential and actual. As a perfection of a kind, each person's potential worth is absolute, while his actual worth is qualified by degree. Because it is qualified by degree, actual worth furnishes differential entitlement, while worth as pure potential establishes a lower limit of entitlement that is alike for all.[30]

Aron and Munsey also would give a different phenomenology in their interpretation of what happens when we respect the human rights of others than the one we gave. They would interpret decisions to respect the rights of others as occurring within a consequentialist search for fulfillment on the part of the agents. But, as we indicated above, this does not seem to represent what actually occurs in more mature human beings when they respect the rights of others; and, as Aron admits, it entails not an absolute exigency to respect the rights of others, but only a hypothetical necessity, that is, provided we want the consequences of such manifestations of respect. The exigency, we would hold, most basically derives from good or value constituted by my human being as social and the intrinsic dignity or worth of others as human. It has a deeper root than self-defined values; rather, a human being shows greater maturity or completeness as a human being when he or she relates to others in a way that accepts this absolute exigency that derives from the human good. We must evaluate "consequences" as moral criteria in the way that Edward Purcell evaluates "what works" when used as moral criteria: "The test of 'what works' was essentially delusive and circular, for practical efficacy was not an objective criterion. Utility as a rationale demanded an answer to two questions: useful for what and what was the justification of that purpose."[31] What I wrote in another context on the human good, may help to clarify our present evaluation of the adequacy of Aron and Munsey in the question under consideration:

> If consequences are good because they help one grow toward the human good, then action is good more because it relates one to the human good in accord with reason than because it has good consequences. Similarly, an action contrary to this human good is morally evil more because it is against the human good proper to man in this action than because it has bad consequences for him and society, immediate and remote. To divorce consequences from the human good (and this includes the common good as well as individual human good) as a moral norm is to leave us without criteria for discerning good from bad consequences. To give them priority over the human good as norms is intrinsically contradictory, since their value depends upon their relation to the human good.[32]

Of course, both Kohlberg and Munsey and Aron would hesitate to accept the phenomenology given above because it would appear to suppose that we can make ontological statements about what constitutes being human. I acknowledge that it does involve such a supposition and that ontological statements are beyond the capacity of empirical psychology as such. However, to assert that we cannot make such statements is a philosophical position, and both those who use a formalist and those who use a consequentialist basis for their study of moral development in children are in fact making philosophical judgments about what it is to be and to act humanly. A phenomenology such as that which we presented above is leading many contemporary philosophers to assert that we do in fact know something of what it means to be human and that this is basic for moral judgment. For example, W. D. Hudson writes:

> Can we say that there is a logical connection between what any man finds it intelligible to regard as a *good* man and what he believes man to be? If so, there would be that much connection between fact and value at least. And should we not be entitled to go on and to say that, if we could settle what man is, we could demonstrate what he ought to do? At the very least, the connection between what we take man to be and what we find it intelligible to consider morally good or bad, obligatory or disobligatory, seems to me to call for closer considerations.[33]

Similarly, G. J. Warnock writes:

> It appears at least enormously plausible to say that one who professes to make a moral judgment *must* at least profess that what is in issue is the good or harm, well-being or otherwise, of human beings--that what he regards as morally wrong is somehow damaging, and what he regards as right is somehow beneficial.[34]

The epistemological question, namely, that of the validity of such knowledge, is a serious one. But as we see from above, a number of modern philosophers no longer consider an empiricist or a Kantian epistemology able to explain what actually happens in the moral judgment. This question is treated elsewhere in this volume, and specifically in Chapter IX.

An Objection and An Answer

Some modern moralists would claim that the interpretation we have offered to the effect that there is a constitutive human orientation or intentionality and a constitutive human good represents a pre-modern anthropology. For example, Paul Taylor would characterize this as an ethics based on an "essentialistic conception of happiness":

> because it presupposes that there is such a thing as an essential human nature. . . . Essentialist philosophers view the good for man as an ideal of human perfection, a perfection which is uniquely suitable to characteristically human capacities. When this conception of happiness is used as the standard of intrinsic value, that standard becomes identical with the essentialist's standard of human perfection or virtue.[35]

In the modern world we are much more aware than previously of the great diversity among cultures and people. This diversity comes from human self-making and creativity in different environments. To assert the existence of a constitutive human good appears to many to be a rejection of the evidence that what is good for human beings depends

228 The Human Good and Moral Choice

upon this diversity and self-making that characterize human existence.

In answer to this, we fully acknowledge that modern evolutionary biology, psychology and cultural anthropology do support a great pluralism or diversity of interpretations of the good life and its dependence upon the creativity and self-making of human beings in differing environments. What these sciences have discovered has significance for philosophical anthropology and for ethics because they show us something of what it means to be human; their findings modify earlier anthropology and moral theory. Through showing us that the structure of human as well as of animal life is pluralistic in a way that is correlated with the spontaneity of the organism or of human beings in interacting with diverse environments, they do show us that what is considered the human good is historically conditioned. We do not dispute this, but we contend that this pluralism is compatible with there being intrinsic standards of the human good and reflects different opinions about those standards. Human beings' interaction with an environment or world is correlated with the environment itself, with the spontaneity and freedom of the subjects, and also with a distinctively human potential. Spontaneity and adjustment to the immediate environment do not of themselves assure that the resulting choice and action will enhance the humanity of the agent or be morally good. It is worthwhile showing briefly that there is much in the sciences mentioned above that supports this viewpoint or even presupposes it in a way appropriate to the limits of these sciences.

(a) *Biology*. Man is an animal, and so the findings of evolutionary biology show us something about human nature as well as about animals. The human zygote takes twenty-three chromosomes from each parent with the accompanying genes that are determinants of hereditary traits. Thus there is a commonality among human beings as well as diversity, and this diversity and commonality exist not only among human beings living at the present time but also among those and human beings who lived in the past, even the distant past. It is characteristic of human beings to interact with an environment, but the way such interaction, according to one theory, may benefit a lower organism shows that there are standards such interaction must fulfill if it is to be beneficial. C. H. Waddington shows us, for example, how the horse of the present time has evolved from an animal closer in size to the fox with much less developed lungs and limbs compared to the horse of today. It is more the phenotype (namely, the organism identified on the basis of behavior) than the genotype (namely the organism identified on the basis of its genetic constitution) that is the unit of evolution. To explain the evolution of an animal, e.g., the horse, one must call upon such factors as the challenge presented by the environment (e.g., that posed by enemies of the horse in the Tertiary period), the spontaneous response of organisms to these challenges (e.g., the horses' strategy of running away rather than standing and fighting), and the feedback of both the environment (e.g., through the survival of the horses that became proficient at this strategy) and behavior (e.g., the mating of horses that have genes capacitating them for this response and thus enhancing the capacity of their offspring) on the genetic system. These affect the gradual changes in this system resulting in a population of organisms that show an appropriately altered phenotype.[36] Granting that the continued life of the species horse is good for it and better than extinction, the aforementioned responses of horses were appropriate to the environment and to the horses' potential, and thus were beneficial to them.

Recently biologists and specifically sociobiologists have found in this reality a basis not only for the diversity of human beings but for their unity, and have built a moral theory on this. While this has led to a reductionist interpretation of human behavior on the part of some representatives of sociobiology, that is not the case with all. For example, Mary Midgley concludes her evaluation of sociobiology by stating that "All moral doctrine, all practical suggestions about how we ought to live, depend on some belief about what human nature is like," and the "traditional business of moral philosophy is attempting to understand, clarify, relate, and harmonize so far as possible the claims arising from different sides of our nature."[37] We can make moral judgments adequately only if we admit claims appropriate to the fulfillment of human nature. Thus contemporary evolutionary biology is not contrary to but, within its own limits, supportive of the existence of a constitutive humanity and human good; in fact, it presupposes this.

(b) *Developmental Psychology*. Recent developments in psychology get beyond the earlier nurture vs. nature disputes and support the view that the development of human beings is due to the active interaction of the growing person with his or her environment or world in a way that leads to a progressive restructuring of the self, of knowledge and of moral judgment. It is a part of being human that there is in the person a "tendency for new characteristics to emerge from previous, global characteristics" and a "tendency (for behavior) to become hierarchically organized, . . . for earlier developments to be continuously subsumed under later developments."[38] This new orientation in psychology is a break with reductionist approaches which characterized much of academic psychology through this century.[39] With this, however, developmental psychologists presuppose the reality of human nature that sets standards and criteria for what may be understood as development and what as regression or failure to develop. For example, Kohlberg recognizes that it is through the subject's active restructuring of his or her moral judgments that he develops, but he accepts that some forms of moral judgment are more adequately and maturely human than others. Piaget finds that the individual cognitive subject restructures his mode of knowing the environment through interaction with that environment, but he presupposes that some cognitive structures are more advanced than others. Erikson shows the personality structure of the adult to be the result of the growing person's restructuring of the self through stages of interaction with an expanding social environment and stages of unfolding inner potential, but he holds that some personality structures are more appropriate to the adult than others. For example, the mature person should be characterized by generativity, i.e., a sustained interest in the development of the next generation in spite of its costs. All this supports the viewpoint that we offered.

It may be particularly appropriate here to recall that Erikson's work supports the existence of constitutive principles of human development. Although there remain elements of Freud's mechanistic metapsychology in his work, Erikson's findings call for kinds of constitutive principles of human development that transcend Freud's reductionism. While Freud interpreted later forms of ego development as epiphenomena, simply as secondary manifestations of the energies or motivation of the id and the ego's service of the id, Erikson acknowledged emergents in human development that cannot be reduced to their origins or to the sum of their parts.[40] The growing person interacts with his or her social environment more out of search for meaning than by being driven through displaced energies. And in this interaction the child develops new forms of relatedness (e.g., basic trust) and modes of being (e.g., imaginative projections in the child of about three years old that enable him to become "a part of a larger whole, which is his relatedness to himself and the world around him"[41]). There is a schedule for maturation and structure formation and the need for suitable experiences being offered to the child at successive stages of his or her growth to support such formation and maturation. Erikson's findings suggest that we should go further than he himself in getting beyond present concepts of ego, id and super ego as used by many psychoanalysts, for they presume "that there is no such entity as a human person aside from the sum of these subdivisions of the psychic apparatus."[42] His findings also support our giving consciousness a more central place than did Freud or behaviorism, for it is through consciousness and specifically freedom (see Chapter V above on freedom and moral choice as well as chapters in the companion volume, *Psychological Foundations of Moral Education and Character Development*, edited by R. Knowles) that the individual has some, though limited, control over his life and can change himself and his circumstances. All of this presupposes the reality of a human nature that sets standards for the way the growing subject interacts with his or her environment and the way the social environment interacts with the child.

In particular, we must acknowledge a "specific knowable and instinctive human nature" and "some instinctual and maturational tendencies . . . common to the species as a whole."[43] Freud accepted the existence of instincts (at least in the sense that the id is instinctual), and in accepting them also acknowledged that there is such a reality as human nature. In this he is joined by developmental psychologists, ethologists and behavioral geneticists, though not by existentialists such as Sartre or by behaviorists such as Watson and Skinner. However, Freud's understanding of instinct is very defective. This notion has been difficult to specify, particularly since it is now recognized that none of man's behavior is totally independent of learning or culture. For this reason one can no longer define the instinctive in man as totally dissociated from experience. A more modest definition is needed of the instinctive than that offered in the past, one that even some behaviorists recognize as existing in man. We may, as Yankelovich and Barrett note, accept D. O. Hebb's definition:

> The term 'instinctive' will be used to refer to behavior other than reflexes in which innate factors play a *predominant* part. Empirically, this is behavior in which the motor pattern is variable but *with an end result that is predictable from a knowledge of the species* without knowing the history of the individual animal.[44]

In this definition of the instinctive, even such human developments as language are included. Thus this descriptive definition releases the instinctive from being confined to blind drives, and "places the phenomenon of the instinctual within the world of significant meanings."[45]

The human being then is a subject who not only does but must restructure himself through interaction with the environment for the purpose of actualizing his being. This actualization of his being as an intrinsic lure calls forth the subject's activity. Human nature here then is not simply that which precedes human action and explains the kinds of action that are distinctive of him. Rather the actualization of his humanity faces the subject as a possibility in need of actualization, a possibility that has not only distinctiveness but also a possibility that demands variety according to the environment of nature and history, differences of age, sex and many other individuating circumstances. The human good is achieved only through an historical process that rightly involves great pluralism without relativism.

Even with the above said, many would still feel the creativity and self-definition we find in men and women to be opposed to a pre-given human nature. Such a reservation may find support in Erikson's analysis of adolescence. In our pluralistic and changing socio-cultural environment, the possibilities that face a young person in life styles, world views, occupation and marriage are quite varied. As a distinctive task of this stage the young person must shape his own identity. The adolescent "from among all possible and imaginable relations . . . must make a series of ever-narrowing selections of personal, occupational, sexual and ideological commitments."[46] For this purpose, the young person is in need of "a system of ideas that provides a convincing world image." As Erikson writes: "It is in adolescence . . . that the ideological structure of the environment becomes essential for the ego, because without an ideological simplification of the universe the adolescent ego cannot organize experience according to its specific capacities and its expanding involvement . . . ."[47] But Erikson seems hesitant to say that the young person needs some ontological understanding of what constitutes humanity and its good. To this extent at least, it may appear to many that developmental psychology does not support the view we have advanced in this chapter.

It is true, we must agree, that the active self-definition that is so much a part of modern Western experience and so central to the task of adolescence has for many philosophers been an argument against considering certain orientations, goals, values, relationships and attitudes as normative for man because they are correlated with a human potential. But is not this viewpoint a misinterpretation of our human self-definition? Is not the meaning of adolescence, for example, found largely in the fact that it is a stage of the person's orientation to a good or kind of be-ing and relatedness that is specifically human, a good or way of be-ing on which man's completion or actualization as human depends? I suggest that this is the case for the following reasons.

There is a certain parallel between the adolescent's knowledge of the world about him and his self-definition at this stage. Piaget shows that at adolescence the cognitive subject has developed a structure of knowledge that capacitates him for simple scientific reasoning. By formal operations, the young person can construct the physical world about him through making and testing hypotheses. Scientific knowledge does involve a cognitive construction of the physical world through the use of mathematics. While many have concluded from this that we do not know the structure of the physical world itself in any real fashion, for Piaget man's cognitive construction of the physical world in science is the *means* by which we reach structures actually present in this world. From the fact that Piaget grounds the formal operational period in the young person's development of the schemes of the actual and the possible, I have argued elsewhere that it is the knowledge of being that enables the young person to advance to this mode of knowledge.[48] Thus the condition of possibility for his cognitive construction of the physical world in science is his knowledge of being; the constructivist character of this knowledge is not counter to or independent of his knowledge of objective reality or reality as being. Moreover, the knowledge that makes science possible is not only constructive or structuring knowledge, but also discrimination of qualitative differences in the world by perception and insight.

If this is the case, can we say that the adolescent's construction of his personal life through the choices he is called upon to make is adverse to, or independent of, his orientation to a good or a way of be-ing appropriate to him as human? In his consideration of alternative life styles, occupations, marriage or the single life, the adolescent is evaluating possibilities of human life. He makes his decisions within the context of his human possibilities and their actualization. True, the growing boy or girl lives human life within a particular environment, both physical and socio-cultural, and correlated with individuated potentials and opportunities. But human life itself, as is evident in Erikson's study of stages leading up to adolescence, has certain kinds of defining possibilities and calls for certain kinds of relationships, values and attitudes for its fulfillment.

The *manner* in which the adolescent or youth orients himself toward the good that completes him as human differs in part from that of the child. Correlated with the formal operational period of his cognitive development, the adolescent presents to himself hypotheses or possibilities of human living that are not limited to adjustment to the present. A greater degree of openness and reflective intentionality is possible and normative for him, as an adolescent. His construction of his life at this stage depends more than earlier on his own knowledge, his own evaluation of possibilities, and his own interests and choices. The consequent freedom which is or should be present in his decisions is no guarantee that he will make decisions that will truly enhance his life as human and that are fitting to him and others. He can as easily, and perhaps more easily, make decisions only on the basis of his unreflected present likes and dislikes or those of his peer group, etc. The possibilities for good or evil are in any case larger in adolescence and youth than they were in childhood, and his responsibility is greater than at earlier stages of his growth. In later adolescence he is given more responsibility for himself and others in his society. The fact that the life he leads as an adult is due to his own construction manifests the *manner* of his orientation toward his fulfillment as human, rather than the disengagement of choice from a good that is proper for human beings.

In fact, if there were not some ways of living humanly that had intrinsic value, that enhanced and actualized a person and contributed to his completion as human, then how much meaning would there be to the choices that adolescents or adults make? If an understanding of themselves as human beings and of the human world in which they live does not offer them criteria for their choices, they seem to be left with only the criteria of their own sub-culture or their own interests. To see these latter bases as the adequate context of a young person's decisions is to reduce severely the meaning that is present in this stage of life; it is to distort rather than explain the problems and, indeed, the mystery that encompass them during periods of decision in adolescence and youth. It is to deny that there are right or wrong decisions, or good and better decisions, and to settle for decisions that are successful or unsuccessful by some immediate criteria, pleasurable or painful, conventional or unconventional. On this basis there would be no moral meaning to adolescence and its choices, for moral meaning occurs within the context of man's orientation to the specifically human dimension of living and what is intrinsically valuable for that living.

Neither Erikson nor those who accept his basic interpretation of adolescence conclude from the fact that the adolescent has to construct his life that there is not a character to human life that constitutes a context of meaning and a norm for the identity that adolescents form. It is essential for the adolescent to gain as deep an understanding as he can about who he is and about the full dimensions of his environment as human, as well as about what his environment is as a member of a particular society and culture. Without this he cannot know what are his possibilities as a human being and thus the meaning and norms for his choices in life. What he needs then is not only an 'ideological simplification of the universe' or 'a convincing world image,'[49] but the truth that is available about the human dimensions of his environment and his possibilities and relationships within it. The fact that the youth constructs his life makes not less but more necessary his understanding of the real dimensions of his humanity and what fulfills it.

(c)Cultural Anthropology. Most anthropologists at present reject relativism.[50] Clifford Geertz, as a good example, acknowledges a unity of human nature; indeed, anthropology presupposes this. He does not affirm a unity of nature as did the enlightenment view of man, namely, by stripping away diversity. This view is defective, because it held that the great variety among men "is essentially without significance in defining his nature. . . . [and] consists of mere accretions, distortions even, overlaying what is truly human--the constant, the general, the universal--in man."[51]

Counter to this view is the empirical finding that humans do not exist unmodified by the customs of a particular place and time. On the other hand, Geertz does not avoid relativism "by seeking in cultural patterns themselves the defining elements of a human existence which although not constant in expression, are yet distinctive in character."[52] Seeking in cultural universals the unity of mankind is another way of looking for the lowest common denominator of humanity, and this is not what we want. Most human behavior is the vector outcome of both intrinsic and cultural controls, and so Geertz adopts an interactive view of man as do Piaget, Kohlberg and Erikson. It is in man's career that we best discern his nature, for it is through this that his innate capacities are transformed into his actual behavior.[53] Culture is one, though not the sole, determinant of this career, and thus cultural particularities themselves can be made to reveal natural processes.

Geertz understands culture not so much as complexes of concrete behavior patterns but "as a set of control mechanisms--plans, recipes, rules, instructions (what the computer engineers call 'programs')--for the governing of behavior."[54] Man is the animal who most needs these "extragenetic, outside-the-skin control mechanisms, such cultural programs, for ordering his behavior,"[55] since he does not have such programming from his instincts or genes save in a most general way. We can see this particularly in childhood practices in many areas of the world, but this is not to deny that there is in the subject an active self-structuring agency that the culture has to take into account and adjust itself to, as Erikson has shown so well.[56] Culture is not simply an ornament of human existence but its essential condition. (See Chapter XI below on the moral environment.) An indication of this is found in the fact that man's physical evolution and cultural evolution overlap rather than being wholly sequential. Man's physical evolution (e.g., the anatomy of the thumb, the representation of the thumb on the cortex, and the size of the brain) is in part dependent upon man's development and use of tools, which by a feedback process affected in turn even the evolution of man's central nervous system, the shape of his thumb and the size of his brain. The development of his tools created for man a new environment, and:

> By submitting himself to governance by symbolically mediated programs for producing artifacts, organizing social life, or expressing emotions, man determined, if unwittingly, the culminating stages of his own biological destiny. Quite literally, though quite inadvertently, he created himself.[57]

The recognition of diversity in cultures, then, while opposed to an ahistorical interpretation of humanity and morality, contradicts neither the unity of human nature nor the reality of the human good as a criterion of moral choice. To deny this is to consider all cultural conditionings and all human behavior as morally equal, for it is to abdicate a criterion for judging morally that is other than particular customs, cultures and conditions. On the other hand, we must acknowledge the dependence of values on culture as well as on man's intrinsic drives and potential; no other view does justice to the cultural diversity of which we are aware. Yankelovich and Barrett express this well:

> The whole lesson of modern anthropology has been that man, even among the most primitive cultures we can find, is ever and always the value-seeking and value-driven animal. There is no necessary conflict between ethical values (superego) and instinct (id). Like any other synergistic structure, values are the joint product of the instinctual and the cultural. The ethical and moral dimensions of man's life have a thoroughly natural basis not reducible either to infantile origins or to social custom. The reality of the ethical, as difficult as it may be to define and clarify, belongs as a primitive concept in any new metapsychology.[58]

There is in this the realization that the culture in which we live can distort as well as support our search for, and interpretation of, true human values. In fact, we have suggested that what is lacking in Kohlberg's view may be partially due to the influence of a democratic process where so many political questions become those of a conflict of interests. Thus he tends to interpret moral judgment somewhat restrictedly in this context. Similarly, we suggest that the interpretations of moral decision by disciples of Dewey may in part be limited by the model of technological intelligence that is used, for in this model it is means rather than human ends or goals that are frequently given primary importance. The final part of this chapter will be relevant to this influence that the culture can have on our interpretation of values.

In this section we first of all presented an hypothesis of a constitutive human dynamism or thrust and a constitutive human good as normative in morality,with the suggestion that if Kohlberg, Munsey and Aron would accept this, they would overcome the dichotomy that divides them. An acknowledgement of this would give a basis for the universality and prescriptiveness that Kohlberg sees as criteria of moral judgments. It would give also a context for a teleological approach since the value of consequences of human action are secondary to, and dependent upon, the constitutive human good and humanity that this fulfills. We defended this hypothesis by the use of a phenomenology of moral judgment, using the case of what actually happens when we treat others justly out of a moral conviction. Finally, we presented the objection to such an interpretation that may derive from the diversity of human cultures and the creativity and autonomy of human moral experience. Here we showed that to acknowledge the reality of a constitutive humanity and human good is not specifically the view of a pre-modern philosophy. Rather, it is supported by contemporary interpreters of the evolutionary process, human development and cultural diversity inasmuch as they understand these processes in the context of an interaction between an organism or humankind and the environment or world, for this interaction presupposes and supports a unity in human nature and its constitutive fulfillment or good, as well as a pluralism consistent with this.

TYPES OF VALUES

It may be helpful here, in view of our whole project, to consider certain types of value since an essential part of moral education is an education in values and in the capacity to choose among them. By 'value' here, we do not mean primarily what an individual or society in fact chooses or toward which they have a positive attitude. Rather, we mean some thing, act, attitude, relationship or person or group that has instrumental or intrinsic worth because of its humanity or because it enhances our humanity--in short, because of its relation to the constitutive human good. The affective reaction we have to this reality should give us access to its value, as is shown in Chapters III and VII of this volume. This was acknowledged by classical philosophy; for example, Thomas Aquinas notes that: "the virtuous man judges correctly about the goal of virtue, because as each person is so does the proper end seem to him, as is said in *Ethics*, 3. Therefore for judging rightly about what is to be done, i.e., for prudence, it is required that man have the moral virtue."[59]

But we usually or frequently cannot trust our affective reaction so totally that in important matters we can do without a critical reflection by which we compare a projected action, relationship, etc., with what we have previously called the constitutive human good. Does it enhance this good or support it, or does it diminish it for ourselves or for others? Is it appropriate for me in my particular circumstances, even if it does enhance the human good? (See Chapter VI above on how we make concrete moral decisions.) For values the primary point of reference then is the human person, as we have seen previously. This view is not egocentric, since it calls for respect for the worth of other persons. Nor is it anthropocentric, for the constitutive human good which is the perfection of our humanity may well involve, as religions hold, a larger than human good. That is, the human person is called to value and seek his human good within the context of a relationship to God as the ultimate horizon of human development.

Within this context, we now ask how we might distinguish some major types of human values. Of course, there are many different ways in which we can classify values.[60] In examining books on this topic, one finds almost as many ways of dividing types of values as there are books.[61] At times it does not seem that this division of values into types is of much practical benefit in reference to moral education, because some divisions aim more at theoretical inclusiveness than at practical relevance. If our interest here is more the latter than the former, then it would seem helpful to offer first some suggestions on what endangers valid insight into human values in our time and then present a viewpoint on types of values that may be helpful in these circumstances.

The Threat of Nihilism

If there is validity to what we have written so far in this chapter, it is of overriding importance in our time that we acknowledge the claim of a human good upon us that precedes our choices and individual or social interests--namely, one that is appropriate to the human dynamism or intentionality from which our choices and interests come, and that is the value to which we should adapt our choices and interests if these are to promote our real human development. The danger that threatens this attitude in our time is perhaps primarily one that lies close to a central strength of our modern western culture, namely, its spirit of creativity shown in our institutions and technology. To many in this culture it seems that values are most basically the creation of human beings in varied cultures, and that to be human is most basically to create the values we will live by. Iris Murdoch describes a type of current reflection on values as follows:

> The center of this type of post-Kantian moral philosophy is the notion of the will as the creator of value. Values which were previously in some sense inscribed in the heavens and guaranteed by God collapse into the human will. There is no transcendent reality. The idea of the good remains indefinable and empty so that human choice may fill it. The sovereign moral concept is freedom, or possibly courage in a sense which identifies it with freedom, will, power . . . the guarantor of the secondary values created by choice. . . . It must be said in its favour that this image of human nature has been the inspiration of political liberalism.[62]

In this perspective freedom and creativity are set in opposition to the givenness of values; claims upon us come most basically from acts of our will rather than from human values that precede our choice. This viewpoint seems to be present in both Kohlberg's interpretation of moral judgment as deriving from an equilibration process and in Aron's and Munsey's interpretation of moral choice as deriving from a person's autonomous action after a consideration of consequences. In practice, for most people this creativity and freedom attaches itself to interests they have antecedently and unreflectively in a particular kind of activity. "Business is business," "art for art's sake," "that's politics," "it's all right as long as it doesn't hurt anyone" are all contemporary phrases that reflect human engagement in different areas of human activity where freedom and creativity may be evident for self-defined values, but where the values sought are not subjected to critical examination. This results in a disintegration of the person, and a subjection of the worth of the person to the achievement, products or pleasures that these particular types of activity offer. It is to subvert the human good and results in a loss of a sense of the worth of the person.[63]

The view that we are ultimately creator of our values and modern practices that reflect this view lead to nihilism and, perhaps, express it before this nihilism is conscious. To quote Nietzsche on the nature of nihilism:

> What does nihilism mean?--*That the highest values devalue themselves.*
>
> The aim is missing: "Why?" finds no answer. According to this view, our existence (action, suffering, willing, feeling) has no meaning: the pathos of "in vain" is the nihilists' pathos--at the same time, as pathos, an inconsistency on the part of the nihilists.[64]

It is described differently by different authors, but all recognize a void at its center.

> The nature of the void called nihilism is described, with varying degrees of clarity, as the "loss of the centre", an "encounter with nothingness," the "'incapacity to escape boredom," the "lack of a proper philosophy of life." Most writers revert to Nietzsche's terms: the loss of sense and purpose, the devaluation of all values, the sense of nothingness.[65]

The source of this in modern western culture seems to be the premise that there are so many conflicting claims to truth about reality that each claim is itself undermined by objections from others. Claims to a truth about life that would give a ground for values are undermined particularly by modern science and historicism. All of this shows that "The deeper one looks, the more our valuations disappear--meaninglessness approaches! We have *created* the world that possesses values!"[66] Thus the view that our creation is the source of our values ends in a sense of meaninglessness and nihilism. This attitude has in the last hundred years spread from humanists to very wide sections of the population in the west.

Thus if one puts creativity and freedom at the source of human values, the result is a sense of meaninglessness and nihilism. Human beings know that they are not by way of their choices and interests as such the creators of value in any ultimate sense; a life led on the illusion that they are leads to a void. If, on the other hand, one recognizes that basic human values are given antecedent to our choice, this need not result in creativity and freedom; witness many traditional cultures that are custom-bound. However, these cultures do frequently sustain a strong sense of meaning in people's lives. The acknowledgement of human values as claims on our choice and interest rather than as creatures of our choice and interest can itself lead to creativity and can be freely given. For example, at the foundation of the United States was the acknowledgement of certain God given human rights that it was the function of government to protect. This free acknowledgement led to the creativity evident in establishing structures likely to defend such rights. Freedom then is more properly itself or more humanly perfect when it acknowledges such values than when it takes it upon itself to create such values. Creativity contributes to human life and value when it is exercised within such acknowledgement. This is true in individual life as well as in political, economic, cultural and social life.

Relationships Among Human Values

In our culture where the loss of the recognition of human values as antecedent to, and criteria for, human freedom and creativity leads to a sense of meaninglessness, there is a need for a renewed sense of the primacy of the human good or human values. And in our non-traditional culture where calls from values of all sorts constantly bombard people because of the pluralistic society in which we live, there is need for some integration of values. The following three areas of reflection seem to me to contribute toward such a restoration of a sense of the human good and the integration of varied values. These reflections are no more than an initial sketch, but they may contribute to an understanding of the relation of the human good and moral choice.

In the first place, the insights of developmental psychology and specifically those offered by Erik Erikson seem to contribute both toward a restoration of the sense of the priority of human good over human choice in a way that is appropriate to our time and toward an integration of varied human values. This is the case because Erikson's analysis uncovers a schedule of unfolding potentialities in the growing person and an interaction between the social environment and the growing person correlated with this maturation. It is then a value for the society around the child to support its development in a way appropriate to its maturing capacities. And it is a value for the child to interact with his or her expanding social environment in a way proportionate to individuating circumstances and gifts, but also in a way that contributes to the emergence of strengths or virtues that lead toward the maturity which Erikson calls generativity.[67] This theme will be developed more fully and appropriately in the psychological volume in this series. Here we simply want to note that the virtues the growing person is called to develop throughout his interaction with society and the care that society is called on to take in reference to the growing person, all form a kind of integrating principle for values that are truly human because they enhance the constitutive humanity of both child and caring agents.

Secondly, if we mean by types of values the different general forms of good "that can be participated in or realized in indefinitely many ways on indefinitely many occasions,"[68] we could divide them as follows: knowledge, life, play, aesthetic experience, sociability or friendship, practical reasonableness and religion.[69] However, without underestimating the validity of this distribution, our earlier phenomenology of non-discriminatory action perhaps gives us a context for a more concrete and personal division. What was the human value involved in such an instance that gave rise to a moral obligation in the given circumstances? We noted that this value was both the worth or dignity of the other and the orientation that is part of the agent's humanity as a social being toward relating to others in society through giving and receiving and through mutual respect. The principle on which we identified this value involved an object pole and a subject pole. The other with his worth as human in himself and as part of the horizon or the good that completes the individual agent is the object pole here; the subject pole is the orientation proper to the agent to relate to other human beings through respect, justice and, let us add, love.

The value we are speaking of here is not exhausted by the specific relation of justice to an individual other. It involves also a community ordered in justice and love and an attitude on the part of the subject toward the formation, support or reformation of such a society or political order that respects the rights or dignity of all the individuals within it. Thus we largely agree with the positions of Kohlberg and Rawls we summarized earlier, though we differ from them through grounding justice in the dignity of the human person and our orientation as social beings to respect that dignity. This value involves too those special relationships of friendship and in particular that found in a marital relationship and the family; all of these are human values or integral dimensions of the human good that fulfills man. Developmental psychologists show us that individuals must restructure themselves progressively through childhood, adolescence and early adulthood if they are to freely and consistently appreciate this dimension of human value. We should note that the modern world is tragically marred by unbelievable atrocities committed against this basic human value; we see this in the many millions killed, tortured and maltreated in concentration camps and elsewhere in the twentieth century.

Using this same basic principle of an integral dimension of the human good to identify other basic types of human value, we can specify another as body or bodily values, namely that order of our life that is primarily physical and our orientation to its preservation and enjoyment, and to growth in it. This could include values external to man such as property that is instrumental in supporting our physical life, as well as our orientation toward these external goods within our orientation to the preservation and enhancement of our life. Food, clothing, shelter, energy, much of our technology, means of transportation, healthy environment, etc., and the money that can purchase these come to mind here. This includes also and even more than external goods the goods internal to the human person such as life, health, physiological maturation, physical skills, pleasure, physical exercise and play, etc.; many of these are both intrinsically valuable and instrumentally valuable. There is a certain priority in time that these values enjoy over the values of human relationships, because it takes a certain physiological development and other developments on this level before the individual is able to appreciate and honor human relationships such as those we described above.

There are, of course, human relationships essential for the child from the first moment of his existence, such as the mutuality of mother and infant; these are largely expressed through the mother's caring for the infant's specifically physical needs and the infant's responding to her as he responds to the goods of the physical order being offered him or her. This instance of the parent caring for the child shows us that this level of bodily values is frequently or even commonly caught up into a more fully human level. For example, we build a museum or a school; food is consumed in the context of human companionship; parents provide food for their children; individuals and a political community seek to feed the poor, clothe the naked, heal the sick; bread and wine are used as sacramental signs. Thus activities directed toward such physical or bodily needs are animated by, and expressive of, a person's or society's orientation to the values of knowledge or beauty, the values of human relationships, and religious values. However, in our society marked by consumerism and hedonism the pursuit of possessions and satisfactions of physical needs or desires frequently crowd out awareness of the deeper human values needed for our human fulfillment. It is engaged in at the cost of the denial of justice, love, beauty, knowledge and, many of us would add, God.

We may roughly associate a number of values such as knowledge, beauty, identity, aliveness to values, and many forms of play as a third generic type of value which we may designate personal or self values as distinct from bodily and social values. There is obviously a melding of one type of value with other types, but there is a family of values that is not primarily bodily or social. These are goods that are far better to have, other things being equal, than not to have; they are dimensions of the constitutive human good that enhance human be-ing, and by the orientation constitutive of being human we tend toward these values or goods. There is an object pole here such as truth or beauty and a subject pole such as knowledge and aesthetic appreciation and creativity. Many human skills can be included here that are enhancing for the person to exercise as well as being instrumental for others, such as skills exercised in many different professions and occupations in life. Not all of these values are on the same level. For example, some areas of truth and knowledge are more centrally human values, or of intrinsic worth, and they enhance human existence more than others. There has to be choice among these values, of course, for one cannot equally seek them all. There is a legitimate and necessary pluralism among individuals and societies in the ways that these values are appreciated, ordered and expressed. Engagement in the pursuit of these values may and frequently is, as we said in reference to bodily values, expressive of and animated by concern for social and religious values. Unfortunately in our culture which is so oriented toward the external, these values are frequently given little prominence in the lives of many people.

We may add that moral values can be understood as personal values that reach the root of the human self; they are far more closely related to the self than, for example, some areas of knowledge (e.g., of the physical sciences). Or moral values may preferably be understood as pervading all genuine human action rather than as a distinct generic order of values. They are present whenever a person orients himself freely toward the constitutive human good in accord with practical reason. For example, personal integrity, justice, honesty, courage, openness to the deeper human values are included here as the subject pole that represents a responsiveness to human values as they are appropriate to the individual person. (See Chapter V on moral character.) Fidelity to conscience that is formed by practical reasonableness or, if properly understood, love may sum up the aspect in which these values can be considered personal or self values. Realistic appreciation of these values obviously calls for a certain restructuring in the normal human life so that the individual does not give prime importance to his individual and material needs.

In the estimation of most people in history, there is a fourth basic type of value that we can designate as religious. Here the object pole is found in the Sacred or, in western religions of Judaism, Christianity, and Islam, God understood as transcendent yet immanent personal being. The subject pole is found in human openness to the Sacred or God, as found in faith, trust, and love, and in liberation from what subverts such openness. There is an intrinsic worth or dignity in the Sacred or God that merits or deserves our acknowledgement. For those who believe that God is the source and goal of all values, God and relation to or communion with him is the apex of fulfillment for human life. Moral values may be understood as implicitly religious since the absoluteness that is a characteristic of certain moral injunctions (e.g., not to directly kill an innocent person) and the sacredness of the other that is the basis for certain moral injunctions are themselves participations in the Sacred that is God. (For a treatment of the relation of morality and religion, see Chapter X.)

John Farrelly 243

According to Christians and many others, love of God is not opposed to appreciation and pursuit of human values in history, but is the ultimate meaning of the human search. Man is meant for more than simply human values, which are participations in a larger and ultimate value. For human beings to acknowledge this, however, calls for a conversion or enlightenment that is a gift of God to those who are open to it.

Thirdly, and finally, one may wonder what value the physical world around us has when we take as criterion of value the constitutive human good. Does this mean that the physical world has only an instrumental value for man; is it without intrinsic value? Certainly we find many traditional societies that look upon the physical world not only as something usable, but as a whole order of reality with which they have a tie of kinship. Thus they respect it and its inner dynamism and beauty, for they consider that they came from the same womb as did nature. St. Francis of Assisi called nature "sister." It is particularly our utilitarian civilization that has reduced it to the status of a quarry that is used but need not be respected.

In recent years there has been, fortunately, a reaction against a simply exploitative approach to the physical world. Many are adopting a viewpoint that we are part of this physical world and that we should preserve with it an ecological balance while we use it. There seems to be more than sentimentalism to this new or renewed attitude, and our approach to value in this chapter supports it. We have not developed an egocentric criterion of value, for we acknowledge man as a social and indeed a religious being, and so we acknowledge that we are oriented and must orient ourselves to a constitutive human good that involves other human beings and God himself.

How does the physical world fit into this picture? In a way analogical to our experience of our own desires and the human dynamism from which they come, we can recognize that the physical world is shot through with intentionality or dynamic inner directedness toward being. (Chapter III in this book also affirms this.) The world is not simply a machine that moves as part mechanically moves part. Teleology is evident in animals for they seek food, sex and play. It is evident also in the very organisms of both animals and plants, since in organisms there is an inner orientation to growth, to reproduction, to the preservation of their being and resistance to what threatens this being. The part of modern evolutionary theory that ascribes this process to chance and natural selection alone has had to suppress evidence for this teleology.[70] Teleology is also evident in the non-living world for here too the pull of a molecular or larger structure is operative in the movement of matter. The characteristics of a machine are no longer adequate as an explanation even though this is all that physics may describe. This does not mean that we have to be panpsychists in order to acknowledge the presence of purpose,[71] but rather that we need to accept the existence of teleology in physical reality that has neither consciousness nor life.

Classical philosophy recognized that each being seeks or holds on to its being in some real though analogical sense. The contemporary study of physical reality by the physical sciences manifests, as Koestler and others bring out, that physical things strive for an order of being that is larger than their own individual being. One conclusion we may draw from this is that it is not opposed to a recognition of the goodness or value of animals, plants and non-living physical reality to use them for human purposes. This too can be a fulfillment for such physical beings. Though this is not without loss, loss is frequently involved in a reorientation to a more than immediate purpose; and we have no basis for ascribing to animals, plants, and non-living physical reality the kind of intrinsic worth that we ascribe to human beings and that prohibits us from subjecting their good to our own.

We can and, it seems, must hold that there is an intrinsic value--or goodness, if some would wish to reserve the term "intrinsic value" for human beings specifically--in physical reality and an orientation in this reality toward such goodness or being. It befits us to respect this and indeed admire it, for it is admirable. It befits us to be basically at peace and harmony with this order, not only because that is a way to respect our own being, but also because it is a way to respect the degree of being had by physical reality below the human scale. This attitude of respect is one of the ways that many of our contemporaries seek to achieve an approach to human life and reality at large that is integrative in the sense that it seeks a fulfillment proper to human beings in a way that subordinates rather than excludes lesser values.

In conclusion, we have in this chapter sought to show that an integration of a constitutive human good and a distinctive moral choice offers a better basis for moral judgment and creative life decisions that either Kohlberg's deontology or Aron and Munsey's consequentialism taken alone. In fact, we have suggested that the view we have developed provides more adequate foundations for the efforts of these psychologists and educationists to promote the moral education of children and adolescents: that it integrates the valuable work they have already done while overcoming the dichotomy between their views.

DeSales School of Theology
Washington, D.C.

NOTES

1. See L. Kohlberg, "From Is to Ought: How to Commit the Naturalistic Fallacy and Get Away with It in the Study of Moral Development," in Theodore Mischel, ed., *Cognitive Development and Epistemology* (New York, Academic Press, 1971), pp. 152, 154.

2. See, for example, Jean Piaget, "Piaget's Theory," *Carmichael's Manual of Child Psychology*, ed. Paul H. Mussen (3rd ed., New York: Wiley, 1970), vol. 1, 722.

3. Kohlberg, "From Is to Ought," pp. 214-215.

4. *Ibid.*, p. 215.
5. *Ibid.*, p. 221.
6. See L. Kohlberg, "Educating for a Just Society: An Updated and Revised Statement," in Brenda Munsey, ed., *Moral Development, Moral Education, and Kohlberg* (Birmingham: Religious Education Press, 1980), pp. 463-464 where he speaks of two forms of participation helpful to the moral education of high school students: "participation in the outside community . . . (and) real power and democratic participation in the governance of the high school itself. The general educational rationale for both is still best given by Dewey's . . . theory as this has been elaborated in the psychological theory of Piaget. . . . According to both, the fundamental aim of education is development, and development requires action or active experience. The aim of civic education is the development of a person with the structures of understanding and motivation to participate in society in the direction of making it a better or more just society. This aim requires experience of active social participation as well as the learning of analytic understandings, of government, and the moral discussion of legal and political issues."
7. See Brenda Munsey, "Cognitive-Development Theory of Moral Development: Metaethical Issues," *ibid.*, pp. 161-181.
8. *Ibid.*, p. 165.
9. *Ibid.*, p. 174.
10. See I. Aron, "Moral Education: The Formalist Tradition and the Deweyan Alternative," *ibid.*, pp. 401-426.
11. *Ibid.*, 412. This is a quotation from John Dewey, *Human Nature and Conduct* (New York: Modern Library, 1930), p. 179.
12. *Ibid.*, p. 413.
13. *Ibid.*, p. 420.
14. *Ibid.*, p. 421.
15. See Bill Puka, "Kohlbergian Forms and Deweyan Acts: A Response," *ibid.*, pp. 429-454.
16. See articles by Puka and Kohlberg, *ibid.*
17. Clifford Geertz, *The Interpretation of Cultures. Selected Essays* (New York: Basic Books, 1973), pp. 130, 141.
18. See also the study of the epistemological question in my book *God's Work in a Changing World* (Washington D.C.: University Press of America, 1985), chap. 9, "Developmental Psychology and Knowledge of Being," pp. 287-314. As noted there, our knowledge of reality is explained in contemporary psychology, on the one hand, by perception that is studied by experiments on people discriminating shapes, etc. (e.g., James and Eleanor Gibson), and, on the other hand, as mediated by the cognitive subject's equilibration process via assimilation and accommodation of the environment to cognitive schemes (Piaget). It can be shown that both perception and equilibration processes--and insight mediated by these--are present in our knowledge of reality or being. One thing that this means is that when we make a factual judgment about what is, we are already dependent upon human action (i.e., the equilibration

process). And since our human action is for the human good or value, because it is for our human being in the sense of the protection, enhancement, actualization of our being, etc., our judgments about facts are already dependent on our orientation to, and action for, values. For example, our judgment about the meaning of the fulfillment or flourishing of our humanity reflects not only knowledge dependent upon perception, but knowledge dependent on our values and action for values. It follows that in being derived from our knowledge and judgment of what is, the prescriptivity present in moral judgments is in part derived from our value knowledge. Thus the exigency that exists in the moral judgment is not without basis in our judgment about what our humanity is. There is not the fact-value dichotomy that much contemporary moral philosophy claims, unless one's epistemology is Kantian or empiricist. Further development of this theme can be found in Chapter III.

19. *The American Heritage Dictionary of the English Language* (New York: Houghton Mifflin Co., 1969), p. 1414.

20. *Ibid.*, p. 567.

21. John Finnis, *Natural Law and Natural Rights* (Oxford: Clarendon Press, 1980), p. 61.

22. (Cambridge: Harvard University Press, 1973). See the statement by Dwight Boyd, "The Rawls Connection," in Munsey (ed.), *Moral Development*, p. 185, that Kohlberg holds that "the central achievement of Rawls' theory is that it represents the first clear systematic justification of the principles and methods of decision we call 'Stage 6,' which were only partly articulated by Kant."

23. *Ibid.*, p. 302.

24. D. F. Scheltens, "The Social Contract and the Principal of Law," *International Philosophical Quarterly*, 17 (1977), 331-332. The enclosed quotations are from Rawls' book.

25. *Ibid.*, p. 528.

26. *Ibid.*, p. 335.

27. E. Sullivan, "A Study of Kohlberg's Structural Theory of Moral Development: a Critique of Liberal Social Science Ideology," *Human Development*, 20 (1977), 362.

28. T. A. Spragens, *The Dilemma of Contemporary Political Theory: A Post-Behavioral Science of Politics* (New York: Dunellen, 1973), pp. 105-106.

29. E. Barker, *Principles of Social and Political Theory* (London: Oxford University Press, 1967), p. 123. This is cited by Scheltens, art. cit., p. 338.

30. David Norton, *Personal Destinies. A Philosophy of Ethical Individualism* (Princeton: Princeton University Press, 1976), p. 311.

31. Edward Purcell, Jr., *The Crisis of Democratic Theory. Scientific Naturalism and the Problem of Value* (Lexington: University Press of Kentucky, 1973), p. 268. Also see Victor Ferkiss, *The Future of Technological Civilization* (New York: Braziller, 1974) for a similar critique of liberal society. For example, he writes: "Reform liberalism

today lacks . . . a vision of the good society because it is liberal and focuses on means rather than ends." (p. 62).

32. J. Farrelly, "*Human Sexuality*: A Critique," chap. 5 in Farrelly, *op. cit.*, p.102. Perhaps it is relevant here to note that elsewhere I support the view that there are occasions when it is morally permissible to act directly contrary to an *immediate* dimension of the human good to which a human act is oriented when the *full* human dimension of the good to which it is directed cannot be preserved from serious harm by lesser means. See J. Farrelly, "The Principle of the Family Good," chap. 4 in Farrelly, *op. cit.*, pp. 77-91. In this specific matter I differ from the position presented by Joseph Boyle on moral reasoning in Chapter V above. We hold much in common concerning moral reasoning--such as our acceptance of the human good as basic to moral reasoning and choice and our rejection of consequentialism. Perhaps the different adjectives we use to designate the human good--he uses "entire" or "total" or "integral" while I use "constitutive"--reflect somewhat different reactions against consequentialism. While his reaction seems primarily focused on the difficulty of comparing one human good with another in consequentialism, my reaction is primarily focused on the self-defined character of the good in this theory. Thus he insists that the basic principle of the human good demands that we not undertake action against one or another human good, while I insist that it demands that we not act against the constitutive human good. I would interpret an amputation of a gangrenous leg to preserve the health of the whole body as morally permissible action against one dimension of the human good to preserve a larger dimension of the same kind of human good. And on analogous grounds I would defend the moral permissibility of contraception in some circumstances. He would accept the moral permissibility of the amputation, although he would describe this as not being direct action against a human good; and he would judge contraception differently.

33. W. D. Hudson, *The Is-Ought Question* (London: Macmillan, 1969), p. 29.

34. G. J. Warnock, *Contemporary Moral Philosophy* (London: Macmillan, 967), p. 57.

35. Paul Taylor, *Principles of Ethics. An Introduction* (Encino, Calif., Dickenson Pub. Co., 1975), pp. 132-133.

36. See C. H. Waddington, "The Theory of Evolution Today," in Arthur Koestler and J. R. Smythies (ed.), *Beyond Reductionism* (Boston: Beacon Press, 1969), pp. 357-395.

37. Mary Midgley, *Beast and Man: The Roots of Human Nature* (Ithaca: Cornell University Press, 1978), p. 166.

38. Richard Lerner, *Concepts and Theories of Human Development* (Reading, Mass.: Addison-Wesley, 1976), p. 117.

39. See Bernard Rosenthal, *The Images of Man* (New York: Basic Books, 1971) for a critique of reductionism in modern psychology.

40. See D. Yankelovich and Wm. Barrett, *Ego and Instinct. The Psychoanalytic View of Human Nature--Revised* (New York: Random

Books, 1970), particularly chapter 17, "The Core of Reconstruction."
41. *Ibid.*, p. 314.
42. *Ibid.*, p. 323.
43. *Ibid.*, p. 317.
44. *Ibid.*, p. 377. The quotation is from D. O. Hebb, *Organization of Behavior: A Neuropsychological Theory* (New York: Wiley, 1949), p. 166. Italics added.
45. *Ibid.*, p. 375.
46. E. Erikson, *Identity: Youth and Crisis* (New York: Norton, 1968), p. 245.
47. *Ibid.*, pp. 31, 27.
48. See "Developmental Psychology and Man's Knowledge of Being," cited in footnote 18.
49. We go beyond Erikson's formulation in one place by what we say here. Largely because of the formulation Erikson gives there, which is weaker than some he gives elsewhere, Peter Homans argues that while there is some 'theological coloration' in Erikson: "his formulations are also clearly psychological in character. For this reason we may say that Erikson has created a system of psychological meaning which both assimilates and secularizes (repudiates) traditional theological meanings. Identity-formation is the assimilation and secularization of the activity of justification by faith." See Homans, "Protestant Theology and Dynamic Psychology," *Anglican Theological Review.* Supplemental Series, #7 (Nov., 1976), 135. Also see his article, "The Significance of Erikson's Psychology for Modern Understanding of Religion," in P. Homans (ed.), *Childhood and Selfhood. Essays on Tradition, Religion and Modernity in the Psychology of Erik Erikson* (Lewisburg: Bucknell Univ. Press, 1978), pp. 264-292 For an interpretation of Erikson as bringing together "an Aristotelian essentialism and a more modern evolutionary and adaptive point of view," see Don Browning, "Erikson and the Search for a Normative Image of Man," ibid., pp. 264-292.
50. See Clifford Geertz, "The Impact of the Concept of Culture on the Concept of Man," in *The Interpretation of Cultures*, p. 37.
51. *Ibid.*, p. 35.
52. *Ibid.*, p. 37.
53. See *ibid.*, p. 52.
54. *Ibid.*, p. 44.
55. *Loc.cit.*
56. Waud Kracke, "A Psychoanalyst in the Field: Erikson's Contributions to Anthropology," in Homans, *Psychology and Childhood*, pp. 147-188, shows the strengths and weaknesses of Erikson's anthropological studies.
57. Geertz, *ibid.*, p. 48.
58. Yankelovich and Barrett, *Ego and Instinct*, p. 326.
59. Aquinas, *Summa Theologica*, I-II, 58, 5. His reference is to Aristotle's *Nichomachean Ethics*.
60. Nicholas Rescher orders classifications of values according to

whether these classifications refer to subscribership to values, the objects valued, the sort of benefit at issue, the sort of purposes at issue, the relation between subscriber and beneficiary, or the relation of the values to other values. See Rescher, *Introduction to Value Theory* (Englewood Cliffs: Prentice-Hall, 1969), chapter 2.

61. See, for example, Louis Lavelle, *Traite des Valeurs*, Tome Second, *Le Systeme des differentes valeurs* (Paris. Universitaires de France, 1955); Donald Walhout, *The Good and the Realm of Values* (South Bend, Ind.: University of Notre Dame Press, 1978); J. N. Findlay, *Values and Intentions. A Study in Value-Theory and Philosophy of Mind* (London: George Allen & Unwin, LTD, 1961); Georg H. von Wright, *The Varieties of Goodness* (London: Routledge & Kegan Paul, 1963); John Finnis, *Natural Law*, chapters 3 and 4.

62. Iris Murdoch, *The Sovereignty of Good* (New York: Schocken Books, 1971), pp. 80-81.

63. See David Norton, *Personal Destinies*, p. 216 for a comparison of this modern widespread approach with Aristotle's "eudaimonism" expressed by his assertion, "No one chooses to possess the whole world if he has first to become someone else." "Aristotle's words (*Nich. Eth.* 9.4. 1166a) epitomize a radical disparity between moral sensibilities of his time and our own. For surely the motto of our time runs, 'Show me how to possess the whole world and I will become whomever you please.' ... The precondition of eudaimonia is the unique, irreplaceable, potential worth of the person. It is his readers' sense of this personal worth on which Aristotle relies in his confident assertion that no one would wish to exchange himself, even 'to possess the whole world.' Today we are without this sense, and rush to exchange ourselves at the prospect of the most trivial rewards. To persons who have no knowledge of who they are, much less of anything in the way of irreplaceable personal worth, nothing is to be lost by such exchange."

64. Friedrich Nietzsche, *The Will to Power*, tr. Walter Kaufmann and R. J. Hollingdale (London: Weidenfeld and Nicolson, 1968), pp. 9, 318.

65. Johan Goudsblom, *Nihilism and Culture* (Totowa, N.J.: Rowman and Littlefield, 1980), pp. 16-17.

66. Nietzsche, *The Will to Power*, p. 326.

67. See E. Erikson, *Childhood and Society* (New York: Norton, 1963), chapter 7, "Eight Ages of Man," pp. 247-274.

68. Finnis, *Natural Law*, p. 61.

69. *Ibid.*, chapters 3 and 4. See also G. Grisez and R. Shaw, *Beyond the New Morality: The Responsibilities of Freedom* (South Bend, Ind.: University of Notre Dame, 1974), chapter 7.

70. See Arthur Koestler, *Janus. A Summing Up* (New York: Random House, 1978), ch. 11, "Strategies and Purpose in Evolution," pp. 205-222 for a documentation of this cover up and evidence for teleology. He notes (226): "The purposiveness of all vital processes, the strategy of the genes and the power of the exploratory drive in animal and man, all

250 The Human Good and Moral Choice

seem to indicate that the pull of the future is as real as the pressure of the past. Causality and finality are complementary principles in the sciences of life; if you take out finality and purpose you have taken the life out of biology as well as psychology."

71. Koestler notes that interpretation of physical phenomena by statistical probability works because there is a tendency in random phenomena toward order. He notes a half-dozen words that different physicists and others have coined to describe this reality, and adds (270): "What all these theories have in common is that they regard the morphic, or formative or syntropic tendency, Nature's striving to create order out of disorder, cosmos out of chaos, as ultimate and irreducible principles beyond mechanical causation."

CHAPTER X

THE FOUNDATIONS OF MORALITY

DAVID L. SCHINDLER

The central problem of philosophical ethics is whether it is possible to provide rational justification for our moral values.[1] This problem typically comes to expression in the form of the relation between "facts," or "what is the case," and "values" or "what ought to be the case."[2] The problem of course looms large in any intended program of moral education. For as the etymology of the word indicates, education involves a drawing out or leading ("*e*" and "*duco*"), and moral education thus involves some sort of drawing out or leading in the area of morality. I leave aside here the question of whether or in what sense this entails some form of indoctrination.[3] My concern bears rather on the nature of the substantive moral values one might wish to build into one's educational program. If and to the degree that moral values are intrinsically irrational or nonrational matters, it would seem that there can be no good reason for urging their appropriation in any such program. My question, then, is whether it is possible to affirm moral values as rational sorts of affairs. Is it possible, as a matter of principle and hence in any given instance, to distinguish rationally between moral good and evil? As this formulation of the question suggests, my intention is to consider, not *which* particular substantive moral judgments are to be taken rationally as good,[4] but rather *whether* and in what sense substantive moral judgments as a matter of principle might be so taken.

It is a commonplace that much of contemporary educational practice and indeed of contemporary philosophy provides us with forms of a negative answer to this question. For example, the influential values-clarification approach to moral education, as the name itself suggests, tends to focus its concern on helping a student to clarify or elucidate the values which he or she already has, rather than on trying to move to a critical judgment about the content or substance of such values.[5] The reason for this restriction of focus to the process of valuing rather than to the specific character of particular value judgments seems to be the assumption, adopted at least provisionally or for operational purposes, that there exists no objective, rationally justifiable, moral standard in terms of which such judgments might be assessed.[6] The values-clarification approach to moral education, in other words, seems to instantiate a mixture of the types of ethical theory called naturalism and noncognitivism.[7] On the one hand, moral values are assumed, at least provisionally, to be a simple function of the contingent facts of one's culture or psychology. On the other hand and often simultaneously, moral values are assumed, again at least provisionally, to be matters of simple preference, and thus the sorts of things about which one cannot, strictly speaking, argue. The common import of such assumptions, then, is that they serve to remove morality from the arena of argumentation and justification.

One of the overarching concerns of the studies which make up this volume is to develop a philosophy which justifies some sort of education in the area of substantive moral claims. Such a concern commits one in principle to a rejection of the relativism and noncognitivism carried in the philosophic assumptions of values-clarification as just noted, and hence to the task of defending some kind of objective standard for morality. But I should like to suggest at the outset that even the values-clarification theorists who adopt the above assumptions cannot so easily dismiss the foundational question about an objective standard for morality, that is, even from within their own assumptions. For as values-clarification theorists themselves have increasingly come to acknowledge, however much they may disparage efforts to make, or to evaluate critically, substantive moral claims in any direct or straightforward way, their very adoption of clarification as the "correct" mode of education carries within it, at least implicitly, an espousal of such values as tolerance, self-actualization, authenticity, and the like, over their opposites.[8]

Of course, as Ellrod notes, the fact that values-clarification theorists increasingly acknowledge their own implied values does not mean that they have thereby justified those values.[9] But this serves to focus just the point I wish to make here: namely, that if in fact the very practice of value-neutrality or value-relativity in one sense (for example, in terms of whether it is good to steal in this particular instance), carries within it a non-neutrality or non-relativity in another sense (for example, in terms of whether it is good to be tolerant of different views regarding the goodness of stealing in this particular instance), then it would seem to follow that the question of the warrants or foundations of morality does in fact arise even for one who adopts the assumptions of value-neutrality or relativity.

The possibilities are twofold: (1) the values-clarification theorist can deny that he or she implies in his or her practice the "correctness" of such values as democratic tolerance and the like. In such a case there is no demand for providing a warrant for one's practice, but only because one is thereby saying that one has exactly no reason, implicit or explicit, for subjecting students to the process of clarification--rather than, say, to a shoot-out--and for encouraging other educators to do the same. Since it is difficult to maintain such a position if one continues to defend the practice of clarification in preference to a shoot-out, (2) the valuesclarification theorist increasingly acknowledges his or her implied judgment of preference for the values of democratic tolerance and the like. In acknowledging such an implied value judgment, the values-clarification theorist is committed to showing the warrants for exempting such a value from the neutrality and relativity which he or she assumes regarding values generally.

It is important that this brief suggestion not be taken in a stronger sense than is intended. For the values-clarification theorist might respond simply by saying that selecting the value, say, of democratic tolerance for preferred status has no other warrant or "reason" than the fact that it is a value which happens to be shared in the society in which we live. The value of democratic tolerance, in other words, might be taken to be non-relative only because it is as a matter of convention taken to be such by--and for--those who live in our society, and not because there are good reasons in the strict or strong sense for taking it, reasons, that is, which could be defended as binding in a cross-cultural or indeed universal sense. My initial suggestion, then, is only that, insofar as the practice of values-clarification implicitly involves taking exception in some form to the values clarificationist's professed value-neutrality, there is an internal demand for one who engages that practice to give some accounting for the exception.

On the one hand this should not, *a priori*, be taken to signify a demand that such accounting be made in terms of good reasons which hold trans-culturally or universally, for that would beg the question of whether there are such--a possibility which the values-clarificationist, in offering conventionalism as a response, precisely rejects. On the other hand, and this is the point of my initial suggestion, the demand for an accounting does seem to me to commit the values-clarificationist *a priori* to considering all the logically possible ways of explaining the exception involved in his or her performance. One cannot simply or *a priori* assume that the conventionalist response is the only, or indeed the most adequate, way of accounting for the exception, for this would also beg the question, now from the other direction: given some elements of non-neutrality and non-relativity carried in any performance of values-clarification, the issue which demands adjudication is precisely that of the sort of "reasons" which suffice finally to account for these elements. That conventionalism is the most adequate explanation available must therefore be argued in light of other possibilities, notably the possibility that there are "natural" reasons or foundations for non-neutrality and non-relativity.

This demand for argument, then, sets both the context and limits of the present article. My purpose will be to show (a) that there is a basic philosophical claim which is operative in the conventionalist account of morality and indeed serves precisely to dictate that account, and to show (b) that there is available an alternative, contrary philosophical claim which makes possible a "natural"[10] account of morality. My purpose, in other words, will be to show the logical possibility of a morality which is natural rather than merely conventional, and thereby to establish the gratuity of the claim that conventionalism is the only possible, and hence most adequate, response to the question of morality.

Among contemporary moral education theorists Lawrence Kohlberg has stood out as one who rejects the claim that we can adequately account for morality in conventionalist terms. He claims that good reasons, that is, reasons which bind cross-culturally or universally, can be given for our conception of morality and thus for our moral judgments. In a word, Kohlberg challenges the non-cognitivism and relativism operative in much of contemporary ethical theory. He does this in the name of a kind of "naturalistic" morality, that is, a morality which has a "natural" and hence both cognitive and universal foundation. Such a position is consistent with the intention of this chapter which therefore will proceed by examining the position of Kohlberg, both in terms of the criticisms he makes of contemporary trends in ethical theory, and in terms of the warrants he provides for his own alternative theory. The purpose of the chapter in so doing will be threefold: it will attempt to distill what I take to be the central philosophical claim operative in the intention of his argument, a successful defense of which is consequently necessary to sustain that argument. Secondly, it will attempt to show that this (implicit) philosophical position is in an important way in tension with the (Kantian/formalist) philosophical tradition on which he explicitly relies for support for his theory. Finally, the chapter will suggest that there is available another philosophical tradition (Aristotelian-Thomistic) which makes just the sort of claim which seems to me to be necessary to allow Kohlberg to realize the intention of his argument. The overarching aim, then, in engaging this threefold task, will be both to call attention to the (assumed) philosophical position which has dictated the rise of noncognitivism and relativism, and to show the logical possibility of an alternative philosophical position which makes possible a view of morality which is both cognitive and normative.

I

There is no need to rehearse the details of Kohlberg's stages of moral development. The major point relevant to our topic is Kohlberg's claim that these developmental stages translate into a moral hierarchy, that is, his claim to "have successfully defined the ethically optimal end point of moral development."[11] Our concern bears on the warrants which Kohlberg provides for such a claim, and this concern leads us into consideration of what is called the "naturalistic fallacy."[12]

Stated broadly, the naturalistic fallacy is taken to consist in the claim to have established ethical conclusions beginning from factual premises. Or, to put it in the terms used at the outset of this article, the naturalistic fallacy as ordinarily understood consists in making values, or what ought to be the case, a function simply of facts, or what is the case. I have already noted above the assumptions connected with this fallacy in much of contemporary social science. On the one hand, insofar as contemporary social science subscribes to the mode of reasoning reflected in the naturalistic fallacy as stated, that science collapses into relativism. If it is not possible to make any distinction between facts and moral value, then a factual variety of moral values from person to person and culture to culture implies a relativism of moral value. On the other hand, insofar as contemporary social science rejects this position of naturalism, it typically does so by separating moral values from facts. That is, moral values are not taken to be matters of fact at all, but rather matters of preference. Strictly speaking, then, values are no longer taken to be relative, but only because they are not the sorts of things about which one can argue whether they are absolute or relative. Values, in short, are not cognitive matters at all. The upshot of these assumptions, then, as we have seen, is that values are either relative or cognitively meaningless. In either case, they are not susceptible of rational justification. Kohlberg claims to have developed a theory which warrants rejection of these assumptions. In order to see how and indeed whether his theory does so we turn to an examination of Kohlberg's position in relation to naturalism.

Kohlberg gives a summary statement of that position as follows:

> To begin with, there are two forms of the 'naturalistic fallacy' we are not committing. The first is that of deriving moral judgments from psychological cognitive-predictive judgments or pleasure-pain statements, as is done by naturalistic notions of moral judgment. Our analysis of moral judgment does not assume that moral judgments are really something else, but insists that they are prescriptive and *sui generis*. The second naturalistic fallacy we are not committing is that of assuming that morality or moral maturity is part of man's biological nature, or that the biologically older is the better. The third form of the 'naturalistic fallacy' which we *are* committing is that of asserting that any conception of what moral judgment ought to be must rest on an adequate conception of what it is (*FITO*, p. 222).

The second form of ethical naturalism which Kohlberg is rejecting here is rather straightforward, and for our purposes can be disposed of quickly. For the kind of moral development Kohlberg suggests is not identified with growth in biological maturity. It is simply not the case that, as one becomes older, one necessarily moves to higher stages of moral reasoning. The move from stage to stage is a logical, not a biological sequence. Of course it is true that an ethically higher stage must come later, but this is precisely because it is ethically higher or more adequate; it is not ethically higher because it comes later (*FITO*, p. 18-1). In short, for Kohlberg it is philosophic adequacy, and ontogenesis, which determines moral hierarchy (*FITO*, p. 181).[113] There are therefore two forms of naturalism with which we must concern ourselves here: the first one noted above, which Kohlberg rejects, and the third one, which he embraces. Why does Kohlberg reject the first and accept the third?

Kohlberg's criticism of the first or bad form of naturalism consists in pointing out what he takes to be a series of confusions among contemporary social scientists which locks them into this bad form. The first confusion is that between ethical and cultural relativism. The cultural relativist affirms that "moral principles are culturally variable in a fundamental way" (*FITO*, p. 156). The ethical relativist makes the further claim that such divergence is logically unavoidable, that is, that there are not rational principles and methods which could reconcile observed divergencies of moral beliefs" (*FITO*, p. 156). Stated in a positive form, then, the confusion is between the notion that everyone has his or her own values and the notion that everyone ought to have his or her own values (*FITO*, p. 156). Stated in negative form, the confusion is manifest in the "move from 'There are no universal human values' to 'There ought not to be any universal human values,' every person or culture ought to do his thing.'" (*FITO*, p. 158). Kohlberg argues that such a move commits the naturalistic fallacy by identifying a factual judgment with a value judgment. More specifically, the collapsing of cultural relativism into ethical relativism involves an ignoring of what is called the "open question": granted that person or culture "x" values "y," we can sensibly ask, "But is that good?" or "Is it right?" To deny the legitimacy of this further question would be to continue to assert the very assumption for which some warrant is being sought.[14]

The second confusion which leads to a fallacious and relativistic form of naturalism is that between "ethical relativity" and "ethical tolerance," that is, between "the relativity of moral principles" and "the relativity of blaming or punishing persons or groups who do not act in accordance with those principles" (*FITO*, p. 159). The claim here, in other words, is that, to avoid sitting in judgment on others and assuming moral superiority for ourselves, we must accept an equality of moral principles, which is to say we must deny that there are any universal moral principles. Kohlberg's response to this position is twofold: first, the universal moral principles of obligation do not oblige one to blame the persons who deviate from these principles; and, secondly, the very urging of the principle of tolerance as applying to all human beings itself entails a denial of ethical relativity, for the principle itself is affirmed thereby as non-relative.

In short, then, Kohlberg rejects a kind of reverse of the "naturalistic fallacy" just discussed: namely, that wherein an "ought" (value) of tolerance, linked with an "is" (fact) of cultural relativism, generates ethical relativism. The "ought" of tolerance is assumed (falsely) to require an identification of ethical relativism and cultural relativism.

The third fallacy behind much of contemporary social-scientific thinking has been its "confusion of ethical relativism with 'value neutrality' or 'scientific impartiality'" (*FITO*, p. 161). Kohlberg cites as an example here the claim of Berkowitz that it is neutral to define moral values as "evaluations of actions generally believed by members of a given society to be either 'right' or 'wrong'" (*FITO*, p. 161). Kohlberg's response is that this is not neutral because it prejudges the facts. To put it another way, it fails to distinguish between "an *a priori* definition of morality in terms of cultural relativity, and the conclusion that morality is culturally relative" (*FITO*, p. 161). The point here is that Berkowitz's definition is not necessarily wrong but that, because it involves a theory which is adopted in advance of inquiry and hence informs the inquiry, it is not a *neutral* approach. On what grounds, for example, other than *a priori* definition, does Berkowitz rule out as an adequate understanding of moral value that of the Catholic priest who defines it in terms of belief in the catechism (*FITO*, p. 162)? In short, the point here is, once again, not that Berkowitz is wrong, but merely that he is not being value-neutral, that he is arbitrarily ruling out of court alternative understandings of morality, and that their thus being ruled out requires justification.

Furthermore, suppose a similar strategy were employed with respect to scientific beliefs. That is, suppose that scientific beliefs were defined as "beliefs about the world generally believed by members of a given society to be true or false" (*FITO*, p. 161). This would entail that we accept as equally "scientific" the most sophisticated forms of scientific theory and the crudest imaginable forms of superstition. But this simply belies what we do as scientists. We would recognize one who equalized matters in this fashion simply to be a poor scientist. Hence, argues Kohlberg contra Berkowitz, we must at least consider the possibility that the same situation obtains in the moral sphere (*FITO*, p. 161). A simply *a priori* rejection of this possibility will not suffice.

Kohlberg contends that Berkowitz's position derives from the view of men like Weber "who distinguish between a rational sphere of social--science methods and findings ('is'), and a sphere of value ('ought'), toward which a rational man or a scientist must take a stance of 'value neutrality,' that is, recognize that his position is personal, arbitrary, and historically conditioned" (*FITO*, p. 162). Hence we are led to a fourth confusion, namely, that "between the 'rational' as 'the scientific or factual' and the 'rational' as the value neutral." (*FITO*, p. 162). Kohlberg argues that this position once again assumes ethical relativity rather than justifies it. On what grounds does one rule out the possibility of establishing rational methods of coming to ethical agreement without a critical assessment of those methods? Indeed, Weber himself is taking a value stand in defense of the value of value-neutrality, and in doing so he attempts to support it with careful rational arguments. The point here, then, is twofold: first, the rejection of rational arguments in the area of ethical value should not be assumed, as it is in the case of men like Berkowtiz and Weber; rather such rejection demands a justification. Secondly, the defense of neutrality exemplified in Berkowitz and Weber itself involves taking a value stance, and doing so by an, at least implicit, appeal to the kind of rational argumentation they have already ruled out in such a context (*FITO*, p. 162).

What is common to these confusions, then, which are linked with the first form of the naturalistic fallacy, is the assumption that moral judgment, as distinct from factual judgments, finally have no cognitive status. Rational methods or modes of rational argumentation are identified with what is understood to be scientific method. The latter is limited to description of the facts of valuing among different persons or cultures. Since these facts of valuing are seen to vary, they are, given the assumed identification of the rational (hence "objective,") with the scientific/descriptive, labelled mere preference, that is, something of a non--cognitive sort.

Kohlberg's criticism of this form of naturalism, which makes moral valuing simply derivative from and finally reducible to psychological fact, is that at least as operative in much of the thinking of contemporary social scientists, it is advanced, not as a conclusion but rather is asserted in the form of *a priori* assumption. There is no justification for assuming in advance of any inquiry into the matter that we cannot find moral development of a genuinely hierarchical sort, and that it is impossible in principle for moral thinkers to come to agreement regarding moral matters on the basis of rational argumentation (*FITO*, p. 163). This assumption by social scientists is belied by their practice, which would seem both to instantiate some sort of ethical non-relativity and non-neutrality, and to carry at least an implicit appeal to some sort of rational argumentation on their behalf.

Kohlberg's criticism of the dominant form of naturalism, then, is similar in many ways to the criticism I sketched at the outset of this article in relation to values-clarification. But his criticism would be incomplete and indeed innocuous without a second, more positive claim: namely, that careful empirical inquiry suggests findings which contradict the assumption of relativism built into the prevalent fallacious form of naturalism (*FITO*, pp. 163ff). As this suggests, Kohlberg at once understands himself to be involved in a form of naturalism, and claims that his form is of a sort which justifies non-relativism. This position claims both to involve a description of the facts of moral development, and that this very description in turn allows a prescription in terms of a hierarchy of kinds of moral judgment. Consideration of how Kohlberg advances this claim will situate us properly to begin reflection on the philosophical issue(s) which I take to be involved in the defense of his claim.

II

If Kohlberg is to be successful in his claim to offer a distinct alternative to the form of naturalism which he considers defective in its assumed relativism, then it seems he must, on his own terms, meet two requirements. First, he must show that moral judgments have some internal connection with facts in the ordinary sense, in order to be able to sustain the third or benign sort of naturalism which would seem necessary to maintain the cognitive status of moral judgments. Secondly, he must show that moral judgments at the same time are in some sense distinct from facts in the ordinary sense, in order to elude the (first or fallacious) sort of naturalism which would collapse moral judgments into relativism. How does he manage to walk this tight-rope?

To begin with, Kohlberg claims that empirical studies of moral development disclose as a matter of scientific fact that "there is a universal moral justice" (*FITO*, p. 223; see also pp. 163-180). It is important to be clear about the nature of this claim. This moral form about which Kohlberg intends to be making a factual claim assumes a distinction between fact and value. As Kohlberg puts it, and this is the second crucial element in his position, "the moral man assumes that his moral judgment is based on conformity to an ideal norm, not on conformity to fact" (*FITO*, p. 223). In other words, the form of naturalism to which Kohlberg thinks it necessary for any moralist to subscribe requires that judgments about what morality ought to be must begin with some characterization of what it is (*FITO*, pp. 222-223). If we attend carefully to the nature of morality as revealed in cross cultural studies, however, we find that in the minds of moral men morality is something distinct from what is taken to be fact in the ordinary sense. Moral men in various cultures consider their moral judgments to be founded on conformity to an ideal, rather than on conformity to facts, in the sense of what happens to be the case in their culture. To put it another way, moral men in various cultures consider what they *ought* to do in any given instance to be logically distinct from the empirical *fact* of their (or their culture's) doing it. Even if what one judges ought to be done coincides with what one does, empirical cross cultural studies of the facts of moral experience reveal that the moral man does not found his sense of obligation on fact in this sense. Rather, they show that the moral man experiences his moral judgment as prescriptive on its own terms, that is, precisely as distinct from his or his culture's psychological facts in the ordinary sense.

These two elements in Kohlberg's position, then, lead us to affirm the following regarding his understanding of the relation between facts and moral judgments (see *FITO*, p. 223). On the one hand, moral judgments are *sui generis*; hence what is ordinarily understood to be a scientific description of the facts can never justify them or pronounce on their worth. On the other hand, such a description of the facts does play an integral role in that it can tell us whether this distinctive concept of moral judgments accurately obtains. In other words, the claim that "x" is what morality is in the minds of moral men is a factual claim of the usual sort which can be tested through empirical study: morality either is this in the minds of moral men, or it is not. Only empirical qualitative observation of various cultures can determine this. But, secondly, the qualitative dimension of the claim made on behalf of one's conception of morality precisely as normative involves a mode of reflection distinct from empirical observation. Disclosure of what moral men do consider to be an adequate conception of morality leaves us in the domain of facts in the ordinary sense. That men *do* as a matter of fact claim that "x" is an adequate conception of morality is logically distinct from whether they *ought* to. The latter claim, therefore, requires a distinct justification.

The following quotations from three of Kohlberg's studies will I think serve to summarize both how he understands the relationship between fact and morality and how he justifies that understanding.

(The) isomorphism of psychological and normative theory generates the claim that a psychologically more advanced stage of moral judgment is more morally adequate, by moral-philosophic criteria. The isomorphism assumption is a two-way street. While moral philosophical criteria of adequacy of moral judgment help define a standard of psychological adequacy or advance, the study of psychological advance feeds back and clarifies these criteria. Our psychological theory as to what individuals move from one stage to the next is grounded on a moral philosophical theory which specifies that the later stage is morally better or more adequate than the earlier stage. Our psychological theory claims that individuals prefer the highest stage of reasoning they comprehend. This claim of our psychological theory derives from a philosophical claim that a later stage is "objectively" preferable or more adequate by certain *moral* criteria. This philosophic claim, however, would for us be thrown into question if the facts of moral advance were inconsistent with its psychological implications.[15]

However, we do hold a stronger position, claiming that while psychological theory and normative ethical theory are not reducible to each other, the two enterprises are isomorphic or *parallel* .... [We] have argued for a parallelism between a theory of psychological development and a formalistic moral theory on the ground that the *formal psychological* developmental criteria of differentiation and integration of structural equilibrium, map into the *formal moral* criteria of prescriptiveness and universality. If the parallelism were correct in detail, then formalist philosophers could incorporate an equilibrium concept as part of their normative ethical theory, and vice versa. The ultimate result would be a theory of rational moral judgment like that now present in economics, in which the theory of how people ought to make economic decisions and the way they do make decisions are very closely linked. What can warrant such a "parallelist" claim is only the fruitfulness of its results. I have argued that the fruitfulness of the parallelist assumption is revealed in the clear success of the psychological work based on it (*FITO*, pp. 224-5).

Epistemological and ethical principles guide psychological inquiry from the start. Thus, the strategy attempts to avoid the naturalistic fallacy of directly deriving judgments of value from judgments about the facts of development, although it assumes that the two may be systematically related. It takes as an hypothesis for empirical confirmation or refutation that development is a movement toward greater epistemological or ethical adequacy as defined by philosophic principles of adequacy (*DAE*, p. 484).

III

Let us move on, then, to our foundational question: given that Kohlberg's conception of the relation of psychology and morality is one of isomorphism, namely, that the criteria of moral development parallel the criteria of psychological development, what is his warrant for this conception? What warrants his adoption of these criteria of moral development, precisely *as moral*. If I have accurately described Kohlberg's position, there are three elements in the answer to this question: (1) Kohlberg assumes his principles of moral adequacy (prescriptiveness and universality) to be established on distinctly philosophical grounds, that is, in the context of a reliance on "the formalistic tradition in philosophic ethics from Kant to Rawls."[16] (2) He then uses this distinctly philosophic assumption interactionally, or hypothetically, in relation to the facts of psychological development. That is, empirical study of the facts of psychology will either confirm or refute this original assumption. (3) Finally, Kohlberg claims that empirical study does confirm the original assumption. Hence his conclusion: the originally assumed and distinctly moral-philosophic criteria are justified.

The point I wish to introduce here is that this answer of Kohlberg seems to harbor an unresolved tension, and hence to need further unpacking. On the one hand, Kohlberg says that moral principles, precisely in their character as moral, must be justified on distinctly philosophical grounds, which he takes to be provided by the formalistic tradition stemming from Kant. In other words, the adequacy of these principles as moral is not dependent upon empirical inquiry. On the other hand, operating as a psychologist, Kohlberg takes over this philosophic justification, which then functions as a hypothesis subject to empirical confirmation or refutation. The second part of his argument thus seems to be that empirical studies play an intrinsic or internal role in determining what are finally to count as adequate moral principles. There results the following tension: namely, that morality is at once independent of facts and dependent upon facts.

Now it seems to me clear that some such position as this is necessary if one is to meet squarely the problem posed by the dominant forms of contemporary ethical theory: if morality is simply a function of facts in the ordinary sense relativism would seem to ensue; if morality is simply not a function of facts non-cognitivism tends to result. Kohlberg's intention is to elude these alternatives by--correctly in my judgment--- entering a qualification: In one sense morality is a function of the facts, while in another sense it is not. But this serves to focus exactly the point I wish to make: namely, that, given his intention, the task incumbent upon Kohlberg is just that of justifying the sense of his proposed qualification, namely, the precise sense in which he takes morality to be at once internally related to facts and distinct from facts.

This statement of the task incumbent upon Kohlberg requires still further precision, for a third form of ethical theory, called nonnaturalism[17] has received support in recent thought, at least among philosophers. I take this theory to involve a threefold claim: first, that moral judgments are cognitive matters (in contrast to noncognitivism); secondly, that moral judgments are nonetheless not cognitive matters of the ordinary sort, that is, the sort of factual matters which can be verified by empirical observation (in contrast to naturalism); and thirdly, that moral judgments are cognitive matters which involve a special sort of cognition, typically called something like "intuition" or "rational insight." Clearly, the whole weight of Kohlberg's argument is in agreement with nonnaturalism in the first sense. My concern here bears on what the line of Kohlberg's argument entails in terms of its being situated relative to the second and third features of nonnaturalism.

As we have seen, Kohlberg is explicit in his intention to embrace a form of naturalism, that is, to overcome a dichotomy between "is" and "ought" (*FITO*, pp. 154-55). He considers it possible, *precisely within the context of this intention*, to defend the claim that moral judgment possesses a distinctly necessary and categorical, and hence a normative, character. It seems clear, therefore, that Kohlberg is in agreement with nonnaturalism in ascribing to moral judgment a categorical or normative character. Nonetheless, at the same time he differs from nonnaturalism regarding the possibility of defending such an understanding of moral judgment in "naturalistic" terms, that is, in terms of "what is" or "fact." In short, Kohlberg, in agreement with nonnaturalism, is committed to defending the distinct categorical or normative character of morality. But, in contrast to nonnaturalism, Kohlberg is committed at the same time to defending such a distinct character in terms of an internal or intrinsic connection with facts.

What I wish to suggest here, then, is that Kohlberg's ethical theory, in sharing simultaneously the concerns of both naturalism and nonnaturalism, is thereby distinct from either (as they are commonly understood). To put it more broadly in light of what I have written above, the theory which Kohlberg advances is an alternative to all three of the dominant forms of ethical theory. If I have correctly identified the central thrust of his theory vis-a-vis those dominant forms, then the philosophical task to which he is committed is that of justifying that/how morality is at once a fact, in contrast to noncognitivism and nonnaturalism, and a fact of a distinct sort, in contrast to naturalism of the usual variety. In a word, Kohlberg must justify the distinctness of morality precisely as a kind of fact.

In the face of this suggestion regarding the central philosophical claim to which the intention of Kohlberg's argument seems to commit him, my concern in what follows will be to make a threefold argument: first, I shall attempt to show that there has been in the tradition of Western modernity a common understanding of fact which has served to generate the three dominant contemporary forms of ethical theory. Secondly, I shall argue that the philosophical tradition on which Kohlberg expressly relies, namely the Kantian, does not break from this common understanding in a way which is sufficiently radical to provide a foundation for Kohlberg's intention of offering a distinct alternative to these dominant forms of ethical theory. Finally, I shall attempt to show that there is available another philosophical tradition, namely the AristotelianThomistic, which does contain resources for breaking from that common understanding of fact in a way which is sufficiently radical to found the distinct alternative which Kohlberg intends.

IV

First of all, then, as Kenneth Schmitz notes apropos of a contemporary dictionary account (*Oxford English Dictionary*, "Fact," #4) of "fact,"

> [t]he term designates a real occurrence ("actually the case"); it is "a datum of experience;" and it is what is "certainly known." This complex meaning of fact has been shaped within the problematic of human cognition, with attention to how realities can be known. It points, therefore, not only to the matter of evidence, to what is there, but also to the human conditions required to certify it.... In sum, then, the term "fact" has for its foreground, focus and surface what is actually the case, the evidence; but that evidence comes forward from a background of selective attention guided by an implicit understanding of what is significant for a distinctive kind of discourse. To speak of what is there as *given fact* is to speak within the circle of a discourse that directs attention to the matter insofar as the matter is capable of satisfying conditions that are determined a priori and in accordance with the demands of objective method.[18]

In this light I suggest that the salient features of the understanding of "fact" which set the context of the contemporary discussion regarding the nature of morality can be captured in what Schmitz terms an "objectification of nature."[19] That is, a fact is typically taken to be whatever can be gotten at in terms of the external criteria of verification.[20] Such criteria involve an understanding of fact (nature) which can properly be termed at once mechanist, objectivist, and empiricist. Though there are of course numerous different ways in which these features come to expression in the thought of Western philosophers in recent centuries, the meaning I wish to ascribe to them can be indicated by turning first to Descartes.

Descartes, whom one might identify as a *locus classicus* for the distinctly modern understanding of fact, was certainly no empiricist. Nonetheless, his influence was decisive in terms of the development of what I wish to call mechanism and objectivism.[21] That is, he adopts as his criteria for what can be affirmed as true--"real"--what can be gotten at clearly and distinctly. This, in turn, must be accessible in terms of the proportions and relations proper to mathematics (geometry),[22] which is to say external spatial relations. And such relations are exactly the sort of relations which are proper to a machine.

Descartes's criteria for truth (what is to count as "real") do not really get transformed in the empiricist tradition. In other words, the empiricist tradition does not so much challenge Descartes's criteria as restrict the scope of their applicability to what is accessible to the senses. One need only refer here to Hume, who proceeds to give an account of fact ("matters of fact") exhaustively in terms of cause and effect, by which he means the external relations of discrete sense impressions or phenomena.[23] Hume cites as the perfect instance of the relation of cause and effect that of a billiard ball at rest which is then struck by another and thereby acquires a motion.[24]

I do not at all intend to suggest with these brief remarks that the differences between Descartes and Hume are either few or unimportant, or in turn that there are not numerous ways of understanding fact (nature) in modernity which are in significant senses different from either Descartes or Hume. At the same time I do mean to suggest that in what one may call the tradition of Western modernity there has been a common assumption regarding the meaning of fact which is well illustrated by the central claims of Descartes and Hume as just noted.[25] That assumption is that reality or what is to count as real is what can be accounted for in terms of external (spatial) relations. The paradigm of causal activity is taken to be locomotion, or motion understood in terms of the displacement of physical bodies.[26] I call such an understanding of fact (nature) objectivist and mechanist. It is objectivist because it considers nature in terms of how it appears from without, and thus proceeds to give an account of the activities of nature in terms of the external influence of one thing on another (cf. Hume's billiard ball example). It is mechanist because external relations are best exemplified in, most proper to, the external behavior of machines. While Descartes represents a dualist variety of this mechanism and objectivism, Hume illustrates the empiricist variety which has been more common in the Anglo-American tradition. In a word, then, I take the dominant understanding in the modern Anglo-American tradition to be one wherein what counts as a fact (nature) is what is both observable and sufficient to account for motion in the sense of the displacement of physical bodies.[27] In the language of the classical philosophical tradition, the causal activity of things is understood exhaustively in terms of a truncated view of efficient causality, to the exclusion of formal and final causes. Our question, then, is how this common Anglo-American empiricist variety of mechanism and objectivism shapes the problem of the relation between fact and morality.

The answer to this question lies simply in calling attention to the three results of excluding the formalizing and finalizing activities of an entity as proper causes. I suggest that those results, pertinent to the problem of the relation of fact and morality, are three. The removal of necessity in the sense meant here stems from the denial of form as a structural feature of each of the entities which make up nature. By form is meant that act of an entity in virtue of which it is identified as an entity of this or that kind. Form therefore is that which universalizes any given entity in the precise etymological sense ("universe": "turning toward one") of serving to unify or make into one the many aspects of an entity. The removal of form as an internal feature of what we mean by fact entails the elimination of the sort of necessity (necessary structural feature) of any given entity which would make it possible to universalize or make universal statements about that entity.

Secondly, the modern understanding of fact (nature) as described removes finalizing (or teleological) activity as a cause of an entity. By finalizing activity I mean that dynamic activity whereby an entity tends or seeks to be what it is. Finality is form in its dynamic, directional, purposive modality. The significance of such an exclusion of finality is suggested when we note the connection between finality or teleology and value. Whatever additional features we may wish to assign to what we mean by value,[28] a minimal and essential feature is value's connection with this tendency or seeking which we term finality or teleology. Since fact or nature (any given entity) becomes a value in itself or inherently valuable insofar as it is the object of its own finalizing activity, modernity's exclusion of finality from fact or nature makes it impossible to speak of any entities having intrinsic value, that is, value precisely in their character *as fact or nature*.

Thirdly, in understanding fact (nature) in terms of the external influence of one entity on another, modernity excludes form and finality as *internal* causes of an entity. In other words, modernity excludes any internal activity whereby that entity shapes itself and its environment in terms of its own immanent structure. As a result, insofar as modernity might wish to recoup the sort of necessity lost in its denial of form, it must do so in terms of forces outside any given entity. Thus, necessity becomes necessity of a deterministic sort. What an entity is, is not determined in any sense from within; it is in no sense self-determined. Rather what an entity is, is what is done to it, the sum of the forces acting upon it from without.

In sum, the dominant understanding of fact in modernity carries within it: (1) an inability to make universal statements about any of the entities which make up nature; (2) an inability to speak of the value of such entities in their character as factual or natural; and finally (3) an inability to speak of necessity with respect to such entities in anything but a deterministic way. For the problem of the relation of fact and morality this implies that one must break with the modern understanding of fact or nature if one wishes to speak of morality as both a matter of fact or nature and as requiring features such as universality, value, and non-determinism.[29]

But let me be clear about the nature of this suggestion. I have made no claim as to what might count as an argument against the modern understanding of fact, or in favor of some other alternative which would incorporate the features I have noted as missing in the modern understanding. Nor do I mean to suggest that the sort of universality, value and non-determinism one might seek for morality need be, or is, simply the same as that sought for fact or nature generally. My point is simply that, *if* one wishes to affirm morality at once both as a fact and as requiring the features of universality, value, and non-determinism, *then* one must assign *some* universality, value, and non-determinism to what one means by fact.

To put it another way, if one continues to accept the modern understanding of fact, one must conceive morality in terms of the following alternatives. On the one hand, if one wishes to take morality as a kind of fact, one must understand morality as a non-necessary non-universal, and hence as a contingent and relative, matter. Any sense of value or obligation one might wish to assign to morality could be assigned only contingently and relatively. On the other hand, if one wishes to take morality as something universal, then, once again given the modern understanding of fact, one must understand morality not to be a matter of fact or nature. Any sense of value (teleology) or obligation (deontology) one might wish to assign morality could thus be found only outside fact or nature. In a word, given the modern understanding of fact or nature, the following dilemma arises: if naturalism (of the sort described by Kohlberg), then relativism; if non-relativism, then nonnaturalism.[30]

V

The point of the above excursus into modern philosophy's understanding of fact or nature has been to show how such an understanding dictates the rise of relativistic and nonnaturalistic views of morality. My concern has been to show that, if one wishes to be neither a moral relativist nor a nonnaturalist, that is, to be both a naturalist and a non-relativist, one must challenge just so far the modern understanding of fact or nature. The burden of my earlier argument with respect to Kohlberg was that such an intention of non-relativism and naturalism is fundamental to his undertaking. My question now is whether the Kantian tradition on which he expressly relies for philosophical support is able to help him successfully to carry out that intention. More precisely in light of the above discussion, my question is whether the Kantian tradition breaks with the modern understanding of fact in a way which would permit Kohlberg to found the universality and obligatoriness (deontology) of morality in nature as Kohlberg must do if he is to sustain his naturalistic intention.

My answer is that Kantian tradition does not do so, for a reason contained in the very starting point of Kant's philosophy. That starting point consists in an assumption and a question, to wit: given the Humean understanding of fact or nature, how can we rescue the sort of necessity required for an adequate view of both science and (in a different way) morality?[31] Obviously the Humean context of the question shapes the direction of Kant's answer to this question: for in so far as the objects of nature do not, in accord with Hume's analysis, yield any features which are universal and hence necessary in the strict sense,[32] such universality and necessity must be sought elsewhere than in these objects of nature in themselves. For Kant this "elsewhere" is in the human mind. In a word, then, Kant begins by accepting the Humean claim that nature has no necessity "in itself," and this in turn leads him to locate necessity in, and found it upon, the structure of the human mind which is something quite different from nature.

Further, while locating necessity in the human mind and in this way distancing himself from Hume, Kant nonetheless continues in a fundamental sense the mechanism of Hume. In other words, though now the causality proper to motion in the sense of the displacement of physical bodies (cf. Hume's billiard ball model) has necessity in the strict sense due to the structure of the mind, it nonetheless is still causality precisely in this mechanical sense. It is still the causality proper to external spatial relations. In a word, the study of nature for Kant does deliver necessity (due to the structure of the mind), but the necessity is nonetheless still characterized by external succession.[33] Given this mechanistic (if now idealistic) understanding of nature, there follow the sorts of consequences noted in a general way earlier: namely, any purposiveness (teleology) or obligation (deontology) one might be inclined to affirm must be located by Kant outside nature.[34]

Thus, however much one might understand the objects of nature as having some purposiveness or finality, the point is for Kant that one can legitimately so understand them only *as if* they had such. To affirm finality as constitutive of nature in the same way as mechanical or efficient causality is constitutive of nature is precisely to go beyond what has been established as the limit of reason in its natural or empirical employment. In a word, insofar as one wishes to employ reason in a teleological sense, one can do so only insofar as one understands such employment to be merely regulative, rather than constitutive, of our knowledge of nature.[35]

Secondly, the sort of necessity required by the "ought" of morality demands a kind of causality different from that of nature. The "ought" of morality demands freedom, which is "the power of a state beginning spontaneously,"[36] and this sort of spontaneity runs counter to the situation of nature wherein one state of nature at any given moment follows of necessity from an immediately preceding state. In a word, the sponaneity and hence lack of determinism required by the kind of necessity proper to morality demands the positing of an order of freedom, which is other than the order of nature whose necessity is of a mechanical and hence deterministic sort.[37]

The point of these brief considerations, then, is to suggest how Kant's understanding of the place of teleology and deontology (the "ought" of morality) in his system is a function of his assumed mechanistic understanding of nature. I say assumed because, in his starting point, Kant does not challenge but rather takes over Hume's mechanism. It is not a question for Kant of challenging the billiard ball model of causation; rather, having assumed that model as sufficient for the (constitutive) understanding of nature, the problem for Kant becomes one of finding a way of inserting a stronger sense of necessity into that model of causation than is provided by Hume. Of course, in locating necessity exclusively in the mind, Kant thereby affirms a dichotomy or dualism of nature and mind. But the mechanical character of that necessity in turn forces the two further dualisms which are directly pertinent to our concern. Given the mechanical character of the necessity of reason in its constitutive or natural employment, teleology and deontology--though in different ways--must *ipso facto* be extrinsic to reason in its natural employment. This means that, on a Kantian understanding of the matter, it is impossible to have any "natural" conception of morality (which involves teleology and/or deontology). There simply can be no intrinsic relation between the judgments of reason in its natural employment and the judgments of reason in its moral employment. In a word, a Kantian conception of morality is essentially nonnaturalistic.

The implication of this for the argument of Kohlberg is clear: insofar as Kohlberg wishes to realize his intention of a naturalistic morality, he cannot rely on the Kantian tradition for his philosophic justification of that morality. The dilemma is this: if his conception of morality is naturalistic, then it must be non-Kantian; whereas if his conception of morality is Kantian, it just so far must be nonnaturalistic. In other words, the Kantian position forces exactly the disjunction between nature ("is") and morality ("ought") which Kohlberg's naturalistic intention commits him to overcoming. In this sense, then, and for this reason, Kohlberg cannot seek the foundations for his conception of morality in Kant.

VI

The overarching concern of this article requires that we press this Kantian issue further. Granted that Kohlberg faces a dilemma insofar as he tries to defend a naturalistic morality from within a Kantian perspective, why does he not resolve the dilemma simply by abandoning his naturalism? In other words, are there compelling reasons for Kohlberg's remaining a naturalist? It seems to me that there are, and that those reasons are two. First of all, as Kohlberg's research illustrates, people ordinarily do take morality to be connected with what we mean by fact or nature generally. When we defend our conception of morality, whatever the detail of that conception, it would seem that we finally make the claim, at least implicitly, that our conception of morality is adequate because "that is the way things are," or again because such a conception "fits the facts." Insofar as we claim that "x" is the most adequate conception of morality, that "x" therefore is what our conception of morality ought to be, it would seem that we mean to say, at least implicitly, that such a conception is warranted finally because that is the way morality *is*.

The issue raised here is of course profoundly difficult and delicate. For it is clearly the case that we can and do use terms such as "is," "facts," "the way things are" in different senses. Indeed the use of such terms in the context of morality provides an example of such a difference: though I use some such common phrases as "the fact is" in saying both that "the fact is that I ought to do 'x,'" and "the fact is that I do 'x,'" it seems clear that I mean something different in each case. Nonetheless this example serves to focus just the point I wish to make: namely that the meaning of "the fact is" in the two cases is not exhausted in the intention of difference. Rather, it seems to me, and the research of Kohlberg points to the same conclusion, that we mean what we say when we use the *one* phrase in both cases, and that there is thus (at least implicitly) some common/one meaning of fact which is simultaneous with, immanent within, the two distinct meanings of the term as used in the two cases. Insofar as one fails to allude to this commonness or oneness within the difference, insofar, that is, as one attends only to the difference, one is just so far guilty of an equivocation which removes the warrant for continued use of that one term.

In short, then, it seems to me that the possibilities are two: on the one hand, we mean something equivocal when we speak of "fact" or "is" in the context of morality as distinct from the context of "nature." But if this is the case, then we should be able to find a way finally of justifying our conceptions of morality without appealing (at least implicitly) to some such common/one term as "fact" or "is" which we ordinarily use with respect to "nature." But Kohlberg's research shows, and indeed I believe our reflection bears out, that we do constantly--unavoidably---find ourselves making such an appeal. Insofar as this is the case, it becomes incumbent upon us to retrieve some sense of the unity of the meaning of "fact" ("is") within its distinctness as used apropos of nature and morality. This task of discovering some sense of unity between nature and morality commits one to the intention of naturalism. Nonetheless, it bears stressing that such an intention does not entail a rejection of the distinctness between nature and morality which is the concern of nonnaturalism. The above criticism of Kant was not that he defended a difference between nature and morality, but that he defended a difference between the two in a way which neglected, which failed adequately to thematize, any unity between them. Kant thereby collapsed into a dualism which is inadequate, given the above argument regarding the implication of the way we use language.

A second reason for not abandoning some sense of naturalism at least in principle as a way out of the above dilemma is the lesson of history. Though it is impossible to rehearse the whole of modern and contemporary history relative to our problem,[38] it seems to suggest that a rejection of naturalism, a removal of morality from any anchoring in

270 *Foundations of Morality*

"facts" or "nature," leads almost inevitably--because it has in fact so led--to a noncognitivist view of morality. However much one might want to defend the normative character of morality in nonnaturalistic terms, that is, in terms which are different from what we ordinarily mean by "is" or "fact" or "nature," the lesson of history is that such an attempt inevitably gives way to the charge of gratuitousness. If morality is not accessible to us in the way in which "facts"--"reality"--generally are accessible to us, then it becomes increasingly difficult to claim that morality is "really" accessible to us at all. To the degree in which we wish to defend morality as something different from "facts" or "reality" in the ordinary sense, it becomes difficult to say that morality is nonetheless still cognitively meaningful. It seems to me that certain strains of both positivism and existentialism (though in different ways) provide eloquent testimony in support of this point.

VII

For these two reasons, it seems that for Kohlberg the way out of the dilemma posed by his reliance on the Kantian tradition is not to abandon naturalism, but rather to abandon the Kantian tradition. More precisely, it is to seek a form of ethical theory which permits one to protect the distinctly normative or categorical character of morality, which is Kant's concern, but which does so while rejecting Kant's dichotomy between nature and morality which makes it impossible to meet the intention of naturalism. The burden of my argument above was that Kant's dualism of nature and morality was a function of his failing to challenge sufficiently radically the mechanism of Hume. Granted that Hume's nature receives in Kant a necessary character due to the structure of the mind, this necessity is exactly the necessity illustrated best by the operations of a machine. That is, the state of nature at any given instant is understood exhaustively in terms of the external influence of one state upon another. In a word, nature is viewed deterministically and as without purposiveness. It follows that, insofar as one wishes to insert into morality a distinctly purposive or teleological character,[39] or the deontological sort of necessity which requires freedom, one must seek the source of that teleology and deontology in something other than nature. In sum, then, my contention has been that it is Kant's mechanistic understanding of nature which compels his dualistic understanding of the relation between nature and morality. If this is true, it follows that a necessary condition for overcoming a Kantian sort of dualism is to challenge that mechanistic understanding of nature.

It is just here, then, that it seems to me that the Aristotelian-Thomistic philosophical tradition is well equipped to help us. Of course there are different interpretations of that tradition in terms of the issue before us. Nonetheless, there is no need to engage here a discussion of the relative adequacy of these different interpretations. Rather, given the line of my argument thus far, it will suffice to show simply that the Aristotelian-Thomistic tradition *can* be shown to possess the kind of non-mechanistic view of nature needed to move beyond the dilemma of *either* a naturalistic relativism *or* a nonnaturalistic dualism. Indeed, within this context, my intention is to show how that tradition *must* be interpreted if it is successfully to meet the necessary systematic conditions outlined above for overcoming that dilemma. My task, then, will be to show, first, how the Aristotelian-Thomistic tradition challenges a mechanistic understanding of nature, and secondly, how that tradition situates morality within a nature the mechanistic understanding of which has been so challenged.

The sense in which the Aristotelian-Thomistic tradition can be understood to challenge a mechanistic understanding of nature becomes readily apparent upon recall of our earlier description of mechanism. Very simply, the mechanistic view removes from nature the internal causes of the Aristotelian-Thomistic tradition, namely form and finality. Consequently the states or activities of nature are understood exhaustively in terms of the effective influence from without of one entity or group of entities upon another. Successful understanding of any given natural entity thus hinges on understanding the forces outside that entity, given which that entity is (does) what it is (does). Successful understanding of an entity, in other words, requires no appeal to any internal activity of an entity whereby that entity actively determines itself to be what it is, or actively shapes its environment in terms of what it is determining itself to be. In short, nature as so understood is both without any inherent purposiveness and, in so far as it has necessity at all, that necessity can only be of a deterministic sort. The appropriate method for the study of nature so understood is the external one of empirical observation and verification.

Against the background of this mechanistic way of viewing things, then, the Aristotelian-Thomistic tradition affirms three basic metaphysical axioms of agency or effectivity, formality, and finality.[40] To begin with, these axioms are properly metaphysical, which means that they apply not simply to entities of this or that kind, but to *all* entities or instances of being, including those which make up what we call nature.[41] But insofar as principles of agency, formality, and finality are operative in nature, the Thomist is committed to an inherently purposive and non-deterministic view of nature. Nature retains a sort of necessity due to the presence of form in the entities which make up nature, but the necessity is now seen as a dynamic one: what an entity is at any given instant is what that entity is actively shaping itself to be, in relation to the other entities which make up its environment. In a word, then, the three causes of agency, formality, and finality, understood as jointly present in any given natural entity, require a threefold affirmation. (a) Natural entities, possessing these internal causal activities, can no longer be properly understood in a deterministic way, that is, in terms of effective influence upon such entities from without. (b) Natural entities, possessing form, retain a mark of necessity and hence of universality: their activity is always of a specific sort. (c) Natural entities, possessing finality, always act in a way which bears a teleological character. Thus, if it is the case that, as I have argued above, a conception of morality which would be naturalistic, that is rooted in nature, requires a view wherein it is possible to speak of nature as bearing the features of universality, value, and spontaneity (non-determinism), I suggest that such a condition is met in the Thomistic understanding as here outlined. But of course realization of this condition, while *necessary* if morality is to be understood as natural, does not *suffice* if morality is taken at the same time to be in some sense distinct from nature. How then does Thomism meet this second or sufficient condition, which is the central concern of nonnaturalism?

First of all, the causes which are operative in nature generally are for the Thomist operative also in human nature. It is simply the case now that those causes are given a human specificity due to the presence of a distinctly human form. That specificity we may call a rationality whose hallmark is self-consciousness. Thus a human being, like a natural being generally, is a locus of intelligible necessities which is at once dynamic and purposive. But as self-conscious, a human being is active and purposive in a distinct way which we call free. In other words, the non-determinism found in nature generally becomes in human nature, due to the presence of self-consciousness, the self-determination which is properly termed freedom.[42] In a word, just as all natural beings actively seek an end or what is called good, so do humans, though humans do so consciously and freely. This assertion does not yet suffice to characterize human activity as moral: granted that humans do and indeed must act in this manner, does this warrant our saying that they *ought* to do so? Even granted that human activity is essentially or naturally characterized by an active seeking of the good, is there anything in such a claim that warrants our saying that humans therefore *ought* to seek the good?

To ask this question is to enter into a controversy which has plagued Thomistic ethical theory.[43] Relative to that controversy, it will suffice for my purposes to record an interpretation which I take to be both logically possible in terms of the texts of Aquinas, and satisfactory in terms of meeting the systematic requirements for an adequate conception of morality as those requirements have been outlined above. This interpretation makes two claims, which bear on Aquinas's statements that "the first principle of practical reason is one founded on the notion of the good, viz., that good is that which all things seek after," and that the primary precept of law is that "good is to be done and pursued and evil is to be avoided."[44] My twofold claim is simply that, while the truth contained in the first statement is the *necessary* condition for the note of obligatoriness contained in the second statement, that truth does not *suffice* to account for the note of obligatoriness.

On the one hand, then: were it not characteristic of human nature actively to seek the good, humans would not experience the obligation to do so, certainly not in any universal way. Human nature, in the sense of its active tendencies, is an inner condition of, and thus provides a necessary foundation for, morality. This is precisely what I take Aquinas to mean when he says that the first principle of practical reason is "*founded upon* (emphasis mine) the notion of good, viz., that good is that which all things seek after."

At the same time, this interpretation does not seem to entail the further claim that the judgment regarding human tendencies suffices to account for the note of obligation contained in the primary precept of law, which is to say, the first principle of morality. Indeed, that seems to me why Aquinas says that the principle which includes the note of obligatoriness "Good is to be done and pursued" (*faciendum et prosequendum*) is the first principle, which is to say a *per se notum* or self-evident principle of morality. The note of obligatoriness, or "ought," sounded first by Aquinas when he moves to the moral order establishes that order *as moral*. But if this is the case, then it follows that that note of obligatoriness is not reached simply by unpacking or reading off one's human tendencies. My awareness that I ought to seek the good is given immediately with, that is, as a distinct moment within, my tendency to seek the good; such awareness thus does not follow upon, in the sense of being inferred from, that tendency.

In sum, then, Aquinas says that the first principle of morality is founded upon man's natural tendencies. I take this to mean that such tendencies are the necessary foundation for morality: did we not have a tendency to seek the good, we would not experience an obligation to do so. On the other hand, Aquinas adds a distinct note of obligatoriness when he formulates the principle which he takes to be the first principle of morality. I take this to mean that there is a primitive experience of obligation which establishes human activity as moral: however much attention to our basic inclinations may disclose to us that we *do* seek the good (and indeed disclose the nature of the various goods we seek), the experience that we *ought* to seek the good (various goods) is given immediately with, and hence not inferred from, the awareness that we do seek the good.

The key to interpreting Aquinas correctly here and to summarizing the importance of his position relative to our earlier argument lies in recognizing that there is for Aquinas a primitive experience of the *deon* (being obligated) as well as the *on* (being). The use of such language to describe Aquinas' position seems to me both proper and instructive. It suggests that we have experiences of both "ought" and "is" which are irreducibly distinct (because given primitively), but which are nonetheless distinct *within* or as modalities *of* nature (*on*: being, what is). Insofar as this is the case, it seems to me, apropos of my earlier argument, that Aquinas is neither a naturalist nor a nonnaturalist of the usual sort: the "ought" of morality is intrinsically related to (because a distinct modality of) the "is" of nature; but the "ought" of morality is at the same time irreducibly distinct from (because not inferred and hence not following from) the "is" of nature. Such a position, in cutting through the dilemma of *either* naturalism *or* nonnaturalism, meets exactly, I suggest, the intention of Kohlberg's argument vis-a-vis contemporary ethical theories. In so doing it meets also the intention of this chapter.

VIII

In concluding, I think it is important to retrieve the main lines of my argument, and in so doing to focus once again what I take to be its scope. I began by noting that any program of moral education which intended to lead students in the area of substantive moral judgments was committed to rejecting a relativist or noncognitivist view of morality. My further suggestion was that even those, for example the values-clarificationists, who claimed in theory not to be leading students in the area of substantive moral judgments belied such a theory in their practice: their practice seemed in fact to involve a non-neutrality and non-relativity regarding (say) democratic tolerance. My intention with regard to the values-clarificationists, then, was to illustrate that even those who would most explicitly espouse value-neutrality and relativity thus could not successfully carry through such a position. My intention was thus to suggest that even would-be relativists and noncognitivists must face up to the task of foundations, that is, of giving some accounting for the nonrelativity which, however much they deny it in theory, they exercise in practice. Further, then, in this context my contention was that the conventionalist and hence relativist account which might be offered in support of their practice of non-relativity was precisely an account whose adequacies could not be assumed, but which required argument.

The demand for an argument from the conventionalist would be trivial were there not available, at least as a logical possibility, an account of morality which was not conventionalist. This led to what has been the burden of the chapter: to show that there is available such a logically possible alternative account of the foundations of moral value, one which might be properly termed a "natural" account. Since Lawrence Kohlberg has stood out among contemporary moral theorists as one who espouses the sort of "natural" account necessary to meet the challenge of conventionalism, my argument was worked out in relation to that of Kohlberg.

The substance of the argument, then, at once in relation to conventionalism and Kohlberg, was to show how the modern Western understanding of fact had shaped the contemporary discussion concerning ethical theory. Specifically, my argument was that the modern understanding of fact or nature could be properly termed mechanistic, and that such mechanism was precisely what served to dictate the alternative ethical theories of naturalism and nonnaturalism. On the one hand, insofar as morality is taken to be a matter of fact, morality just so far-that is, given the modern (e.g., Humean) understanding of fact--can only be a contingent and hence relative matter. Thus there results naturalism of the relativistic sort as described by Kohlberg. On the other hand, insofar as morality is taken to be non-relativistic, morality just so far--once again given the modern understanding of fact--can only be a non-factual matter. In other words, there results a nonnaturalism which is characterized by a dualism of fact or nature and morality. The burden of my argument, then, was to show that, because it was mechanism that dictated the alternatives of naturalism (of the relativistic sort) and nonnaturalism, a challenge to mechanism was the necessary (though not the sufficient) condition for moving beyond these alternatives. In a word, my effort was to show that, insofar as one wished one's ethical theory to be neither relativist nor dualist, one just so far must defend some sort of non-mechanistic view of nature.

Within this context, the argument was twofold: (1) It was my contention that Kant accepted, in a fundamental way the mechanistic understanding of fact, and hence was forced, in seeking a distinctly normative conception of morality, to found it upon something outside fact or nature. In other words, Kant was seen to illustrate the second or nonnaturalistic alternative noted above. My contention consequently was thus that Kohlberg, insofar as he relied on the Kantian tradition for justification of his ethical theory, was just so far forced into a nonnaturalism which belied his intention of naturalism, that is, of rooting his ethical theory in fact or nature. (2) Secondly, then, I suggested in this context that there was available another philosophical tradition, namely, the Aristotelian-Thomistic, which did in fact challenge the mechanistic understanding of fact of modernity, and which in so doing founded a possible way out of the impasse regarding ethical theory (that is, either relativistic naturalism *or* dualistic nonnaturalism) dictated by that mechanistic understanding.

It is important to be clear about the scope of the argument as recapitulated here. I have not argued the preferability of a non-mechanistic understanding of fact or nature, such as that found in the Aristotelian--Thomistic philosophical tradition, over against the mechanistic understanding of modernity. The intention of this article is met in showing how one's assumptions regarding the meaning of fact or nature, that is, whether fact or nature is to be conceived mechanistically or non-mechanistically, bear upon one's ethical theory. If the argument has been sound, it follows that anyone who would defend the ethical theories of naturalism, noncognitivism, and nonnaturalism, all of which presuppose a mechanism, must provide an argument showing why such presupposed mechanism is to be preferred to non-mechanism as a way of understanding fact or nature. In view of the opening considerations of this article, this task is incumbent upon values-clarificationists just so far as they wish to make anything other than a gratuitous claim upon others on behalf of their conventionalist ethical theory.

On the other hand, it follows that anyone who would defend an alternative to these three dominant forms of ethical theory, that is, who would defend an ethical theory which purports to be at once cognitive, non-relativistic, and natural, must provide an argument showing why non-mechanism is to be preferred to mechanism as an understanding of fact or nature. I would stress here, then, in light of my considerations of Kohlberg, that Kohlberg must either undertake this task, in order to maintain his intention of providing a distinct alternative to the three dominant forms of ethical theory; or he must be prepared to defend the mechanism which I have argued underpins Kantian ethical theory, and in so doing embrace non-naturalism.

Finally, then, I have suggested that an argument on behalf of non-mechanism is contained in principle in the Aristotelian-Thomistic philosophical tradition. Nonetheless I would stress that my suggestion was only that: my brief sketch of the central features of that tradition as it bears upon the problem of fact and morality requires fuller development, both in terms of its adequacy as an interpretation of that tradition, and in properly systematic terms.

Apropos of the requirement for such a fuller development, I must be content here in conclusion with re-focusing the precise issue I take to need arguing. The mechanistic understanding of fact consists essentially in considering things as they appear from without, that is, in their externality. Such an understanding involves both a content and a method. In accord with a method of observation and verification the mechanistic approach proceeds to give an account of things in terms of a truncated view of efficient causality (of effective influence from without). An argument on behalf of a non-mechanistic understanding of fact therefore must consist in justifying that/how things act also from within. Such justification must attend to both content and method. The idea of causality must be expanded to include internal causes (e.g., form and finality), and a method appropriate for the inclusion of such internal causes, that is, a method distinct from the objectivist method of observation and verification, must be worked out. In sum, then, if the argument developed in this article is sound, the need for such a justification of a nonmechanistic understanding of nature must be met, if not in the suggested Aristotelian-Thomistic terms then in some other. Otherwise, I submit, we are necessarily left in the contemporary impasse regarding ethical theory which consists in having to choose between relativism, noncognitivism, and dualism.

University of Notre Dame
Notre Dame, Indiana

NOTES

1. Alan Gewirth, *Reason and Morality* (Chicago: University of Chicago Press, 1978), p. ix.
2. W. D. Hudson, "Editor's Introduction: The 'is-ought' problem," in *The Is-Ought Question*, ed. by W. D. Hudson (London: Macmillan, 1969), p. 11.
3. See Ch. XI below.
4. Apropos of this issue, see Ch. X above.
5. See the works by Sidney Simon, Howard Kirschenbaum and

others cited by Frederick Ellrod in nn. 1-2 in Ch. I above. Ellrod offers a brief description and assessment of the values clarification theory on pp. 10-19 of his article.

6. Cf. Ellrod, *Ibid.*, p. 7 and pp. 4-17, *passim*.

7. For a description of naturalism and noncognitivism, see Richard B. Brandt, *Ethical Theory* (Englewood Cliffs, N.J.: Prentice-Hall, 1959), pp. 151-153, and Ch. 7 and 9.

8. Ellrod, *op. cit.*, pp. 7-11; p. 14.

9. *Ibid.*, p. 14.

10. I use the term "natural" here in the sense of something which holds universally. The connection between "natural" and "naturalist" is of course a matter which is a major concern of this chapter.

11. Lawrence Kohlberg, "From Is to Ought: How to Commit the Naturalistic Fallacy and Get Away With It in the Study of Moral Development," in *Cognitive Development and Epistemology*, ed. by Theodore Mischel (New York: Academic Press, 1971), pp. 151-235, at p. 153. (Hereafter cited as *FITO.)*

12. It has been denied that the "naturalist fallacy" is in fact correctly termed a fallacy at all, and claimed that it is rather simply a mistake or at best but a species of the definist fallacy. See, for example, James M. Giarelli, "Lawrence Kohlberg and G. E. Moore on the Naturalistic Fallacy," *Educational Theory*, 26 (1976), 352. This distinction does not materially affect the line of argument taken in this paper.

13. Cf. also Lawrence Kohlberg and Rochelle Mayer, "Development as the Aim of Education," *Harvard Educational Review*, 42 (1972), 483. (Hereafter cited as *DAE*).

14. Cf. also in this context Kohlberg's rejection of what he terms "the psychologists's fallacy" and defines as follows: "the direct derivation of statements about what human nature, human values, and human desires ought to be from psychological statements about what they are." Kohlberg subjects this fallacy to the same criticism noted here: namely, that it ignores the "open question" of why a given fact of desiring or valuing should be called good. See *DAE*, pp. 466-67.

15. Lawrence Kohlberg, "Moral Development and Moral Philosophy," *The Journal of Philosophy*, LXX (1973), p. 633.

16. *Ibid.*

17. On naturalism, noncognitivism and nonnaturalism as the three prevalent forms of ethical theory, and for a brief description of each, see Richard B. Brandt, *op. cit.*, pp. 15153, and Chs. 7-9.

18. Kenneth L. Schmitz, *The Gift: Creation* (Milwaukee: Marquette University Press, 1982), pp. 40-41.

19. *Ibid.*, p. 88.

20. *Ibid.*

21. Clearly Descartes is responsible in an important way for the turn to the *subject* characteristic of Western modernity. My point is simply that the criteria of knowledge which Descartes employs in his turn to the subject are criteria proper to objects. It is in just this sense

that I take him to be objectivist.

22. Cf. *inter alia, Discourse on Method*, Part II, in: *The Philosophical Works of Descartes*, Vol. I (London: Cambridge University Press, 1973), pp. 92-93.

23. Cf. for example, Hume, *An Inquiry Concerning Human Understanding*, Section IV Part I, and *passim* (New York: Library of Liberal Arts, 1955); see also, "An Abstract of a Treatise on Human Nature," *loc. cit.*, pp. 183-198; and the "Appendix to the Treatise on Human Nature," in *A Treatise of Human Nature*, Vol. II (London; New York; E. P. Dutton & Co., 1952), esp. pp. 317-320.

24. "An Abstract," pp. 186-187.

25. Cf. in connection with this claim: Alasdair MacIntyre, *After Virtue* (Notre Dame: University of Notre Dame Press, 1981), esp. Ch.-1-7; and Schmitz, *op. cit.*, II, III, IV.

26. Schmitz, *op.cit.*, pp. 120-21.

27. *Ibid.*, p. 121.

28. On the additional features required for an adequate conception of value, see my "Whitehead's Inability to Affirm a Universe of Value," *Process Studies*, 13 (Spring 1983), 117-131, especially the remarks regarding the Aristotelian-Thomistic tradition in footnote 2.

29. My principle concern in this article is of course the foundation of the universality of morality as normative, and hence obligatory. For the sense in which this universal obligatory character involves a concern for value, or the good, see John Farrelly's "The Human Good and Moral Choice" in this volume. For the sense in which the universal obligatory character of morality presupposes non-determinism, or more precisely freedom, see my discussion of Kant which follows and ch. IV above.

30. There is of course a third possibility here, namely noncognitivism, which holds that morality is, strictly speaking, neither relative nor non-relative, precisely because it is cognitively meaningless. In terms of the argument of the paper, this collapses into the two possibilities noted. For, on the one hand, noncognitivism is often mixed with naturalism in the thinking of social scientists; and, on the other hand, insofar as noncognitivism is strictly adhered to, it embraces a dualism of fact and morality which, as dualistic, is similar to nonnaturalism in the sense pertinent to my argument.

31. Cf. especially in this connection Kant's Introduction to his *Prolegomena to Any Future Metaphysics*, edited by Paul Carus (Chicago: Open Court Publishing Co., 1933); see also the Preface to the Second Edition and Introduction, *Critique of Pure Reason*, trans. by Norman Kemp Smith (New York: St. Martin's Press, 1965). (Hereafter *CPR*).

32. Cf. e.g., *CPR*, p. 44.

33. Cf. e.g., *CPR*, p. 464.

34. Of course Kant himself does not ascribe a teleological character to morality. My point in what follows is simply that, insofar as he is concerned to find a place anywhere in his system for teleology, that place must be outside nature (in a constitutive sense). My further point,

then, is that anyone who, in disagreement with Kant, might wish to ascribe to morality a teleological character must nonetheless, *like* Kant, locate that character outside nature if nature is interpreted in Kant's mechanical sense.

35. *CPR*, pp. 549-570, esp. pp. 560-61.
36. *CPR*, p. 464.
37. *CPR*, pp. 464-479, esp. pp. 464f and 472f.
38. See in this connection MacIntyre's *After Virtue*, loc. cit.
39. See n. 34.
40. Cf. Schmitz, *op. cit.*, pp. 118-19 and 96-130. For the sense in which these metaphysical axioms bespeak a radical activity or energy (*energeia*) rooted in *esse*, which is act in the fundamental sense in Thomism, see especially the remarks by Schmitz on pp. 117f. For the sense in which these axioms bespeak an activity or energy (*energeia*) in Aristotle, see James P. Etzweiler, "Being as Activity in Aristotle: A Process Interpretation," *International Philosophical Quarterly*, XVIII (1978), 311-334, and Frederick E. Ellrod's response "*Energeia* and Process in Aristotle," *IPQ*, XXII (1982), 175-181. In what follows I am concerned principally with the Thomistic formulation of the issue relative to the problem of a mechanistic understanding of nature.

41. For studies pertinent to this claim see Schmitz, *op. cit.*, and "Immateriality Past and Present," *Proceedings of the American Catholic Philosophical Association*, (1978), 1-15; my "David Bohm on Contemporary Physics and the Overcoming of Fragmentation," *International Philosophical Quarterly*, XXII (1982), 315-327, and my "Whitehead's Inability to Affirm a Universe of Value," cited in n. 28.

42. For the purposes of this paper, I simply abstract from the question whether, or in what sense, beings other than humans might be properly affirmed to be conscious. It suffices for the purposes of my paper to affirm that all beings including human beings are active and purposive, but that human beings are nonetheless active and purposive in a distinct way (a way which is called self-conscious and free).

43. See in this connection the following works: Germain Grisez, "The First Principle of Practical Reason: A Commentary on the *Summa theologiae*, 1-2, Question 94, Article 2," *Natural Law Forum*, 10 (1965), 168-201; John Finnis, *Natural Law and Natural Rights* (Oxford: Clarendon Press, 1980); Ralph McInerny, "The Principles of Natural Law," *American Journal of Jurisprudence*, 25 (1980), 1-15; John Finnis and Germain Grisez, "The Basic Principles of Natural Law: Reply to Ralph McInerny," *American Journal of Jurisprudence*, 26 (1981), 21-31.

44. Aquinas, *Summa Theologiae*, 1-2, Question 94, Article 2.

CHAPTER XI

ENVIRONMENT: THE SOCIAL DIMENSION

OF MORAL DEVELOPMENT[1]

WALTER NICGORSKI

The question considered here is how the environment relates to a person's moral development. Such aspects of the moral agent as character, reasoning, choice, affectivity and judgment are not, of course, isolated factors in an isolated individual. They are aspects of an integrated and complex person who in turn is integrated with an environment. That environment necessarily interacts with, and thus conditions without absolutely determining, the various aspects of the moral agent. The dimension of the environment that is of primary concern here is the human or social ambiance of the person. This is the familiar environment of family, school, peers and media which has long seemed an immensely powerful influence on moral development and the moral life.

Before considering this human dimension of the environment in detail, it is useful to comment on that other facet of the environment which is excluded in what follows, namely the physical environment. - That the person's response to nature is a moral matter is now widely recognized, as is evident in the burgeoning field of environmental ethics and the notable public interest in the moral dimension of environmental issues. John Farrelly has earlier in this volume stressed that the person's respect for physical nature as a given is part of the constitutive human good. Not only does the physical environment pose moral issues, it also provides the initial hindrance or assistance to overall human development that entails or culminates in moral development. Thus Kohlberg's view of moral development is based on an understanding of cognitive development that Piaget had developed and that entails a coming-to-terms with the physical environment.

That the disposition of the physical environment is implicated in and usually a condition for moral development is generally apparent. Severe hardships or dire circumstances often diminish self-respect and respect for others. There is always the tendency to think that moral responsibility disappears in an oppressive environment marked, for example, by lack of food or shelter. Barbarism in all forms including cannibalism can be encouraged by a desperately unsupportive physical environment. Such severe tests, however, sometimes reveal moral heroism rather than moral degradation. It is a commonplace in most moral traditions to measure a person's moral stature by how he or she responds to varying circumstances and to expect a minimally decent response even in difficult straits.

In ancient thought, specifically that of Aristotle, a major responsibility of the family or household and of the *polis* or political community is to secure and so dispose material necessities that the ends of those communities may be attained. Material wherewithal, and hence a beneficent physical environment, is a necessary, but by no means sufficient, condition for reaching that moral goal of full human development. Clearly how a community utilizes and disposes the physical environment is a major determinant in how that environment will serve or detract from the genuine moral aspirations of its time and subsequent generations. Shortage of necessities, inhuman crowding and aesthetic sterility are among environmental conditions that will pose obstacles to a community's moral development. In its own way, abundance too can be an obstacle.

Environmental issues are fraught with moral significance because their determination affects the well-being of other persons as well as those immediately involved. Whether one adopts this common and clearly persuasive consequentialist perspective on the moral significance of the physical environment or simply expects a reverence or respect for the given of the physical environment as a mark of moral maturity, it is clear that the person's response to the physical environment is one great sphere in which he exercises moral agency. How he exercises it here as well as in other spheres will be affected in important ways, not primarily by the physical, but by the social or moral environment in which he develops and acts.

The more or less active work of the human environment upon the moral agent is the process commonly called socialization. This term appears to be of recent vintage, yet the process that it denotes has been a concern to educators, civic leaders, priests and scholars as far into the human past as one can peer. The process of socialization is the passage into participation in some community by coming to share its convictions and ways of acting. Education is often encouraged and supported as a major instrument of socialization though in some communities and, perhaps to a degree in all, it is seen also as a threat to effective socialization. All communities have some convictions and ways of acting which go more to the heart of the community, those that are more central and primary. Most often these reflect the morals or ethics of the community. Moral education, then, is the most important part, the very substance, of socialization.

The fact that education is often seen as a threat to socialization can mean from another perspective, that socialization is often a threat to the person understood as essentially autonomous. Contemporary man, living in an age of individualism which highlights his self-determination and his right to assert himself in the face of the community, is likely both to overlook his own socialization and to underestimate the necessary formative power of communities with respect to morals. The very words morals and ethics, which presently often evoke the dramatic sense of individual responsibility and confrontation suggesting images of standing with Antigone or marching with Martin Luther King, have origins which point up the dominant role of the community. The Latin "mos, moris" means ancestral way or custom, while the Greek "ethos" means custom, general usage or habit. Philosophers, historians and anthropologists give substantial support to the conclusion of such etymological analysis, namely that morals and ethics at one time were simply the work of the community and remain largely so today. No person is an island even in finding, embracing and standing by the formative convictions of life. Socialization is inadequately understood if it is seen simply as the work of the community upon the individual, for in most instances it is the effort of one community and its authorities to overlay the work of other communities. Antigone and Martin Luther King are themselves formed by the moral tradition of communities even as they resist certain social and political demands of their societies.

The emphasis on the community's role in setting morals can, no doubt, be overdone. It is at times forgotten that though a person is enmeshed in communities he experiences some capacity to stand apart, and that such capacity to transcend is necessary if he is to have any basis for uplifting or reforming his communities. To seek collective or individual consciousness or awareness is at its best to educate in order to protect persons and subcommunities against the socialization of a dominant community. Some theories and forms of socialization are dehumanizing, denying to the person any sense of self, autonomy, or real significance for one's rationality. Crippling indoctrination by collectivist states and other movements provide well-known examples in this century. Philosophers, historians and anthropologists, most notably in the nineteenth century and on into the present, have lent support to various forms of historicism that restricted a person's horizons to his time and culture and frequently implied a temporal and/or cultural relativism with respect to morals. In this century such approaches find a powerful ally in the Skinnerian underpinnings of the behavior-modification movement, which engages in what might be called total socialization. Such theorizing and practice deny individual autonomy and go far to undermine personal significance. They call forth the dominant philosophical response of this century in the form of existentialist insistence on the reality of freedom and responsibility. At the popular level in the West, contemporary man at best uneasily accepts the value and reality of processes called "formation" and "socialization"; he outrightly rejects "indoctrination."

The contemporary philosophies of moral education which have grown partly in reaction to traditional practices and were sketched early in this volume have reflected the dominant Western emphasis on individual autonomy and have seen moral development largely in those terms. This is an important aspect of the morally developed person, and in the remainder of this essay there is an effort to appreciate autonomy in the face of the practices of total socialization and/or crippling indoctrination. On the other hand, autonomy is shown to be the outcome of relatedness and dependency, and radical autonomy or individualism is found to be illusory. A contextualized autonomy embracing the person's dependency and relatedness and the consequent responsibilities of this condition is indicated as the way of true self-fulfillment.

THE CRITIQUE OF TOTAL SOCIALIZATION

One encouraging and common dimension of the contemporary philosophies described by Ellrod in Chapter I is an emphasis on the significance of the individual subject and his or her thinking in moral development. That emphasis stands in contrast to the powerful behavior modification school which either banishes individual consciousness as Samay observed above or notably undermines its importance. Kohlberg's theory explicitly developed in active opposition to this dominant behaviorism.

Behavior modification or the social learning school is seen by him as the "scientific" manifestation of the long established cultural transmission tradition in moral education. As noted in the chapter on "Moral Character," Kohlberg seems unjustifiably to lump together Aristotle's teaching, traditional American approaches (the "boy scout" approach) and behavior modification as varieties of a defective form of moral education called cultural transmission. Not only does behavior modification claim for itself a "scientific" foundation, it also turns habit formation into a technology which it considers as constituting the whole of moral education. Kohlberg's sound critique of behavior modification focuses on the moral relativism this technology implies in its destruction of autonomy, an essential element of the moral sphere proper, and on the incapacity of the technology to succeed on its own terms.

In one sense of socialization, the behavior modification school represents the complete or total socializers, for in this view, man is entirely what he is conditioned to be while other people or society itself are the conditioners. In his article "Indoctrination Versus Relativity In Value Education," Kohlberg calls attention to the fact that the term "socialization" is frequently used to make outright indoctrination more palatable.[2] There is no doubt that "socialization" is often a euphemistic way to speak of the processes of simply conditioning. Both general and scientific usage do not, however, tie the term "socialization" to indoctrination or conditioning. This is reflected in Kohlberg's most important piece on socialization, entitled "Stage and Sequence: The Cognitive-Developmental Approach to Socialization," where behavior modification is described as among "associationist-learning approaches to socialization."[3] In Kohlberg's usage, behavior modification is but one of a number of approaches in the "associationist-learning" species and within the genus of methods of socialization.

Examining both the associationist-learning and the psychosexual--maturational approaches to socialization he finds that studies of moral development based on these approaches have yielded few empirically powerful predictors of moral behavior."[4] Earlier in the same piece he was more specific in concluding that "neither early parental handling of basic drives nor [sic] amount of various types of discipline have been found to directly correlate with moral attitudes or behavior in the studies surveyed."[5] Kohlberg then argues that one does not reach the basis of social behavior by simply understanding it as "reversible situation-specific behavior" as do the social learning theorists. His studies of morality draw him to hypothesize that "there are stages or directed structural age-changes in the area of social-personality development just as there are in the cognitive area."[6] Stage development of this sort can account for the non-reversibility, situation-generality and longitudinal predictability of aspects of social behavior.

For Kohlberg, however, social-personality development is not independent of cognitive development, but a broader type of development which involves the cognitive in a central way in moral judgements about social behavior. Apparently a central aspect of social-personality development, moral development is critically dependent on cognitive development but not on it alone. The heightened role of the cognitive becomes clear when Kohlberg contrasts his understanding of "internalization" of a norm, such as self-control, with that of social learning theory. Note how his sense of self-control reflects an Aristotelian understanding of this virtue with an essential rational or cognitive dimension.

> ... it becomes clear that the child conditioned to feel anxiety over kinesthetic cues of incipient action has no more made a gain in self-control than has the dog conditioned in a similar fashion or the child whose conditioned anxiety represents a phobia. Self-control implies control and inhibition of action by an organized self or ego with cognitive representations of itself and the world, and with an intelligent flexibility as to the cues and conditions of inhibition or release of action. Insofar as inhibition of action is determined rigidly by the paradigms of classical conditioning, it indicates the absence of self-control in the usual sense.[7]

This critique of association-learning or behavior modification was continued and stated less technically in the article with Mayer in the *Harvard Educational Review*. Here the emphasis is directly on education rather than upon the broader notion of socialization. The alternatives to the cognitive-developmental or "progressive" approach are called the "romantic" model built on the maturationist theory of development and the cultural transmission model built on an associationist learning theory.

> In contrast to the child-centered romantic school, the cultural transmission school is society-centered. It defines educational ends as the internalization of the values and knowledge of the culture. The cultural transmission school focuses on the child's need to learn the discipline of the social order, while the romantic stresses the child's freedom. The cultural transmission view emphasizes the common and the estab-

lished, the romantic view stresses the unique, the novel and the personal.[8]

Kohlberg takes A.S. Neill as a spokesman for the "romantic" position and cites his advice to "Abolish authority. Let the child be himself. Don't push him around. Don't teach him. Don't lecture him. Don't elevate him. Don't force him to do anything."[9] This emphasis on individual freedom as opposed to the social control emphasized by Skinner's cultural transmission ideology is "not justified as an ethical principle but as a matter of psychological fact, leading to 'mental health and happiness.'"[10] In the end Kohlberg finds both the "romantics" and "cultural-transmitters" denying a specifically human end to development. Kohlberg's words are sharp and memorable on this occasion.

> ... in spite of their libertarian and non-indoctrinative emphasis, romantic ideologies also have a tendency to be elitist or patronizing. Recalling the role of Dostoievsky's Grand Inquisitor, they see education as a process which only intends the child to be happy and adjusted rather than one which confronts the child with the ethical and intellectual problems and principles which the educator himself confronts. Skinner and Neill agree it is better for the child to be a happy pig than an unhappy Socrates. We may question, however, whether they have the right to withhold that choice.[11]

Neill's romantic position is representative of a widespread modern outlook checked only at times by persistent common sense. Freedom and individualism in this outlook falsely appear to gain strength from a skepticism regarding true values and ways of life. The idea of the self that emerges from this standpoint has recently been called the "emotivist self" by Alasdair MacIntyre. This "specifically modern self," he argues "finds no limits set to that on which it may pass judgment for such limits could only derive from rational criteria for evaluation and, as we have seen, the emotivist self lacks any such criteria.[12] For many the Nazi phenomenon, other mass movements and popularly chosen tyrannies have exposed the danger to democratic values of such an unqualified skepticism and the fact that freedom and individualism are themselves values requiring some sort of defense or grounding in the nature of the person. Such experiences appear to contribute to Kohlberg's insistence that moral education theory be freed of relativism and skepticism, that it is senseless and doomed to futility if it is not formed around some understanding of the objectively right and just, and that there are in fact democratic values that are universal.

As his above comment on Neill indicates, the "libertarian and non-indoctrinative" features of such romantic ideologies appeal to Kohlberg as they do to most modern peoples, at least in the West. These features reflect the assumptions at the root of one of the dominant myths of self-understanding in the modern world, that of the isolated individual standing alone in the state of nature, starting with a clean slate, making up his own mind on all things and fashioning his morality and political associations by contracts with others.[13] Until very recently, much work in moral education seems to serve and accentuate these atomistic assumptions of modern thought and instrumentalist and contractarian approaches to interpersonal relations.[14] These principles of modern thought throw light on the apparent tendency for some time among Kohlberg and others to be uncomfortable with an explicit role for habituation or formation, that is, whatever scents of indoctrination, in moral education and to reject too comprehensively all forms of moral education of the cultural transmission type. Habituation has been, of course, a primary mode of socialization across cultures and down through the ages.

As indicated in the earlier chapter on "Moral Character," the place of habit cannot be readily overlooked and tends to surface in a number of ways even in Kohlberg's analysis. As will be discussed shortly, a social dimension and social factors are assumed in the practices of the values clarification, cognitive-analytic and cognitive-developmental schools. Like habit, the social dimension is an ineluctable and important aspect of a complete view of the development of the moral agent and must be fully integrated in any adequate theory. If that is to be done, the social dimension requires more development than it has received by Kohlberg or the theorists of the other dominant schools. Despite this limitation, the contribution of moral educators to a renewed emphasis on the person's thinking in moral development is important and welcome, for autonomy encompassing both freedom and rationality is an essential part of the moral person.[15]

AUTONOMY: AN ESSENTIAL DIMENSION

The person's dependence, interrelatedness (being in relation or being with) and inevitable sharing in communities must not detract from his or her fundamental individuality. Human beings are, in part, distinct particular consciousnesses in whom moral life is most deeply and properly rooted.

> The human individuals constitute, each of them, the basic order of action. The term 'community,' like 'society' or 'social group,' indicates an order derived from the first one. Being and acting 'together with others' does not constitute a new subject of acting but only introduces new relations among the persons who are the real and actual subjects of acting.[16]

Earlier in this century William James stressed the psychic basis for individuality. He observed that "the elementary psychic fact were [sic] not *thought* or *this thought* or *that thought*, but *my thought*, every thought being *owned*. James added

Neither contemporaneity, nor proximity in space, nor similarity of quality and content are able to fuse thoughts together which are sundered by this barrier of belonging to different personal minds. The breaches between such thoughts are the most absolute breaches in nature.[17]

To call for and to develop autonomy as a central task of moral education is no modern heresy but an important concern of all the great moral thinkers. It is not simply contemporary man but the mainstream of at least the Western tradition which resists the swallowing of the individual in the engines of one or another society's acculturation. It is, after all, Socrates who marks for the tradition a heroic and ever-renewing beginning to moral philosophy and a kind of moral education that involves reason's capacity to transcend any given society. The prevalent and orthodox view is that Socrates emerges from a movement of Sophists who challenged the old and general truth that the community's ways are the right ways. That movement was without the serious purpose and the transcendent hope that marked Socrates. His intent, masked somewhat by his partly feigned ignorance, was to hold up a standard of full human development and, of course, to display a method by which both teacher and student can move through and past the opinion-laden ways of society toward that goal.

The approaches to moral education now influential have manifest, if not explicit, Socratic affinities. The values-clarification school, the cognitive-analytic school and cognitive developmentalists, as evident in Ellrod's initial paper in this volume, encourage the challenging and questioning of traditional ways, which usually are community-enforced. They highly value individual autonomy, promise to do something for moral education in a time of especially felt need and propose methods that are intended to be consistent with the pluralism and constitutional restraints of a free society. These Socratic affinities explain much of the enthusiasm among educators and others for these approaches which *seem* to be an outgrowth or renewal of the efforts of one of the most notable moral educators in the West. Kohlberg, in particular, sees his effort in the Socratic tradition, drawing attention to the fact that the autonomy he seeks in moral development is not independence from objective truth and values. Autonomy will not develop, he says, "through an education of 'do your thing.'"[18] In another place he finds Socrates to be the father of the cognitive-developmental approach to moral education and explores the kinship as follows:

> Socrates believed in a universal conception of justice which was rational or cognitive. While rational, justice was also to be loved, lived, and died for, as Socrates demonstrated. Socrates believed that a universal conception of justice was latent in every person (including Meno's slave), that it developed through levels, and that its development depended

upon questioning, the arousal of doubt, and social dialogue.[19]

In the tradition of Socrates autonomy inheres in the individual person not as the source or maker of the moral law but as the receiver who recognizes, and is hence the proper acknowledger of moral principles and the maker of moral choices.[20] The individual's freedom and rationality is then at the core of autonomy; the person's capacity to reason is the very basis of freedom. Personal autonomy is the fruit of an appropriate habituation and socialization. Autonomy becomes radical, illusory, and destructive when the individual and the exercise of his moral freedom are decontexualized and the *dependency* of the individual's very being as well as of his freedom and rationality is ignored or minimized. The undervaluing of this dependency is often accompanied by a diminishment of *responsibility* for the good of others and the community in moral choices. In this conception of man's condition the ligatures with others are cut; nothing is seen as taken and nothing owed. Thus appears the aggrandizing of the modern self without limits, as described earlier by MacIntyre.

Such radical autonomy pervades modern thought and appears to influence the dominant approaches to moral education. Kohlberg, at least, has taken one clear step away from this extreme conception of autonomy and the wholly self-determining self to which it leads. He holds the person responsible to a standard of justice not of his own making. However, as noted earlier in these essays, that conception of justice or morality seems restricted to the principles necessary to settle conflicts between individuals. It does not incorporate a conception of the good that would describe the person's flourishing in terms of his relationships to others and the good of communities of which he is a part.[21] Furthermore the social dimension of the development of the moral agent has been left until recently largely implicit and unattended by Kohlberg as well as by the other leading current schools. With respect both to the means of moral development and to an understanding of the nature of the goal, man's essential sociality needs to be more manifest in an integrated and complete theory of the moral agent.

SOCIALITY: IMPLICIT AND INESCAPABLE

Perhaps the best initial step in the effort to direct attention to the largely underemphasized social factors in the dominant approaches to moral education is to point out some obvious features of the Socratic model. Three points are notable about the social dimension of Socrates' work. First, the person develops in the most important respect, the moral respect, through a close and candid relationship with a teacher. This is the maieutic relationship, and in the best of circumstances it is one-to--one. The person's development is critically tied to his dependence on another. Second, the student comes to the teacher disposed somewhere along a continuum from well (e.g., Glaucon and Adeimantus in the *Republic*) to ill (e.g., Thrasymachus) for seeing and responding to that to which the teacher's queries can lead. Presumably nature and the socializing efforts of family, friends and society as a whole have worked to shape this disposition using an appropriate habituation. Third, the maieutic relationship of reasoning together about even the most important things is supported only in a certain kind of society: either the best kind of society that encourages such activity or a free and tolerant one that allows such activity. Being the latter, Athens was for Socrates a decent and defensible place, worthy of dying for, even as she was acting unjustly in a given instance.

Against this Socratic model, consider the approaches of values clarification and the cognitive-analytic school. They are comparable in that they depend on interpersonal relationships, involve parties in various states of disposition or readiness to benefit from the discussion involved, and assume an engulfing society that is supportive of the values of openness and autonomy. To a degree both, but especially values clarification, lack a well-defined notion of the human good, give scant explanation of states of readiness and of the social and political ambiance of moral development. They lack what Plato or at least the Platonic account supplied to the Socratic method, namely an understanding of the soul or human person and of social and political theory. Such an understanding gives the basis for knowing the conditions, limitations and desirable goals of such approaches to moral education. As it stands, these contemporary approaches to moral education simply graft themselves onto a modern liberal society and its traditional communities (families, schools, business organizations, etc.). Any technique or method, but especially one engaging the issues likely to be most formative for life, calls out for an effort to understand the context in which its use is proposed. Only such an understanding yields in turn an understanding of conditions, limitations and goals that can provide an ultimate defense for such a method.

Kohlberg and cognitive developmentalists seem, on the other hand, to offer more of a contribution to a detailed and larger social and political theory in which moral education might be set. Like the other leading approaches, these moral educators have centered their attention on the school and the operation there and elsewhere of the elemental social relationship (that of dialogue of teacher and student as well as of student with student) that tends to appear when societies are no longer considered primitive and simple. Even before his recent turn to close interest in the moral impact of the group, Kohlberg has reached out from this relationship to consider the environment's impact and has found it to be critical. This aspect of his work may be appreciated by understanding the significance of his tendency to describe the process of cognitive moral development as *interactionist* and *dialectical*. The former is the key to Kohlberg's understanding of proper socialization, for it is interaction between the self, specifically the mind, and the environment, primarily society, that stimulates the self's movement along the invariable stages of moral development. The process is dialectical when one views the mind's internal processes throughout interaction. The dialectical process is described by Kohlberg as one in which

> a core of universal ideas are redefined and reorganized as their implications are played out in experience and as they are confronted by their opposites in argument and discourse. These reorganizations define qualitative levels of thought, levels of increased epistemic adequacy. The child is not a plant or a machine; he is a philosopher or a scientist--poet.[22]

Proper interaction stimulates dialectical movement in a definite and invariant direction.

> Autonomy ... is not born, it develops .... Autonomy will not develop through an education of 'do your thing,' but through educational stimulation which leads first to the level of understanding the standard of the group and then to autonomy, to constructing standards held through reflection and self-judgment.[23]

In order to appreciate in more detail the social dimension of Kohlberg's cognitive-developmental approach to moral education it is necessary to take a more microscopic view of the broad notion of interactionism. Interaction occurs when the mind processes experience; it is at the center of cognitive development. In social experience it operates in a parallel manner resulting in social and moral development that extends beyond cognitive development. "Our values tend to originate inside ourselves as we process our social experience."[24] The developed or, more likely, developing mind does not assure social and moral development, but is a necessary condition of such development. Appropriate social experience does not assure social and moral development, but is a necessary condition of such development. Among the requisites for understanding interaction in more detail is an appreciation for what Kohlberg calls "the universal structural features of the environment."

> The universal structural features of the environment relevant to moral stages are partly those of the general physical environment since moral stages presuppose cognitive stages. At the first moral stage, the regularities of the physical and the social environment are confused and the basis of conformity to social laws is not much different than the basis of conformity to physical laws. More fundamentally, however, there are universal structures of the social environment which are basic to moral development. All societies have many of the same basic institutions of family, economy, social stratification, law, and government. In spite of great diversity in the detailed definition of these institutions, they have certain transcultural functional meanings.[25]

These institutions apparently all provide the framework for "systems of defined complementary role expectations.[26] Increased self-awareness of such structure through experience is a necessary phase in the route to moral development.

In cognitive-developmental or "symbolic-interactional" theories of society, the primary meaning of the word "social" is the distinctively human structuring of action and thought by role-taking, by the tendency to react to the self's behavior in the role of the other (Mead, 1934; Baldwin, 1906; Piaget, 1948). There are two subsidiary meanings of "social," the first that of affectional attachment, the second that of imitation. Both human love and human identification, however, presuppose the more general sociality of symbolic communication and role-taking. Before one can love the other or can model his attitudes, one must take his role through communicative processes (Mead, 1934; Kohlberg, 1966b). The structure of society and morality is a structure of interaction between the self and other selves who are like the self, but who are not the self.[27]

The broad theory of interactionism encompasses both of Kohlberg's major strategies of moral education, namely dilemma discussions and the just school or just community emphasis. These are not, as sometimes suggested, poles of his work that are in tension; they are rather complementary strategies based on a theoretical understanding of interactionism's role in moral development. Dilemma discussions are tests or dialectical challenges to an existing moral framework; interaction is highly focused in a dilemma discussion. The just (and democratic) community or school operates more in a supportive capacity or in the ambiance of the focused interaction in a dilemma discussion. It provides the social experience that increases the likelihood that dilemma resolution will contribute to stage advance. Better than other social systems, it provides role-taking opportunities and accessible and supportive examples, and it also provides the most effective of dilemmas, those of real life.

Role-taking opportunities which are available and encouraged to a greater extent in some classes and cultures than others are the key to understanding Kohlberg's finding that there are positive relationships between culture or class and stage of moral advance, but no such relationship between religious belief and practice and stage of moral advance.[28] Family, school, neighborhood and society in general can all be more or less supportive of role-taking opportunities which play a critical part in the interaction and mutual development of the cognitive and the affective dimensions of man. "What development and socialization achieve, is the organization of empathic phenomena into consistent sympathetic and moral concerns, not the creation of empathy as such."[29] It is especially noteworthy that Kohlberg has not regarded the family as uniquely necessary for moral development; this follows from the function assigned the family, that of facilitating role-taking in the immediate environment. Research on children of the kibbutz is taken to support the non-essential character of the family.[30]

A noteworthy aspect of this phase of his thought is the awareness that clashes between communities or levels of society (e.g., family loyalties set against the society in general) can be stimulants to moral development.[31] In a pluralistic society it is a matter of chance whether a specific clash presents the kind of dilemma that contributes to moral development in a given individual.

With some justice Kohlberg has offered his cognitive-developmental approach to moral education as non-indoctrinative. This rests essentially on his claim that it is based on human nature (the universal and invariable stages of advance) and that moral advance is primarily attained by cognitive realization of a higher set of principles for moral decisions rather than by an emotional or coercive inducement. Furthermore he has offered his insistence on a democratic environment for the processes of moral development as additional support for his non-indoctrinative approach. From the beginning of his work, in accord with his non-relativistic position, he has recognized that democracy itself implies certain values or moral principles.[32] More recently, he has accepted indoctrination of a limited, "democratic" kind in order to gain adherence to the principles necessary for an environment conducive to moral development.[33] The acceptance of a limited role for indoctrination is one of the "revisions" alluded to earlier in this chapter and throughout this volume. The overall character of these revisions is to give much more emphasis to the role of the group and its atmosphere in the process of moral development and specifically in moving an agent from moral judgment to moral action.[34]

There is, it seems, much work to be done in this school to understand how the influence of the group penetrates individual character. Kohlberg himself seems to resist a development that would restore emphasis on character and the social sector's important traditional function of contributing to moral development through proper habituation or formation of character. In writing of his new concerns, Kohlberg says that he and his students "have passed from a study of the internal mental structure of moral reasoning to an analysis of . . . group norms and expectations, ethnographically defined." Although insisting that the new concern is not then limited to external behavior, he writes that behavior is to be examined "not in terms of individual moral character but in terms of the character or 'moral atmosphere' of a group or community."[35]

One might wonder how it is possible to avoid restoration of an emphasis on character as one enlarges the significance of the group's influence or formative power. Even in the case of providing role-taking opportunities, a community function long stressed by Kohlberg, one can ask what leads one person rather than another to maximize role-taking opportunities when available. Clark Power and Joseph Reimer whose research has played an important part in the new emphasis on group moral norms among Kohlberg and his students seem more receptive to the role of moral character and turn to Durkheim for assistance in interpreting their research. Durkheim is introduced as having argued "that moral character develops in a context in which students have to limit their behavior for the sake of the community," as having seen "in human nature a profound harmony between the good of the individual and the good of the group," and as having concluded that "true happiness could only be found in self-sacrifice for the group."[36] There is then increasing evidence that Kohlberg and his students seem on the verge of some reconciliation with the approach of cultural transmission or the traditional approach to moral education.

SOCIALITY: THE DEPTH OF HUMAN SOLIDARITY

It may then be especially timely and useful to recall that the Socratic model of moral educator, so admired in the contemporary moral education schools, has often been assimilated to an Aristotelian understanding of man's relationship to his community and to recall that understanding. Aristotle is, of course, the primary Western source or *locus classicus* for a reasoned and grounded defence of the truism that man is a social and political being. Man is born for the political community; he can be fully human, that is, a just or wholly virtuous person only in and through the community. Human completeness or flourishing is the work of the community.[37] Latter-day Christian Aristotelians would extend this approach to human completeness to include a supernatural dimension, the responsibility of the larger community known as the Church.

For Aristotle the natural and proper community for the person is that which is adequate to bring him to physical, intellectual and moral development. This community (the polis) is in his time an association of households. This community completes and supports the work of the family and friends in the effort of human development. That effort of the larger political community, insofar as it directly concerns moral development, takes the form of supporting the family in disposing the young for virtue by appropriate habituation, of supporting and encouraging adults in the practice of virtue, and of providing the opportunity for the exercise of virtue on a scale appropriate to human fullness or justice.[38] The person's fullness or flourishing is found in participating in just communities, in the activity of virtue both intellectual and moral. Reason is to be brought to full life in the soul; it is brought to attunement with, and arises as a friend to, natural inclination and proper habituation.[39] The person's beginning and end are integrally bound up with a supporting community. The clearest signs of this are his radical physical dependence in birth and infancy, his inclination and desire to be with others, and the capacities for language and reason which are instruments for communication and the forging of society.

That Aristotelian framework is complemented and developed in modern thinking by a deeper appreciation of human interdependency at the level of consciousness and perception. A person's grip on reality rests on his shared perception of it. "Where there is no sharing," writes Buber, "there is no reality."[40] Hannah Arendt adds in the same voice that "the reality of the world is guaranteed by the presence of others, by its appearing to all . . . ."[41] The world then is only accessible through an initial encounter and joining with others whose powers, depths and kinship we recognize. The very realization of existence and selfhood is found through the co-existing other person and what Buber calls "the natural solidarity of connection."[42] Here it is fitting to recall John Caputo's earlier observations that it is the "interpersonal world" which is primarily given to the human being and that a person's debt to others reaches to the very depths of his being. Accordingly Buber speaks of the fundamental reality being "man with man" and his warning to the sciences of man is obviously applicable to theories of moral education.

> The philosophical science of man, which includes anthropology and sociology, must take as its starting-point the consideration of this subject, "man with man." If you consider the individual by himself, then you see of man just as much as you see of the moon; only man with man provides a full image. If you consider the aggregate by itself, then you see of man just as much as we see of the Milky Way; only man with man is a completely outlined form. Consider man with man, and you see human life, dynamic, twofold, the giver and the receiver . . .[43]

The ordinary giving and receiving among persons, as has been recently pointed out, can be seen as "symbols of a deeper giving and receiving" in "shared being" of a "dynamic plurality." At its deepest point, gift-giving is a "celebration" of co-presence.[44]

The thoroughness of a person's dependency, his very existence in relationship with the other, are the most powerful indicators of his natural embeddedness in a human environment. His good or happiness, because of his very nature, is to be found in acting together with others.[45] The person's autonomy must be developed in accord with the social property of his being. An environment that allows and encourages this development gives hope of a harmony between the person's natural inclination to develop his freedom and reason, and his social nature. As the goal for moral development of both persons and communities, this harmony can be described as contextualized autonomy.

Radical autonomy or individualism cannot conceive of a person's fulfillment as being in relationship, not to speak of the specific relationship of giving and service entailed by any relationship that is not merely instrumental. As long as the human being is not seen as fulfilled in relationship, no functional concept of man can be recovered and thus is lost the basis that has traditionally provided the ground for value, a content-rich basis for the constitutive human good.[46]

In addition, radical autonomy or individualism invites an environmental response that is hostile to genuine human autonomy. Again Buber has described this well in his treatment of the illusory character of both a solitary individualism and the collectivism that often arises from it. In saying that "modern individualism has essentially an imaginary basis," Buber highlights the fundamental unlivability of individualism. It cannot withstand the test of given real situations. Collectivism, he perceives, "essentially follows upon the foundering" of individualism. "Here the human being tries to escape his destiny of solitude by becoming completely embedded in one of the massive modern group formations." The modern collective, however, is an illusory comfort; while he is mesmerized man remains anomic. Buber continues,

> the person is joined to the reliably functioning "whole," which embraces the masses of men; but it is not a joining of man to man. Man in a collective is not man with man. Here the person is not freed from his isolation, by communing with living beings, which thenceforth lives with him; the "whole," with its claim on the wholeness of every man, aims logically and successfully at reducing, neutralizing, devaluating, and desecrating every bond with living beings. That tender surface of personal life which longs for contact with other life is progressively deadened or desensitized.[47]

Collectivism that attempts to swallow the individual, his consciousness, human sensitivity and responsibility is the twin of behaviorism. Totalitarian collectivism attempts in political action what behaviorism seeks in analysis and self-understanding. Both undermine meaningful autonomy.

Karol Wojtyla, like Buber and others, has seen a relationship between modern individualism and totalitarian collectivism. He wrote of the latter as "totalism" a "reversed individualism," that tends to coercion precisely because it shares the understanding of man of individualism and views him as radically alone and self-seeking.

> The dominant trait of totalism may be characterized as the need to find protection *from* the individual, who is seen as the chief enemy of society and of the common good. Since totalism assumes that inherent in the individual there is only the striving for individual good, that any tendency toward participation or fulfillment in acting and living together with others is totally alien to him, it follows that the 'common good' can be attained only by limiting the individual. The good thus advocated by totalism can never correspond to the wishes of the individual, to the good he is capable of choosing independently and freely according to the principles of participation; it is always a good that is incompatible with and a limitation upon the individual. Consequently, the realization of the common good frequently presupposes the use of coercion.[48]

Human nature calls for a fulfillment that avoids the Scylla of radical individualism and the Charybdis of loss of autonomy to total socialization or a coercive collective state. Hence, it is not surprising to find moral educators like Kohlberg moving to incorporate more explicitly and more completely than earlier the social dimension of the person. It is also significant that in America, often seen as the paradigmatic achievement of John Locke's individualism, there is to be found a recurrent call to community by the nation's prime moral thinkers.[49] Royce called for fulfillment in loyalty and dedication to a cause, James for faith and risk in the open-ended demands of love, and Dewey for a principle of continuity which leads a person to join his endeavors to the work of a community that preceded him, developed him and will go on beyond him. All of these indicate a conception of fulfillment and happiness, a moral goal, in tension with the American myth and often the reality of individualism and struggle.

CONTEXTUALIZED AUTONOMY: THE TRUE SELF

It may be said that a person is human only insofar as he is of others, with others and for others. He is autonomous, and his dignity is found partly in that autonomy. But his fulfillment and the basis of that dignity is found in life in accord with his nature, a life of acknowledgement of his dependence and his relatedness. The person is an essentially related being, not simply because of his or her need for others and the necessity of encounter with them, but also because it is in activity with and for others that the self is fulfilled. A person is born into the riches of human consciousness and is born to share them. It is in extending the self that the self is found. In other words, a person's distinct humanness or full dignity is found not simply in autonomy - what has here been called radical autonomy - but in autonomy exercised in accord with what he is. Both the means and the goal of moral education must be tuned to this somewhat paradoxical fact of a human's existence.

Some features of contextualized autonomy require special emphasis. The first concerns the mutuality of personal and community moral development. A person is *giving* and *receiving* in relationship to his human context. The community is rooted in the individual and is formed, led and enriched by distinct responsible persons. Rather than a collectivity of people, it is a mutual sharing of their particular endowments. The community, however, plays a critical role in preparing and drawing individuals to their fullness of being.

The person cannot serve the community in development or reform without the capacity to transcend its formation of him. Efforts to attain historical or national consciousness can be at their best endeavors to stand aside and understand the formative influences of a dominant class and the existing community. This distance and transcendence requires an openness and accessibility to a horizon or community other than that of a person's particular historical community. Socrates cannot be critic and gadfly of Athens if he is a conformer who has simply been led to share the way of life and moral principles of Athens.

At the same time, a person's particular historical community makes a justifiable moral claim on the individual, for man's social and political dimensions must always be realized in some particular family, neighborhood, and political society. Those communities are never perfect; at best they are pointed toward and more or less on their way toward the fullness and justice appropriate to them. Moral stirring and development made possible by man's capacity to transcend his embedding in particular societies should not lead to an intemperate and immature moral utopianism. Socrates' example is again instructive, for in the end he remained loyal to an Athens he had often sought to uplift; he did this even as this city was unjustly sentencing him to death. Moral education must be sensitive to the great goods such as rule of law and public accountability of officials achieved in far from perfect societies. The unifying fabric of societies like the family and well-established political communities is not to be readily sundered in the pursuit of what might appear a greater good.

Another feature of contextualized autonomy that warrants comment concerns the ultimate context or horizon in which the person finds himself. The essential relatedness of man emphasized hitherto in this essay has consisted in human relationships. Those interpersonal relationships though primary in the order of experience seem to take on greater significance in the context of meaning that an Ultimate Other or Thou can provide. In such a context, the feel for responsibility and obligation that genuine interpersonal relations call forth can be grounded, for then the person is accountable beyond the transient human world.[50] In the light of this Person, man's best conceptions of justice become duties to which he must respond. In the light of this Person's beneficence in providing man's being and environs, a life of self-giving love seems congruent with the whole order of reality.

Finally, it is hard to see how interpersonal relations can rise beyond individualism and its attendant instrumental personal relations without the presence of the Ultimate Person. The increasing interest of moral educators, specifically Kohlberg, in the social dimension of the person as it pertains to moral education may well indicate, if not necessitate, a freer and easier movement in the future between the effort to provide moral education and the endeavor to work out an ultimate context of meaning. Moral development at every stage need not necessarily involve a grappling with the most fundamental questions of human existence, but moral development conceived of as independent of wider horizons of meaning seems to do violence to the wholeness of experience out of which persons inevitably draw their moral ideals and principles.[51]

University of Notre Dame
Notre Dame, Indiana

NOTES

1. I am grateful to the various contributors to this volume for their critical assistance and to my colleague, M. Katherine Tillman for bibliographical direction for an aspect of this study and overall editorial assistance.
2. Lawrence Kohlberg, "Indoctrination Versus Relativity in Value Education," *Zygon*, (1971), 286-87.
3. Kohlberg, "Stage and Sequence: The Cognitive-Developmental Approach to Socialization," in *Handbook of Socialization Theory and Research*, ed. by D. Goslin (Chicago: Rand McNally, 1969), pp. 361ff.
4. *Ibid.*, p. 364.
5. *Ibid.*, p. 363.
6. *Ibid.*, p. 369.
7. *Ibid.*, p. 410.
8. Kohlberg and Rochelle Mayer, "Development as the Aim of Education," *Harvard Educational Review*, 42 (1972), 454.
9. *Ibid.*, p. 469.
10. *Ibid.*, p. 472.
11. *Ibid.*
12. Alasdair MacIntyre, *After Virtue* (Notre Dame, Indiana: University of Notre Dame Press, 1981) p. 30.
13. Stephen Rogers, "The Myth of the 'Self-Centered Person,'" *Pace* 10 (1979), 1-4.
14. See Kohlberg's affirmation of the liberal contractarian tradition specifically the expression of it by John Rawls in Kohlberg's "The Future of Liberalism as the Dominant Ideology of the West," in *Moral Development and Politics*, ed. by Richard W. Wilson and Gordon J. Schochet (New York: Praeger, 1980), p. 56. This collection also contains a critique of Kohlberg's liberalism from the perspective of "critical theory." See Herbert G. Reid and Ernest J. Yanarella, "The Tyranny of the Categorical: On Kohlberg and the Politics of Moral Development," pp. 107-132.
15. William Alston, though critical of Kohlberg in certain respects, has praised him "for producing evidence that should force psychologists to take the cognitive aspects of morality seriously as an important influence on behavior." "Comments on Kohlberg's 'From Is To Ought,'" in *Cognitive Development and Epistemology*, ed. by Theodore Mischel (New York and London: Academic Press, 1971), p. 278.
16. Cardinal Karol Wojtyla, *The Acting Person*, trans. by Andrzej Potocki (Dordrecht, Holland: D. Reidel, 1979), p. 277. For more development of this idea of the person as the free, self-conscious subject, see Ch. XII below.
17. William James, *Psychology: Briefer Course* (New York: Collier Books, 1962), p. 168.
18. Kohlberg, "Moral Education For A Society in Transition," *Educational Leadership*, 33 (1975), 47-48.

19. Kohlberg, "This Special Section in Perspective," *Social Education*, 40 (1976), 213. Also see his strong identification with Socrates in "From Is To Ought: How to Commit the Naturalistic Fallacy and Get Away With It in the Study of Moral Development," in *Cognitive Development* ed. by Mischel, p. 232.

20. See Ch. IV on "Freedom and Moral Choice."

21. Kohlberg's efforts (assisted by Clark Power) to relate moral development to ego development, ultimate meaning and religious development are found in "Religion, Morality and Ego Development," in *Toward Moral and Religious Maturity*, ed. by J. Fowler and A. Vergate (Morristown, New Jersey: Silver-Burdett, 1980), pp. 343-372, and in "Moral Development, Religious Thinking, and the Question of a Seventh Stage," *Zygon*, 16 (1981), pp. 203-259. These essays are explored in part in Ch. XI below.

22. Kohlberg and Mayer, p. 456.

23. Kohlberg, "Moral Education," pp. 47-48.

24. Kohlberg, "Indoctrination," p. 293.

25. Kohlberg, "Stage and Sequence," p. 397.

26. *Ibid.*, p. 398.

27. *Ibid.*

28. *Ibid.*, p. 427. See also Kohlberg, "From Is To Ought," pp. 174, 190-91; Kohlberg and Mayer, pp. 406ff.; Kohlberg, "Moral Development and the Education of Adolescents," in *Adolescents and the American High School*, ed. by Richard F. Purnell (New York: Holt, Rinehart, and Winston, Inc., 1970), p. 155.

29. Kohlberg, "Stage and Sequence," p. 394.

30. *Ibid.*, pp. 399ff. and 428.

31. *Ibid.*, p. 402.

32. Kohlberg and Mayer, p. 475.

33. See Ch. I above. See also Kohlberg, "Revisions in the Theory and Practice of Moral Development," in *Moral Development*, ed. by William Damon (San Francisco: Jossey-Bass Inc., 1978), pp. 84-85. Kohlberg goes only so far to allow "'indoctrination' without violating the child's rights, as long as teacher advocacy is democratic (or subject to the constraints of recognizing student participation in the rulemaking and value-holding process), recognizing the shared rights of teachers and students." Depending on the degree of participation of students Kohlberg would require, the new approach may be no more workable in schools than that which prescinded from all "indoctrination." "Indoctrination" includes exhorting and influencing for Kohlberg. Also see Kohlberg, "High School Democracy and Educating for a Just Society," in *Moral Education: A First Generation of Research and Development*, ed. by Ralph L. Mosher (New York: Praeger Publishers, 1980).

34. *Ibid.* See Ch. I of this volume. See especially Kohlberg's second Clark lecture in his *The Meaning and Measurement of Moral Development* (Worcester: Clark University Press, 1981), pp. 35-52. Also see Clark

Power and Joseph Reimer, "Moral Atmosphere: An Educational Bridge Between Moral Judgment and Action" in Damon. See also Joseph Reimer, "Moral Education: The Just Community Approach," *Phi Delta Kappan* (1981).

35. Kohlberg, "Revision," p. 85.
36. Power and Reimer, p. 34. See also Kohlberg's discussion of Durkheim in *The Meaning* and specifically his suggestion on p. 51 that "a history of action" in terms of certain norms might through individuals have carry-over impact to the larger less moral society beyond the school.
37. Aristotle, *Politics*, 1253a.
38. Aristotle, *Nicomachean Ethics*, 1180a14-24; *Politics*, 1277a14--b29, 1325b10-32, 1328b33-1329a2, and 1336a29-b35.
39. Aristotle, *Politics*, 1332b, 1334b.
40. Martin Buber, *I and Thou* (New York: Charles Scribner's Sons, 1958), p. 63.
41. Hannah Arendt, *The Human Condition* (Garden City, New York: Doubleday and Co., Inc. 1959), p. 178. She cites Aristotle in making this observation.
42. Buber, p. 62.
43. Buber, "What is Man?" in *Reality, Man and Existence: Essential Works of Existentialism*, ed. by H. J. Blackham (New York: Bantam Books, 1965), p. 234. Sabastian Samay above has offered powerful support for this social interpretation of personhood in his report and interpretation of the work of Kurt Goldstein.
44. Kenneth L. Schmitz, *The Gift: Creation* (Milwaukee: Marquette University Press, 1982), p. 81.
45. Wojtyla, p. 274.
46. MacIntyre, p. 56.
47. Buber, "What is Man?" p. 270.
48. Wojtyla, p. 274.
49. See Mann's detailed account of these thinkers in Ch. II above.
50. H. Richard Niebuhr, *The Responsible Self* (New York: Harper and Row, 1963). Niebuhr writes that the "encounter of I and Thou takes place, as it were, always in the presence of a third, from which I and Thou are distinguished and to which they also respond," p. 79 and *passim*.
51. Ralph B. Potter, "Justice and Beyond Moral Education," *Andover Newton Quarterly*, 19 (1979), p. 148. See Ch. XI below for an exploration of the religious factor in moral development.

CHAPTER XII

THE INTEGRITY OF MORALITY

IN RELATION TO RELIGION

DAVID L. SCHINDLER

The several papers in this volume take up in turn various aspects of an integrated theory of the moral agent. Recognizing that cognitive factors are extremely important in moral action, these papers attempt at the same time to show the indispensable role of emotion, volition, character, social environment and the like in the making of moral judgments. Within this context, then, the present paper considers the role of the religious factor in moral judgment. This issue is analogous to that running through many of the earlier papers. If it is the case that the existential factors of emotion, character, and the like are indeed integral to the development of adequate moral judgments, then these factors must be incorporated into one's theory of moral agent and subsequently attended to in one's program of moral education, if the latter is to have any chance for success. And so it would seem to be with respect to the religious factor in moral agency. Indeed in the instance of religion the issue would seem to be intensified. For if religion makes any claim on us at all it would seem to be a more comprehensive claim than that of other factors noted: the very nature of religion would seem to be such as to require recognition of its primacy in relation to morality.

But, of course, it is just the meaning of such a suggestion which must be examined here. For if an affirmation of a primacy of religion in relation to morality were seen to require making morality simply a function of religion, there would seem to result a direct challenge of the legitimacy in principle of any programs in value or moral education just so far as they are understood as distinct from programs in religious education. It is in this context that Lawrence Kohlberg, together with Clark Power, has seen it necessary, in order to carry through his program in moral education, particularly in public schools, to defend the autonomy of morality over against what he calls the "divine command theorists,"[1] that is, those who hold that morality is simply a function of God's revelation as recorded in the Bible.

The thesis Kohlberg and Power advance is that development of moral thinking is necessary but not sufficient for development of religious thinking.[2] That is, their claim is that religion serves primarily to reassure one in one's moral judgments: it serves to support one in the face of the question as to why one should be moral, in a way proportionate to the form of that question as it emerges at any given stage of morality. Thus, while religion goes beyond morality, a certain stage of morality nonetheless precedes or is the necessary presupposition for a correlative stage of religion. In a word, then, morality is at once distinct from, but related to, religion: morality is autonomous but nonetheless in the limit needs religion. Kohlberg and Power are of course concerned to confirm their thesis with appropriate empirical studies, and in the course of their argument offer evidence which they take to testify to such confirmation. Nonetheless, they are also clear that their thesis involves distinctly philosophical-theological assumptions (*MD*, p. 227, and *passim*).

In what follows I shall be concerned to outline a theoretical position which defends the simultaneous distinctness and relatedness of religion and morality, but which does so by qualifying Kohlberg's and Power's philosophical/theological assumptions, particularly as those assumptions bear on the nature of religion. Kohlberg and Power seek to defend the autonomy of morality, and their intention is to do so precisely within the context of an authentic--non-reductionist--view of religion. To carry this through, they see it necessary to support the thesis that morality is logically prior to religion in human experience, but that morality nonetheless does not replace religion. I shall argue that such a thesis is not necessary for the maintenance of a legitimate distinctness of morality in relation to religion. Indeed, my argument will be that it is logically possible to defend such distinctness in a way which is more faithful to the integrity of religion--more faithful, that is, to what is legitimate in the concerns of the "divine command" theorists regarding the centrality of God (or of whatever functions as ultimate) in human experience.

To this end I shall suggest a theoretical position which provides warrant for the converse of the thesis of Kohlberg and Power: namely, that there is a sense in which religion is prior to, but does not replace, morality.[3] To carry through this suggestion we must make a number of important distinctions, and I therefore propose to begin by examining more carefully the warrants Kohlberg and Power advance in support of their thesis and indeed of the meaning they assign to its crucial terms.

I

Kohlberg and Power situate their understanding of the relation of morality and religion between what they regard as two extreme current views of that relation, namely, the fundamentalist or divine command theory on the one hand, and the Freudian atheistic emotivistic theory on the other (*MD*, pp. 203-208). Those who espouse the divine command theory hold that morality is ultimately defined by and rests upon revelation as recorded in the Bible or other texts taken to be sacred. Those who espouse the emotivistic theory regard morality and religion as cognitively empty. In its specifically Freudian formulation, this theory understands moral judgments as "expressions of the constellation of emotional structures termed the *superego*" (*MD*, p. 207). While "morality" in this sense is taken by the Freudian to have a necessary function in the maintenance of social order and survival, religion does not fare so well. Sharing with morality its irrational and relativistic character, religion has the additional quality of being an illusion, something akin to a collective neurosis. Kohlberg and Power take these two views of morality and religion, despite their vast differences in other respects, to be similar from the perspective of educational theory: for, in linking morality essentially with attitudes of respect for some authority figure, both hold a non-rational basis for morality (*MD*, p. 208) and indeed are guilty of the "naturalistic fallacy" which consists in making "ought" statements a function of "is" statements (see for example *MD*, p. 206). Both, therefore, regard religious thinking and scientific thinking as opposed to one another and see a rational and Socratic approach to moral and religious education as not viable (*MD*, p. 208).

In response to these alternatives, Kohlberg and Power propose a class of theories, which they term theories of natural law, which they understand as giving more adequate expression to the nature of morality and religion and their relation (*MD*, pp. 209-213). They term these theories natural law theories because they contend that the human conceptions of moral law are the "outcomes of universal human nature developing under universal aspects of the human condition" (*MD*, p. 210). That is, these conceptions, illustrated for example in the lives of Socrates and Martin Luther King, are not tied to any specific theology, creed, or divine command to which Socrates or King had privileged or private access. At the same time, Kohlberg and Power argue that their understanding of "natural law" theory escapes the naturalistic fallacy into which the divine command theory inevitably falls: for the "nature" which humans share in the moral order and which is thematized in moral philosophy is parallel with, but not derived from or reducible to, "nature" as thematized in science, metaphysics, and religion.

In considering the relationship between religious thinking and moral thinking, Kohlberg and Power, following Stephen Toulmin, take religion to be a form of reassurance (*MD*, p. 212f; *RM*, pp. 346-48). Religion addresses questions which arise at the boundary of moral reasoning, such as "Why be moral at all?," and thereby provides support proportionate to one's moral level for continued acceptance of one's duty to be moral. Thus Kohlberg and Power state in summary that

> this essay's central claim is that religion is a conscious response to and an expression of, the quest for an ultimate meaning for moral judging and acting. As such, the main function of religion is not to supply moral prescriptions but to support moral judgment and action as purposeful human activities. If this is true, it implies that a given stage of solutions to moral problems is necessary, but not sufficient, for a parallel stage of solutions to religious problems (*MD*, p. 226).

There are, then, two philosophical assumptions which Kohlberg and Power single out as giving rise to their hypothesis (*MD*, p. 227). The first assumption is that morality is autonomous, that is, a realm logically independent of religion. This is consistent with the fact that only a small minority of persons explicitly appeals to religious concerns to justify its moral judgments and that persons in even the highest stage of moral development hold widely differing religious views. The second philosophical assumption is that the development of metaphysical reasoning presupposes the development of moral or practical reasoning. The point once again is that the metaethical question which religion and metaphysics seek to answer, such as why be moral at all, *presupposes* the existence of a normative moral structure which is being called into question. A certain stage of morality thus precedes a comparable stage of religion, and hence is necessary for religion: but religion in turn goes beyond morality, in that morality does not suffice to answer the question it (morality) raises.

It is important to note that, up to this point, Kohlberg and Power see their philosophic position as having affinities with Dewey and Kant (*MD*, pp. 227-228; 243-247). That is, Kohlberg and Power share with them the view that morality precedes religion, but that religion in turn goes beyond morality. But when one presses for the fuller meaning of this common claim, a crucial difference emerges. Dewey and Kant share an agnosticism regarding any speculative, metaphysical claims as proper to the religion which goes beyond morality, whereas Kohlberg and Power in their understanding of religion proceed on a "natural law" basis which they take to be properly metaphysical (*MD*, pp. 228 and 246).

Kohlberg and Power adopt a natural law theory because they take such a theory to be more adequate in terms of accounting for the experiences contained in the examples of persons who seem most mature religiously, that is, who have moved to the highest or sixth stage of religious development (*MD*, p. 228 and p. 246). Kohlberg terms this sixth stage of religious development a "seventh stage" in relation to his well--known six stages of moral reasoning. In accord with his general thesis that a given stage of moral maturity precedes a comparable level of religious maturity, his contention is that only at the sixth stage of moral maturity is one motivated to move to the highest (sixth) stage of religious reasoning. One is forced to move beyond the realities of the human social order to an ultimate stage of religious orientation only when one's experience presses one to seek justification for acting in accord with the universal ethical principles proper to Stage 6.

This new stage is genuinely a "seventh" stage in relation to Kohlberg's six moral stages because in it one's thinking goes beyond the sixth moral stage. Nonetheless, the term "seventh stage" is at the same time properly to be taken as a metaphor because it does not add any new content or formal criterion to the formulation of specifically moral judgment. Rather, "Stage 7" provides support for the structure of morality already expressed in Stage 6, and does so by way of integrating that structure into an overarching perspective on life's ultimate meaning (*MD*, pp. 233-34). In a word, for Kohlberg and Power only one who is fully morally mature moves on to seek a mature solution to the question of the meaning of life in a properly religious context, and indeed in a religious context understood to involve properly ontological or metaphysical claims (*MD*, p. 234).

It is this demand for a cognitively or speculatively satisfying answer to the question of the meaning of life which arises out of the experience of the morally mature person, then, that both leads one into a "seventh stage" and does so in a way which seems to Kohlberg and Power to warrant distancing themselves from the agnostic philosophic positions of Dewey and Kant. That is, mature moral experience seems to demand a "realistic" or metaphysical, rather than an "idealistic" or "imaginative," kind of religion.[4] But Kohlberg and Power nonetheless go on to note that the exact form which such a metaphysical religion must take is not unitary and definable (*MD*, p. 257). Indeed they offer Marcus Aurelius and Andrea Simpson as examples of persons who embody "seventh stage" reasoning but nonetheless do so while espousing different metaphysical/religious views (see *MD*, pp. 234-43). While Aurelius describes his experience in a way consistent with a pantheistic form of religion, Simpson does so in a manner more consonant with a theistic form.

In the final section of their argument, then, Kohlberg and Power describe how Spinoza and Teilhard de Chardin afford us examples of the kinds of religion/metaphysics which provide the required rational underpinnings for the experience of Aurelius (pantheistic) and Simpson (theistic-Christian) (*MD*, pp. 246-55). And again the rational character of their accounts is crucial: however much Teilhard's position, for example, might draw its inspiration from Christian revelation, it nonetheless contains within it a theology of nature or creation which is offered as a way of accounting most adequately for the totality of experience (*MD*, p. 253). The point bears stressing: it is not at all the case for Kohlberg and Power that views such as Teilhard's, which are offered as "seventh stage" "foundations" for a Stage 6 morality, must not have explicitly "supernatural" sources; the point rather is simply that such views, even if "supernatural" in origin, contain within them claims which are *also* distinctly rational in the sense that they can be advanced as satisfying the demands of human intelligence for meaning.

It is just this final claim of Kohlberg and Power, then, which distances them from the emotivist on the one hand and the fundamentalists on the other, who would both, though with vastly different motivations, disallow any distinctly natural knowledge of the Ultimate Reality, God. But once again these "natural law" religious views offered by Kohlberg and Power are not to be understood as themselves directly generative of morality. Rather they are parallel with, and supportive of, what remains the distinctly moral reasoning of Stage 6. In a word, religion, in its most adequate stage, informs "a general natural law, ontological orientation and supports principles of justice" (*MD*, p. 212).

II

The views of Kohlberg and Power as described here seem to me to make an important contribution to the contemporary discussion regarding the theoretical foundations of programs in moral education. Kohlberg's non-reductionist account of the stages of morality, expanded now in the articles under discussion to include a more detailed description of how metaphysical and religious concerns with ultimacy function in moral judgment and action, serve to open for educators a whole range of questions which long have been taken as purely private matters. Both the emotivists (positivists) and the "divine command" theorists, though in different ways and for vastly different reasons, have failed to challenge the private character of morality, precisely because they make morality a function of what is non-rational and thus not naturally accessible to all. More exactly, they construe morality as of a piece with a metaphysics or a religion taken to be essentially non-(or extra) rational, and hence non-natural and private. Kohlberg's position all along has served generally to challenge traditions which subscribe to the private character of morality. What he attempts to fill out in the more recent articles with Power is the sense in which it is possible to be genuinely religious *while* respecting the legitimate autonomy --the public character or cognitive status--of morality. He does this by assuming an analogous form of his earlier arguments regarding a parallelism between the structures of moral reasoning and scientific and (here) religious thinking, rather than a simple derivation of one from the other.[5] But he does it also by showing us views of religion which allow us to affirm such autonomy on intrinsically religious grounds. That is, he shows that, if one wishes to be genuinely religious while nonetheless defending the public character of morality, one must develop an understanding of religion which allows, on inner-religious grounds, a metaphysics or natural theology. Put another way, one must espouse a form of religion which permits affirmation of the integrity of the distinctly "natural" structures of the world.

For present purposes, then, I shall assume with Kohlberg and Power the correctness of the thesis regarding the need for affirming a realistic metaphysics, a natural theology, as intrinsic to religion properly understood, if one is to sustain the public character of morality from within a religious context. At the same time, I should like to raise a question about the way in which they see this thesis as entailing an affirmation of the relative primacy of morality over religion. In granting an understanding of religion which affirms the integrity of the "natural" structures of things, is it not more adequate to situate that understanding within a context wherein religion is taken as having primacy over morality?

In what follows I shall argue for a sense in which this is the case on intrinsically religious and philosophical grounds. But I should nonetheless note at the outset what seems to me to be the importance a priori of facing up to the full implications of this issue. For what if it is the case that religion is needed, not only to support a level of moral judging and acting already reached, but rather, precisely, to generate that level of judging and acting in the first place? Or, put in a way similar to the broader form of the question raised by Tocqueville with respect to the political-cultural trends he saw developing in nineteenth century America: what if it is the case that we cannot successfully generate morality in our children without situating that morality explicitly in a context of religion?

III

I should like to begin my discussion by returning to Kohlberg and Power and calling attention to an important ambiguity in their position which is directly pertinent to the thesis I should like to advance. In the context of their general argument regarding the primacy of morality over religion seen as emerging at the "limit" of morality (*RM*, p. 350), Kohlberg and Power identify another way of considering the relation of morality and religion, namely, from the perspective "of the psychological unity of the two provided by the ego" (*RM*, p. 350; see also *MD*, p. 226). They then go on to say

> Insofar as religion serves to strengthen the self which makes moral decisions, it has an effect, not on the particular formulation of the moral judgment, but on whether any judgment is to be made at all and whether and how, if it is made, that judgment will be carried into action (*RM*, p. 251).

Drawing on the work of Fowler, Kohlberg and Power then offer three illustrations of ways in which the strengthening of the self on the part of religion can occur:

> First, a religious interpretation of one's life as a vocation can renew one's sense of moral purpose and commitment (*RM*, p. 351).

> Second, religion can serve to encourage the self confronted by the abyss between the moral ideals of the self and the injustice of the world (*RM*, p.351f)

> Third, a religious perspective can heighten one's moral sensitivity by offering a vision of the self as intrinsically related in a familial bond with other selves .... Thinking of strangers as brothers and sisters [can have] the effect of making what [might be] construed as a non-obligatory situation, one in which moral action [is] obligatory. In addition, the motivation to act [can be] intensified (*RM*, p. 252).

Finally, in the same article from which these quotations are taken, we find the following statement:

> The claim that moral stages are necessary but not sufficient for religious stages ... is compatible with the theistic position that implicit, universal faith grounds the very possibil-

ity of making a moral judgment or acting morally. That is, in every moral judgment there is a tacit further judgment that the activity of moral judging is, in fact, necessary. Such a judgment is based not on the fulfillment of moral criteria for an ethically right act but on the fulfillment of "religious" criteria for an ultimately meaningful act (*RM*, p. 365).

I quote these passages because they seem to open up a way of defending a form of a primacy of religion over morality. Indeed they suggest a genuine tension with the more general thesis of Kohlberg and Power outlined above. But since Kohlberg and Power apparently do not see such a tension, we must sort further through their meaning.

The crucial distinction for Kohlberg and Power in founding the affirmations just cited is that between faith and religion. Faith, as Fowler understands it, is holistic; it is a basic stance, a system of loyalties and beliefs, which includes in its sweep both cognitive and affective factors (see for example *RM*, p. 347 and 355; *MD*, pp. 213-14; 223 and 226; Fowler, *op.cit.*, pp. 174-74). In contrast, Kohlberg and Power would restrict religion to "that part of faith in which there is a conscious reflection on that which provides ultimate reassurance and meaning for life. Through the symbols, concepts, and theo-logic of religion, the concerns of one's faith are openly addressed in a reasonable way" (*RM*, p. 347). As they put it elsewhere, they would distinguish within the broad matrix of faith what they take to be the partially separable domains of morality and religion, while in fact redefining this broad matrix as a matter of ethical rather than faith development (*MD*, p. 226). - Thus, though there may indeed be a certain unity in a person's ethical development, of which Aristotle's *Ethics* provides a good picture, within this unity moral judgment or thinking remains clearly distinguishable logically from religious judgment or thinking (*MD*, p. 226).

Within the context of this distinction between faith and religion, then, the claims recorded in the quotations cited above would seem to fit as follows into Kohlberg's and Power's "necessary but not sufficient" hypothesis. First, insofar as one is speaking of faith, that is, of a fundamental though largely tacit system of loyalties and beliefs, it would seem to be permissible--logically possible and indeed necessary--to affirm such faith as anterior to morality. Such faith would seem to provide the initially necessary confidence in the very worthwhileness of acting morally at all (See *RM*, p. 365; *MD*, pp. 223 and 226). But secondly, insofar as one is speaking of religion (a) a certain level of morality or moral judgment must precede a parallel level of religion or religious judgment.[6] (b) Insofar as religion in turn positively influences moral judgment, it does so by providing after-the-fact reassurance, namely, a proportionate measure of support for an already achieved level of morality which has been pressed to its limit. Finally, (c) religion provides such support, not by adding anything specific to the particular formulation of moral judgment, but by providing the person making the judgment with a general reason "for being and for purposeful human activity" (*RM*, p. 368).

Just what are Kohlberg's and Power's warrants for making the distinction between faith and religion which is central to the priority they accord morality over religion? I can discern two. First and generally, they seem to take some such understanding of religion as alone capable of protecting the autonomy of morality--that is, in the face of the challenge from divine command theorists. Secondly, a distinction between faith and religion makes possible a more careful and detailed empirical study of the relation of religion and morality (see for example *MD*, p. 226; *RM*, p. 355).

Now I simply reject the second reason as an adequate warrant for making a theoretical distinction. Susceptibility to clearly delimited empirical study is not, of itself, a sufficient criterion for determining the intrinsic meaning of something. It would be such only on the basis of an assumed form of empiricism which I regard as indefensible and which I take it Kohlberg and Power themselves would not want to espouse. The question I wish to raise, then, is that connected with the first warrant: is there some broader understanding of religion which would allow us to affirm a priority of religion while permitting continued affirmation of the rational and hence public character of morality? In the remainder of this paper I shall be concerned to outline a form of an affirmative response to this question.

IV

First of all, it is important to recall that Kohlberg and Power do not deny the reality in human experience of a stance bearing on ultimacy, termed by them faith, which includes tacit and affective features. They simply do not wish to call such a stance religious, that is, except insofar as it gets expressed in a cognitively explicit way. But they have offered no adequate warrant for so restricting, a priori and as a matter of principle, the meaning of religion.[7] Their argument, in other words, does not suffice to rule out the logical possibility of a broader notion of religion which can nonetheless maintain the integrity of morality. It is within just this context, then, that I shall begin by adopting such a broader notion of religion. Specifically, I shall begin by accepting an understanding of religion as a stance bearing on ultimacy which includes both tacit or implicit and explicit features, and which is at once cognitive and affective.[8] To aid in explaining the meaning of the various elements of this understanding of religion, and the bearing of such understanding on the question under consideration, I shall employ the classical terms of the philosopher-theologian Thomas Aquinas.[9]

To begin with, apropos of the affective-volitional factor in human cognition, Aquinas writes as follows:

> From this we can easily understand why these powers include one another in their acts, because the intellect under-

stands that the will wills, and the will wills the intellect to understand. In the same way, the good is contained under the true, inasmuch as it is a desired good.[10]

The will moves the intellect as to the exercise of its act, since even the true itself, which is the perfection of the intellect, is included in the universal good as a particular good. But as to the determination of the act, which the act derives from the object, the intellect moves the will; for the good itself is apprehended under a special aspect as contained in the universal true.[11]

Of course Aquinas uses faculty-psychology terms which may be offensive to many contemporary ears, but I do not think we need engage that debate here. For Aquinas's point can easily be translated for our purposes here as meaning (a) that there are distinctly volitional/affective and cognitional factors in each human act, which (b) are nonetheless mutually internal to one another and hence unified in the exercise of each such act. Further, there is a sense in which the volitional/affective factors have priority as what moves one to know in the first place. That is, any given act of knowing presupposes as its anterior, immanent condition a distinct tendency (wanting-seeking-desiring) to know.

This distinctly affective/volitional factor does not destroy the integrity of the cognitional process: on the contrary, it in turn precisely presupposes that integrity. Volition and cognition are given simultaneously as distinct aspects of any one conscious act: they cause the act of consciousness efficiently. Cognitional factors on the other hand have priority in the order of specification: they cause the act or consciousness formally.[12]

The upshot of Aquinas' position here is that some form of love, that is, some form of tending or seeking or desiring, is always distinctly internal to each act of consciousness, and hence to each act of knowing and judging. It is just this position which founds Aquinas' general claim that love is the "form" of the virtues, in the sense, that is, that it is love which is the internal dynamism which moves a person to each of his or her specific human acts.[13] It follows that any adequate account of cognition, and hence in turn of moral cognition, must incorporate this distinct but internal factor of love as a necessary condition for, and in this ontological (or logical--i.e., not temporal) sense prior to, any act of cognition.

The dimension of ultimacy proper to religion emerges when we press the above description of Aquinas' position to its fuller implications. That is, each human act, when pressed to its limit, discloses itself as carrying a dimension of ultimacy. As Aquinas puts it, "of necessity everything that one desires one desires for the sake of the ultimate end."[14] Now such a drive for ultimacy, as a human drive, involves in principle both affective/volitional and cognitive factors in the way and for the reasons already described. This is exactly the import of Aquinas's referring to the drive here as a "desire" (hence involving affectivity/volition) "for the sake of" (hence involving awareness or cognition). His point, then, is that in each human act there is disclosed in the limit some volition and cognition which bears on ultimacy. This does not mean that one is always explicitly aware of ultimacy or of what is functioning as ultimate in one's conscious acts. It means rather that in one's conscious acts there is some at least implicit (but with the possibility of becoming explicit in varying degrees) affirmation bearing on ultimacy which is at once cognitive and affective/volitional. In a word, each of our human acts in the limit discloses something which we value the most or ultimately, and such valuing is at once a matter of love and knowledge (cognition).[15]

V

Religion, then, as I understand the term, is a stance bearing on ultimacy which includes simultaneously both love and knowledge, and does so in both implicit and explicit ways. As the terms of this brief description suggest, this understanding of religion has roots in at least one major philosophical/theological tradition. But before considering the significance of this understanding of religion for the thesis of Kohlberg and Power, I think it is important here to record disclaimers in connection with two features which are commonly affirmed of religion, at least in its Christian form.

First of all, is it not the case that participation in community, or indeed affiliation with some institution, is integral to what we mean by religion, and hence that any adequate definition of religion ought to include this feature? My response to this question is this: (a) if one accepts, as I do, the ontological claim that human being is essentially social and historical, it of course follows that a historical community is in principle involved in, internal to, each of one's acts. There is no such thing as an action by a human being--and hence in turn a specifically religious action-which is atomic or simply an act of an individual. (b) But the relevant point in the present context, in my judgment, is that what specifies particular actions, and hence communities organized around such actions, as religious in the first place is precisely the bearing of those actions or communities on ultimacy.

The point, in other words, is not that religion does not--that is, given the social-historical character of human being--entail participation in a historical community. Rather the point is that it is the bearing on ultimacy which originally specifies *as religious* any given instance of human participation in community, which is to say, any given historical community. In the present chapter I restrict myself to a consideration of the sense in which love and knowledge, both tacitly and explicitly, are in principle involved in this stance bearing on ultimacy which essentially characterizes religion. Clearly a more comprehensive and systematic treatment of religion would require a thematizing of the elements of participation in community--for example, such factors as particular

314 *The Integrity of Morality in Relation to Religion*

rituals, symbols, stories, and the like--which, in light of the social-historical character of human being, are internal to one's basic love and knowledge. But I nonetheless abstract from these factors in the present chapter for the simple reason that their inclusion, however much it would enrich and amplify my thesis regarding the primacy of religion in relation to morality, is unnecessary in terms of establishing the basic sense of that thesis.

The second disclaimer I should like to make surfaces in connection with the possible charge that religion in the sense adopted here is defined in terms of the human relation to what is ultimate rather than, for example, in terms of the God who is ultimate. This objection will be addressed more fully later in connection with the challenge raised by the "divine command theorists." Nonetheless, I should like to stress in the present context that the understanding of religion as outlined here does not rule out the possibility that the proper way of understanding the human relation to God is in terms of a relation of a created being to its creator, that is, in the first instance in terms of gift to giver. It may well be the case that we are properly related to what is ultimate only when we see our actions as already in some fundamental way consequent upon the primary and gracious acting of an ultimate and personal agent. But the initial point of my definition here is exactly that it *may* turn out to be the case. That is, the definition does not preclude such a way finally of conceiving religion; it simply leaves the question open. In a word, my definition of religion is concerned in the present context to express what is necessary for religion; it is not concerned to express what suffices finally for an adequate conception of the necessary features of religion.

VI

What follows, then, from an understanding of religion as I have formulated it, specifically in terms of the thesis advanced by Kohlberg and Power regarding a relative priority of morality over religion? First of all, insofar as religion involves a fundamental affectivity/volition, it is thereby anterior to, as immanent within, any given moral judgment; it is precisely a necessary ontological condition for such a judgment. That is, as a human act each moral judgment presupposes love as its immanent or "moving" condition, and in the limit some ultimate love (love bearing on ultimacy).

Further, such basic or ultimate love which characterizes religion carries within itself, however implicitly, some cognitive claim. It follows that the basic loe which is a presupposition for moral judgment is not blind or simply irrational, but already carries within itself a cognitive direction. To put the point more sharply, it already carries within it, however implicitly, a cognitive claim about the nature of what is ultimate.

Does this sense of the priority of religion, then, destroy any possible integrity of the process of moral judging? I suggest that it does not. The key to defending this suggestion lies in making a number of distinctions: first, insofar as religion is a matter of love, one must recall that love was affirmed to be prior *in its own order*. That is, love never replaces the cognitive factors involved in any human act. On the contrary it presupposes them as given simultaneously. It follows that, while, on the one hand, the love bearing on ultimacy which characterizes religion does condition the knowing process in a real or internal way, it nonetheless always and as a matter of principle leaves that knowing process formally intact. It therefore follows further that it leaves morality, insofar as morality is a matter of knowing (that is, moral judgment), formally intact. To put the matter more precisely: however much one's basic love might impede or assist one's intelligent inquiry in matters of morality, that love can never *specify* what is true in such matters. What constitutes justice in the moral order, for example, remains distinctly a matter of the formal requirements of moral intelligence.

In sum, then: (1) insofar as religion, as basic love or love bearing on ultimacy, presupposes the distinctness of the cognitive factor in morality, and in this sense depends on it to *specify what* it is that is moral, one can legitimately affirm with Kohlberg and Power the "autonomy" of morality. For morality can never be simply or formally absorbed into religion; and religion, as basic *love*, adds no new content to the particular formulation of moral judgment. At the same time, the initial point I wish to stress here is that moral judgment already and always presupposes the immanent and hence anterior moving force of basic love. In this sense moral judgments are conditioned, indeed transformed: while not *specifically* or *formally* different, they are nonetheless still *internally* different in the sense that they are suffused with one's basic love. It is in this sense, then, that the function of religion is not only to reassure but, anteriorly, to assure.

(2) Secondly, as we have seen, the basic love which characterizes religion carries within it, however implicitly, a cognitive claim about the nature of what is ultimate. If this is true, it follows, in light of the preceding analysis, that such a cognitive claim also exercises some influence on moral judgment. One's implicit claim regarding the nature of the ultimate internally affects one's understanding of the nature of morality. To illustrate this point in relation to Kohlberg and Power, I would suggest that their very conception of morality as prior to religion presupposes, precisely as an anterior, immanent condition, an implicit claim about the nature of ultimacy--that is, an implicit religious claim: namely, that whatever it is that is ultimate is such that its existence is compatible with the existence of the "natural" structures of the world as we know it. They already presuppose, as the necessary immanent condition for advancing their understanding of morality intelligently, a certain natural theology of a sort they eventually work out explicitly, but then only in the context of its providing support *after the fact* for their conception of morality.

My second point, then, is that there is already a fundamental metaphysical or natural theological claim built into the basic love which characterizes religion, and that this claim, as carried within that basic love, is itself already and always internal to, and hence presupposed by, any given moral judgment. As a matter of principle, then, the quality of such a claim has an internal bearing on the quality of one's conception of morality. Thus, in the case of Kohlberg and Power, their non-relativist conception of morality already presupposes as its anterior, immanent condition some non-relativist claim about the nature of ultimacy. Once again, religion not only reassures after the fact of moral judgment; it provides an anterior assurance--which in this case is cognitive--that is necessary for the fact of moral judgment at all.

(3) Finally, there is the difficult question of how the affirmation made in principle here regarding the relation between religion and morality works out in the detail of the several stages of religion and morality described by Kohlberg. Given the correctness of my general thesis, there should follow a correlation between the stages of religion and the stages of morality. That is, all along the way there should be some correlation between the quality of one's basic love and basic cognitive claims, on the one hand, and the quality of one's moral judgment, on the other. And it would seem that the particularities of such correlation can be determined only by relevant empirical studies.[16] I would only suggest, apropos of such empirical studies that, if they are to be undertaken in critical fashion, they must face up to two theoretical issues which I believe are raised by my general thesis: first, if the relation between love and knowledge is in the first instance an ontological rather than temporal one, it would seem to follow that love and knowledge will always be found in mutual relation, that is, as *simultaneously* affecting each other in the unity of one act. This implies a problem for any empirical effort to ascertain clearly the priority of one factor over the other as these factors come to expression in the context of religion and morality. In what sense is it possible to engage an empirical study of the mutual relation of love and knowledge in the context of religion and morality without collapsing that relation into a simply temporal one? Secondly, religion as basic love or love bearing on ultimacy carries within it tacitly (but not only tacitly) affective/volitional and cognitive factors. What are the consequent systematic limitations involved in trying to assess the influence of religion on one's moral life, in terms of how explicitly a given person is able to formulate his or her basic love and knowledge? How does one measure or make explicit what essentially includes a tacit or implicit character?

VII

But we must press on. As suggested in connection with my second disclaimer above, does not the priority of religion over morality in the sense in which I have outlined it precisely fail to meet the thrust of the challenge coming from the divine command theorists? That is, does not this defense of a certain priority of religion remain in the kind of human or "natural law" context which is exactly in question when one sees religion and morality as radically a function of God's gracious acting?

Resolution of the challenge arising from the divine command understanding of God seems to me to hinge on a proper grasp of the Christian understanding of God.[17] I take the heart of that understanding to be a sense of God as creator of the world *ex nihilo*, and hence of the world as created.[18] The significance of this understanding in terms of the present context seems to me to be twofold: on the one hand, it establishes God as agapic love, and hence as an utterly gracious actor or agent. God, as the plenitude of being, has no inner lack or need, and hence acts gratuitously in creating the world. It thus follows further that the world and the things within it are, in their inner reality, gifts. To be, for anything in the world, is at once to be given.[19] This leads to the second key feature of this understanding of God: namely, that the things of the world, all of which have their own nature and hence an excellence according to their kind, are seen at the same time to have those natures by virtue of the ongoing gracious activity of God.[20]

The point, then, is twofold: on the one hand, the natural necessities structured into the things of the world are transformed by being placed in the context of God's agapic love; but, on the other hand, those natural necessities are maintained within that love. To put it another way, God's will is disclosed precisely through the intelligible structures of the natural world. In a word, this understanding of God in relation to the world allows one to cut through, by transforming its context, the classical dilemma set by Plato in the *Euthyphro* as to whether God commands something because it is inherently right, that is, right by virtue of its own natural necessity, or whether it becomes right by virtue of God's command. For the Christian understanding of God as creator implies affirmation of a coincidence of God's will and the natural necessities of things.[21] It should be noted, then, that this understanding of God is at once a faithful and a reasonable claim. That is, the disclosure of God in revelation as loving Lord of the universe carries within it a certain metaphysical claim about the ways things are.[22]

The upshot of this understanding of Christianity for the present discussion seems to be twofold: on the one hand, such an understanding affirms the radical primacy of God's gracious activity as interior to and immanent within, the activity of the things of the world. In so doing, there is affirmed a transformation of the context of the activity of the things of the world. At the same time, this inner transformation is not seen as destroying the integrity of the natural necessities involved in the activity of the things of the world: on the contrary such a "graced" transformation is seen to coincide with such natural necessities. It seems to me, therefore, that such an understanding suffices in principle to meet the legitimate sense of the concern of the divine command theorists regarding the primacy of God; and to do so while protecting the integrity of the "natural" world necessary to maintain the legitimate sense of the autonomy of the "natural law" morality sought by Kohlberg and Power.

To put the matter more specifically in terms of the context of the salient aspects of the relation between religion and morality as recorded above, I would note the following. First, the general primacy of religion in the sense recorded above is now understood in terms of the radical primacy of God's graciousness. That is, my loving activity, the distinctly moral specificity of that loving activity, and indeed the entire sweep of the activities which make up the world, are all now seen as founded upon, and sustained by, God's loving activity. Secondly, it remains the case that, while religion in its Christian form does not add any specific content to the particular formulation of moral judgment,[23] it nonetheless transforms the context of that formulation: (a) the love which internally transforms justice while maintaining its formal integrity is now seen in the first and founding instance to be God's love; and (b) the necessary condition regarding one's conception of ultimacy, that is, in terms of sustaining the integrity of the "natural" moral order is met in the understanding of God as creator *ex nihilo*, and hence of the world as creation. Finally, then, regarding the question of the correlation between one's stages of maturity as a Christian and one's stages of moral maturity, I should suggest that the comments made above regarding the correlation between religious maturity generally and moral maturity, as well as the limitations involved in an empirical study of such correlation, hold in the present context.

VIII

It remains for us to say a word about the implications of the primacy of religion over morality as defended here in terms of programs in moral education projected for use in public schools. Though religion in some form (some set of ultimate convictions) is a necessary condition for morality, and thus must be incorporated into any program in moral development which would be complete, it does not follow that such a thesis has the practical effect of forcing programs in moral education out of public schools--to the would-be satisfaction of both the divine command theorists and the atheistic/agnostic emotivists. But this suggestion of course hinges on the correctness of the thesis whose meaning I have sketched above. I would reformulate that thesis for the present context as follows: there is a concern structured into every human being which bears on what is ultimate and which carries in principle, though in varying degrees of explicitness, a cognitive claim about the nature of what is ultimate. This concern, as fundamental, is thus operative (again in varying degrees of explicitness) in each of one's conscious activities. In the present context bearing on political life, it follows that this concern is operative in the conscious activities of constructing cultural (social-political) institutions.

What I wish to suggest here, then, is that, given the general ontological claim outlined in this paper, it follows that there can be no society or group of human beings which is simply without some set of convictions in matters of ultimacy and hence religion. No society can avoid reflecting such convictions, however implicitly, in its cultural--and hence educational--institutions.[24]

This brief theoretical claim makes no pretense of solving the enormous difficulties involved in trying to spell out its exact implications for educational practice. The claim nonetheless does entail a transformation of the conventional context of the discussion of religion in public life as undertaken in light of the Establishment Clause of the First Amendment. By conventional here I mean the positivist context which assumes the possibility of simple neutrality in public life in matters of religion. If such neutrality is not possible, then it is a matter not of *whether* the institutions of society, including its educational institutions, will reflect such convictions regarding ultimacy, but rather of *which sort of* convictions they will reflect. The issue which should thus set the context for discussion of religion in public schools, specifically here that discussion as it emerges in the debate between the divine command theorists and Kohlberg and Power, is not whether but how religion in the sense affirmed in this paper, that is, some set of convictions bearing on ultimacy, should be incorporated into public schools and indeed integrated into programs of moral education in such schools. In light of the position sketched in this paper, the answer would seem to involve an effort by educators, first, to become self-conscious about the convictions bearing on ultimacy which are de facto operative in their current educational practice and, secondly, to assess the adequacy of those convictions. Such assessment should be careful to show how the religious convictions maintain the integrity, which is to say the public character, of morality.

In a word, then, though the understanding of religion outlined above provides some theoretical guidelines relevant to the problem of religion in public moral education, this paper makes no pretense of solving the profoundly difficult and complex issues bearing on educational practice which are involved in carrying through a solution to this problem. My minimal suggestion here is simply that Kohlberg and Power, in their legitimate concern to protect the autonomy of morality in the face of the constitutional challenge, have too readily conceded the positivist understanding of the place of religion in public life--which is to say, the positivist assumption that it alone is without an "orthodoxy" in matters of religion. What is needed, in my judgment, is rather an approach which begins by recognizing the de facto presence of religion (a set of convictions bearing on ultimacy) in public life, and then, within this context, goes on to elaborate an understanding of religion which both retrieves an adequate sense of religion on its own terms, and secures the gains on behalf of the freedom of individuals made in the development of democracy in the modern West.

In conclusion, I should like to recall the limits of the argument I have sketched in relation to Kohlberg's and Power's understanding of the relation between morality and religion. In an effort to defend the autonomy of religion in the face of the challenge from fundamentalists, Kohlberg and Power consider it necessary to advance the thesis that morality is a necessary and prior, but not sufficient, condition for religion. In advancing this thesis, they make religion coextensive with the explicitly cognitive elements of faith. In response my argument has been, first, that they do not provide an adequate warrant for so restricting the meaning of religion and thus leave open the legitimate possibility of a broader understanding. Within this context, then, I have offered a form of a broader definition of religion and have attempted to show how such a broader definition would permit accommodation of Kohlberg's and Power's concern to protect the integrity of morality, while nonetheless entailing a form of the converse of their thesis regarding the relation between morality and religion: namely, that religion is a necessary and prior condition for, but does not simply replace, morality. As all of this suggests, the intention of my argument has not been to justify an alternative view of religion simply, but rather to show that it is possible to defend the integrity of the moral order from within a context of a primacy of religion. In so doing, my intention has been to suggest an alternative to the views of both Kohlberg and Power and the divine command theorists, which nonetheless would accommodate what is legitimate in the concerns of each. Finally, then, I have suggested a sense in which, given the understanding of religion developed in the paper, there follows a transformation of the conventional--positivist--context of the discussion of the place of religion in public life and hence education.

University of Notre Dame
Notre Dame, Indiana

FOOTNOTES

1. Lawrence Kohlberg and Clark Power, "Moral Development, Religious Thinking, and the Question of a Seventh Stage," *Zygon*, 16 (1981), pp. 203-207. (Hereafter *MD*). This article also appeared in Kohlberg's *The Philosophy of Moral Development*, Vol. I of *Essays on Moral Development* (New York: Harper & Row, 1981).

2. *MD*, p. 255. See also F. Clark Power and Lawrence Kohlberg, "Religion, Morality, and Ego Development," in *Toward Moral and Religious Maturity*, ed. by J. Fowler and A. Vergote (Morristown, N.J.: Silver-Burdett, 1980), p. 365. (Hereafter *RM*.)

3. See James Fowler's criticism of Kohlberg in Fowler's "Stages in Faith: The Structural-Developmental Approach," in *Values and Moral Development*, ed. by Thomas C. Hennessey, S.J. (New York: Paulist Press, 1976), pp. 207-211.

4. But, of course, in itself this precisely does not meet directly the challenge posed by Kant: namely, granted that the drive to understand things in their ultimate roots and foundations--which emerges in the experience of those who are most advanced morally--is a necessary feature of the human spirit, how do we know that that drive is not profoundly misleading and even destructive if understood "realistically," that is, as leading to a disclosure of the way things ultimately are? In a word, Kohlberg and Power show that our experience leads us away from Kant's

idealism, but Kant's challenge bears precisely on the ontological warrant for "giving in" to experience on this point. I do not raise this issue here in criticism of Kohlberg and Power; indeed, they clearly do not intend their argument as a "proof" of their suggested metaphysical turn (see for example *MD*, p. 246). I raise the issue only to note that, while such "proof" is a distinct task yet to be engaged, I will nonetheless assume, with Kohlberg and Power and for the purposes of this paper, the "correctness" of their metaphysical turn.

5. Kohlberg's understanding of the relation between moral reasoning and scientific reasoning is taken up in Ch. IX above.

6. Kohlberg and Power note that this claim is ambiguous at the lower stages (1-3) (*RM*, p. 359), but this is not crucial to my basic concern in this paper.

7. Indeed, it is not clear that Kohlberg's and Power's formulation, if interpreted literally, can itself legitimately disallow a broader understanding of religion which would include faith: for in distinguishing religion from faith, they nonetheless define religion as "*that part of faith . . .*" (*RM*, p. 347) (emphasis mine). But if that is what is meant, then religion would seem to be, on their own terms, a *specification* of faith. And since a specification (specific differentiation) occurs within, not outside, its appropriate genus, it would seem to follow, on Kohlberg's and Power's own terms, that religion must carry *within* it the element of faith.

8. My understanding of religion here, then, is similar to what Fowler means by faith. I would only note that I specify faith as religious in the first instance by virtue of its bearing on ultimacy, and not, as Fowler apparently does, by virtue of its connection with some particular institution taken to be religious. (Cf. J. Fowler, "Faith and the Structuring of Meaning," in Fowler and Vergote, *op. cit.*, p. 53). But see my further qualification of this point in Section V below.

9. For an expansion of my argument as sketched here, see my "History, Objectivity, and Moral Conversion," *The Thomist*, 37 (1973), esp. pp. 578-588. For what I take to be an analogous form of this argument cast in a more contemporary idiom, see the effort of Michael Polanyi to retrieve, in the context of the modern Western tradition of critical thought, the Augustinian--hence fiduciary, volitional, affective--roots of knowledge: *Personal Knowledge* (New York: Harper Torchbooks, 1964), p. 266 and *passim*.

In connection with my claim outlined here in the context of religion, see the arguments developed elsewhere in this volume regarding the importance, for adequate moral judgment and action, of volitional and affective factors (cf. especially the chapters on choice, character, and emotion).

10. *Summa Theologiae*, 1, q. 82, a. 4 *ad primum*.

11. *Ibid.*, I-II, q. 9, a. 1 *ad tertium*.

12. See the following quotation from Andre Hayen, which I think captures the heart of Aquinas's position as I have tried to express it here:

"Saint Thomas's perspective is . . . concrete; it is that of the actual exercise of human activity. The will is intrinsically constitutive of intellection, not as intellectual, but as *act* of intellection: the judgment finds its completion in a willed engagement, not as an act of intelligence, but as an *act* of knowledge" (my translation) "Le lien de la connaissance et du vouloir dans l'acte d'exister selon saint Tomas d'Aquin," *Doctor Communis*, 3 (1950), p. 88.

13. Strictly speaking, of course, Aquinas's claim is that charity, that is, love as a "supernatural" virtue, is the form of the virtues (See *S.T.* II-II, q. 23, a. 8; and *De Caritate*, a. III). The purpose of my suggestion here is merely to record one of the ontological foundations for such a claim.

14. *Summa Theologiae*, I-II, q. 1, a. 6.

15. See in this connection Karl Rahner, *Hearers of the Word* (New York: Herder and Herder, 1969), p. 105 and *passim*.

16. See the various studies cited by Fowler and Kohlberg and Power in the articles noted above. I would stress here, however, that though the studies of Kohlberg and Power may seem to be at odds with the general thesis I have advanced in this paper, I take those studies to be inconclusive insofar as they presuppose the restricted understanding of religion which I have rejected.

17. The analysis that follows does not necessarily carry the implication that the Christian understanding of God is the only one that involves, or could involve, the type of resolution I propose regarding the relation between God's acting and the acting of the entities of the world. I simply abstract from this question in light of the theme of the present paper, which concerns the fundamentalist Christian challenge to Kohlberg's program. Secondly, it suffices for the purposes of this paper that the understanding of God offered here in the name of Christianity be one of the logically possible ways of understanding the Christian God. It is not necessary for my purposes to defend the stronger claim that it is the only possible way of understanding the Christian God.

18. By this statement I do not mean that a full-blown sense of God as a creator *ex nihilo* is explicit in the Christian scriptures, but only that this is the interpretation of scripture which retrieves the full and proper sense of the Lordship of God which is central to scripture. For a study of the meaning of creation, see Kenneth L. Schmitz, *The Gift: Creation* (Milwaukee: Marquette University Press, 1982). Cf. also in connection with my brief treatment of the Christian understanding of God here: Robert Sokolowski, *The God of Faith and Reason* (Notre Dame: University of Notre Dame Press, 1982); John Courtney Murray, *The Problem of God* (New Haven: Yale University Press, 1964); and Joseph Ratzinger, *Introduction to Christianity* (New York: Seabury Press, 1970). Perhaps I should note, in view of some current tendencies to oppose creation and evolution, that creation as I understand it here--and indeed in what I take to be its properly Christian understanding--is quite compatible with a theistic theory of evolution.

19. For a rich sense of the way the notion of creation *ex nihilo*, and hence of the world as gift, transforms the conventional meaning of "the given," see Schmitz, *op. cit.*, pp. 34ff and *passim*.

20. See Sokolowski, *op. cit.*, pp. 21-23.

21. A good illustration of this general claim here might be found in Aquinas's working out of the meaning of natural law in light of St. Paul's understanding of law (See his *Treatise on Law*).

22. See the works of Murray and Sokolowski cited above. The claim is put trenchantly by Murray: "How odd of God it would have been had he made man reasonable so that, by being reasonable, man would become godless" (*op. cit.*, p. 76).

23. A different context would require a fuller development of the sense of this assertion. Briefly, its basis is that God's will as creator is manifest in the natural necessities of the things created. On the one hand, this seems to transform the context of morality by personalizing it, though such a personalization does not seem to involve the addition of another *formal* content or criterion for moral judgment. On the other hand, religion in its Christian form may legitimately make, if not "natural," then "positive," additions to morality, provided that those additions be interpreted as fulfillments rather than destructions of the natural order of things. A detailed treatment of this issue is beyond the scope of the present paper.

24. In connection with my argument here see the following: Walter Berns, *Freedom, Virtue, and the First Amendment* (Baton Rouge: Louisiana State University Press, 1957); Herbert Marcuse, "Repressive Tolerance," in *A Critique of Pure Tolerance*, edited by Robert Wolff, Barrington Moore, Jr., and Herbert Marcuse (Boston: Beacon Press, 1969); Glenn Olsen, "You Can't Legislate Morality: Reflections on a Bromide," *Communio: International Catholic Review*, 2 (1975), pp. 148-162; Walter Nicgorski, "Democracy and Moral-Religious Neutrality: American and Catholic Perspectives," *Communio*, 9 (1982), pp. 292-320; and my "On the Critical Study of Religion: Positivism, the First Amendment, and the *Roemer* Case," *Communio*, 3 (1976), pp. 300-317.

PART III

THE UNITY OF THE MORAL AGENT

CHAPTER XIII

THE PERSON, MORAL GROWTH

AND CHARACTER DEVELOPMENT

GEORGE F. McLEAN

For the last half century, from John Dewey's emphasis upon socialization to the more recent emphasis upon character, education has retained one general goal, namely, not merely to provide information but to develop the integral person. Though the need for content has often required reaffirmation, the time is long passed when schools were considered to be only repositories of knowledge upon which students might draw. The ancient respect and even veneration of one's teacher as one who creatively affected the student's life and personality survives in the conviction that, along with information and even knowledge in its broadest sense, real education and character development must promote the development of the student's powers to examine and evaluate, to create and communicate, to feel and to respond.

Nowhere is this more true, or more specifically intended, than in programs of moral education. Values clarification programs aim at bringing students to a greater consciousness of the values they possess; cognitive-developmental programs are directly concerned with the growth of the student's ability to make moral judgments. Progress in identifying more adequate goals and in enriching the content of such moral education programs depends upon improving our understanding of the nature of moral growth.

This, in turn, requires clarifying both the place of moral growth and character development in the life of the person and the nature of the person as a distinct and responsible agent in the community. Such understanding is not, of course, fabricated upon the moment, but is derived from the long experience of humankind. Hence, we should review our heritages for answers to three crucial questions about the person as the subject of a moral life and of moral education.

(a) Is the person only a set of roles constituted entirely in function of a structure or system in which one plays a particular part? If so, one could not refuse to do whatever the system demanded or tolerated. Or is the person a subject in his or her own right, with their proper dignity, heritage, goals and standards?

(b) Is there merely a stream of consciousness which becomes a person only upon the achievement of a certain level of self-awareness? If so, it becomes difficult to integrate the experiences of early childhood and the emotions of adult life which play so central a role in moral maturity. Or is the person an essentially free and responsible psychophysical subject?

(c) Finally, does a person's freedom consist merely in implementing a pattern of behavior encoded in one's nature. If so, there would be little place for the anguish of decision, the pains of moral growth, or the creativity of a moral life. Or is this free subject a creative center whose basic dynamism consists in realizing a unique inner harmony and outer community for which moral education should contribute both form and content?

To respond to such basic concerns those involved with education must have available the full resources of their heritages. At the same time, because the task of self-creation on the part of the student will reflect one or more of the multiple modes of our contemporary self-understanding, it can be expected that not everyone will subscribe to all the possible dimensions of meaning, nor certainly in the same mode or to the same degree. Hence, one involved in the moral education of others in a pluralistic society must be clear about the potential dimensions of the person: what they are,[1] how they are rooted in our cultural heritages, how they affect the aims and methods of moral education, and how they can be interrelated in a mutually reinforcing manner toward the development of a more integrated person and a more cohesive society. Indeed, there might be a certain correlation of the abovementioned questions both with the dimensions of the subject as a distinct-yet-related responsible moral agent and with the progressive development of the person throughout his or her life.

For orientation in this task let us begin by delineating the person by contrasting it to a number of other notions. These contrasts will serve subsequently as guideposts for a series of positive and progressively deepening insights regarding the nature of the person, their moral growth, and self- fulfillment.

First and most notably, persons are contrasted to possessions. We object most strongly to any suggestion whether in word, gesture, or deed by which a person is treated as a commodity subject to manipulation or as a mere means by which others attain their goals. This, indeed, has become a litmus test for acceptable behavior.[2] Secondly, persons are considered to be irreducible to the community. Any structures or situation which considers only the whole without taking account of the individual and his concerns is rejected precisely as depersonalizing. (See W. Nicgorski in Chap. XI above.) Thirdly and conversely, those who are so individualistic as to be insensitive to the concerns of others are themselves considered impersonal. These exclusions direct our search for the meaning of the human person toward a responsible self which is neither reducible to, nor independent of, the physical and human context in which one abides.

This positive notion of the person has not always had an identical or unchanging meaning. By natural growth, more than by mere accretion, the notion has managed to incorporate the great achievements of human self-discovery, for which it has been both the stimulus and the goal. This continuing process has been central to philosophy from its earliest days. Like all life processes, the search for the person has consisted in a sequence of important steps, each of which has resulted in a certain equilibrium or level of culture. In time each has been enriched and molded by subsequent discoveries. Seen over time this search appears to be the very heart of our personal life.

To look into this experience it will be advantageous to study the nature of the person through reflection on a series of paired and progressively deeper dimensions: first, as a role and as the one who lives out this role; second, as free self-consciousness and as the subject of that freedom; and third, as moral agent and as searching for one's moral development and fulfillment. The first member of each pair is integral to an understanding of the human person, moral growth and character development, but it requires also the corresponding member of that pair and evokes the pair on the next and deeper level.

ROLE AND INDIVIDUAL

Role

One means for finding the earliest meaning of a particular notion is to study the term by which it is designated. As earliest, this meaning tends to be more manifest and hence to remain current. The major study[3] on the origins of the term 'person' concludes that, of the multiple origins which have been proposed, the most probable refers to the mask used by actors in Greece and subsequently adopted in Rome. Some explain that this was called a *'persona'* because by 'sounding through' (*per-sonando*)[4] its single hole the voice of the wearer was strengthened, concentrated, and made to resound clearly. Others see the term as a transformation of the Greek term for the mask which symbolized the actor's role.[5] Hence, an original and relatively surface notion of person is the assumption of a character or the carrying out of a role. As such it has little to do with one's self; it is defined rather in terms of the set of relations which constitutes the plot or story-line of a play.

This etymology is tentative; some would document an early and more rich sense of person in homeric literature.[6] There can be no doubt, however, that the term has been used broadly in the above ethical sense of a role played in human actions. Ancient biblical literature described God as not being a respecter of persons, that is, of the roles played by various individuals.[7] The Stoics thought of this in cosmic terms, seeing the wise person either as writing their role or as interpreting a role determined by the Master. In either case, to be a wise person was to be consistent, to play out one's role in harmony with oneself and with reason as the universal law of nature. From this ethical sense of person as role it was but a short step to a similar legal sense. This generally is a distinct and characteristic relation, although, as Cicero noted, it could be multiple: "Three roles do I sustain . . . my own, that of my opponent, that of the judge."[8]

Far from being archaic,[9] the understanding of person as the playing of a role seems typical of much modern and American thought. John Dewey in *Reconstruction in Philosophy* characterized the essence of the modern mentality in just these terms: in the case of ancient or classic usage "we are dealing with something constant in *existence*, physical or metaphysical; in the other [modern] case, with something constant in *function* and operation."[10] The social and psychological sciences focus upon these roles or functions and in these terms attempt to construct, through operational definitions, their entire conceptual field.

This undergirds much of the progress in the social and behavioral sciences. As the same individual can play multiple roles, even in the same circumstances, studying the person in terms of roles makes it possible to identify specific dimensions of one's life for more precise investigation and to analyze serially the multiple relations which obtain in an interpersonal situation. William James, for example, distinguishes in this manner the self shown to family from that which one shows to professional colleagues or to God. Further, determining to pursue this exclusively on the basis of data which is subject to empirical verification[11] has made possible an immense collaborative effort to achieve a scientific understanding of human life.

Though much has been accomplished through understanding the person in terms of roles, there may have been a distant early warning of the limitations of this approach in Auguste Comte's (1798-1857) *Cours de philosophie positive*. By rejecting psychology as a scientific discipline and reducing all data concerning the person to either biology or sociology he ignored introspection and the corresponding dimensions of the individual's conscious life. The person was not only one who could play a role, but one whose total reality consisted in playing that role.

More recently Gabriel Marcel has pointed up a number of unfortunate consequences which derive from considering the person only in terms of roles or functional relations. For in that case no account can be taken of one's proper self-identity. If only "surface" characteristics are considered, while excluding all attention to "depth,"[12] then the person is empty; if the person can be analyzed fully in terms of external causes and relations it becomes increasingly devoid of intrinsic value. What is more, lack of personal identity makes it impossible to establish personal relations with others. Even that consistency between, or within, one's roles--which the Stoics as early proponents of this understanding of person considered to be the essence of a personal life--is left without foundation. Life could be reduced "in the words of Shakespeare 'to a tale told by an idiot'."[13]

The Individual

These difficulties suggest that attention must be directed to another level of meaning if the person is to find the resources required to play its roles. Rather than attempting to think of a role without an actor, it is important to look to the individual who assumes the role and expresses him or herself therein. Caution must be exercised here, however, lest the search for the subject or the self appear to reinforce the excesses of self-centeredness and individualism. This could be a special danger in the context of cultures whose positive stress on self-reliance and independence has been rooted historically in an atomistic understanding of individuals as single, unrelated entities. This danger is reflected, for example, in the common law understanding of judicial rulings, not as defining the nature of interpersonal relations, but simply as resolving conflicts between individuals whose lives happen to have intersected.

In this context it is helpful to note that when Aristotle laid the foundations for the Western understanding of the person he did so in the context of the Greek understanding of the physical universe as a unified, dynamic, quasi-life process in which all was included and all were related. Indeed, the term 'physical' was derived from the term for growth and the components of this process were seen always with, and in relation to, the others. (Similarly, modern physical theory identifies a uniform and all-inclusive pattern of relations such that any physical displacement, no matter how small, affects all other bodies). Within this unified pattern of relations the identification of multiple individuals, far from being destructive of unity, provides the texture required for personal life. Where individuals are differentiated by the moral tenor of their actions which in turn make a difference to other persons, distinctiveness becomes, not an impediment to, but a principle of, community.[14] (See Ch. XI above.)

In order better to appreciate the members of a community it is helpful to consider them on three progressively more specific dimensions, first as instances of a particular type, that is, as substances; secondly as existing, that is, as subsisting individuals; and thirdly as self-conscious, that is, as persons. The order in which these three will be considered is not accidental, for while it is necessary to be of a certain definite type, it is more important to exist as an individual in one's own right; for the person, finally, it is important above all that one be self-conscious and free. Hence, our exposition begins with substance and the subsisting individual in order to identify some general and basic--though not specific or exclusive--characteristics of the person, whose distinctive self-awareness and freedom will be treated in the following sections.

1. *Substance*. It was Aristotle who identified substance as the basic component of the physical order; his related insights remain fundamental to understanding the individual as the subject of moral life. His clue to this first discovery appears in language. Comparing the usage of such terms as "running," and "runner" we find that the first is applied to the second, which in turn, however, is not said of anything else.[15] Thus, one may say of Mary that she is running, but one may not say that she is another person, e.g., John. This suggests the need to distinguish things that can be realized only in another (as running is had only in a runner) whence they derive their identity, from those which have their identity in their own right (e.g., John, the runner). A first and basic characteristic of the moral subject, and indeed of any substance, is that it have its

identity in its own right rather than through another; only thus could a human being be responsible for one's action. Without substances with their distinct identities one could envisage only a structure of ideals and values inhabited, as it were, by agents. In this light the task of moral education would be merely to enable one to judge correctly according to progressively higher ideals. This, indeed, would seem to be the implicit context of Kohlberg's focus upon moral dilemmas which, as seen earlier in this volume, omits not only the other dimensions of moral development but this personal identity as well. Aristotle points instead to a world of persons realizing values in their actions. In their complex reality of body, affections and mind they act morally and are the subjects of moral education. (See W. Kirkpatrick in R. Knowles, ed., *The Psychological Foundations of Moral Education and Character Development*, the second volume of this series.)

Secondly, as the basic building blocks in the constitution of a world, these individuals are not merely undetermined masses. As the basic points of reference in discourse and the bases for the intelligibility for the real world these individual components must possess some essential determinateness, they must be of one or another kind or form. The individual, then, is not simply one thing rather than any other; he or she is a being of a definite--in this case, a human--kind,[16] relating to other beings each with its own nature or kind. Only thus can one's life in the universe have sense and be able to be valued.

Thirdly, being of a definite kind the individual has its own proper characteristics and is able to realize a specific or typical set of activities. These activities derive from, or are "born of" (from the latin, *natus*), the specific nature of the thing. The determination of what activity is moral will need to include not only the good to be derived from the action, but respect for the agent and his or her nature. (See Chs. VII and IX above.)

In the search for the subject of moral education, the work of Aristotle has made an essential contribution by directing our attention to three factors, namely: (a) individual beings, (b) who are particular instances of a definite kind, and hence (c) capable of specific types of activities. It should be noted that all three are concerned with the kind or type of the agent.[17] This is important, but it is not enough for moral education. One can know well enough what kind of thing a unicorn is but, as none has ever existed, they have never acted or entered the field of activity in which morality is found. Similarly, one might know what kind of musician is needed in order to complete an orchestra, but this does not mean that one is available to be engaged for a concert. In sum, in order to consider the field of moral action it is important to take account not only of the nature or kind of agent involved, but also of his or her existence and actions.

2. *Subsisting Individual*. Something of the greatest importance was bound to take place, therefore, when the mind expanded its range of

awareness beyond the nature of things to what Shakespeare was to call *the* question: "to be or not to be." At that point the mind became able to take explicit account not only of the kind, but of the existence of the individual, by which it is constituted in the order of actual, and hence of acting, beings.

From this there followed a series of basic implications for the reality of person. It would no longer be considered as simply the relatively placid distinct or autonomous instance of some specific type. Rather, it would be understood in a much more dynamic manner as existing. This means not only being in its own right or, as it were, 'standing on its own two feet' (subsisting), but bursting in among the realities of this world as a new and active center (existing). This understanding incorporates all the above-mentioned characteristics of the individual substance, and adds three more which are proper to existence, namely, being complete, independent, and dynamically open to actions and to new actualization. Since existing or subsisting individuals include not only persons but rocks and trees, however, these characteristics, though fundamental, still will not be exclusive to the person.

First, a person must be whole or complete. As regards its nature it must have all that is required to be of its distinctive kind, just as by definition a three digit number cannot be made up of but two digits. Hence, if humans are recognized to be by nature both body and mind or body and soul, then the human mind or soul without the body would be neither a subsisting individual nor, by implication, a person for it would lack a complete human nature. This is of special importance in view of the tendency of some to reduce the human person to only the mind, soul, or consciousness or to consider the person to be adequately protected if these alone are cared for. In fact the essential inclusion of body in the human person is as central to education as it is to human rights. The same, of course, is no less true of the mind or spirit in view of the tendency of others described by William James,[18] to reduce the person to "nothing but" the inert by-products of physiology, or functions of the structure of production and distribution of goods.

Further, the existing individual requires not merely a complete nature, but his or her proper existence. As existing the individual is not merely an instance of a specific nature or kind, but a concrete reality asserting oneself and dynamically struggling to achieve one's fulfillment. In the person this goes beyond merely walking a course whose every step is already charted; it includes all the unique, fully individual choices by which a life is lived. It is subject then to combinations of the precarious and the stable, of tragedy and triumph in its self-realization (See Ch. VI above). These were described by the American pragmatists and Continental existentialists as the very stuff of life, and hence by Dewey as the very stuff of education.

Secondly, as subsistent the person is independent. Being complete in its nature it is numerically individual and distinct from all else. In accord with this individual nature, one's existence is, in turn, unique, and establishes the subject as a being in its own right, independent of all else. This, of course, does not imply that the human or other living subject does not need nourishment, or that it was not generated by another: people do need people and much else besides. There is no question here of being self-sufficient or absolute. What is meant by independence is that the needs it has and the actions it performs are truly its own.

In turn, this means that in interacting with other subsistent individuals one's own contribution is distinctive and unique. This is commonly recognized at those special times when the presence of a mother, father, or special friend is required, and no one else will do. At other times as well, even when as a bus driver or a dentist I perform a standard service, my actions remain properly my own. This understanding is a prerequisite for education to responsibility in public as in private life. It is a condition too for overcoming depersonalization in a society in which we must fulfill ever more specialized and standardized roles.

Another dimension of this independence is that the human person as subsisting cannot simply be absorbed or assimilated by another. As complete in oneself one cannot be part of another, for as independent in existence one is distinct from all else. Hence, one cannot be assumed or taken up by any other person or group in such wise as to lose one's identity. In recent years awareness of this characteristic has generated a strong reaction against the tendencies of mass society totally to absorb the person and to reduce all to mere functions in a larger whole called the state, the industrial complex, or the consumer society. (See Ch. XI above.)

As noted above it is perhaps the special challenge of the present day, however, to keep this awareness of one's distinctive independence from degenerating into selfishness, to keep individuality from becoming individualism. The individual existent, seen as sculpted out of the flow and process of the physical universe, cannot be rightly thought of as isolated. Such an existent is always *with* others, depending on them for birth, sustenance and expression. In this context, to be distinct or individual is not to be isolated or cut off, but to be able to relate more precisely and intensively to others. My relation to the chair upon which I sit and the desk upon which I write is not diminished but made possible by the distinction and independence of the three of us. Their retention of their distinctness and distinctive shapes enables me to integrate them into my task of writing. Because I depend still more intimately upon food, I must correlate more carefully its distinctive characteristics with my precise needs and capacities. On the genetic level it is the careful choice of distinctive strains that enables the development of a new individual with the desired characteristics. On the social level the more personable the members of the group the greater and more intense is its unity. Moving thus from instruments such as desks, to alimentation, to lineage, to society suggests that as one moves upward through the levels of beings distinctness, far from being antithetic to community, is in fact its basis. This gives hope that at its higher reaches, namely, in the moral life, the distinctiveness of autonomy and freedom may not need to be compromised, but may indeed be the basis for a community of persons bound together in mutual love and respect.

The third characteristic of the subsistent individual to be considered is this openness to new actualization and to interrelation with others. The existence by which one erupted into this world of related subjects is not simply self-contained; it is expressed in a complex symphony of actions which are properly one's own: thus, running can be said only of an existing individual, such as Mary, who runs. What is more, actions determine their subject, for it is only by running that Mary herself is constituted precisely as a runner. This will be central to the last part of this study: the person as moral agent.

It is important too for our relations to and with others. For the actions into which our existence flows, while no less our own, reach beyond ourselves. The same action which makes us agents shapes the world around us and, for good or ill, communicates to others. All the plots of all the stories ever told are about this; but their number pales in comparison with all the lives ever lived, each of which is a history of personal interactions.[19] The actions of an individual existent reflect one's individuality with its multiple possibilities, and express this to and with others. It is in this situation of dynamic openness,[20] of communication and of community that the moral growth of persons takes place. As subsistent therefore the person is characteristically a being, not only in oneself, but *with* other beings. About this more must be said below.

To summarize: thus far we have seen the early derivation of the notion of person from mask. For this to evolve into the contemporary notion of person a strong awareness both of the nature and of the existence of independent individuals needed to be developed. The first was achieved by the Greeks who identified within the one physical process basically different types of things. Substances are the individual instances of these specific types or natures. This provides the basis for consciousness of one's own nature and for relating to others in its terms within the overall pattern of nature(s).

There were limitations to such a project, for in its terms alone one would be ultimately but an instance of one's nature; in the final analysis the goal of a physical being would be but to continue one's species through time. This was true for the Greeks and may still be a sufficient basis for the issues considered in sociobiology. It does not allow for adequate attention to the person's unique and independent reality. This required the subsequent development of an awareness of existence as distinct from nature or essence, as that by which one enters into the world and is constituted as a being in one's own right. On this basis the subsisting individual can be seen to be whole and independent, and hence the dynamic center of action in this world.

Still more is required, however, for the above characteristics, while foundational for a person, are had as well by animals and trees. These too, each in its own way, are wholes that are independent and active in this world. In addition to the above realities of substance and of subsisting individual, therefore, it is necessary to identify that which is distinctive of the human subsistent and constitutes it finally as personal, namely, self-consciousness and freedom.

THE PERSON: A SELF-CONSCIOUS AND FREE SUBJECT

Self-consciousness and will had been central to philosophies of the person in classical times; indeed, at one point Augustine claimed that men were nothing else than will. After Descartes' reformulation of metaphysics in terms of the thinking self, however, the focus upon self-consciousness by John Locke and upon the will by Kant brought the awareness of these distinctive characteristics of the person to a new level of intensity and exclusivity. This constituted a qualitatively new and distinctively modern understanding of the person. It is necessary to see in what these characteristics consist and how they relate to the subsisting individual analyzed above.

Self-Consciousness and Freedom

John Locke undertook to identify the nature of the person within the context of his general effort to provide an understanding which would enable people to cooperate in building a viable political order. This concentration upon the mind is typical of modern thought and of its contribution to our appreciation of the person. By focusing upon knowledge Locke proceeded to elaborate, not only consciousness in terms of the person, but the person in terms of consciousness. He considered personal identity to be a complex notion composed from the many simple ideas which constitute our consciousness. By reflection we perceive that we perceive and thereby are able to be, as it were, present to ourselves and to recognize ourselves as distinct from all other thinking things.[21] Memory, which is also an act of consciousness, enables us to recognize these acts of consciousness in different times and places. Locke saw the memory, by uniting present acts of awareness with similar past acts, as not merely discovering but as creating personal identity. This binding of myself as past consciousness to myself as present consciousness constitutes the continuing reality of the person. Essentially, it is a private matter revealed directly only to oneself, and only indirectly to other persons.

Because Locke's concern for knowledge was part of his overriding concern to find a way to build social unity in a divided country he saw his notion of the self as the basis of an ethic for both private and public life. As conscious of pleasure and pain the self is capable of happiness or misery, "and so is concerned for itself."[22] What is more, happiness and misery matter only inasmuch as they enter one's self-consciousness as a matter of self-concern directing one's activities. He sees the pattern of public morality, with its elements of justice as rewarding a prior good act by happiness and as punishing an evil act by misery, to be founded upon this identity of the self as a continuing consciousness from the time of the act to that of the reward or punishment. 'Person' is the public name of this self as open to public judgment and social response; it is "a forensic term appropriating actions and their merit."[23]

This early attempt to delineate the person on the basis of consciousness locates a number of factors essential for personhood such as the importance of self-awareness, the ability to be concerned for oneself, and the basis this provides for the notions of responsibility and public accountability. These are the foundations of his *Letters Concerning Toleration* which were to be of such great importance in the development of subsequent social and political structures in many parts of the world.

There are reasons to believe, however, that, while correct in focusing upon consciousness, he did not push his analysis far enough to integrate the whole person. Leibniz, in his *New Essays Concerning Human Understanding*, was quick to point out some of these reasons in a detailed response. Centering personal identity in consciousness, Locke distinguished it from the notion of the person as that which could be identified by a body of a particular shape. This led him to admit that it is conceivable that the one consciousness, self or person could exist in different bodies a thousand years remote one from another[24] or, conversely, that multiple selves could inhabit the same body.

This is more than an issue of "names ill-used";[25] it is symptomatic of the whole cluster of problems which derive from isolating human consciousness from the physical identity of the human self. These include problems not only regarding communication with other persons for which one depends upon physical signs, but regarding the life of the person in a physical world in whose unity and harmony one's consciousness has no real share, and indeed in contrast to which it is defined.[26] Recently, existential phenomenologists have begun to respond to the perverse, desicating effect this has had even upon consciousness itself, while environmentalists have pointed up the destruction it has wrought upon nature.

This implies a problem for personal identity itself. Locke would claim that this resides in the continuity established by linking the past with the present in one's memory.[27] But, as there is no awareness of a substantial self from which this consciousness proceeds,[28] what remains is but a sequence of perceptions or a flow of consciousness recorded by memory.

Finally, Leibniz would question Locke's claim to have provided even that public or forensic notion of the self by which he sought to provide a sufficient basis for legal and political relations. Memory can deal with the past and the present, but not with the future; whereas planning and providing for the future is the main task of a rationally ordered society. Further, Locke's conclusion, that since the self is consciousness the same self could inhabit many bodies of different appearances, would undermine the value of public testimony, and thereby the administration of justice.[29] Though self-consciousness is certainly central and distinctive of the person, more is required for personhood than a

338 *The Person, Moral Growth and Character Development*

sequence of consciousness, past and present.

Another approach was attempted by Kant whose identification of the salient characteristics of the person has become a standard component for modern sensitivity. Whereas Locke had developed the notion of the person in terms of consciousness predicated upon experience, Kant developed it on the requirements of an ethics based upon will alone. Both the strengths and the weaknesses of this approach to the person lie in his effort to lay for ethics a foundation that is independent of experience. (See Ch. XII above.) He did so because he considered human knowledge to be essentially limited to the spatial and temporal orders and unable to explain its own presuppositions. Whatever be thought of this, by looking within the self for a new and absolute beginning he led the modern mind to a new awareness of the reality and nature of the person.

For Kant the person is above all free, both in oneself and in relation to others; in no sense is the person to be used by others as a means. From this he concluded that it is essential to avoid any dependence (heteronomy) on anything beyond oneself and, within oneself, on anything other than one's own will. The fundamental thrust of that will is its unconditional command to act lawfully; this must be the sole basis for an ethics worthy of man. In turn, "the only presupposition under which . . . (the categorical imperative) is alone possible . . . is the Idea of freedom.[30] (See Ch. VII above.)

As free the person must not be legislated to by anyone or on the basis of anything else; to avoid heteronomy one must be an end-in-oneself. It was Kant's self-described goal to awaken interest in the moral law through this "glorious ideal" of a universal realm of persons as ends-in-themselves (rational beings).[31] The person, then, is not merely independent, as is any subject; he is a law-making member of society. This means that the person has not only value which is to be protected and promoted, but true dignity as well, for he is freely bound by and obeys laws which he gives to himself.[32] As this humanity is to be respected both in oneself and in all others one must act in such wise that if one's actions were to constitute a universal law they would promote a cohesive life for all rational agents.

This "glorious ideal" has been perhaps the major contribution to the formation of our modern understanding of ourselves as persons. At the minimum, it draws a line against what is unacceptable, namely, whatever is contrary to the person as an end-in-him-or-herself, and sets thereby a much needed minimal standard for action. At the maximum, as with most *a priori* positions, it expresses an ideal for growth by pointing out the direction, and thereby providing orientation, for the development of the person. In Kohlberg's schema of moral development it constitutes the sixth or highest stage, and hence the sense and goal of his whole project--though he notes rightly that this is not an empirically available notion. (See Ch. XII above.)

Further, this bespeaks a certain absoluteness of the individual will which is essential if the person is not to be subject to domination by the circumstances he encounters. If one must be more than a mere function of one's environment-whether this be one's state, or business, or neighborhood-then Kant has made a truly life-saving observation in noting that the law of the will must extend beyond any one good or particular set of goods. (In Ch. V above.)

Nevertheless, there are reasons to think that still more is needed for an understanding of the person. In Part I of his *Foundations of the Metaphysics of Morals* Kant correctly rules out anything other than, or heteronomous to, human freedom and will as an adequate basis for ethics, at least as far as using one's own ability to think and to decide are concerned. Nor does he omit the fact that these individuals live their lives with others in this world. As the good is mediated by *their* concrete goods, however, a role for experience must be recognized if right reason is to conform to the real good in things. (See Chs. IX and X above.) Further, there is need to know more of the reality of the person in order to understand, (a) not only how will and freedom provide the basis for ethical behavior, but (b) by what standards or values behavior can be judged to be ethical and (c) how ethical behavior is integral to the project of the person's self-realization. (Various facets of this are treated in all the chapters above.) Something more than a postulation of freedom (along with the immortality of the soul and God) is essential to enable the development of the person to be guided throughout by his "glorious ideal."

In sum, Locke and Kant have contributed essentially to delineating the nature of the person for the modern mind. Both have pointed up that which distinguishes the person from other subjects. Focusing upon knowledge, Locke showed the person to be an identity of continuing consciousness which is self-aware and "concerned for itself." Focusing upon the will and its freedom, Kant showed the person to be an end--in-itself.

By attending directly to consciousness and freedom, however, both left problems which are similar and of great importance to the present project. The first regards the way in which consciousness and freedom are realized in the person as a unique identity with a proper place in society and indeed in reality as a whole. It is true, as Locke says, that the term person expresses self-aware and continuing consciousness, as well as its status in the public forum. But, for moral education one needs more than an isolated view of that which is most distinctive of man; one needs to know what the person is in his or her entirety, how one is able to stand among other persons as a subject, and how in freedom one is to undertake one's rightful responsibilities. One educates not consciousness or freedom, but conscious and free subjects or persons. Further, it is necessary to understand the basis of the private, as well as the public, life of the person, for one is more than a role, a citizen, or a function of state. The second problem regards the way in which the person can attain his goal of full self-awareness, freedom, and responsibility, namely, how the person can achieve his or her fulfillment through time and with others.

In sum, what Locke and Kant discovered about the person by considering self-awareness for the political arena, or in the abstract, needs now to be integrated with what was seen regarding the individual in Part I in order to constitute the integral person as a rational and free subject.

The Self Conscious and Free Subject

While it has been said that ancient thinkers had no concept of the person, a very important study by Catherine De Vogel[33] has shown that there was indeed a significant sense of person and of personality among the ancient Greeks and Romans, as well as a search for its conditions and possibilities. It will be helpful to look at this in order to identify some of the cultural resources for understanding the way in which self-consciousness and freedom are rooted in the subject and constitute the person with which moral education is concerned. Above, we saw a certain progression from the Greek philosophical notion of the individual as an instance of a general type to a more ample existential sense of the subject as an independent whole, which nonetheless shares with others in the same specific nature. It is time now to see how this relates to self-consciousness and freedom.

The Greeks had a certain sense for, and even fascination with, individuals in the process of grappling with the challenge to live their freedom. T.B.L. Webster notes that "Homer was particularly interested in them (his heroes) when they took difficult decisions or exhibited characteristics which were not contained in the traditional picture of the fighting man."[34] In the final analysis, however, the destiny of his heroes was determined by fate, from which even Zeus could not free them. Hence, an immense project of liberation was needed in order to appreciate adequately the full freedom of the moral agent.

This required establishing: (a) that the universe is ruled by law, (b) that a person could have access to this law through reason, and (c) that the person has command of his relation to this law. These elements were developed by Heraclitus around 500 B.C. He saw that the diverse physical forces could not achieve the equilibrium required in order to constitute a universe without something which is one. This cosmic, divine law or Logos is the ruling principle of the coherence of all things, not only in the physical, but in the moral and social orders. A person can assume the direction of his life by correcting his understanding and determining his civil laws and actions according to the Logos, which is at once divine law and nature. In this lies wisdom.[35]

This project has two characteristics, namely, self-reflection and self-determination. First, as the law or Logos is not remote, but within man--"The soul has a Logos within it"[36] --the search for the Logos is also a search for oneself: "I began to search for myself."[37] Self-reflection is then central to wisdom. Second, the attainment of wisdom requires on the part of man a deliberate choice to follow the universal law. This implies a process of interior development by which the Logos which is within "increases itself."[38]

A similar pattern of thought is found in the Stoic philosophers for whom there is a principle of rationality or "germ of logos" of which the soul is part, and which develops by natural growth.[39] A personal act is required to choose voluntarily the law of nature, which is also the divine will.

These insights of Heraclitus, though among the earliest of the philosophers, were pregnant with a number of themes which correspond to Kant's three postulates for the ethical life: the immortality of the soul, freedom and God. The first of these would be mined by subsequent thinkers in their effort to explore the nature of the person as a physical subject that is characteristically self-conscious and free. The implications of Heraclitus' insight that the multiple and diverse can constitute a unity only on the basis of something that is one gradually became evident, binding the personal characteristics of self-consciousness and freedom to the subject with its characteristics of wholeness, independence and interrelatedness. The first step was Plato's structure for integrating the multiple instances of a species by their imitation of, or participation in, the idea or archetype of that species.[40] This, in turn, images still higher and more central ideas, and ultimately the highest idea which is inevitably the Good or the One.

Aristotle took the second step by applying the same principle to the internal structure of living beings. He concluded that the unity of their disparate components could be explained only by something one, which he termed the soul or *psyche*, whence the term 'psychology.' The body is organized by this form which he described as "the first grade of actuality of a natural body having life potentially in it."[41] For Aristotle, however, the unifying principle of a physical subject could not be also the principle of man's higher mental life, his life of reason. Hence, there remained the need to understand the person as integrating self-consciousness and freedom in a subject which is nonetheless physical.

Over one-thousand years later Thomas Aquinas took this third step, drawing out of Heraclitus' insight its implications for the unity of the person with its full range of physical and mental life. He did not trace the physical to one form or soul and the higher conscious life to another principle existing separately from the body as had the Aristotelian commentators, nor did he affirm two separate souls as did Bonaventure. Rather, Thomas showed that there could be but one principle or soul for the entire person, both mind and body. He did this by rigorously carrying out under the principle of non-contradiction the implications of the existence of the subject noted above. One subject could have but one existence --lest it be not one but two. This existence in turn could pertain to but one essence or nature, again lest it be and not be of that nature; and for the same reason the one essence could be of but one form. Hence, there could be only one formal principle or soul for both the physical and the free self-conscious dimensions of a person. This rendered obsolete Aristotle's duality of these principles for man and founded the essential and integral humanness of both mind and body in the unity of the one person.[42]

This progression of steps leading to the one principle, which enables that which is complex to constitute nonetheless a unity, points in the person to the one form which is commonly called the soul. By this single formal principle what Locke articulated only as a disembodied consciousness and Kant as an autonomous will are able to exist as a properly human subject. This is physical truly but not exclusively, for it transcends the physical to include also self-consciousness and freedom. Similarly, it exists in its own right, yet does so in such wise that it exists essentially with others as a person in society.

There are pervasive implications for education in such an integration of the physical with the self-conscious dimensions of the person through a single principle. One does not become a person when one is accepted by society; on the contrary, by the form through which one is a person one is an autonomous end-in-oneself and has claim to be responded to as such by others. Hence, though for his or her human development the person has a unique need for acceptance, respect and love, the withholding of such acceptance by others--whether individuals, families or states--does not deprive them of their personhood. One does not have to be accepted in order to have a claim to acceptance. (Hence, even in circumstances of correction and punishment, when a person's actions are being explicitly repudiated, he cannot be treated as a mere thing). The right to an education is based within the person who has claims or human rights which must be responded to by family and society.

Similarly, it is not necessary that the person manifest in overt behavior signs of self-awareness and responsibility. From genetic origin and physical form it is known that the infant and young child is an individual human developing according to a single unifying and integrating principle of both its physical and its rational life.[43] The rights and the protection of a human person belong to a person by right prior to an ability consciously to conceive or to articulate them. Further, the physical actions of young children through which they express themselves in their own way and respond to others are truly human. Indeed, though the earlier the stage in life the more physical the manner of receiving and expressing affection, the earliest months and years appear to be the most determinative of one's lifetime ability to relate to others with love and affection.

Finally, attempts to modify the behavior of a person must proceed according to distinctively human norms if they are not to be destructive. Despite at earlier life stages greater operational similarities to some animals, only by an abstraction can infants and very young children be said to be small animals. They are, in fact, human persons and integrally so in each of their human actions and interactions. Not to attend to this is to fail to realize who in fact is being educated to the detriment and dishonor of both the person and the educative process.

There is a second insight of great potential importance in the thought of Heraclitus. When he refers to the Logos[44] as being very deep he suggests multiple dimensions of the soul. Indeed, it must be so if human life is complex and its diverse dimensions have their principle in the one soul. Plato thought of these as parts of the soul; in these terms the development of oneself as a person would consist in bringing these parts into proper subordination one to another. This state is called justice, the "virtue of the soul."[45] Both the *Republic* and the *Laws* reflect amply his concern for education, character formation, and personal development understood as the process of attaining that state of justice. The way to this is progressive liberation from captivity by the objects of sense knowledge and sense desires through spiritual training, as described in the *Phaedo* and the *Republic*. All this prepares the way for what is essential, namely, the contemplation of the transcendent Good. This alone establishes that inner harmony of soul through which the person is constituted as free and responsible, both in principle and in act. Because this vision, not only of some goods, but of the transcendent Good, cannot be communicated by teaching but remains "an extremely personal interior vision,"[46] the uncalculating and unmeasured love shared in family, Church and other communities has special importance for moral education.

By the human form or soul the human individual as a person is open in principle, not only to particular states of affairs or events, but to the one source, logos and goal of all. (See Ch. XI above.) Through this, in turn, one is able to take account of the full meaning of each thing and freely to relate oneself to others in the coordinating virtue of philanthropia, the love of all mankind.[47] As it is of foundational importance for a truly moral life to have not merely access to some goods, but an ability to evaluate them in terms of the Good, the form or soul as the single organizing and vivifying principle of the person is the real foundation for the person as an end in oneself.

Correlatively, recent thought has made crucial strides toward reintegrating the person in one's world. The analytic process of identifying the components of the world process initiated by the Greeks was inherently risky, for any imperfection in the understanding of personal identity would distract from grounding the person in the One. Cumulatively, the intensive modern concentration upon freedom in terms of self-consciousness would generate an isolating and alienating concentration upon self.[48]

Some developments in recent thought have made important contributions to correcting this individualist--even potentially solipsist---bias. One is the attention recently paid to language and to the linguistic character of the person. Our consciousness is not only evoked, but shaped, by the pattern of the language in which we are nurtured. In our highly literate culture--many would say in all cultures--the work of the imagination which accompanies and facilitates that of the intellect is primarily verbal. Hence, rather than ideas being developed and then merely expressed by language, our thought is born in language. As this language is not one's private creation but that of our community over a long period, conscious acts, even about ourselves, involve participation in that community. To say that our nature is linguistic is to say that it is essentially with others.

A similar point, but on another level of insight, was developed by Martin Heidegger and laid the basis for the stress among many existential thinkers on the importance of considering the person as being in community. As conscious and intentional, one is essentially, not closed within oneself, but open to the world; one's self-realization depends upon and indeed consists in one's being in the world. Therefore it is not possible to think of persons in themselves and then to add some commerce with their surroundings; instead persons exist and can be conceived only as beings-in-the-world. Here the term 'in' expresses more than a merely spatial relation; it adds an element of being acquainted or familiar with, of being concerned for, and of sharing. At root this is the properly personal relation.[49]

From what was said of being-in-the-world it follows that the person is also being-with-others, for one is not alone in sharing in this world. Just as I enter into and share in the world, so also do other persons. Hence, as essentially sharing-in-the-world, our being is also essentially a sharing-with-others; the world of the person is a world in which we are essentially with others. In this light a study of the existence of the rational subject with its hopes and its efforts toward self-realization with others must center ultimately upon understanding the moral development of the person through education. (See Ch. XI above and its reference to the work of K. Schmitz.)

MORAL GROWTH AND THE DEVELOPMENT OF CHARACTER

Recent advances in this project are being made by interweaving two main streams of thought regarding the person: one considers the subject as existing in one's own right as conscious and free; the other situates this consciousness and freedom in the person as acting in the world with other persons. Together they provide a context for understanding the development of the moral awareness of the person.

The Person as Moral Agent

In Aristotle's project of distinguishing the components of the physical process actions and attributes were found to be able to exist and to be intelligible only in a substance which existed in its own right. (There could be no running without a runner.) Actions, as distinct from the substantive nature or essence, could appear to be added thereto in a relatively external or "quantitative" manner. Subsequent developments in understanding the subject in terms of existence have provided a protection against this exernalism. In relation to existence, essence does not merely specify the specific nature or kind of the thing; it is rather the way in which each thing is or each living being lives. Hence, for a person it implies and calls for the full range of activities of a human being. Indeed, essence is often termed nature (from *natus* or born) precisely as that from which these life acts derive.[50] These actions, in turn, cannot be mere additions to the person; they are the central determinants of the quality of one's very life. It is not just that one can do more or less, but that by so doing one becomes a more or less kind, loving, or generous person.

A person should be understood also in terms of his or her goals, for activities progressively modify and transform one in relation to the perfection of which one is by nature capable and which one freely chooses. Thus, though infants are truly and quite simply human beings, they are good only in an initial sense, namely, as being members of the human species. What they will become, however, lies in the future; hence they begin to be categorized as good or bad people only after and in view of their actions. Even then it is thought unfair to judge or evaluate persons at an early age, before it can be seen how they will "turn out" or what they will "make of themselves," that is, what character and hence constant pattern of action they will develop.

Further, one's progress or lack thereof can be judged only in terms of acting in a manner proportionate to one's nature. A horse may be characterized as good or bad on the basis of its ability to run, but not to fly. One must be true to one's nature, which in that sense serves as a norm of action; in this new sense I am a law to myself, namely, I must never act as less than one having a human nature with its self consciousness and freedom. (See Chs. VII and IX above.) Below we shall see a way in which being true to this nature implies constituting both my self and my world.

Boethius defined classically the person as "an individual substance of a rational nature."[51] In this Locke focused upon self-consciousness. Conscious nature can be understood on a number of levels. First, it might be seen as a reflection or passive mirroring in man of what takes place around him. This does not constitute new being; but merely understands what is already there. Secondly, if this consciousness is directed to the self it can be called self-knowledge and makes of the subject an object for one's act of knowledge. Thirdly, consciousness can regard one's actions properly as one's own. By concerning the self precisely as the subject of one's own actions, it makes subjective what had been objective in the prior self-knowledge; it is reflexive rather than merely reflective.

This self-conscious experience depends upon the objective reality of the subject with all the characteristics described above in the section on the self conscious and free subject. This, in turn, is shaped by the reflexive and hence free experiences of discovering, choosing, and committing oneself. In these reflexive acts the subject in a sense constitutes oneself, being manifested or disclosed to oneself as concrete, distinct, and indeed unique. This is the distinctively personal manner of self actuation of the conscious being or person.

The result for the person is a unique realization of that independence which above was seen to characterize all subsistent individuals. Beyond the mirroring of surrounding conditions and of those things that happen to one, beyond even the objective realization of oneself as affected by those events, the person exists reflexively as their subject and as a source of action. As a person one has an inward, interior life of which one alone is the responsible source. This implies for the person an element of mystery which can never be fully explicated or exhausted. Much can be proposed by other persons and things, much can even be imposed upon me. But my self-consciousness is finally my act and no one else's. How I assess and respond to my circumstances is finally my decision, which relates to, but is never simply the result of, exterior factors. Here finally lies the essence of freedom, of which the ability to choose between alternatives (see Ch. V above) is but one implication. What is essential for a free life is not that I always retain an alternative, but that I can determine myself and carry through with consistency the implications of my self-determination even, and at times especially, in the most straightening of circumstances. In this the personal finally transcends that growth process originally called the *physis* or the physical and has been considered rightly to be spiritual as well.

This, of course, is not to imply isolation from one's physical and social world; rather it bespeaks in the world a personal center which is self-aware and self-determining. More than objective consciousness of oneself as acting, the inward reflexion at the origin of my action is that according to which I freely determine[52] and experience myself as the one who acts in freedom. The bond of consciousness with action as deriving from self-determination is crucial for a full recognition of subjectivity. It protects this from reduction to the subjectivism of an isolated consciousness which, being separated from action, would be finally more arbitrary than absolute.

Self-determination in action has another implication: in originating an action the person's experience is not merely of that action as happening to or in him, but of a dynamism in which he participates efficaciously. As a self I experience myself immanently as wholly engaged in acting and know this efficacy to be properly my own, my responsibility. Hence, by willing the good or evil character of an action, I specify, not only the action which results, but myself as the originator of that action.

Finally, I am aware of my responsibility for results of my actions which extend beyond myself and shape my world. The good or evil my actions bring about is rooted in good or evil decisions on my part. In making choices which shape my world I form also myself for good or evil. By their subjective character actions become part of the person's unique process of self-realization.[53]

Action then manifests an important dimension of the person.[54] On the one hand, the need to act shows that the person, though a subject and independent, is not at birth perfect, self-sufficient or absolute. On the contrary, persons are conscious of perfection that they do not possess, but toward which they are dynamically oriented. The person is then essentially active and creative.

On the other hand, this activity is essentially marked by responsibility. This implies that, while the physical or social goods that one can choose are within one's power, they do not overpower one. Whatever their importance, in the light of the person's openness to the good as such one can always overrule the power of their attraction. When one does choose them it is the person--not the goods--that is responsible for that choice.

Both of these point to two foundations of the person's freedom, and hence of one's ability to be a self-determining end-in-oneself. First, one's mind or intellect is oriented, not to one or another true thing or object of knowledge, but to truth itself and hence to whatever is or can be. Second and in a parallel manner, the person's will is not limited to--or hence by--any particular good or set of goods. Rather, because oriented to the Good itself, it is freely open to any and all goods.

Moral Growth and Character Development

In view of this it is time to look more closely into the relation of the person to the good, for it is there that one finds the drama of the self-realization of the person and the development of one's moral life. The good is first manifest in one's experience as the object of desire, namely, as what is sought when absent. (See Chs. III, VIII and X.) This implies that the good is basically what completes a being; it is the "per-fect," understood in its etymological sense as that which is completed or realized through and through. Hence, once the good or perfection is achieved it is no longer desired or sought, but enjoyed. This is reflected in the manner in which each thing, even a stone, retains the being or reality it has and resists reduction to non-being or nothing. The most that we can do is to change or transform a thing into something else; we cannot annihilate it. Similarly, a plant or tree given the right conditions grows to full stature and fruition. Finally, an animal protects its life--fiercely if necessary--and seeks out the food needed for its strength. Food, in turn, as capable of contributing to animal's realization or perfection, is in this regard an auxiliary good or means.

In this manner things as good, that is, as actually realizing some degree of perfection, are the basis for an interlocking set of relations. These relations are based upon both the actual perfection things possess and the potential perfection they lack but to which they are directed. The good is dynamic both as attracting when it has not yet been attained and as constituting one's fulfillment upon its attainment. Goods then are not arbitrary or simply a matter of wishful thinking; they are rather the full development of things and all that contributes thereto. In this ontological or objective sense all beings are good to the extent that they exist and thereby can contribute to the perfection of others.

1. *Values*. The moral good is a more narrow field; it concerns only one's free and responsible actions. This has the objective reality of the ontological good noted above, for it concerns real actions which stand in distinctive relation to our own perfection and that of others, and indeed to the physical universe and to God as well. Hence many possible patterns of actions could be objectively right because they promote the good of those involved. Others, precisely as inconsistent with the real good of the persons or things, are objectively disordered or misordered.

Because the realm of objective relations is almost numberless whereas our actions are single it is necessary not only to choose in general between the good and the bad, but in each case to choose which of the often innumerable possibilities one will render concrete. However broad or limited the options, the act as responsible and moral is essentially dependent upon its being willed by a subject. In order to follow the emergence of the field of concrete moral action, it is important to examine therefore not only the objective aspect, namely, the nature of the persons, actions, and things involved. In addition one must consider the action in relation to the subject, namely, to the person who in the context of their society and culture appreciates and values the good of this action, chooses it over its alternatives, and eventually wills its actualization.

The term 'value' here is of special note. It was derived from the economic sphere where it meant the amount of a commodity by which it attained a certain worth. This is reflected also in the term 'axiology' whose root means "weighing as much" or "worth as much." It requires an objective content-the good must really "weigh in," and make a real difference. But the term 'value' expresses this good especially as related to wills which actually acknowledge it as a good and as desirable.[55] Thus, different groups of persons or individuals, and at different periods, have distinct sets of values. They are sensitive to and prize a distinct set of goods or, more likely, establish a distinctive ranking in the degree to which they prize various goods. By so doing they delineate among the limitless order of objective goods a certain pattern of values which, to an extensive degree, mirrors their corporate free choices and constitutes a basic component of their culture.

By giving shape to the culture this constitutes as well the prime pattern and gradation of goods which persons born into that culture experience from their earliest years. In these terms that they interpret their developing relations. Young persons peer out at the world through a lens, as it were, formed by their family and culture and reflecting the pattern of choices made by that community throughout its history, often in its most trying circumstances. Like a pair of glasses this does not create the object; but it does focus attention upon certain of the goods involved rather than upon others. This becomes the basic orienting factor for one's affective and emotional life. In time, it encourages and reinforces certain patterns of action which, in turn, reinforce this pattern of values.

2. *Virtues.* Martin Heidegger describes a process by which the field of moral action is gradually shaped by a subject. It consists in the person's transcending oneself or breaking beyond mere self-concern. In this one projects outward as a being whose very nature is to share with others for whom one cares and is concerned. In this process one constitutes new purposes or goals for the sake of which action is to be undertaken. In relation to these goals certain combinations of possibilities, with their natures and norms take on particular importance and begin thereby to enter into the makeup of one's world of meaning. In this light freedom becomes more than mere spontaneity, more than choice as examined in Ch. V above, and more even than self-determination in the sense of causing oneself to act as described above in the present chapter. It shapes--the phenomenologist would say even that it constitutes--my world as the ambit of my human decisions and dynamic action.[56] This is the making of myself as a person in a community.

To see this it is necessary to look more closely at the dynamic openness and projection which characterize the concrete person--not only in one's will, but in one's body and psyche as well. In order to be truly self-determining the person must not merely moderate a bargaining session among these three, but constitute a new and active dynamism in which all dimensions achieve their properly personal character.[57]

Bodily or somatic dynamisms, such as the pumping of blood, are basically non-reflective and reactive. They are implemented through the nervous system in response to stimuli; generally they are below the level of human consciousness, from which they enjoy a degree of autonomy. Nonetheless, they are in harmony with the person as a whole, of which they are an integral dimension. As such they are implicit in my conscious and self-determined choices regarding personal action with others in this world.

Dynamisms of the psyche are typified by emotivity. In some contrast to the more reactive character of lower bodily dynamism and in a certain degree to the somatic as a whole, these are based rather within the person. They include, not only affectivity, but sensation and emotions as well. These feelings range from some which are physical to others which are moral, religious and aesthetic. Such emotions have two important characteristics. First, they are not isolated or compartmentalized, but include and interweave the various dimensions of the person. Hence, they are crucial to the integration of a personal life. They play a central role in the proximity one feels to values and to the intensity of one's response thereto. Secondly, they are relatively spontaneous and contribute to the intensity of a personal life. This, however, is not adequate to make them fully personal, for as personal life is not only what happens in me, but above all what I determine to happen. This can range beyond and even against my feelings.

It is necessary, therefore, to distinguish two directions or dimensions of one's personal transcendence. The first relates to one's world as the object of either one's knowledge or one's will. This might be called horizontal as an activation of a person inasmuch as he or she relates to other things and especially to other persons. This relation would be poorly conceived were it thought to be merely an addition to a fully constituted person. On the contrary, the person as such is essentially transcendent, that is, open to others. One requires this interaction with others in order to have a language and all that this implies for the formation of thought, to have a moral code to assist one in the direction of one's will, and above all to have a family and community and thus the possibility of sharing in the hope and anguish, the love and concern, which gives meaning to life.

The other, or vertical dimension of transcendence characterizes the person and his action in their most properly personal sense. Personal actions are carried out through a will which is open and responsive to *the* Good and as such able to respond to, without being determined by, any particular good or value. Thus, it is finally up to the person to determine him or herself to act. One is able to do this because personal consciousness is not only reflective of myself as an additional object of knowledge, but reflexive or self-aware in its conscious acts.

If such actions derived merely from my powers or faculties of knowledge or will, in acting I would determine only the object of my action. Instead, these actions derive from my self as subject or person; hence, in acting I determine equally, and even primarily, myself. This is self-determination, self-realization, and self-fulfillment in the strongest sense of those terms. Not only are others to be treated as ends in themselves; in acting I myself am an end.

This process of deliberate choice and decision manifests a dimension of the person which transcends the somatic and psychic dynamisms. Where the somatic was extensively reactive, the person through affection or appetite is fundamentally oriented to the good and positively attracted by a set of values. These are not merely known by the mind, but evoke an active response from the psychic dynamisms of the emotions in the context of a responsible freedom. (See Chs. III and VIII above.)

It is in the dimension of responsibility that one encounters the properly moral dimension of life. For in order to live, oneself and with others, one must be able to know and choose what is truly conducive to one's good and that of others. To do this the person must be able to judge the true value of what is to be chosen, that is, its objective worth both in itself and in relation to others. This is moral truth: the judgment whether the act makes the person good in the sense of bringing true individual and social fulfillment or the contrary.

In this I retain that deliberation and voluntary choice whereby I exercise my proper self-awareness, self-possession, and self-governance. By determining to follow this judgment I am able to overcome determination by stimuli and even by culturally ingrained values, and to turn these instead into openings for free action in concert with others. This vertical transcendence in one's actions as willed enables the person to shape his or her self, as well as one's physical surroundings and community.

This can be for good or for ill, depending on the character of the actions. Only morally good actions contribute to the fulfillment of the person, that is, to one's development and perfection as a person. It is the function of conscience as man's moral judgment to identify this element of moral goodness in action.[58] Moral freedom consists then in the ability to follow one's conscience. This must be established through the dynamisms within the person, and must be protected and promoted by the related physical and social realities. This is a basic right of the person---perhaps *the* basic social right--because only thus can one transcend one's conditions and strive for self-fulfillment. Moral education is directed particularly at capacitating the person for the effective exercise of this right.

3. *Character*. The work of conscience is not a merely theoretical judgment (see Ch. VII above), but the development and exercise of self-possession through one's actions. In this one's reference to moral truth constitutes one's sense of duty, for the action that is judged to be truly good is experienced also as that which I ought to do. As this is exercised or lived patterns of action develop which are habitual only in the sense of being repeated. They are modes of activity with which we are familiar; in their exercise--along with the coordinate natural dynamisms they require--we are practiced; and with practice comes facility and spontaneity. These constitute the pattern of our life, its basic, continuing and pervasive shaping influence. For this reason they have been considered classically to be the basic indicators of what our life as a whole will add up to or, as is often said, "amount to." Since Socrates the technical term used for these specially developed capabilities is virtues. (See Ch. VI above.)

It is possible to trace abstractly a general table of virtues required for particular circumstances in order to help clarify the overall terrain of moral action. As with values, however, such a table would not articulate the particulars of one's own experience nor dictate the next steps in one's project toward personal realization with others in relation to the Good. This does not mean, however, that such decisions are arbitrary; conscience makes its moral judgments in terms of real goods and real structures of values and virtues. Nevertheless through and within the breadth of these categories it is the person who must decide, and in so doing enrich his or her unique experience of the virtues. No one can act without courage and wisdom, but each exercise of these is distinctive and typically one's own. Progressively they form a personality that facilitates one's exercise of freedom as it becomes more mature and correlatively more unique. This is often expressed simply by the term more 'personal.'

A person's values reflect then, not only his culture and heritage, but within this what he has done with its set of values. One shapes and refines these values through one's personal and hence free search to realize the good with others in one's world. Hence, they reflect not only present circumstances which our forebears could not have experienced, but our free response to the challenges to interpersonal, familial and social justice and love in our days.

In the final analysis, moral development as a process of personal maturation consists in bringing my pattern of personal and social virtues into harmony with the corresponding sets of values along the vertical pole of transcendence. In this manner we achieve a coordinated pattern of personal capabilities for the realization of our unique response to the Good.

Though free and hence properly personal, as was seen above, this is done essentially with others. For this reason the harmony sought within oneself for moral development must be mirrored in a corresponding harmony between modes of action and values in the communities and nations in which persons live. (Thus, Aristotle considered his ethics of individual moral action to be an integral part of politics). If that be true then the moral development of the person as a search for self-fulfillment is most properly the search for that dynamic harmony both within and without which is called peace. (See Ch. XI above.)

The Catholic University of America
Washington, D.C.

NOTES

1. For a psychological analysis of the person see Volume II in this series, *The Psychological Foundations of Moral Education and Character Development*, ed. by Richard Knowles and George F. McLean; as well as Gordon Allport, *Personality: A Psychological Study* (New York: Holt, 1948) and *Pattern and Growth in Personality* (New York: Holt, Rinehart & Winston, 1961); M. Arnold and J. Gasson, *The Human Person: An Approach to an Integral Theory of Personality* (New York: Holt, Rinehart & Winston, 1971); R. Ruddock, ed., *Six Approaches to the Person* (London: Routledge Kegan Paul, 1972); and J. Dagenais, *Models of Man: A Phenomenological Critique of Some Paradigms in the Human Sciences* (The Hague: M. Nijhoff, 1972).

2. Some, notably those sensitive to environmental concerns, extend this to the need to promote the natural qualities of the land even in our use of it.

3. Adolf Trendelenburg, "A Contribution to the History of the Word Person," *The Monist* 20 (1910) 336-359. This posthumously published work is now over 100 years old. See also "Persona" in *Collected*

Works of F. Max Muller (London, 1912), vol. X pp. 32 and 47; and Arthur C. Danto, "Persons" in *The Encyclopedia of Philosophy* (New York: Macmillan, 1967), vol. VI, pp. 110-114.

4. This was pointed out by Gabius Bassus. See Aulus Gellius, *Noctes Atticae* V, 7.

5. *Prosopeion*. This explanation was given by Forcellini (1688-1769), cf. Tendelenburg, p. 340.

6. C. J. De Vogel, "The Concept of Personality in Greek and Christian Thought," *Studies in Philosophy and the History of Philosophy*, ed. John K. Ryan (Washington, D.C: The Catholic University of America Press, 1963), II, 20-60.

7. "That accepteth not the persons of princes." *Job* 3 and 4:19. See also *Deut* 10:17; *Acts* 10:34-35; *Rom* 2:10-11.

8. Cicero, *De Officiis* I, 28 and 31; *De Orator* II, 102; and Epictetus, *Enchiridion*, 17.

9. A. Danto. See n. 2 above.

10. (Boston: Beacon, 1957), p. 61.

11. Rudolf Carnap, Hans Hahn, and Otto Neurath, "The Scientific World View: The Vienna Manifesto," trans. A. E. Blumberg, in *Perspectives in Reality*, eds. J. Mann and G. Kreyche (New York: Harcourt, Brace & World, 1966), p. 483.

12. R. Carnap *et al*, *Wissenschaftliche Weltaufassung: Der Wiener Kreis*, ch. 2, trans. A.E. Blumberg, in J. Mann and G. Kreyche, *Perspectives on Reality* (New York: Harcourt, Brace and World, 1966), pp. 483-87.

13. Gabriel Marcel, *The Philosophy of Existence*, trans. Manya Harari (New York: Citadel Press, 1956), p. 14.

14. See Pierre Teilhard de Chardin, *The Phenomenon of Man* (New York: Harper, 1959); Wilfrid Desan, *The Planetary Man* (New York: Macmillan, 1961).

15. Aristotle, *Posterior Analytics* I, 4 73 a 3-b 25.

16. Rene Claix "La statut ontologique du concept de sujet selon le metaphysique d'Aristot. L'aporie de *Metaphy*. VII (Z) 3," *Revue philosophique de Louvain*, 59 (61), 29.

17. *Metaphysics* VII 4-7.

18. William James, *Pragmatism* (New York: Meridian Books, 1955), ch. I.

19. See also Hannah Arendt, *The Human Condition* (Chicago: Univ. of Chicago Press, 1958), pp. 181ff.

20. Gabriel Pastrama, "Personhood and the Burgeoning of Human Life," *Thomist*, 41 (1977), 287-290.

21. John Locke, *An Essay Concerning Human Understanding*, Book II, ch. 27, n. 11 and 9-10, ed. A. C. Grasser (New York: Dover, 1959), Vol. I, 448-452. The person is "a thinking, intelligent being, that has reason and reflection and can consider itself as itself."

22. *Essay*, n. 17.

23. *Essay*, nn. 18 and 26.

24. *Essay*, n. 20.
25. *Essay*, n. 29.
26. G. W. Leibniz, *New Essays Concerning Human Understanding*, Bk. II, ch. 27, 9, trans. A. G. Langley (Chicago: Open Court, 1916).
27. Locke, *Essay*, ch. 27, n. 15.
28. Leibniz, *New Essays*, II, ch. 27, n. 14. This consequence was recognized and accepted by Hume who proceeded to dispense with the notion of substance altogether.
29. *New Essays*, nn. 20-66.
30. Immanuel Kant, *Foundations of the Metaphysics of Morals*, III, trans. Lewis White Beck (New York: Bobbs-Merrill, 1959), p. 80.
31. *Foundations*, III, p. 82.
32. *Foundations*, II, pp. 53-59.
33. C. J. De Vogel, 20-60.
34. T.B.L. Webster, *Greek Art and Literature, 700-530 B.C.* (London, 1959), pp. 24-45 (cited by C. De Vogel, p. 27, fn. 17a).
35. Heraclitus, fgs. 2, 8, 51, 112 and 114 (trans. by C. De Vogel).
36. Heraclitus, fg. 115 (trans. by C. De Vogel, p. 31). See also fg. 45.
37. Heraclitus, fg. 101 (trans. by C. De Vogel, p. 31).
38. Heraclitus, fg. 115 (trans. by C. De Vogel, p. 31).
39. Diog. L. VII 136; Marcus Aurelius IV 14, VI 24.
40. Plato, *Republic* 476, 509-511: *mimesis*.
41. Aristotle, *De Anima* II, 2 412 a 28-29.
42. George F. McLean, "Philosophy and Technology," in *Philosophy in a Technological Culture*, ed. G. McLean (Washington: Catholic Univ. of America Press, 1964), pp. 14-15. The same Heraclitean line of reasoning is reflected by recent structuralist insights regarding the need which structures have for a single coordinating principle. Inasmuch as the structure is continually undergoing transformation and being established on new and broader levels this principle must be beyond any of the contrary characteristics or concepts to be integrated within the structure. It must be unique and comprehensive in order to be able to ground and to integrate them all. Jean Piaget, *Structuralism* (New York: Harper and Row, 1970), pp. 139-142. Cf. also George F. McLean *Plenitude and Participation* (Madras: Univ. of Madras, 1978), pp. 12-15.
43. For a detailed consideration of the first weeks after conception and of the point at which an individual life is clearly present see Andre E. Helligers, "The Beginnings of Personhood Medical Consideration," *The Perkins School of Theology Journal*, 27 (1973) 11-15; and C. R. Austin, "The Egg and Fertilization," in *Science Journal*, 6 [special issue] (1970).
44. Heraclitus, fg. 45.
45. Plato, *Republic* I 353 c-d; and IV 43 d-e, 435 b-c, and 441 e-442d.
46. *Republic* VI 609 c. See De Vogel, pp. 33-35.
47. De Vogel, pp. 38-45.
48. Different cultures, of course, are variously located along the

spectrum from individualism to collectivism.

49. Martin Heidegger, *Being and Time* (New York: Harper and Row, 1962), pp. 52-57 and 118; see Joseph J. Kockelmans, *Martin Heidegger* (Pittsburgh, Pa.: Duquesne Univ. Press, 1965), pp. 24-25 and 56-57.

50. H. Rousseau, "Etre et agir," *Revue Thomiste*, 54 (1954); Joseph de Finance, *Etre et agir dans la philosophie de Saint Thomas* (Rome, P.U.G., 1960).

51. Boetius, *De duabis naturis et una persona Christi*, c. 3.

52. Karol Wojtyla, *The Acting Person* (Dordrecht: Reidel, 1979), pp. 48-50; "The Person: Subject and Community," *Review of Metaphysics*, 33 (1979-80), 273-308; and "The Task of Christian Philosophy Today," *Proceedings of the American Catholic Philosophical Association*, 53 (1979), 3-4.

53. Wojtyla, pp. 32-47.

54. This goes beyond Piaget's basic law that actions follow needs and continue only in relation thereto. Jean Piaget, *Six Psychological Studies* (New York: Vintage Books, 1968), p. 6.

55. Ivor Leclerc, "The Metaphysics of the Good," *Review of Metaphysics*, 35 (1981), 3-5.

56. Mehta, pp. 90-91.

57. Wojtyla, *The Acting Person*, p. 197.

58. *Ibid.*, p. 156.

CONCLUSION

THE EDITORS

I

The foregoing presents the broad outlines of an integral theory of moral action. It should, therefore, provide the tools with which to understand moral problems as to both decision-making and execution. To illustrate this, let us return to the example considered in section III of the Introduction.

We supposed that an employer was faced with the decision whether to use racial factors to discriminate among job applicants. This is a reasonably typical instance of a moral decision, though there are many others that might be taken. That the individual recognizes the situation as problematic at all requires a certain moral sensitivity. This is in part a function of *emotional empathy and cognitive alertness, and in part a function of the social environment which provides interpretations of such acts which may highlight or obscure the relevant qualities of the situation. Once the issue is recognized, the moral agent may confront it directly by choosing to think it through; or he may allow his action to be governed by whatever feelings and opinions are already present. This initial decision to consider the question openly will itself be determined by the affective commitments, the previous habituation to clear or muddy thought, and the willed choice of the agent. Thus thoughtfulness or thoughtlessness about moral issues may already be a matter for which the agent may be worthy of praise or blame.

On the one hand, thinking through the situation could then be relatively unproblematic if it is immediately evident that the matter is covered by some previous reflection and commitment. Thus the employer may well have met with such issues before, have grappled with them, and have resolved to act without prejudice in the future. If so, and if this decision has become fixed in his or her habits of action, little active consideration here will be necessary. They will simply act according to the well- or ill-formed structures of his character, as guided by the particular features of this situation and the previous deliberations which that character embodies. If, on the other hand, the individual has not yet faced such a problem squarely, or if this particular case seems to present unusual and unforeseen problems, then the more active process of thought which Aristotle called "deliberation" will begin.

Once individuals have begun deliberating, if they are to deliberate well, they must have in the background of their thought the fundamental nature of the constitutive human good. Many valuable or disvaluable factors will be involved in the possible actions the agent may take. These will include: the effect on the job candidate who may be discriminated against (or for), the effect on the system or institutional structure, the effect in the character of the agents themselves; and perhaps the worth of the action as such. Some of these, of course, will be more important than others. As discussed above, the agent's judgments about good and bad results aim at being accurate understandings of possible objective goods and evils, at supplying the content of moral judgment, and at being based upon a critically analyzed affective and emotional response. These will be taken into account by a well-balanced scheme of moral reasoning, which will involve attention to such results along with formal or "deontological" guides such as considerations of justice and impartiality.

The agent should be aware that justice demands fair consideration for each candidate; knowledge of the end for which hiring occurs enables one to see which of the qualities of the candidate are relevant to fitness for the position; and from this it becomes clear that racial factors are not relevant (unless, for example, it is a matter of casting for "Othello" or some similarly unusual case). To use such factors to make one's decision, then, would not only deprive the candidate of an important good, but might be said to show disrespect for him or her as a person whose abilities and excellences are to be considered on a par with those of others. Reinforcing this will be the agent's consciousness that to set such a precedent, particularly in the current social and economic situation, would have harmful ramifications in addition to constituting a fundamental injustice. The ordinary answer to such deliberations, then, should be: racial factors should not be taken into account.

It is now necessary to *enact* the decision arrived at. Here the primarily cognitive factors of deliberation (underpinned by habits of thought, emotional awareness of the good, and the affective drive to act well and to fulfill one's own good in the situation) give way to the largely non-cognitive factors of execution. The employer may have to overcome a certain habitual reluctance to act impartially (prejudice), or to take risks in doing so (lack of courage); they will, however, be assisted in doing so by what courage and fidelity to the truth they may possess as character traits. It may be necessary for them to encourage or discourage certain of their own feelings about the situation in order to do the right thing, calming trepidation and dwelling on what is admirable in carrying out one's duty.

How this is to be carried out will depend on the situation; it may be necessary to win over certain persons, to convince or rebut, to work through certain channels. All this will be directed by the free choice of the agent, operating *within* the limitations of his situation, to rouse some reactions and suppress others, to make certain efforts and take certain actions (telephone calls, writing documents, signing forms). One's ability to act rightly will be influenced by one's accustomed patterns of feeling and action, which may make easy or difficult certain types of actions in certain ways with certain individuals, such as compromising, apologizing, persuading or commanding. In particular the agent's religious beliefs and commitments will affect the way in which he views himself, other people, and their actions. Just as they, in turn, may generate much of the practical motivation which leads one to take a difficult rather than an easy course, one that is in harmony with one's beliefs about what God would have one do rather than against this.

The integrated moral agent, then, must both *think* and *act* within a complex social *context* in order successfully to carry out moral actions. All the aspects of such an agent discussed in the preceding chapters are required in order to explain how such action may be performed rightly--or wrongly.

II

Clearly, further development of the scheme described here is possible. More detail may be given on many of the topics sketched broadly above; some points may be amplified or corrected by the progress of further work. Nonetheless, it is our argument that the above model of the moral agent is substantially correct, and that it incorporates the real necessities of the moral life more fully than the theories of moral education described at the beginning of this volume.

Some of this further development and specification will be done in the volumes to follow. In *The Psychological Foundations of Moral Education and Character Development*[1] an integrated account from the point of view of the psychology will be presented to further articulate these points and in particular to elaborate the way in which persons *acquire* such abilities and learn to exercise them over the course of their lives. Thus it is necessary now to turn to a thorough psychological account of the factors which have been identified here as crucial to moral action, and to describe, as far as current research permits, their genesis and functioning in the acting person. From this an expanded psychological model of the moral agent can emerge.

In *Character Development in Schools and Beyond*[2] a further articulation of the implications of this model for moral and character education will be drawn out, providing guidance for its application in practice. Such application should in time enable still further refinement of the original model. It is clear from the range of the topics covered that programs of moral education may require a number of different types of work, including, for example, character training *as well as* rigorous and critical cognitive advance, emotional growth as well as self-discipline and a growing ability to live with others. All these are among the aspects of the human program which affect moral action, and all must enter into an effective education of the responsible person in the present world.

Subsequent volumes[3] will consider more in detail the relation of values to the social context, *The Social Context and Moral Values,* to specific cultures such as *Philosophical Foundations of Moral Education and Character Development in China,* and to patterns of cultural interaction and change, *Culture, Human Rights and Peace in Central America* and *The Relation Between Cultures,* in order to draw on the multiple cultural heritages as resources for contemporary life.

NOTES

1. (Washington: University Press of America, 1986).
2. (New York: Praeger, 1986).
3. To be published in this series by The University Press of America, Washington, D.C.

INDEX

Abstraction 79-86
Action 1-4, 9-12, 21-32, 106-111, 125-157
Adolescent 231-233
Affectivity 61-93, 119, 158, 191-202, 205-208, 225, 281, 313-314, 349
Allport 352
Alston 92, 148, 160, 299
Analytic philosophy 13
Anthropology 234-248
Application 107
Aquinas 57, 63, 142, 162, 178-179, 188-189, 236, 248, 272-279, 311-312, 321-323, 341
Arendt 142, 295, 301, 353
Aristotle 17, 27, 50-58, 94, 101, 109-142, 145-162, 191, 206, 210, 215, 248-249, 279, 281-301, 310, 331-357
Arnold 352
Aron 211-226, 236-245
Atherton 160
Atkinson 97
Austin 140, 161, 354
Authority 30-31, 37, 43, 105
Barker 225, 246
Barrett 231, 235, 247, 248
Becker 59
Behaviorism 76, 230, 284, 296
Benevolence 24
Bentham 173, 187
Berkeley 33, 45, 162
Berkowitz 97, 256, 257
Berns 323
Biology 228-229
Bleiker 119
Boetius 355
Bok iii, 58, 186
Boyle v, 140, 142, 157-163, 187-188, 247
Brandt 277
Broad 28, 76-77, 107, 169-187, 291-292, 310, 348, 357
Broughton 41
Browning 248
Buber iii, 295, 296, 301

Buchler 74, 75, 94, 95
Callahan iii, 58, 186
Campbell 131, 141
Caputo 104, 105
Carlyle 59
Carnap 119, 353
Cassirer 97
Cause 125-137, 264, 265, 297,
Chapman 161
Character 1-4, 29-32, 89-91, 123-142, 284
Choice 4, 11-14, 123-141, 191-209, 350
Chomsky 141
Christianity 48, 192, 194, 242, 317, 322, 365
Claix 353
Clifford 49, 216, 234, 245, 248
Cochrane 35
Cognitive development 21-22
Colby 35-37, 41
Collectivism 219, 296, 355
Communication 100
Community 105, 282-301, 328-335
Conation 67, 82
Concrete 72-74
Confidence 11, 90, 310
Conscience 144, 351
Consciousness 69-99
Consequentialism 170-187, 221, 244-247
Conservatism 30, 103
Content 192-233
Control 123-125
Cotton, J. 46, 59
Coughlin 60
Criteria 3, 260-264
Critique 116
Cultural Anthropology 231-236
Culture 88, 99
Cybernetic 89
Dagenais 352
Damon 35-41, 159-160, 300-301
Daniels 35
Danto 353
Deism 46

Deliberation 140-146, 165, 214, 350-358
Dependency 283-285
Descartes 102, 114, 119, 195, 203, 263-264, 277-278, 336
Determinism 126-134, 265-267
Development 341-365
Developmental psychology 18, 21, 229-239
Dewey 4, 34, 44-60, 67-68, 93, 104, 119, 145, 159-162, 211-215, 235, 245, 297, 306-307, 327-333
Dialectic 115
Dilemmas 20, 22, 48,
Discipline 30, 31
Divine command 303-320
Donagan 177, 187, 188
Durkheim 294, 301
Education 282-295
Efficiency 15
Ellrod 1, i, v, 1, 9, 38, 43-46, 123, 141-143, 158, 186-187, 212, 252, 277-279, 284, 288
Emotion 4, 65-66, 92-93, 303, 321
Environment 32, 281
Epicurean 128, 129
Erikson 31, 40, 161, 229-249
Ethics 43-46
Existentialism 301
Experience 80-85
Fact 66-70, 220-236
Faith 50, 309-311, 320-322
Family 105
Farrelly v, 96, 178, 187-188, 211, 247, 278, 281
Feeling 71, 191-192
Ferkiss 246
Fichte 59
Finality 265-267, 271-276
Findlay 131-132, 141, 208, 249
Finnis 34, 186, 187, 246, 249, 279
Forcellini 353
Formalism 221
Fowler iii, 35, 159, 300, 309-310, 320-322

Frankena 187
Franklin 40, 46, 59
Freedom 13, 113, 123-142, 150-157, 186-189, 237-239, 270-272, 328-352
Freud 76, 97, 153, 230
Frings 96
Fromm 31
Function 330
Fuss 59
Gabius Bassus 353
Gaddamer 113-119
Gasson 352
Geertz 216, 234, 245, 248
Generosity 157, 203
Gewirth 276
Gibson 245
Gilligan 37
God 50, 101, 314-323, 330
Golden rule 28-29, 175-181, 186
Goldstein 76, 79-81, 95-96, 301
Good 55-57, 211-249, 345-348
Goslin iii, 38, 158, 299
Goudsblom 249
Gratitude 157, 168
Greeks 335, 340, 343
Grim 144
Grisez 140, 187-189, 249, 279
Growth 54-55
Gulley 92
Habermas 41, 115, 117, 119
Habits 25-26, 54-56, 143-162
Hahn 353
Hamm 35
Hare 21, 25, 26, 40
Harmin 10, 33, 34, 41
Harriman 92
Hart 33, 40
Hartshorne 40, 143-161
Hayen 321
Hebb 231, 248
Hegel 52, 59, 76, 114
Heidegger 117-119, 191-209, 344-355
Helligers 354
Hennessy 37
Heraclitus 340, 341, 343, 354

Hermeneutics 99, 101, 110, 113, 116
Hermes 99
Hesiod 101
Historical 110, 116
Historicity 107
History 104, 105, 112, 335
Homans 248
Homeostasis 65
Howard 1, 5, 10, 33, 41, 276
Hudson 227, 247, 276
Human good 236-247
Hume 264-270, 278, 354
Husserl 73, 76, 192, 208
Id 230, 235
Idealism 106
Ideals 46-48
Imagination 102
Impulse 71
Independence 74, 334
Indeterminism 126-133, 152
Indignation 157
Individualism 219, 286, 295-298, 331-355
Indoctrination 16, 32-33, 303-325
Inhibition 85
Insight 81, 86
Instinct 84-86
Intellectualism 62-64, 92
Intentionality 198
Interactionism 291-292
Interest 90
Intuitionism 168, 170, 179
Islam 242
James 34, 38, 44-60, 156, 162, 188, 245, 277-279, 287, 297-299, 320, 330-333, 353
Jaspers 75, 95
Jefferson 46, 59
Johnson 187
Judaism 242
Judgment 62
Justice 24, 27, 223-225
Kant 21, 37, 47, 48-59, 65, 76, 81-93, 108, 114, 130-131, 139-142, 171-180, 188, 192, 195-210, 246, 261, 266-270, 275-279, 306-307, 320-321, 336-342, 354
Kierkegaard 192-198, 202, 208
Kindness 96
King 20, 107, 282, 283, 305
Kirkpatrick 332
Kirschenbaum 1, 5, 10, 14-17, 33-41, 142, 276
Knowledge 61-78, 102, 114
Knowles 230, 332, 352, 363-365
Koestler 244, 247, 249, 250
Kracke 248
Kreyche 119, 353
Kristol 34
Kuhn 33, 41
Language 114
Laplace 127, 141
Lavelle 249
Laws 137, 340, 343
Leibniz 337, 354
Lerner 247
Levinas 210
Liberation 103
Locke 45-46, 297, 336-345, 353-354
Lockwood 34, 35, 39, 40
Logos 72, 118, 201, 340, 341, 343
Love 24, 47-49, 63-64, 96, 312-18
Loyalty 47
Lucretius 128, 141
M'Naghten 40
MacIntyre 165, 187, 278-279, 286-289, 299-301
Maller 40
Mann i, v, 43, 119, 143, 156, 160, 301, 353
Marcel 59, 330, 353
Marcus Aurelius 307, 354
Marcuse 323
Marx 73, 114-117
Mather 46
May 39, 144-46
Mayer 146, 159, 277, 285, 299, 300
McCosh 45, 46, 58
McDermott 59

McLean 99
Mehta 119, 355
Memory 85-86, 102
Merleau-Ponty 76-78, 95, 202
Midgley 229, 247
Mill 173, 187
Miller 58
Mischel 35, 160, 244, 277, 299, 300
Modesty 157
Moods 194-97
Moore 171, 277, 323
Moral agent 9-10, 344
Moral decision 21, 163-89
Moral Norms 182-84
Moral reasoning 163-186, 305-308
Morality 261-76, 303-25
Mosher 20, 36-38, 300
Motivation 97
Muller 353
Munsey 211-226, 236-246
Nagel 94, 141
Naturalism 255-78
Nature 27
Neill 286
Neurath 353
Nicgorski v, 143, 158, 160, 281, 323, 328
Niebuhr 301
Nietzsche 238, 249
Nihilism 237-39, 249
Noncognitive 23
Nonnaturalism 272-75
Norton 40, 161, 225, 246-249
Objectivity 86-87
Obligation 212, 256
Ought 16, 35-38
Palmer 118
Passion 191-194
Pastrama 353
Pathos 192-194
Patience 157
Person 3, 9-17, 27, 100, 327-55
Peters iii, 97, 149, 159, 160
Phenix 35, 41, 142
Phenomenology v, 73-76, 94-95, 191-210, 216-226, 236, 240
Philibert 5, 147, 159, 160
Piaget 5, 18-24, 36-37, 47, 59, 71, 212, 229-234, 244-245, 281, 292, 354-355
Pieper 142, 162
Piety 157
Plato 18, 27, 101-107, 127, 143-149, 158, 171, 192, 206-210, 215, 290, 317, 341-343, 354
Polanyi 321
Potter 301
Power 35-38, 300-303, 347
Pragmatism 46, 353
Prejudice 76, 102, 111, 114, 357, 358
Prichard 165, 186
Principle 15
Prizing 12
Protention 64
Prudence 36-38, 108
Psychology 1
Puka 245
Punishment 40
Purcell 226, 246
Purpel 33-36, 38, 162
Raths 10, 16, 33
Rationalism 107
Ratzinger 322
Rawls 18-25, 59, 220-25, 240, 246, 261, 299
Realism 45
Reasoning 4, 18-23, 29, 31
Reid 45, 58, 299
Reimer 36, 38, 92, 159, 293, 301
Reinforcement 32, 85
Relativism 1, 13, 254-256, 283-286
Religion 35-39, 303-323
Rescher 248, 249
Respect 198-205
Responsibility 124, 153-157, 180-185, 342, 350
Rest 37-38
Ricoeur 117
Right judgment 158
Risk 49-50

Rogers 15, 34, 40, 138, 142, 299
Role 26, 294, 327-30
Ross 160, 168-171, 179, 187
Roth 59, 60
Rouse 158, 358
Rousseau 355
Royce 4, 44-59, 297
Ruddock 352
Rules 21, 24-26, 28-30
Ryan 33-36, 38, 162, 353, 365
Ryle 97
Sagacity 108
Samay v, 61, 106, 119, 161-162, 208, 284, 301
Sartre 34, 70, 76, 93, 137, 142, 150, 203, 230
Schachter 92
Scharf 33-41
Scheffler 35, 92, 162
Schelling 59
Scheltens 224, 246
Schmitz 263, 277-279, 301, 322-323, 344, 363
Schneider 77, 78
Schools 2, 32-35, 53-54, 105-106, 287-303, 318-319, 327, 359, 365
Schopenhauer 93
Schrag 73
Scientific method 55-57
Scriven 38, 39, 41
Self conscious 340, 345
Shaw 189, 249
Shuttleworth 40
Simon 1, 10, 16, 25, 33-35, 41, 142, 276
Singer 92
Sizer 35, 159
Skinner 230, 286
Sloan 45, 58
Socialization 32, 282-299
Sociobiology 229, 335
Socrates 56, 62, 92, 101, 160, 173, 197, 202, 286-300, 305, 351
Sokolowski 161,·322, 323
Solidarity 294, 295
Solomon 34, 142, 208
Soul 339-343

Spinoza 64, 307
Spirit 86-87, 96
Spragens 225, 246
Stewart 33, 35, 41, 45
Subject 327-50
Subjectivity 116, 118, see affectivity
Sublimation 87-88
Sullivan 40, 224, 246
Taylor 132, 141, 227, 247
Teilhard de Chardin 307, 353
Teleology 243, 265-68
Temperament 144, 151-53
Tillman 299
Tollefsen 140
Tradition 21-31, 63, 103-106, 115
Transvaluation 87
Trendelenburg 352
Trust 90
Truth 112
Truthfulness 157
Ultimate reality 304-07
Unconscious 24, 82, 90, 153
Universals 146
Utilitarian 51
Values 1, 10-35, 68, 73, 86-97, 99-104, 198-206, 214-44, 274-275, 348-52, 361
-violence and, 106
Values Clarification 10-18, 43, 327 see S. Simon
Van Doren 59
Vergote iii, 35, 159, 320, 321
Virtues 27, 137, 145-147, 157, 349-352
Vital urge 83-85
Voluntary 54
von Uexkull 72, 94
von Wright 249
Waddington 228, 247
Walhout 249
Warnock 227, 247
Watkins 34
Webster 340, 354
Whitehead 72, 94, 278-279
Wick 188

Will 16, 48, 126, 133, 312
Wilson iii, 23-29, 38-40, 157, 299
Windmiller 161
Wolff 94, 209, 323
Wolman 92
Wynne 161
Yanarella 299
Yankelovich 231, 235, 247, 248
Yulish 39, 40
Zeus 99

THE COUNCIL FOR RESEARCH IN VALUES AND PHILOSOPHY

PURPOSE

Today there is urgent need to attend to the nature and dignity of the person, to the quality of human life, to the purpose and goal of the physical transformation of our environment, and to the relation of all this to the development of social and political life. This, in turn, requires philosophic clarification of the basis upon which freedom is exercised, that is, of the values which provide stability and guidance to one's decisions.

Such studies must be able to reach deeply into the cultures of one's nation---and often of other parts of the world from which they derive--in order to uncover the roots of the dignity of persons and of the societies built upon their relations one with another. They must be able to identify the conceptual forms in terms of which modern industrial and technological developments are structured and how these impact human self-understanding. Above all, they must be able to bring these elements together in the creative understanding essential for setting our goals and determining our modes of our interaction. In the present complex circumstances this is a condition for growing together with trust and justice, honest dedication and mutual concern.

The Council for Studies in Values and Philosophy is a group of scholars who share the above concerns and are interested in the application thereto of existing capabilities in the field of philosophy and other disciplines. Its work is to identify areas in which study is needed, the intellectual resources which can be brought to bear thereupon, and the financial resources required. In bringing these together its goal is scientific discovery and publication which contributes to the promotion of human life in our times.

In sum, our times present both the need and the opportunity for deeper and ever more progressive understanding of the person and of the foundations of social life. The development of such understanding is the goal of the Council for Research in Values and Philosophy (RVP).

PROJECTS

A set of related research efforts are currently in process, some developed initially by the RVP and others now being carried forward by it either solely or conjointly.

1. *Cultural Heritage and Contemporary Life: Philosophical Foundations for Social Life.* Sets of focused and mutually coordinated continuing seminars in university centers, each preparing a volume as part of an integrated philosophic search for self-understanding differentiated by continent. This work focuses upon evolving a more adequate understanding of the person in society and looks to the cultural heritage of each for the resources to respond to its own specific contemporary issues.

2. *Seminars on Culture and Contemporary Issues.* This series of 10 week seminars is being coordinated by the RVP in Washington.

3. *Joint-Colloquia* with institutes of philosophy of the national Academies of Science, university philosophy departments, and societies have been underway since 1976 in Eastern Europe and, since 1987, in China concerning the person in contemporary society.

4. *The Mediation of Values to Social Life.* The development of a four volume study on the mediation of values to social life is a corporate effort of philosophers throughout the world.

5. *Foundations of Moral Education and Character Development.* A study in values and education which unites philosophers, psychologists and scholars in education in the elaboration of ways of enriching the moral content of education and character development.

The personnel for these projects consists of established scholars willing to contribute their time and research as part of their professional commitment to life in our society. The Council directly sponsors some projects and seeks support for projects sponsored by other organizations. For resources to implement this work the Council, as a non-profit organization incorporated in the District of Colombia, looks to various private foundations, public programs, and enterprises.

PUBLICATIONS ON CULTURAL HERITAGE AND CONTEMPORARY CHANGE

Series I.   *Culture and Values*
Series II.   *Africa*
Series IIa. *Islam*
Series III. *Asia*
Series IV. *W. Europe and North America*
Series IVa. *Central and Eastern Europe*
Series V.   *Latin America*
Series VI. *Foundations of Moral Education*

THE COUNCIL FOR RESEARCH IN VALUES AND PHILOSOPHY

VOLUMES ON

CULTURAL HERITAGE

AND CONTEMPORARY CHANGE

VALUES AND CONTEMPORARY LIFE

Series I. Culture and Values

Vol. I.1 *Research on Culture and Values: Intersection of Universities, Churches and Nations,*
George F. McLean,
ISBN 0-8191-7352-5 $45.00; paper ISBN 0-8191-7353-3 $14.00.

Vol. I.2 *The Knowledge of Values: A Methodological Introduction to the Study of Values,*
A. Lopez Quintas,
ISBN 0-8191-7418-1 $45.00; paper ISBN 0-8191-7419-x $14.00.

Vol. I.3 *Reading Philosophy for the XXIst Century,*
George F. McLean,
ISBN 0-8191-7414-9 $45.00; paper ISBN 0-8191-7415-7 $15.00.

Vol. I.4 *Relations Between Cultures,*
John Kromkowski,
ISBN 1-56518-009-7 $45.00; paper ISBN 1-56518-008-9 $17.50.

Vol. I.5 *Urbanization and Values,*
John Kromkowski,
ISBN 1-56518-011-9 $45.00; paper ISBN 1-56518-010-0 $17.50.

Vol. I.6 *The Place of the Person in Social Life,*
Paul Peachey and John Kromkowski,
ISBN 1-56518-013-5 $45.00; paper ISBN 1-56518-012-7 $17.50.

Vol. I.7 *The Humanities, Moral Imagination and Character Development,* Richard Graham and Richard Knowles, in preparation.

Vol. I.8 *The Humanization of Social Life: Dilemmas of Contemporary Change,* Ronald Calinger, in preparation.

Vol. I.9 *Democracy, Culture and Values,* Habib C. Malik, in preparation.

Vol. I.10 *Freedom and Choice in a Democracy,* Richard Khuri, in preparation

Vol. I.11 *Ethics at the Crossroads: Vol. 1. Normative Ethics and Objective Reason,*
Richard Wollack and George F. McLean,
ISBN 1-56518-023-2 $45.00; paper ISBN 1-56518-022-4 $15.00.

Vol. I.12 *Ethics at the Crossroads: Vol. 2. Personalist Ethics and Human Subjectivity,*

Richard Wollack and George F. McLean,
ISBN 1-56518-025-9 $45.00; paper ISBN 1-56518-024-0 $15.00.

Vol. I.13 *The Emancipative Theory of J. Jürgen Habermas and Metaphysics*,
Robert Badillo,
ISBN 1-56518-043-7 $45.00; paper ISBN 1-56518-042-9 $14.00.

CULTURAL HERITAGES AND THE FOUNDATIONS OF SOCIAL LIFE

Series II. Africa

Vol. II.1 *Person and Community: Ghanaian Philosophical Studies: I*,
Kwasi Wiredu and Kwame Gyeke,
ISBN 1-56518-005-4 $45.00; paper ISBN 1-56518-004-6 $15.00.

Vol. II.2 The Foundations of Social Life: Ugandan Philosophical Studies: I,
A.T. Dalfovo,
ISBN 1-56518-007-0 $45.00; paper ISBN 1-56518-006-2 $14.00.

Series IIA. Islam

Vol. IIA.1 *Islam and the Political Order*,
Muhammad Saïd al-Ashmawy,
ISBN 1-56518-046-1 $40.00; paper ISBN 1-56518-047-x $15.00.

Series III. Asia

Vol. III.1 *Man and Nature: Chinese Philosophical Studies, I*,
Tang Yi-jie, Li Zhen,
ISBN 0-8191-7412-2 $45.00; paper ISBN 0-8191-7413-0 $15.00.

Vol. III.2 *Chinese Foundations for Moral Education and Character Development, Chinese Philosophical Studies, II*.
Tran van Doan,
ISBN 1-56518-033-x $45.00; paper ISBN 1-56518-032-1 $14.00.

Vol. III.3 *Confucianism, Buddhism, Taoism, Christianity and Chinese Culture, Chinese Philosophical Studies, III*,
Tang Yijie,
ISBN 1-56518-035-6 $45.00; paper ISBN 1-56518-034-8 $14.00.

Series IV. W. Europe and North America

Series IVA. Central and Eastern Europe

Vol. IVA.1 *The Philosophy of Person: Solidarity and Cultural Creativity: Polish Philosophical Studies, I*,
A. Tischner, J.M. Zycinski,
ISBN 1-56518-048-8 $45.00; paper ISBN 1-56518-049-6.

Vol. IVA.2 *Public and Private Social Inventions in Modern Societies: Polish Philosophical Studies, II*,
L. Dyczewski, P. Peachey, J. Kromkowski,
ISBN 1-56518-050-x $45.00. paper ISBN 1-56518-051-8 $15.00.

Vol. IVA.3 *Knowledge and Morality: Georgian Philosophical Studies, 1*,
N.V. Chavchavadze, G. Nodia, P. Peachey,
ISBN 1-56518-052-6 $40.00; paper ISBN 1-56518-053-4 $15.00.

Vol. IVA.4 *Morality and Public Life in a Time of Change: Bulgarian Philosophical Studies, I,*
V. Prodanov, M. Stoyanova,
ISBN 1-56518-054-2 $45.00; paper ISBN 1-56518-055-0 $15.00.

Vol. IVA.5 *Traditions and Present Problems of Czech Political Culture: Czechoslovak Philosophical Studies, I,*
M. Vejrazka, M. Bednar,
ISBN 1-56518-056-9 $45.00; paper ISBN 1-56518-057-7 $15.00.

Series V. Latin America

Vol. V.1 The Social Context and Values: Perspectives of the Americas,
O. Pegoraro,
ISBN 0-8191-7354-1 $45.00; paper ISBN 0-8191-7355-x $15.00.

Vol. V.2 Culture, Human Rights and Peace in Central America,
Raul Molina, Timothy Ready,
ISBN 0-8191-7356-8 $45.00; paper ISBN 0-8191-7357-6 $14.00.

FOUNDATIONS OF MORAL EDUCATION AND CHARACTER DEVELOPMENT

Series VI. Foundations of Moral Education

Vol. VI.1 *Philosophical Foundations for Moral Education and Character Development: Act and Agent,*
G. McLean, F. Ellrod,
ISBN 1-56518-001-1 $45.00; paper ISBN 1-56518-000-3 $17.50.

Vol. VI.2 *Psychological Foundations for Moral Education and Character Development: An Integrated Theory of Moral Development,*
R. Knowles,
ISBN 1-56518-003-8 $45.00; paper ISBN 1-56518-002-x $17.50.

Vol. VI.3 Character Development in Schools and Beyond,
Kevin Ryan, Thomas Lickona,
ISBN 1-56518-058-5 $45,00; paper ISBN 1-56518-059-3 $17.50.

Vol. VI.4 The Social Context and Values: Perspectives of the Americas,
O. Pegoraro,
ISBN 0-8191-7354-1 $45.00; paper ISBN 0-8191-7355-x $15.00.

Vol. VI.5 *Chinese Foundations for Moral Education and Character Development,*
Tran van Doan,
ISBN 1-56518-033-x $45.00; paper ISBN 1-56518-032-1 $14.00.

The series is published by: The Council for Research in Values and Philosophy, Cardinal Station, P.O. Box 261, Washington, D.C. 20064, Tel. 202/319-5636, Fax. 220/319-6089; RVP Distribution Center, P.O. Box 605, Herndon, Va 22070, tel: 800/659-9962, fax: 703/689-0660.